Library of
Davidson College

CONSTITUENT QUESTIONS

STUDIES IN LINGUISTICS AND PHILOSOPHY

(Formerly SYNTHESE LANGUAGE LIBRARY)

Managing Editors:

ROBIN COOPER, *University of Wisconsin*
ELISABET ENGDAHL, *University of Wisconsin*
RICHARD GRANDY, *Rice University*

Editorial Board:

EMMON BACH, *Department of Linguistics, University of Massachusetts, Amherst, U.S.A.*

JON BARWISE, *CSLI, Stanford, U.S.A.*

JOHAN VAN BENTHEM, *Filosofisch Instituut, Rijksuniversiteit Groningen, The Netherlands*

DAVID DOWTY, *Department of Linguistics, Ohio State University, Columbus, U.S.A.*

GERALD GAZDAR, *Cognitive Studies Programme, University of Sussex, Brighton, U.K.*

EWAN KLEIN, *School of Epistemics, University of Edinburgh, Scotland*

BILL LADUSAW, *Cowell College, University of California Santa Cruz, U.S.A.*

SCOTT SOAMES, *Department of Philosophy, Princeton University, U.S.A.*

HENRY THOMPSON, *Department of Artificial Intelligence and Centre for Cognitive Science, Edinburgh, Scotland*

VOLUME 27

ELISABET ENGDAHL

Department of Linguistics, Lund University, Sweden and
Department of Linguistics, University of Wisconsin, Madison, U.S.A.

CONSTITUENT QUESTIONS

The Syntax and Semantics of Questions
with Special Reference to Swedish

D. REIDEL PUBLISHING COMPANY

A MEMBER OF THE KLUWER  ACADEMIC PUBLISHERS GROUP

DORDRECHT / BOSTON / LANCASTER / TOKYO

Library of Congress Cataloging-in-Publication Data

Engdahl, Elisabet.
  Constituent questions.

  (Studies in linguistics and philosophy ; v. 27)
  Outgrowth of thesis (doctoral).
  Bibliography: p.
  Includes indexes.
    1. Grammar, Comparative and general–Interrogative. 2.
  Swedish language–Interrogative. 3. Generative grammar. 4.
  Grammar, Comparative and general–Syntax. 5. Semantics. I. Title.
  II. Series.
  P299.I57E53   1985   439.7'5   85-25581
  ISBN 90-277-1954-3
  ISBN 90-277-1955-1 (pbk.)

Published by D. Reidel Publishing Company,
P.O. Box 17, 3300 AA Dordrecht, Holland.

Sold and distributed in the U.S.A. and Canada
by Kluwer Academic Publishers,
190 Old Derby Street, Hingham, MA 02043, U.S.A.

In all other countries, sold and distributed
by Kluwer Academic Publishers Group,
P.O. Box 322, 3300 AH Dordrecht, Holland

All Rights Reserved
© 1986 by D. Reidel Publishing Company, Dordrecht, Holland
No part of the material protected by this copyright notice may be reproduced or
utilized in any form or by any means, electronic or mechanical
including photocopying, recording or by any information storage and
retrieval system, without written permission from the copyright owner

Printed in The Netherlands

CONTENTS

Preface   xi

CHAPTER I. INTRODUCTION

1.	Theoretical and Methodological Issues	1
2.	Unbounded Dependencies	4
3.	Questions in Swedish	5
3.1.	Extractions Out of Indirect Questions	6
3.2.	Bound Anaphors in Preposed Constituents	6
4.	The Semantics of Questions	8
5.	Extensions of the Present Study	11
	Notes	12

CHAPTER II. RECENT APPROACHES TO UNBOUNDED DEPENDENCIES

0.	Introduction	13
1.	Short Overview of Relevant Data from Swedish	13
2.	Arguments for Transformations	17
3.	Generalized Phrase-Structure Grammars	19
3.1.	Syntactic Rules	19
3.2.	Semantic Rules	24
3.2.1.	Designated Variables	24
3.2.2.	Lambda Conversion	28
3.3.	Evaluating the GPSG Framework	32
4.	Cooper's Proposal	34
4.1.	Free Quantification and Controlled Quantification	35
4.2.	Interpretation Through Substitution	37
5.	Phrase Linking Grammars	41
5.1.	An Outline of PLG	42
5.2.	Linked Trees	44
5.3.	Semantics	48

6.	Unbounded Dependencies in the Government-Binding Framework	51
7.	Choosing a Framework	52
	Notes	54

CHAPTER III. A FRAMEWORK FOR SWEDISH

1.	Introduction	58
2.	The Format of Rules	59
2.1.	Syntax	60
2.2.	Semantics	65
3.	Quantification	66
3.1.	Free Quantification	66
3.2.	Controlled Quantification	71
4.	Questions	77
4.1.	Questions Out of Questions	78
4.2.	Multiple Questions	78
4.2.1.	Mixed *yes/no* and Constituent Questions	83
4.2.2.	Do We Need a Syntactic Category Q?	84
4.2.3.	Linked Trees and Token Indexing	86
4.3.	Subject Questions	88
4.4.	Infinitival Questions	91
5.	Pronouns	94
5.1.	Free and Bound Pronouns	95
5.1.1.	Resumptive Pronouns	98
5.1.2.	Epithets	102
5.2.	Reflexives	106
5.3.	Restrictions on Binding of Pronouns	114
6.	Gaps	119
6.1.	Alternation Between Gaps and Pronouns	121
6.2.	Pronoun-Gap Alternation as a Disambiguating Device	126
6.3.	Parasitic Gaps	129
7.	Constraining the Framework	132
7.1.	How Many Extractions?	133
7.2.	Structural Constraints	137
8.	Summary	145
	Notes	146

CHAPTER IV. THE INTERPRETATION OF QUESTIONS

1.	Some Previous Approaches to Questions	151
1.1.	Karttunen's Treatment of Constituent Questions	156
1.2.	Some Problems for Karttunen's Approach	157
2.	Quantifying Into Questions	159
2.1.	Karttunen and Peters' Proposal	160
2.2.	Belnap's Proposal	162
3.	Some Arguments Against Quantifying Into Questions	163
3.1.	Relational Questions Without Wide Scope Antecedents	163
3.2.	Negative Antecedents	166
3.3.	Questions Into Opaque Contexts	167
3.4.	Summary	168
4.	A Relational Approach to Interrogative Quantifiers	169
4.1.	Similarities Between Pronouns and Interrogatives	169
4.2.	The W Function	174
4.3.	Questions With Bound Anaphors	183
4.3.1.	Bound Personal Pronouns	183
4.3.2.	Reflexive Pronouns	190
5.	Interaction Between Interrogative Quantifiers and Other Quantifiers	195
5.1.	Quantifiers and Pronoun Interpretation	195
5.2.	Constituent Questions With Quantifiers	197
5.3.	Excursus on Wide Scope Interpretation of Embedded NPs	204
6.	The Internal Structure of Interrogative Constituents	206
6.1.	Possessives	206
6.1.1.	**vems** (*whose*)	208
6.2.	PP Complements	210
6.3.	Partitive Questions	210
6.4.	More on Control of Reflexives	217
7.	Multiple WH Questions	220
7.1.	Simple 'unmoved' WH Phrases	221
7.2.	Embedded WH Phrases	227
7.3.	Embedded WH Phrases in Comp	231
8.	Questions Involving Other Categories	234
8.1.	Pied-Piping	234
8.2.	Adverbial, Adjectival, and Predicate Nominal Questions	236

viii CONTENTS

8.3.	Questions With Quantifier Type Answers	240
9.	An Alternative Approach	241
9.1.	Analyzing *which* as a Quantifier	241
9.2.	Temporally Ambiguous Questions	245
9.3.	Arguments Against Splitting up the Interpretation of Interrogative Quantifiers	250
10.	Conclusion	251
	Notes	252

CHAPTER V. A COMPARISON WITH EST-GB

1.	Introduction	259
2.	Semantic Interpretation in Transformational Grammar	259
3.	Characterizing *wh*-Movement	261
4.	*wh*-Interpretation and Reconstruction at LF	267
5.	Bound Anaphors in Moved Constituents	269
5.1.	Anaphora Interpretation in EST	269
5.2.	The Binding Theory in the Government-Binding Framework	273
5.3.	*wh*-Interpretation Reconsidered	275
6.	Higginbotham and May's Theory of Questions	278
	Notes	282

CHAPTER VI. RESTRICTING THE INTERPRETATION OF PRONOUNS

1.	Introduction	284
2.	Disjoint Reference and Non-Coreference	285
2.1.	A Pragmatic Account for Non-Coreference	286
2.2.	Bound Anaphora and Parasitic Gaps	293
3.	Cross-over	302
3.1.	Background	302
3.2.	Higginbotham's Approach	303
3.3.	Accounting for Cross-over Without Indexing of Syntactic Structures	309
3.4.	Weak Cross-over	312
3.5.	Cross-over and the Binding Theory in GB	317
	Notes	320

CHAPTER VII. THEORETICAL POSTSCRIPT

1.	Linked Trees	322
2.	Storage	324
3.	Relational Readings	325

Bibliography 327

Index of Names 338

Index of Subjects 341

PREFACE

This monograph has grown out of some issues that I began to investigate in my dissertation (Engdahl, 1980a). I am extremely grateful to the members of my doctoral committee, Emmon Bach, Chuck Clifton, Lyn Frazier, Barbara Partee, and Edwin Williams, who gave me constructive feedback all through the writing of the dissertation. In particular, I want to thank my chairperson, Barbara Partee, for her detailed comments and insightful suggestions. To a large extent, the research presented in this book represents further developments of ideas and problems that came up in our weekly meetings. During this period I also discussed with Eva Ejerhed, Irene Heim, Per-Kristian Halvorsen, Lauri Karttunen, Bill Ladusaw, Jim McCloskey, Stanley Peters, Arnim von Stechow, and Annie Zaenen who in various ways made me aware of additional aspects of the semantics of questions. Several people gave me helpful comments on my dissertation, most of which have influenced the present study in one way or another. Among these people I would like to mention Mürvet Enc, Gerald Gazdar, Jeroen Groenendijk, Angelika Kratzer, Fred Landman, Alice ter Meulen, Mats Rooth, and Martin Stokhof.

While I was developing the analysis presented in this book, I greatly benefitted from opportunities to present my ideas to other people. I am grateful to Arnim von Stechow and Sonderforschungsbereich 99 in Konstanz for inviting me there in the fall of 1981 and to the Meaning and Cognition group at the Center for Advanced Study in the Behavioral Sciences at Stanford for several interesting discussions in the spring of 1982. I especially want to thank Jon Barwise, Dagfinn Føllesdal, Hans Kamp, Lauri Karttunen, John Perry, and Stanley Peters for insightful discussions. During the fall of 1982 I had opportunities to present part of this material at a workshop on Interrogative Quantification at the University of Groningen, organized by Alice ter Meulen, and at the Linguistics department at the University of Trondheim.

I am especially indebted to Robin Cooper, Östen Dahl, Lars Hellan, and Traugott Schiebe who read an earlier draft of this book and whose comments and questions helped me organize the material in a more accessible fashion. I began writing this book while I had a Sloan Postdoctoral Fellowship at Stanford University. Most of the writing took place at Lund University and I want to thank the Linguistics department there for making this possible. I acknowledge the financial support from the Faculty of Humanities at Lund University as well as a grant from Hvitfeldtska stiftelsen. The manuscript was more or less completed in January 1983 but for various reasons it wasn't until the fall of 1984 that the final form could be prepared. I would like to thank Ann-Marie Gayle for typing the manuscript and Jana Geggus for checking the references. Finally I would like to thank Robin Cooper for writing the index program.

Lund, November 1984

CHAPTER I

INTRODUCTION

1. THEORETICAL AND METHODOLOGICAL ISSUES

The aim of this book is to provide an explicit syntax and semantics for questions, in particular constituent questions, and to do so in a way which relates the linguistic data to certain central issues in linguistic theory. By way of introduction I will briefly mention what these central and often controversial issues are and indicate the nature of the linguistic data that will be brought to bear on them.

One such issue concerns the relation between syntax and semantics in the grammar. I have come to believe that what is most interesting in the study of natural language constructions is the way the syntax and the semantics of the language in question interact and constrain each other. At first sight this view might seem to go against one of the main methodological assumptions in Chomsky's work, the so-called 'autonomy of syntax' hypothesis, at least on certain interpretations of this hypothesis. However, I don't think this is a necessary conclusion. One might very well argue that the most explicit and illuminating syntactic (or semantic) analysis is one that only makes reference to strictly syntactic (or semantic) categories without bringing in semantic (or syntactic) considerations. Still, when it comes to choosing a particular syntactic (or semantic) framework as part of a grammar, it might very well be that this choice has to take into consideration the interaction of the syntax with the semantics, and vice versa. It is at this point that we can argue that a certain syntactic analysis is to be preferred because it fits in more naturally with other systems such as a system of interpretation rules, or a set of parsing strategies. Consequently, although I consider it to be methodologically desirable that syntactic and semantic rules be formulated independently of each other, I still think it is the requirements that specific syntactic and semantic frameworks establish on each other that provide the real challenge for the linguist who is interested in both syntactic and semantic adequacy. In this respect, the study of constituent questions turns out to be a particularly fruitful area. In languages like English and Swedish where interrogative phrases often occur in a syntactically designated position (Comp), it turns out that the syntactic dislocation determines the interpretation possibilities for the question in a way that we will study in detail in Chapter IV. The methodological consequences of this way of looking at autonomy and interaction will show up in the organization of the grammar for Swedish which is presented in Chapter III. I there try to formulate syntactic rules and semantic rules using only categories and terms appropriate for the type of rule in question. However, the application of certain semantic rules will be directly linked to certain syntactic configurations.

Another controversial issue in current linguistics is whether the syntactic representations of phrases and sentences in a natural language can be directly interpreted or whether an intermediate level of representation (or some system of mapping rules) must be postulated between the syntax and the semantics. The first view, viz. that it is possible to do semantic interpretation directly off the syntax of a natural language has been put forward and explored within the framework of Montague Grammar (cf. e.g. Montague, 1974; Cooper, 1975, 1983; McCloskey, 1979; and Ladusaw, 1979). The second view assumes that the relation between form and meaning has to be mediated by a disambiguated representation. This approach is taken in most linguistic analysis within the Chomskyan tradition (cf. e.g. Chomsky, 1975, 1977; Sag, 1976; Williams, 1977). Chomsky (1981) claims that the intermediate level of logical form constitutes an essential linguistic level of representation, and a prerequisite for semantic interpretation in e.g. the model theoretic sense.

In this book we will adopt the first view and explore the possibility of formulating semantic interpretation rules which apply directly to sentences of the language under an appropriate syntactic description. I use the term 'appropriate syntactic description' here in the sense of a syntactic analysis that can be motivated on purely syntactic grounds, as mentioned above. The reason for this modification is obvious. The claim that syntactic structures are directly interpretable is an interesting one only to the extent that the syntax is independently motivated, i.e. that it is not tailored for the sole purpose of fitting the semantics.

Another controversial and methodologically rather far-reaching assumption I will defend in this book is that there is no need to enrich the syntactic representation with indices (numeric subscripts). I here take issue with the practice, common in the Extended Standard Theory and the Government-Binding framework, of annotating syntactic representations with indices in order to be able to formulate constraints on coreference, disjoint reference, etc. directly on the syntactic representation. My position is that relations such as coreference and quantificational binding are essentially semantic and that such facts, although they may be formally reflected in the syntax, should be captured by the semantic rules. This means that one must formulate the semantic rules so that they can handle quantificational binding and obligatory coreference without making reference to coindexing of syntactic constituents. In Chapter III, I will introduce the semantic mechanisms that will make this approach possible. In Chapters V and VI, I will compare the type of approach that relies on coindexing of syntactic constituents with the one presented here where the syntax is kept free from auxiliary notation and where the task of assigning intended interpretations is handled by the semantic rules. We will for instance look at how the two approaches account for restrictions on anaphoric relations such as the cross-over constraint (Chapter VI.3). In this connection I will also discuss the status of the so-called non-coreference facts. I will suggest that such facts should be explained with reference to pragmatic principles of rational language use and that they need not be covered by one of the formal components of the grammar (cf. Reinhart, 1983).

An issue that has recently regained interest in linguistic theory is whether transformations are necessary. In earlier work in transformational generative grammar such as Chomsky (1975, 1965), a central claim was that linguistically adequate grammars for natural languages require a transformational component and much research was devoted to formulating precise transformational rules and stating restrictions on them. The type of data we will be investigating here, constituent questions which involve an unbounded dependency between a constituent and a gap, were thought to provide the strongest motivation for transformations. In the late 1970s, several linguists began to challenge the claim that transformations are necessary. For instance G. Gazdar and S. Peters argued that it was possible to write adequate grammars for natural languages using only phrase structure rules and started to develop non-transformational grammars. A central issue in this book is the question whether a non-transformational account for constituent questions in Swedish is feasible as well as linguistically defensible. It is interesting to note that also within the transformational paradigm, the role of transformations has changed considerably. For instance,

Chomsky (1982) does not consider it to be an important question whether the rule Move α is in fact a syntactic transformation or some other way of relating two levels of representation. What is important, according to him, is the ability to capture certain generalizations which he claims characterize the Move α relation (cf. also Chomsky, 1981, section 2.4.6).

2. UNBOUNDED DEPENDENCIES

Constituent questions in Swedish, like in English, consist of structures where an initial interrogative phrase is matched by a gap somewhere in the sentence. The task of defining the relation between the initial constituent and the gap has played a central role in the development of generative grammar. As we mentioned in the preceding section, it has been commonly assumed that such structures could not be generated by phrase structure rules alone and that they motivated postulating transformations in the grammar. Furthermore, the type of transformation involved in question formation is of a particular kind which is different from the type of transformation that was assumed to account for e.g. passive. These transformations typically involve argument positions within one clause. Ross (1967) pointed out that the rules for questions and relative clauses involve essential variables in their structural descriptions, i.e. variables that could not be replaced by an enumeration of syntactic categories. This class of rules is often called *wh*-movement rules. We will often use the term 'unbounded dependency' to refer to the relation that holds between an initial constituent and a gap. Although there is agreement on the fact that the dependencies displayed in questions hold over an unbounded domain, it is a controversial issue whether this unbounded dependency arises through one application of an unbounded process or through iterated applications of a bounded process (cf. Chomsky, 1973, 1977; Bresnan, 1977).

From the point of view of semantics, unbounded dependencies require a different approach than ordinary phrase structure rules. In Montague Grammar, the rules that build syntactic constituents are interpreted semantically as function-argument applications. The rules that form questions and relative clauses, on the other hand, involve variable binding. B. Partee (1977) points out that it is the unbounded syntactic rules that apparently involve variable binding in the semantics.

In this respect, the interpretation of sentences with unbounded dependencies thus is similar to the interpretation of quantified sentences. Indeed, several linguists have attempted to relate constraints on quantifier scope to constraints on *wh*-movement (McCawley, 1970, quoted in Seuren, 1972; Lakoff, 1971; Rodman, 1976; Cooper, 1977, 1983; May, 1977 *et al.*). To the extent that such correspondences can be established, they bear more or less directly on the nature of the interaction between syntax and semantics in the grammar.

We mentioned earlier that the existence of unbounded dependencies has been taken to provide the clearest evidence for the need for transformations in the syntax. In recent years, several linguists have shown a renewed interest in phrase structure grammars and have begun questioning the assumption that these grammars are inherently inadequate for natural languages. Non-transformational theories such as Generalized Phrase Structure Grammar (GPSG) and Lexical-Functional Grammar (LFG) have developed and linguists working within these frameworks are exploring the possibility of writing linguistically adequate grammars without using transformations. These grammars thus only involve one level of syntactic representation, surface structure. Until recently, unbounded dependencies have provided the most recalcitrant obstacle to such endeavors but now certain specific proposals have been made for how unbounded dependencies can be captured without introducing structure-mapping transformations into the grammar. These proposals are certainly worth considering seriously. If it can be shown that it is possible to write syntactically and semantically adequate grammars for natural languages without transformations, then this will presumably play a major role in the effort to restrict the class of grammars necessary for describing human languages. In this book, we will outline a grammatical framework for Swedish which does not employ transformations.

3. QUESTIONS IN SWEDISH

Most of the discussion about properties of unbounded dependency constructions in natural language has centered around data from English. The theoretical interest of looking at Swedish comes from the fact that questions in this language display certain properties that have implications for linguistic theory in general.

3.1. Extractions out of Indirect Questions

The first property is that in Swedish, as in all Scandinavian languages, it is possible to extract out of indirect questions. In English, on the other hand, *wh*-movement is assumed to be subject to the so-called *wh*-Island Constraint which prohibits extractions out of structures where a *wh*-phrase has been fronted. The question in (1) shows that the *wh*-Island Constraint does not hold for Swedish.

(1) Vilken film$_i$ var det du gärna ville veta vem$_j$ som ___$_j$
which film was it you wanted know who that
hade regisserat ___$_i$?
had directed

*Which film did you want to know who had directed?

In his paper 'On *wh*-movement' (1977), Chomsky gives a characterization of this rule. The central point in this characterization is that the rule observes subjacency, i.e. the rule may not involve positions separated by more than one cyclic node. The subjacency constraint implies the Complex NP Constraint and, given the additional assumption that Comp cannot be doubly filled, the *wh*-Island Constraint. In Chapter V, we will argue that the data from Swedish cast doubt on the assumption that subjacency is a necessary criterion on syntactic movement rules.

The non-transformational approaches to unbounded dependencies we will be discussing have primarily been developed for English, a language that typically allows one extraction per clause. In Chapter II, we will look at proposals made by G. Gazdar, R. Cooper, and S. Peters and R. W. Ritchie and discuss what modifications are needed in order to make these non-transformational approaches syntactically adequate for a language like Swedish which allows more than one extraction out of a clause. We will briefly discuss the possibility of writing a context-free grammar for a language like Swedish. We find that this depends crucially on the assumption that the number of extractions is limited to a finite number.

3.2. Bound Anaphors in Preposed Constituents

The second theoretically significant fact that can be illustrated by data from Swedish, although it is by no means exclusive to this language, is that a preposed constituent may contain bound anaphors such as reflexives, as for instance in the example in (2).

(2)   Vilken av **sina**   böcker brukar varje **författare**
      which of POSS REFL *books uses   every author*
      rekommendera?
      recommend?
      Which of his own books does every author usually recommend?

sina is a possessive reflexive pronoun which, like all reflexive pronouns in Swedish, must normally be bound by the subject of the clause in which it occurs. The problem raised by examples like (2) is how to account for the relation between the antecedent and the anaphor when the anaphor is not within the scope of the antecedent at surface structure.

The presence of bound anaphors in preposed constituents bears directly on the form and place of the semantic rules in the grammar. Within the form of the Extended Standard Theory, the rules for interpreting anaphors apply at surface structure, after the application of movement rules. These interpretation rules make reference to structural relations between antecedents and anaphors. In brief, an antecedent must c-command any item that is anaphorically related to it. When a reflexive pronoun occurs in a preposed position, it is no longer c-commanded by its antecedent. In Chapter V, we discuss how these structures could be handled within the EST framework and propose some revisions of the way the interpretive rules are stated.

Gazdar's, Cooper's, and Peters and Ritchie's non-transformational grammars directly generate questions like (2) as surface structures to which the semantic interpretation rules apply. They all adopt some version of model theoretic semantics and assume that the semantic rules work compositionally. The meaning of a constituent must be a function of the meaning of its parts and how they are put together. On these approaches, the problem raised by (2) can be formulated in the following way: How can we determine the meaning of the initial constituent **vilken av sina böcker** which contains an explicit anaphor independently of the rest of the sentence? Semantically it looks like the interrogative phrase has scope over the rest of the sentence. Still it contains anaphoric material which can only be interpreted with respect to an antecedent within the sentence, even in cases where the scope of the antecedent arguably does not extend outside the sentence. In Chapter II, we will bring out the implications of this fact for the choice of semantics to go with the base generated syntactic frameworks. In Chapter IV, we will develop a formalism which will enable us to interpret questions like (2) directly.

4. THE SEMANTICS OF QUESTIONS

The semantic analysis of questions in this book will be carried out within the brand of formal semantics which originates in the works of Richard Montague (Montague, 1974) and is frequently referred to as Montague Grammar. The reasons for choosing this particular framework are (a) that it is an explicit theory of what 'meaning' is as well as of how 'meanings' can be associated with the syntactic representation of a natural language and (b) that a significant number of linguists and philosophers have become familiar with the formalism of Montague Grammar and thus have the background to follow the by necessity rather technical exposition involved in some of the more complex cases we will analyze. I am not claiming that the distinctions I want to make with respect to the interpretation of questions or the possible results for linguistic theory that they entail can only be expressed in a Montague Grammar. Rather I regard the choice of this particular formalism as providing a convenient means of exposition. There are now several other semantic frameworks available in which the same theoretical distinctions can be expressed and which could presumably be developed to provide coherent and enlightening accounts for these phenomena. See Hintikka (1982) for an illustration in Game-Theoretical Semantics and Engdahl (1984b) for a preliminary formulation in Situation Semantics.

Most work in formal semantics has dealt with declarative sentences. There is by now a whole body of literature on the scope of a semantic theory for declaratives and what criteria of adequacy apply to it. When we turn to questions, the picture is less clear. There is less agreement on what phenomena the semantic theory should account for, and one might even encounter the opinion that it is useless to approach the semantics of questions with the methods of formal semantics, in particular truth conditional semantics. Without going too far into the issue of whether all aspects of the meaning of questions can be accounted for within a formal semantic treatment, I will mention two tests for adequacy that I think every semantic theory of questions should pass.[1] The first is that the theory should enable us to talk about the denotation of a question so that we can individuate questions in a way that corresponds to how speakers of the language differentiate between distinct questions. The second test has to do with the compositionality requirement; that the meaning of a complex expression should be a function of the meanings of its parts and the way they are put together. The meaning we assign to a question should consequently be such that it can contribute to the meaning of a question-embedding verb like *wonder, remember*, or *depend on* in an appropriate way. To this we could add as a further requirement that the semantic characterization of questions should be compatible with an analysis of the illocutionary force associated with the speech act of asking.

Following Hamblin (1973) and Karttunen (1977) we will analyze the meaning of a question in terms of its possible answers. This might at first seem to be an indirect way of approaching the meanings of questions, but we will argue that it is only through speakers' intuitions about what the possible answers to a question are that we can determine what the meaning of a question is. We will also argue that this approach meets the requirement on individuation of questions mentioned above. On Karttunen's approach, a question like (3)

(3) Who is coming to dinner?

denotes the set of true propositions of the form 'x is coming to dinner' where x is a person. So, for instance if only John is coming to dinner, then the question denotes the set containing as a single member the proposition that John is coming to dinner. If both John and Mary are coming to dinner, the question denotes the set containing the propositions that John is coming to dinner and that Mary is coming to dinner.

However, answers do not always take the form of 'individual instantiation' as in the preceding illustration. The question in (3) could presumably just as well have been answered as in (4).

(4) a. I am not.
 b. Someone you don't know.
 c. A man from Canada.
 d. Everybody except John.
 e. Nobody.

I think any one of the alternatives in (4) would count as an informative answer to the question in some context. In this study, I will have very little to say about what answers people actually give to a question. In order to say anything interesting about actually occurring answers one must take into account both large chunks of discourse and the non-linguistic setting of the question and this would go far beyond the scope of the present study. For similar reasons I won't here discuss the interesting issue of what determines whether an answer is appropriate or not in a given situation. I refer the reader to Manor (1982), Groenendijk and Stokhof (1983b), and von Stechow and Zimmermann (1984).²

By letting questions denote sets of propositions, we are also able to comply with the second criterion for adequacy. The meaning of a question, when it occurs embedded as in (5), will contribute to the embedding VP in a straight-forward way.

(5)   Mary wonders who is coming to dinner.

(5) can be paraphrased as follows: Mary stands in the *wonder* relation to the set of true propositions of the form 'x is coming to dinner' where x is a person. Another way of paraphrasing it would be to say that Mary wonders which propositions are in the set denoted by the embedded question.

Most of the literature on questions (a noteworthy exception is Belnap (1982)) has dealt with *individual questions*, i.e. questions which can be satisfactorily answered by individual instantiation as in our discussion of (3). However, there exist questions which cannot be answered in this way. Some examples are given in (6)–(8).

(6) Q: Who does *no man* like?
    A: *His* mother-in-law.

(7) Q: Where do *most people* settle down?
    A: Close to where *they* grew up.

(8) Q: Which of *his* teachers does *every student* like best?
    A: The one *he* feels *he* can talk to.

The point of an example like (6) is that there might very well not be any single woman that isn't loved by any man, but it might still be true that no man loves the woman who stands in the mother-in-law relation to him. Similarly the answers in (7) and (8) don't pick out any particular individuals or places, but rather individuals and places that are somehow related to the NPs *most people* and *every student*. I will call these readings of questions *relational questions*. In Chapter IV, I will argue that the existence of relational questions shows that it is not sufficient to let interrogative quantifiers involve quantification over individuals only. Rather what we need is a way of letting interrogative quantifiers pick out individuals or sets of individuals that are somehow related to the denotation of other NPs in the question. On this approach, (8) comes out as denoting the set of true propositions of the form 'every student x likes $W(x)$ best' where $W(x)$ is a teacher of x's. A particular value for W would be the function that maps each student into the teacher he feels he can talk to.

5. EXTENSIONS OF THE PRESENT STUDY

The approach to constituent questions taken in this book is almost entirely theoretical. I have restricted myself to the formulation of syntactic and semantic rules for a rather large and theoretically interesting body of data in Swedish. The syntactic and semantic rules are intended to generate (or admit) all possible structures in the language and to assign them all possible readings. Very little is said here about how people actually produce and process the kinds of questions discussed here. This does not mean that I don't think it would be fruitful to try to link these rules with considerations having to do with parsing as well as general processing factors. On the contrary, I believe that a very natural extension to this work would be to study what strategies people use when they process the often complex type of sentences analyzed here. I have recently begun some experimental work on how people process sentences with unbounded dependencies (Engdahl, 1982d) which I hope to extend to questions. In particular it would be interesting to investigate whether sentences with preposed constituents containing explicit or potential anaphors are in general harder to process than other sentences with unbounded dependencies. Sentences with preposed anaphors involve a double task. In order to interpret them the hearer must both identify the gap and determine the appropriate antecedent for the anaphor. I believe this kind of experimental work would be a valuable addition to the theoretical discussion here since it would bear directly on the interaction of processing-motivated restrictions and the form of constraints in the grammar (cf. Fodor to appear; Frazier, 1979).

The semantic interpretation has been couched in standard model theoretic terms and again very little has been said about how these interpretation rules relate to what people actually do when they understand sentences of the language. However, it is my belief that this semantic approach is compatible with a more explicit constructivistic approach where the interpretation rules are taken to correspond more or less directly to the types of discourse model construction and checking that people might perform during the production and understanding of questions, answers, imperatives, as well as statements. For some suggestions along these lines see Dahl (1977, 1983), Kamp (1981) and Johnson-Laird (1982).

NOTES

[1] See Peters (1982) for similar considerations.

[2] The authors mentioned in the text are concerned with characterizing the notion *relevant* or *useful* answer. It seems quite likely that in an extension of the present analysis, we could use algorithms for calculating relevant answers to account for how information is organized, either in the individual or in computational data base systems.

CHAPTER II

RECENT APPROACHES TO UNBOUNDED DEPENDENCIES

0. INTRODUCTION

We mentioned briefly in the first chapter that the possibility of writing linguistically adequate grammars that do not employ transformations is currently being explored by several linguists. In this chapter. We will first present some data on unbounded dependencies in Swedish illustrating the type of constructions we are focussing on in this study. We will then look at three non-transformational approaches which have been proposed for English and investigate how readily they can be extended to handle the Swedish data. One interesting point turns out to be what type of semantics is required in order to interpret directly generated surface structures, in particular structures involving unbounded dependencies. After a brief look at how unbounded dependencies are handled in one current version of transformational grammar, the Government-Binding framework, we summarize the reasons behind our choice of a framework for this study.

1. SHORT OVERVIEW OF RELEVANT DATA FROM SWEDISH

The aim of this book is partly to provide an explicit and linguistically motivated syntax and semantics for questions in Swedish, in particular for constituent questions. These types of questions are sometimes referred to as WH questions. They are typically introduced by an interrogative phrase, as in (1).

(1)   What do you think John put in the basket?

Syntactically, constituent questions pattern together with topicalizations and relative clauses in Swedish. These three types of constructions have in common that they relate a preposed constituent to an empty position (a gap)[1] inside the sentence over an unbounded domain. It seems plausible that the same type of syntactic dependency is involved in all three cases. Although we are mainly concerned with questions, we will sometimes consider examples involving other types of unbounded dependencies. What we have called unbounded dependencies here have also been discussed under the terms 'extractions', 'long-distance dependencies', and 'movement phenomena'. The choice of label is of no particular interest. What is of theoretical interest, however, is the implicit assumption that there is a difference between unbounded dependencies and other types of dependencies, which we can call 'local dependencies'. Local dependencies can be illustrated by the type of dependency involved in passive constructions, dative shift, and particle movement. These constructions crucially involve NPs that are arguments to the same verb, as has been pointed out in Bresnan (1978) and Dowty (1978). Hence they can be defined as local operations on the argument structure of verbs. The grammatical function of these NPs can be determined given only information about their surface position and the voice of the verb.

In long-distance dependencies, on the other hand, the grammatical function of the preposed constituent cannot be determined by looking solely at the closest verb. Instead we must identify the gap corresponding to the preposed constituent, since it is only with respect to this position that we can assign the preposed constituent its grammatical role. A preposed constituent may be separated from its deep-structure position over an arbitrarily long string of lexical material, provided that the extraction does not violate any *syntactic islands* in the language under consideration. Exactly what structures constitute syntactic islands varies from language to language. In certain languages, tensed sentences in general may constitute islands, whereas in other languages extractions may occur out of a subset of tensed sentences, such as the declarative sentences. In English it is generally assumed that indirect questions and relative clauses are syntactic islands. In order to prevent extractions out of one or both of these structures, linguists have introduced constraints like the Complex NP Constraint (Ross, 1967), Subjacency (Chomsky, 1973, 1977), the *wh*-Island Constraint (Chomsky, 1977), and the NP Constraint (Horn, 1974). A consequence of these constraints is that not more than one constituent can be extracted from a tensed clause in English.

Within linguistic theory, so far most of the discussion on constraints on unbounded movement has been based on facts from English or similar languages, i.e. languages where extractions are limited to one per sentence. The theoretical interest in looking at long-distance dependencies in Swedish is that this language, like the other Scandinavian languages, allows more than one extraction out of a tensed sentence.

RECENT APPROACHES TO UNBOUNDED DEPENDENCIES

We find extractions out of indirect questions as well as out of relative clauses. However, not all sentences with multiple extractions are equally good and in Chapter III we discuss some factors that may lie behind the variation in acceptability. We also address the issue of whether or not an upper limit on the number of extractions should be stated in the grammar. Some examples of constructions that we want our grammar of Swedish to account for are given in (2)–(5). For perspicuousness, we will indicate gaps by '____' and the relation between a given gap and a preposed constituent by coindexing.

(2)   [$\bar{S}_1$ Vilken film$_j$ var det du ville veta [$\bar{S}_2$ vem$_i$
which film was it you wanted know who

som ____$_i$ regisserat ____$_j$?]]
that   directed

Which movie was it you wanted to know who directed?

(3)   [$\bar{S}_1$ Vilken film$_j$ var det du redan glömt [$\bar{S}_2$ vem$_k$ det
which film was it you already forgotten who it

var som ____$_k$ visste [$\bar{S}_3$ vem$_i$ som ____$_i$
was that   knew   who that

regisserat ____$_j$?]]]
directed

Which movie was it that you had already forgotten who it was that knew who had directed?

(4)   Vilken artikel$_i$ finns det faktiskt [$_{NP}$ en möjlighet
which article exists it in-fact a possibility

[$_{\bar{S}}$ att Dagens Nyheter tar in ___$_i$?]]
that Dagens Nyheter takes in

Which article is there in fact a possibility that Dagens Nyheter accepts?

(5)   Vilken filmstjärna$_i$ skulle du gärna vilja
which filmstar should you with-pleasure want

träffa [$_{NP}$ någon$_j$ [$_S$ som ____$_j$ kan presentera dig
meet someone that can introduce you

för ____$_i$?]]
for

Which filmstar would you like to meet someone who can introduce you to?

In (2)–(3) the extraction sites occur inside an indirect question, in (4) inside a noun complement, and in (5) inside a relative clause.

The relative marker **som**, which we have glossed as *that*, is obligatory if the subject has been relativized, as in (5). Notice that **som** is required in indirect questions as well, if the subject has been questioned and occurs in the Comp adjacent to the empty subject position as in (2). Apparently the intervening clefting phrase **det var** (*it was*) doesn't count for the notion of adjacency assumed here, as shown by the obligatoriness of **som** following **det var** in (3). One might raise the question whether there really are any subject gaps in these structures, or whether **som**, in some sense, acts as a subject place holder. There is some evidence that goes against this assumption. If another clause intervenes between the preposed constituent, and the empty subject position, then **som** can optionally occur adjacent to the preposed constituent, but not adjacent to (or in) the empty subject slot. This is illustrated in (6).

(6) [$\bar{S}_1$ Vilken film$_j$ kunde ingen minnas   [$\bar{S}_2$ vem$_i$ (som)
     which film could no-one remember   who   (that)

   alla trodde [$\bar{S}_3$ ___$_i$/*som hade regisserat ___$_j$?]]]
   *all believed   *that had directed*

   Which movie could no one remember who (that) everyone thought (*that) had directed?

It thus seems plausible that **som** is attached outside S, and that even in examples like (2) and (3), there is really a gap in subject position.[2]

In the examples above, the grammatical function of the initial interrogative phrase cannot be determined until the gap is found, but the preposed constituent itself can be fully interpreted. There are also cases where the preposed constituent contains anaphoric material, for instance a reflexive pronoun. Consequently, the constituent cannot be fully interpreted until the antecedent for the reflexive pronoun has been determined. Consider the example given in (7):

(7) [Vilken av **sina** böcker]$_i$ påstod du att de   flesta
     which of self's books   claimed you that DEF. most

   författare tycker bäst om ___$_i$?
   authors   think best about

Which of their books did you claim that most authors like best?

Sina, glossed as *self's*, is a third-person possessive reflexive pronoun which alternates with the personal possessive **hans** (*his*) and **hennes** (*her*) in the same way that ordinary reflexive and personal pronouns alternate. In order to determine the antecedent for **sina**, we must locate the gap and from this position find a third-person antecedent in a syntactically permissible position, according to the reflexivization rules of the language. The general rule in Swedish is that a reflexive pronoun is controlled by the subject of the smallest tensed sentence in which it occurs.[3] In this case, **de flesta författare** (*most authors*) fulfills both requirements and the question receives the interpretation given in the English paraphrase. Sentences like (7) where a reflexive pronoun occurs outside the scope of its antecedent, both syntactically and, it will be argued, semantically, pose a challenge for any grammatical theory that generates and interprets all constituents in their surface position.

2. ARGUMENTS FOR TRANSFORMATIONS

When one looks at constituent questions, one immediately notices that they are systematically related to the corresponding declarative sentences. Consider the range of data in (8).

(8) a. John thought Mary was here.
    b. *John thought Mary were here.
    c. *Which student$_i$ did John think ___$_i$ were here?
    d. *Which student$_i$ did John think Mary was here?
    e. Which student$_i$ did John think ___$_i$ was here?

In brief, questions and declaratives have the same subcategorization properties. The preposed question constituent triggers the same agreement phenomena as in the corresponding declarative, (8c). It must be correlated with an empty position, (8d). It has been assumed that these correlations can be explained most economically if questions are derived from underlying declarative sentences by a transformation which has the effect of moving a WH-constituent to the front of the sentence.

All through the development of generative grammar, it has been a main issue that natural languages display phenomena which cannot be adequately captured by phrase structure rules, but which require access to transformational rules (cf. Chomsky, 1957, 1965; Postal, 1964).

Formally, transformations are rules that map structures into structures. A consequence of introducing such rules into the grammar is that the grammar exceeds the power of context-free grammars and that the languages generated may fall outside the set of recursive languages (cf. Peters and Ritchie, 1973b). The transformational component thus made the grammars extremely powerful, and much of the linguistic research in the sixties and seventies aimed at constraining the transformational component of the grammar as much as possible.

Recently the position of transformational grammar (henceforth TG) has been challenged by among others Gerald Gazdar. He claims that the move to adopt transformations was made on insufficient grounds and that, contrary to what has been widely assumed, a syntactically and semantically adequate grammar for English can be given using essentially a context-free grammar (Gazdar, 1981, 1982). Several other linguists have developed frameworks which dispense with transformational rules in favor of direct generation of surface structures (Bach, 1980; Brame, 1978; Hudson, 1976; Peters, 1979). Bresnan (1978) argued that all local transformations should be handled by lexical rules. Gazdar has taken one step further in explicitly claiming that all transformations, bounded as well as unbounded, can be handled by devices that are more restricted than transformations and which do not increase the generative capacity of the grammar beyond context-free languages. If non-transformational approaches, employing linguistically motivated rules, can be shown to reach the same level of descriptive adequacy as current transformational approaches, then a non-transformational approach appears very attractive. If it can be shown that grammars that employ only one level of representation, surface structure, are linguistically adequate, then the burden of proof appears to be on those linguists who advocate theories with more levels of representation. Furthermore, the type of rules allowed in a context-free phrase structure grammar is more restricted. There exist efficient algorithms for parsing the context-free languages generated or accepted by context-free grammars, whereas much less is known about the formal properties of non-context-free languages. For an overview of the efficiency of various parsing algorithms, see Perrault (1983) and references therein.

Even if a context-free grammar can be shown to be descriptively adequate, the issue of explanatory adequacy may still be raised. If it turns out that the resulting grammars, although context-free, are totally uninteresting from the point of view of linguistic analysis, then the whole project will not be seen as making progress in the theory of grammar for natural languages. Gazdar claims, however, that so-called linguistically significant generalizations can be equally well expressed in the type of context-free phrase structure grammar he proposes, and this claim is certainly worth investigating seriously. It seems likely that the issue cannot be resolved until a number of transformational and non-transformational grammars for languages of different types are available for comparison. Given the growing interest in writing and implementing grammars for comprehensive fragments of natural language (cf. e.g. Barwise *et al.* (to appear), Berwick and Weinberg (1982), Gawron *et al.* (1982), and Joshi (1983)), the required base for comparison might actually be available within the next couple of years. In this chapter, we will investigate whether a non-transformational approach to Swedish is feasible, and begin by giving an outline of three recent non-transformational grammars.

3. GENERALIZED PHRASE-STRUCTURE GRAMMARS

In a series of recent papers, G. Gazdar has proposed a grammatical framework which he claims will provide an adequate account for the syntax of English without exceeding the power of a context-free grammar (Gazdar, 1981, 1982). A number of rather detailed proposals for various constructions in English and other languages have now been worked out with this framework, which we will refer to as Generalized Phrase-Structure Grammar, henceforth GPSG, (cf. Gazdar, Pullum and Sag (1982), Gazdar and Pullum (1982), Barlow *et al.* (1982), and Gazdar *et al.* (to appear)).[4]

3.1. Syntactic Rules

GPSG uses only phrase structure rules, which are interpreted as node admissibility conditions.[5] Sets of phrase structure rules may be related by *metarules*, which can be seen as inductive devices for predicting the existence of types of rules. The phrase-structure rules introduce syntactic categories which are structured sets of a finite number of syntactic features (cf. Gazdar and Pullum (1982), and Gazdar *et al.* (to appear)) for the formal theory of features assumed in GPSG). The idea of letting syntactic categories be complex symbols has been used by several linguists, e.g. Chomsky (1970), Bresnan (1976), Jackendoff (1977), and

McCloskey (1979). What is new in GPSG is that features can take syntactic categories as values. (9) gives an illustration of a syntactic category, in this case a noun phrase.

(9)
$$\begin{bmatrix} \text{Feature} & \text{Value} \\ \text{N} & + \\ \text{V} & - \\ \text{BAR} & 2 \\ \text{PER} & 3 \\ \text{NUMB} & 1 \\ \text{SLASH} & \begin{bmatrix} \text{N} & + \\ \text{V} & - \\ \text{BAR} & 2 \end{bmatrix} \\ \text{NUL} & - \\ \cdot & \cdot \\ \cdot & \cdot \end{bmatrix}$$

The features are subject to different instantiation conventions such as the *Head Feature Convention*. Features which are subject to this convention are called HEAD features. They include the features which determine the categorical properties of a category, whether it is verbal or nominal, etc., as well as inherent properties that may be relevant for morphological and syntactic agreement processes such as number, person, and gender. The Head Feature Convention ensures that the head features on a mother category are identical to the ones on the head of the phrase. FOOT features indicate that a given constituent either consists of or contains a particular type of phrase such as an interrogative phrase or a reflexive pronoun. The feature SLASH, which takes a category as its value, indicates that the category contains a hole, i.e. that somewhere in the subtree admitted under this category there will be a gap. The example in (9) thus consists of a third-person singular NP with a PP-gap. Instead of representing SLASH as in (9), we will continue to use the informal notation 'α/β', introduced in Gazdar (1981), for a category α whose value for SLASH is β. Categories whose values for SLASH are not null are sometimes referred to as *derived* or *slashed* categories.

Slashed categories are used in order to handle unbounded dependencies. Gazdar's original idea was that such dependencies, which according to several linguists required movement and/or deletion transformations, can be handled by encoding both the information that there

RECENT APPROACHES TO UNBOUNDED DEPENDENCIES

is a constituent missing and the relevant information about this constituent in the syntactic categories which lie on the projection path from the gap to the filler.[6] This is precisely what the feature SLASH does. In GPSG, sentences with unbounded dependencies are admitted by phrase-structure rules of the form given by the rule schema in (10). Rules introducing slashed categories are called *linking* rules.

(10) $S \rightarrow \alpha \ S/\alpha$

Slashed categories may be eliminated by a schema as in (11) which introduces a designated terminal t, the empty string.[7]

(11) $\alpha/\alpha \rightarrow t$

An instance of this schema would be NP/NP, dominating a gap. In this case, t, would be translated by a designated variable h of the appropriate type to translate NPs. We will write this as $h_{\langle NP \rangle}$. (10) and (11) in conjunction ensure that a sentence-initial constituent will always be matched with a gap of the appropriate type somewhere in the sentence.

Linking rules are used for instance to introduce constituent questions, relative clauses, and topicalized sentences. (12) shows a tree for a simple embedded question.

(12)

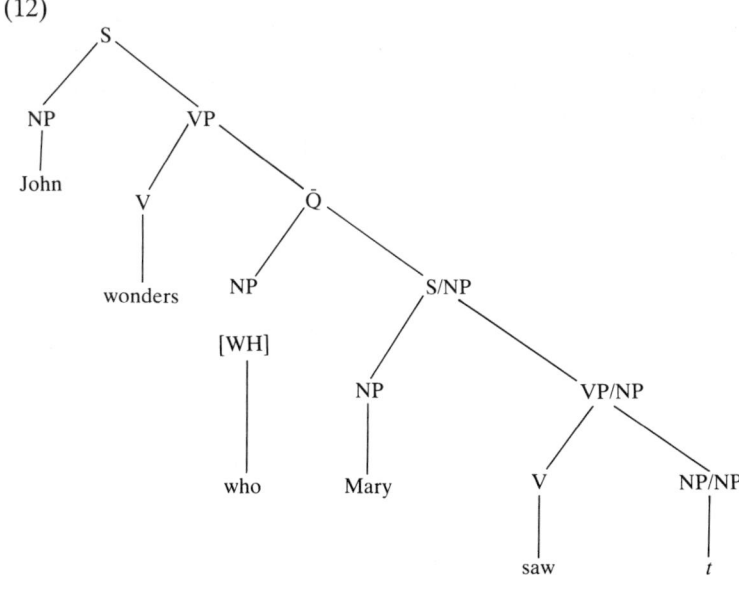

This figure illustrates how the unbounded dependency information is represented in the syntactic tree. Recall that '/NP' is just an abbreviation about number, gender, person, and case of the missing constituent. This information is then passed down and is available for checking that the local context of t is compatible with the dislocated constituent.

The category structure in (9) allows for one value for SLASH, i.e. it will allow syntactic categories that dominate trees with exactly one constituent missing. But as we saw in the data overview in the previous section, Swedish allows more than one extraction out of a clause. English also allows for double extractions, for instance out of infinitival questions, as in (13).

(13)   This problem$_j$ John doesn't know what$_i$ to do ____$_i$ about ____$_j$.

Maling and Zaenen (1982) furthermore point out that cases of multiple extractions in English may arise through the interaction of leftwards and rightwards dependencies, both of which involve the feature SLASH in GPSG. Consequently it appears necessary to extend the category structure in (9) so that it allows for SLASH to take more than one value. Making this extension, however, raises a number of interesting issues. First, will it be sufficient to assume that there is an unordered set of values for SLASH? If there are restrictions on the ways fillers and gaps may be linked up, then one way to encode this would be by having SLASH take sequences of values, where the order in the sequence somehow reflects the order of occurrences of fillers or gaps. Fodor's *Nested Dependency Constraint* for English (Fodor, 1978), which prevents intersecting assignments, suggests that the order of the fillers and gaps matters, when the values of SLASH are of the same syntactic category. However, when the values of SLASH are of distinct categories, intersecting assignments are allowed, which indicates that simply having a sequence of SLASH values might not be appropriate. Chapter III.6.2 contains a discussion of this matter in connection with the question of whether the preference for nested assignments is a property of the grammar or a reflex of parsing strategies used in interpreting sentences.

Second, how many coefficients can SLASH take? If we want the grammar to remain context-free, we clearly have to set an upper limit on the number of SLASH values any syntactic category can contain, or the number of syntactic categories would no longer be finite, which is a prerequisite for context-free grammars. The issue is now whether we want to incorporate a restriction on the number of gaps in the grammar. The examples we have come across so far involve two gaps. In Chapter III.7.1, we will discuss some examples of triple-gap sentences in Swedish. I argue there that restrictions on the number of empty nodes follow from performance limitations and that they should not be stated in the syntax. Whether or not an unlimited number of gaps should be allowed is a purely theoretical issue. For all practical purposes, a grammar with some fixed upper bound on the number of gaps, say n, will be sufficient for a language like Swedish. But I think it would be misleading to argue, on the basis of this factual circumstance, that Swedish has the property of allowing exactly n gaps. To set some numeric limit may be a practical step, but I think it will always be an arbitrary stipulation which does not express any essential property of the language. My argument is that, just as we do not want to impose any numeric limit on the number of center-embedded relative clauses that a grammar should allow, we should not state any limit on the number of extractions out of a sentence either. From the point of view of devising a grammar that could be employed in parsing, we could probably write a context-free grammar for ordinary Swedish, allowing for two, possibly three gaps. But if all that matters is parsability and what constructions are used in the language, then we could equally well argue that the most appropriate grammar for Swedish is a finite state grammar, since the facility for unlimited recursion is never used.[8] A linguistic grammar, on the other hand, focusses on what structures are generable in the language, not on what structures are actually used. It seems to me that a linguistically defensible stand is that a grammar for Swedish should in principle allow for both unlimited center embeddings and unlimited extractions and that restrictions should be attributed to performance factors such as limited processing capacity and short-term memory. If we are interested in providing linguistically adequate grammars for natural languages, then it appears that languages like Swedish put the adequacy of the GPSG approach in question. In order for GPSG to maintain the claim that the grammar is context-free, it is important that the set of rules and symbols in the grammar be finite. Unbounded dependencies are handled by creating new syntactic categories, essentially a new category for each node that can dominate one or more empty nodes, where the number of empty nodes is also a distinguishing feature on the dominating node. It is an open issue how this approach can be extended to account for the apparently recursive gap-generating device which seems to be what we need to reflect the linguistic competence among speakers of languages where there is no fixed upper limit on extraction.[9]

3.2. Semantic Rules

3.2.1. Designated Variables

We now turn to see how the semantic rules in GPSG can handle sentences with multiple long-distance dependencies. The framework assumes a compositional semantics which gives the meaning of a dominating node as a function of the meanings of its daughter constituents. The meaning of a constituent is repesented by its translation into Intensional Logic (IL) (cf. Montague, 1974). For convenience we will represent the translation of a node XP by XP'. As mentioned above, empty categories translate into *designated* variables, $h_{\langle\alpha\rangle}$, one for each syntactic category α. The translation of a linking rule which introduces a dislocated constituent of category α involves abstracting over the designated variable $h_{\langle\alpha\rangle}$. The resulting function applies to the translation of the dislocated constituent, which consequently can be converted into the position held by h in the translation of the sentence with a gap, and which corresponds to the empty node t.

The rule schemata for topicalization and constituent questions could look like that in (14) and (15).

(14) *Schema for Topicalization*
  $\langle S \rightarrow \alpha \quad S/\alpha, \quad \lambda h_{\langle\alpha\rangle}[(S/\alpha)'](\alpha')\rangle \quad \alpha = $ NP, PP, AP, $\bar{S}$

(15) *Schema for Constituent Questions*
  $\langle Q \rightarrow \underset{[WH]}{\alpha} \quad S/\alpha, \quad \lambda p \,\exists n[\lambda h_{\langle\alpha\rangle}[\check{\,}p \,\&\, p = \hat{\,}(S/\alpha)'](\alpha')]\rangle$

The semantic part of the rule in (15) essentially amounts to the interpretation for questions given in Karttunen (1977) and adopted in a way similar to that suggested in Cooper (1978b). We will discuss the semantics in detail in Chapter IV. To simplify this initial discussion, we assume that NPs just translate into individual type variables and we omit intensions in argument expressions.

WH phrases are translated into expressions containing the designated variable n. Actually, there is a correlation between the syntactic feature WH and occurrences of the variable n in the translation. A simple interrogative phrase like *who* will just be translated into n. Notice that the question rule, in addition to abstraction over h, involves existential quantification over n.

We can illustrate how the semantic part of the rule in (15) works by looking at the translation for the sentence whose structure is given in (12). Proceeding bottom-up, we get the following translation for the embedded question *who Mary saw*.

(16) (i) $[_{NP/NP}\ t]$ $h_{\langle NP \rangle}$
      (ii) $[_{VP/NP}\ saw\ t]$ **see**$'\ (h_{\langle NP \rangle})$
      (iii) $[_{S/NP}\ Mary\ saw\ t]$ **see**$'\ (m, h_{\langle NP \rangle})$
      (iv) $[_{NP_2}\ who]$ n
      (v) $[_{\bar{Q}}\ who\ Mary\ saw\ t]$ $\lambda p\ \exists n[\lambda h_{\langle NP \rangle}[\check{}p \wedge p =$
                                          $= \hat{}\mathbf{see}'\ (m, h_{\langle NP \rangle})](n)] =$
                                          $= \lambda p\ \exists n[\check{}p \wedge p = \hat{}\mathbf{see}'\ (m, n)]$

The translation for the entire sentence can be paraphrased as John wonders for which n it is true that Mary saw n, or, equivalently, John stands in the wonder relation to the set of true propositions of the form 'Mary saw n'. In step (v), the translation for *who* goes in for the variable in the translation of the empty node. The existential quantifier will then bind the designated variable n, and we get the desired translation.

There is one major problem with using a designated variable corresponding to an occurrence of an empty node in the syntax. This problem becomes obvious as soon as one considers sentences with more gaps, which as we have seen, are part of the data we want to account for. Sentences with multiple gaps occur not only in Swedish, but also in English, where untensed constructions allow for more than one gap, as for instance in (13), repeated here as (17), where a phrase has been topicalized out of an infinitival question.

(17)   This problem$_j$ John doesn't know what$_i$ to do ____$_i$ about ____$_j$.

The structure for (17) would presumably be something like in (18), assuming some modifications to allow for infinitival questions and double gaps. The number in parenthesis on a node indicates the rule that admits that node.

(18)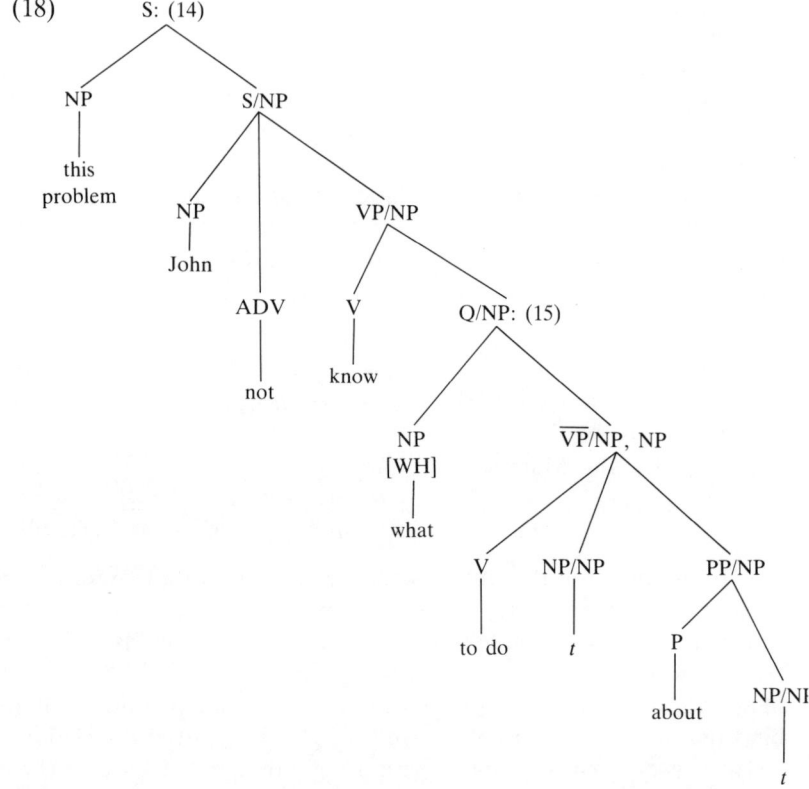

In (18), all NP/NP nodes are expanded as t, which according to the rule schema in (19) is translated by the designated variable $h_{\langle NP\rangle}$.

(19) *Schema for Empty Nodes*
$\langle \alpha/\alpha \to t, h_{\langle \alpha \rangle} \rangle$

Consequently, the translation of the tree rooted in VP/NP,NP will contain two occurrences of $h_{\langle NP\rangle}$ and the translation rule for the indirect question will insert the translation of *what* in both places. The abstraction at the S level will be vacuous and the sentence will come out with an unwanted meaning. If we leave the details of the correct interpretation of infinitival questions aside,[10] (17) will come out meaning roughly that John stands in the *doesn't know* relation to the set of true propositions such that for some n, someone should do n about n. This is clearly not an appropriate interpretation since we have lost the information that John was ignorant about what to do about a certain problem. The same thing happens in sentences with extractions out of *tough* complements as in (20).

(20)   What kind of student$_j$ is subjacency$_i$ hard to explain ___$_i$ to ___$_j$?
(Maling and Zaenen, 1980).

Even if we amend the syntax so that it allows for two gaps, the semantic rules will fail to assign the appropriate meanings, as long as we use only one designated variable for empty nodes. One way to get around this problem would be to let linking rules introduce indexed constituents which are matched with indexed variables as translations for the empty nodes. A translation schema for topicalization along these lines could look like in (21) and the rule for terminal nodes could be as in (22).

(21) $\langle S \to \alpha_i \ S/\alpha_i, \ \lambda h_{i\langle\alpha\rangle}[(S/\alpha_i)'](\alpha_i)\rangle$

(22) $\langle \alpha/\alpha_i \to t, \ h_{i\langle\alpha\rangle}\rangle$

The kind of indexing suggested in (21) and (22) might be sufficient to guarantee a unique pairing between preposed constituents and empty nodes. However, it still would not provide the right semantics for sentences with more than one interrogative phrase, as in the interrogative counterpart to (17), given in (23).

(23)   Which problem$_j$ did John not know what$_i$ to do ___$_i$ about ___$_j$?

If we let all interrogative phrases translate into expressions containing the designated variable n, then all occurrences of n will be bound by the first existential quantification over n and, the result would be the same as in the topicalized version.

To get the desired interpretations for sentences with multiple interrogative phrases, we need to make sure that each variable introduced in the translation of a WH phrase gets bound by a distinct quantifier. If we assume that the index on preposed constituents, proposed in (21), somehow is transmitted down to the WH phrase, then we could link a particular index with the introduction of a particular designated variable. The translation schema for constituent questions would be as in (24) and the rule for interrogative NPs as in (25).

(24) $\langle Q \rightarrow \alpha_i \ \ S/\alpha_i, \ \ \lambda p \ \exists n_i[\lambda h_{i\langle\alpha\rangle}[\check{\ }p \wedge p = \hat{\ }(S/\alpha_i)'(\alpha_i')]]\rangle$

(25) $\langle [_{NP_i} \text{ who}], n_i \rangle$
         [WH]

This way we could get the intended interpretation for (23). Notice, however, that this transmission of indices is triggered by the application of a linking rule. It will not cover those interrogative phrases which occur in situ in multiple questions as in (26).

(26)   Which boy$_i$ did you see ___$_i$ kiss which girl?

If there was no indexing of WH phrases at all, (26) would come out with the meaning we normally associate with (27), assuming that the unmoved WH phrase gets quantified in last.

(27)   Which boy did you see kiss himself?

The indexing schema in (24) will only apply to the preposed WH phrase *which boy*. In order to be able to interpret unmoved WH phrases as well we need an extra convention which assigns them translations with free n variables. Furthermore, one must keep track of exactly which variables are used so as to prevent accidental variable collision and so as to ensure that all WH phrases get quantified in.[11]

If we adopt the kind of correspondence of indices suggested above, the grammar is no longer context-free. G. Gazdar (personal communication) conjectures that the class of languages generated by this type of grammar would probably fall within the indexed languages, a proper subset of the context-sensitive languages, which keep track of dependencies by indexing nodes and distributing the information across daughters (cf. Hopcroft and Ullman, 1979, p. 389).

3.2.2. Lambda Conversion

Granted that we allow the syntactic and semantic rules a limited indexing capacity for distinctness purposes, we could apparently translate structures with, in principle, any number of dislocated constituents. This revised version of Gazdar's framework might then be semantically adequate for a language like Swedish, although the syntax would no longer be provably context-free. We recall that the grammar directly generates sentences with dislocated constituents in their surface positions. The syntactic configurations are interpreted by semantic rules which conform to the principle of compositionality: the meaning of an expression is a function of the meanings of its parts and of the way they are put together. As we saw in the previous section, the semantic part of linking rules use lambda conversion which essentially has the effect of inserting the translation of the preposed constituent into the position of the empty node in the translation of the sentence. There is one major problem with using lambda conversion for this purpose, which we will now address explicitly. The problem arises in sentences where some anaphoric relation holds between a preposed constituent, or some phrase contained in a preposed constituent, and some other constituent in the sentence. The rule schema for topicalization given in (14) will give the correct result for sentences like (28) and (29) where the denotation of the preposed constituent in some sense remains constant.

(28)   Mary, John likes a lot.

(29)   In Paris, Susan met Bill.

Lambda conversion will apply to the topicalized constituent and the sentences will come out meaning the same as their declarative counterparts. But the rule in (14) will not give the correct result for a sentence like (30).

(30)   By herself, Mary couldn't have solved the problem.

In (30) the denotation of the preposed constituent *by herself* cannot be determined until the antecedent for the reflexive pronoun *herself* has been established. Suppose we translate reflexive pronouns by some designated variable, say r, and that we capture the fact that reflexive pronouns, at least in English and Swedish, must be interpreted as controlled by some constituent in the same tensed sentence by a rule that abstracts over r at the VP level, thus ensuring that any occurrence of r will be bound by the subject. This is essentially the analysis of reflexives in GPSG proposed in Gazdar and Sag (1981) and it works for occurrences of reflexive pronouns inside the VP. However, when a reflexive occurs in preposed constituent, as in (30), we cannot use the rule involving lambda conversion in (14) to make sure that the reflexive gets bound by the appropriate antecedent in the sentence. The reason for this is that lambda conversion is a way of relating well-formed expressions to well-formed expressions (cf. Church (1940)).[12] The translation of (30), according to (14) will be a formula with a free r variable occurring in the argument expression. Since a formula where a variable occurs freely is not equivalent to a formula where this variable is bound, r may not get bound during the application of a function to the argument where it is contained. But this is exactly what would happen if we were to convert the translation of *by herself* into the sentence and under the scope of an abstraction operator over r.[13] However, if lambda conversion does not apply, r remains free and we don't get the intended interpretation for the sentence. It thus appears that this approach to topicalized reflexives is not viable. However, there is a way of getting around this problem which exploits the correspondence between the presence of a syntactic feature for reflexives and occurrences of the designated variable r. This approach was outlined by E. Klein at the Amsterdam Colloquium on Formal Methods in the Study of Language in March 1980.[14]

Klein's suggestion amounts to having special rules for constituents with preposed reflexives in which the designated variable r is temporarily bound during the application of the topicalization rule. This avoids the violation of lambda conversion we mentioned above. In addition to (14) and (19), the rule schemata for 'regular' topicalization and 'regular' empty nodes, we would have (31) and (32).

(31) $\langle S \rightarrow \alpha_{[SELF]} \quad S/\alpha_{[SELF]}, \quad \lambda v_{0_{\langle e, \tau(\alpha) \rangle}}[S/\alpha)'](\lambda r[\alpha']) \rangle$

(32) $\langle \alpha/\alpha_{[SELF]} \rightarrow t, \quad v_{0_{\langle e, \tau(\alpha) \rangle}}(r) \rangle$

A reflexive gap is thus translated by a designated variable, v_0, over functions from individuals to objects of the type of the preposed constituent. This function is immediately applied to the designated variable r. Klein's proposal works for topicalized reflexives like in (30). However, it is not clear how to extend this treatment to reflexive pronouns that occur in constituent questions, as for instance in (33).

(33) Which picture of herself does Mary like best?

It can be argued that the scope of the interrogative phrase is determined by its surface position. A rule that converts the preposed constituent in the case of a constituent question into a position inside the sentence would fail to account for this. The problem of how to resolve the apparent conflict between the scope of the WH phrase and the interpretation of anaphors contained in it is the main topic of Chapter IV

and we will delay further discussion of sentences like (33) until then.
Instead we will turn to another respect in which Klein's approach appears to be inadequate as a general technique for interpreting sentences with bound anaphors in preposed constituents. Recall that Klein's proposal makes use of the syntactic feature [SELF] and that the variable used in the translation of a constituent marked with this feature is recoverable. However, we also get sentences like (34).

(34)   On his birthday, every boy is happy.

(34) has two readings. According to one, every boy was happy on some particular boy's birthday, e.g. on Peter's birthday, if Peter is the contextually salient person picked out by *his*. On the other reading, *his* is interpreted as bound by the quantifier *every boy* and does not refer to any boy in particular. In languages with possessive reflexive pronouns, the two readings of (34) are distinguished syntactically, as can be seen in (35), the two Swedish versions of (34).

(35) a. På **hans** födelsedag var varje pojke glad.
$\begin{bmatrix}\text{PERS.}\\\text{POSS}\end{bmatrix}$

b. På **sin** födelsedag var varje pojke glad.
$\begin{bmatrix}\text{REFL}\\\text{POSS}\end{bmatrix}$

Presumably Klein's proposal would give us the correct interpretation for the Swedish sentence in (35b) but not for the English sentence with the same intended interpretation. In order to extend Klein's approach to sentences with bound personal pronouns we would need, in addition to special rule schemata for displaced reflexives, special rule schemata for translating sentences with displaced bound pronouns. If personal pronouns are translated into free individual variables, $x_0, x_1, \ldots, x_n$, then the schemata for topicalization and the corresponding empty nodes could look like those shown in (36) and (37).

(36) $\langle S \rightarrow \alpha \quad S/\alpha, \quad \lambda v_{i_{\langle e, \pi(\alpha)\rangle}}[(S/\alpha)'](\lambda x_j[\alpha'])\rangle \quad j \in N$

(37) $\langle \alpha/\alpha \rightarrow t, \quad v_{i_{\langle e, \pi(\alpha)\rangle}}(x_j)\rangle \quad\quad\quad j \in N$

v_i is a designated variable; j may take any value. We will get the bound interpretation of a sentence like (34) just in case both the variable x_j in the translation of the gap gets bound by some quantifier in the sentence, and λx_j, the lambda operator preceding the translation of the topicalized constituent in (36), actually binds an occurrence of a variable inside it. As given, (36) and (37) will account for cases with one bound pronoun in a preposed constituent. However, it is easy to construct sentences with two bound pronouns, as illustrated by the following example.

(38) *Every boy* misses **his mother** during *his* first separation from **her**.

(39) During *his* first separation from **her**, *every boy* misses **his mother**.

The point is that since there is no limit on the number of bound pronouns in a declarative sentence, and since topicalization isn't sensitive to the presence or absence of bound pronouns, there is no limit in principle on the number of bound pronouns that may occur in a topicalized constituent or in a constituent question. To account for (39), the designated variable in the translation of the gap must be a variable over functions from two individuals to PP-denotations. The possibility to increase the number of bound pronouns leads us to the conclusion that we would need a potentially infinite set of distinguished variables as translations for gaps, one for each number of pronouns that may occur in the displaced constituent. The lack of syntactic motivation for the abundance of rule schemata makes Klein's proposal less appealing as a general solution to the problem discussed here. It seems more desirable to try to formulate a semantics which does not crucially depend on lambda conversion rather than to try to get around the constraints on lambda conversion in the manner illustrated above.[15]

3.3. Evaluating the GPSG Framework

Looking at the GPSG proposal as a whole, the grammar is certainly very attractive, both in its restrictiveness and in the clear way it represents the syntactic-semantic parallelism. However, we have noted that in order to extend a GPSG type grammar to account for multiple gap constructions in English as well as in Swedish, we need to introduce some indexing procedure, conceivably tied to the linking rules. If we want to stay strictly within context-free grammars, we also need to assume some upper limit on the number of gaps in the grammar. With respect to the semantic rules, we found that they cannot be formulated quite as simply as suggested in e.g. Gazdar (1981, 1982). The presence of bound anaphors and quantifier phrases in dislocated constituents in both English and Swedish requires some special handling. One partial solution, available within the framework, was described in some detail in the previous section. This solution has the disadvantage of requiring a multiplication of rule schemata for which there is little or no independent syntactic motivation.

It seems to me that if the claim that all sentences of the language can be directly generated and interpreted in their surface form can be maintained only by adopting such ad hoc modifications, then the framework looses much of its attractiveness as a theoretically interesting model for natural language. It is not clear that e.g. G. Gazdar would accept a grammar modified along the lines suggested here, since it does not satisfy the standards of explanatory adequacy that he assumes must be met by any alternative to transformational grammar that deserves serious consideration (Gazdar, 1979).

In his 1981 article, Gazdar proposes the following strong hypothesis about what classes of grammars are needed: the class of permitted generative grammars should be among those phrase structure grammars that are capable only of generating context-free languages. He points out two important metatheoretical consequences of this position. First, it would reduce the class of grammars that the language acquisition device needs to consider as candidates for the language being learned. However, the class of context-free grammars does not form a natural class from the point of view of learnability, so it is not clear how to evaluate this point. (For an overview of the learnability issue, see Pinker (1979) and references therein.) The second point has to do with language processing. Gazdar argues that it is a particular advantage that

sentences of a context-free language are provably parsable in a time which is proportional to the cube of the length of the sentence or less (Younger, 1967; Earley, 1970). But no such restrictive result holds for the recursive or recursively enumerable sets potentially generably by grammars which include a transformational component (Gazdar, 1981, p. 155).

It is worth pointing out that the results alluded to in this quote hold for classes of grammars, not for any particular grammar. These results don't allow the inference that any given context-free grammar for a language will be faster to parse than any transformational grammar for that language. In order to evaluate the relevance of the claim made in the quoted passage to actual grammars, we need to compare the performance of a context-free grammar with linking rules and metarules and a grammar which handles unbounded dependencies by transformations, for the same language. We should also consider another factor that may influence parsing efficiency. R. Kaplan, quoted in Fodor (1980, p. 50) points out that parsing time in the limit is a function not only of the number of words in a sentence but also of the number of distinct node types that the grammar admits. We have seen that for a language like Swedish, the number of distinct node types will be quite large. Consequently it is not clear that a GSPG grammar for Swedish would be efficient from the point of view of parsing.

In the next section we will look at some other non-transformational approaches to unbounded dependencies, which do not run into the problem of multiplying syntactic categories. We will first look at a proposal by R. Cooper, and then give an overview of the theory of Phrase-Linking Grammars developed by S. Peters and R. W. Ritchie. There is still another non-transformational approach that is currently being developed and which would be worthwhile looking into, namely Lexical-Functional Grammar as presented in the papers in Bresnan (1982), in particular Kaplan and Bresnan (1982). In this framework, unbounded dependencies are accounted for by a procedure that operates on a level of representation called *functional structure*. The framework has now been developed in some detail and contains some specific proposals for how constraints on extractions can be expressed, given the notion of functional structure. We won't discuss this framework here but refer the reader to the discussion of unbounded dependencies in Icelandic in Zaenen (1980) for an illustration of the framework's extendability to other languages.

4. COOPER'S PROPOSAL

In his recent book, *Quantification and Syntactic Theory*, Robin Cooper makes an interesting proposal for how WH constructions such as questions and relative clauses in English can be handled by a phrase structure grammar combined with an explicit model theoretic semantics, developing some ideas which he originally introduced in his dissertation (Cooper (1975) and in a subsequent, unpublished paper (Cooper, 1978b)). In order to be able to present Cooper's proposal for WH constructions, we will first describe certain techniques he uses. This will turn out to be relevant to the grammar of Swedish that we present in Chapter III, as well as to the analysis of questions in Chapter IV, since certain of Cooper's ideas will be exploited there.

4.1. Free Quantification and Controlled Quantification

Sentences with quantifier phrases often have several meanings, depending on the interaction between the quantifier and the scope of other elements in the sentence such as modals, negation, intensional verbs, and other quantifiers. For instance, a sentence like (40) is often considered to have two readings, which can be highlighted by the possible continuations.

(40) Every Englishman admires a woman, (a) namely his mother
(b) namely the Queen

In order to get both readings, Montague in PTQ gave this kind of sentence two distinct syntactic derivations. On one derivation, the meaning of *admire* combines directly with the meaning of *a woman*, which gives us the narrow scope reading, compatible with the continuation given in (40a). On the other derivation, the meaning of *admire* first combines with the meaning of a subscripted pronoun, him_0, which acts as a variable over expressions of the language. *a woman* is then quantified in at the sentential level, thus getting scope over any other NP or modal element in the sentence. This way we get the reading where all Englishmen admire one and the same woman, (40b). Given a compositional semantics like in PTQ, to have a separate syntactic derivation for quantified-in structures provides a way of ensuring that the meaning of some constituent does not combine with the meanings of other constituents until you have reached the level in the three over which the meaning of that constituent has scope semantically. Given a syntactic rule of quantifying-in, we can represent all the readings of sentences with quantifier scope ambiguities. However, having two distinct derivations for a sentence like (40) does not seem to be well motivated on syntactic grounds, since there is no syntactic effect of applying the quantifying-in rule.[16] In order to get a linguistically more motivated way of handling the distinct readings of sentences like (40), Cooper developed a technique for wide scope interpretation which does not involve having a distinct syntactic derivation. Cooper's proposal, which is often referred to as *storage*, handles the multiple scope possibilities entirely in the semantics without syntactic quantifying-in rules. This technique works as follows.[17] At each point in a derivation where we are about to interpret a NP we have the option of 'storing' a binding operator, $\|NP\|_n$, derived from the intension of the NP, and inserting a variable, σ_n, as a placeholder in the derivation. The index on the binding operator and on the variable are the same. The binding operator remains in store until we have reached the part of the tree over which we want the binding operator to have scope. At this point, we retrieve the binding operator from the store and quantify it in.

It is worth noting that Cooper's technique for interpretation still is a compositional semantics. The meaning of an expression is a function of the meanings of its parts. But Cooper takes meanings to be more complex than for instance in PTQ. The grammar assigns compositionally to each phrase a sequence consisting of an intension (or a denotation) followed by zero or more stored binding operators. Notice that all storage and retrieval takes place in the semantics. Identical surface structures will have identical syntactic derivations, but may differ in interpretations assigned to them. Cooper limits the use of storage to quantifiers. In natural language, it is typically the quantifiers which are responsible for scope distinctions and it is this property of quantifiers that is reflected in the storage technique.

The technique we have just described for getting wide scope quantification is referred to by Cooper as *free quantification*. Free quantification is optional. A NP can always be interpreted in situ, which amounts to taking the option of not storing any binding operator. *Controlled quantification* on the other hand is obligatory. Cooper uses this term for the kind of quantification involved in WH constructions in English where there is also a syntactic 'reflex' of the scope assigning quantification rule, namely WH fronting. Cooper captures the obligatory nature of controlled quantification for WH phrases by saying that WH phrases yield only binding operators, no normal NP interpretations. Thus, the meaning of a WH phrase must be stored and cannot interact with the rest of the sentence until it is retrieved. In Cooper (1978b), the retrieval of WH binding operators was linked to the application of a movement rule in the syntax. WH movement was given a special interpretation which amounted to retrieving a stored WH phrase and quantifying it in. In Cooper (1983, Chapter V) he notes that controlled quantification can be linked either to particular lexical items, e.g. WH words, or to particular syntactic rules, e.g. in a non-movement analysis the rule that introduces an interrogative phrase to the left of an S node. In languages like Chinese and Japanese, where interrogative phrases remain in place, we probably want to take the first option.[18] In these languages, too, the interpretation of the WH phrase will involve storage, since the contribution of the WH phrase, i.e. turning the phrase into a question, cannot be integrated until the interpretation procedure has reached a level corresponding to a sentence meaning.

4.2. Interpretation Through Substitution

In Cooper (1983, Chapter V), he proposes a phrase structure grammar for questions and relative clauses in English. In addition to the regular phrase structure rules, he adds the equivalent of a rule schema like in (41).

(41)   X → NP S   where X ∈ {Q, R}. (Q and R are complex symbols that dominate questions and relative clauses, respectively.)

Something more is needed in order to generate well-formed WH clauses. In particular, we need to make sure there is a gap in the sentence and that this gap is correlated with the NP generated to the left of the sentence. Cooper briefly considers Gazdar's proposal, which as we recall, involves encoding the information about what type of constituent is missing into the syntactic node lables. He credits it with being very useful and theoretically important for showing that a large number of constructions in natural language can be defined purely in terms of a phrase structure grammar contrary to what has commonly been assumed among linguists. However, Cooper chooses not to introduce Gazdar's machinery into the syntactic rules. Rather he allows null lexical insertion in the syntax, thereby providing for nodes that dominate the empty string. The grammar thus generates trees like in (42). The syntax will also generate trees where both or none of the NPs in (42) dominate lexical material, but the semantic rules are restricted so that they can only interpret structures where there is a correspondence between stored WH binding operators and gaps. The way this *semantic filtering* works is by distinguishing the interpretation of gaps, i.e. of constituents of the type [$_{XP}$] from the interpretation of any other constituent of category XP. Intuitively, an XP gap plays the role of a variable over XP interpretations in the semantics. When we combine

(42)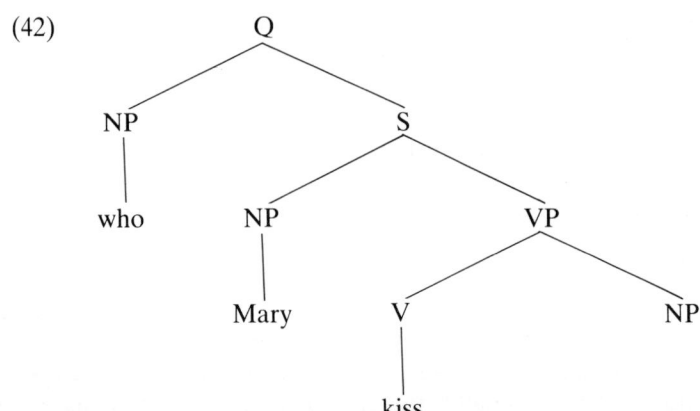

the interpretation of the preposed constituent [$_{NP}$*who*] with a sentence interpretation, we must check that there is a binding operator corresponding to the WH constituent in store and that there is a gap interpretation in store. We then substitute the interpretation of the preposed constituent for the interpretation of the gap. In the derivation in (42), we calculate what the interpretation of the sentence would have been if the interpretation of [$_{NP}$*who*] had been assigned to the gap. Since the interpretation of a WH phrase always involves a stored binding operator, this will not be passed up through the derivation of S and be retrieved at the point of interpreting the embedded question.

Note that it is only the WH binding operator that remains stored after the substitution. Any other material in the preposed constituent will hence be interpreted as if it occurred in the gap position. The interpretation-by-substitution thus correctly handles pied-piping facts as in (43) as well as questions where the interrogative phrase contains a bound pronoun as in (44). We noted earlier that this type of construction remains problematic for the GPSG approach.

(43)   In which year were you born?

(44)   Whose picture of *him* does *every man* like best?

We are here interested in the reading of (44) on which *him* is understood as bound by *every man*.

We will illustrate the interpretation-by-substitution technique by a schematic derivation of (44). To simplify the exposition, we will let $\|\alpha\|$ simply denote the interpretation of α. (Cooper assumes that the denotation depends on a world, w, and a sequence of individuals, σ. σ_i represents the ith member of the sequence, cf. Cooper (1983, p. 119)).

(44′)

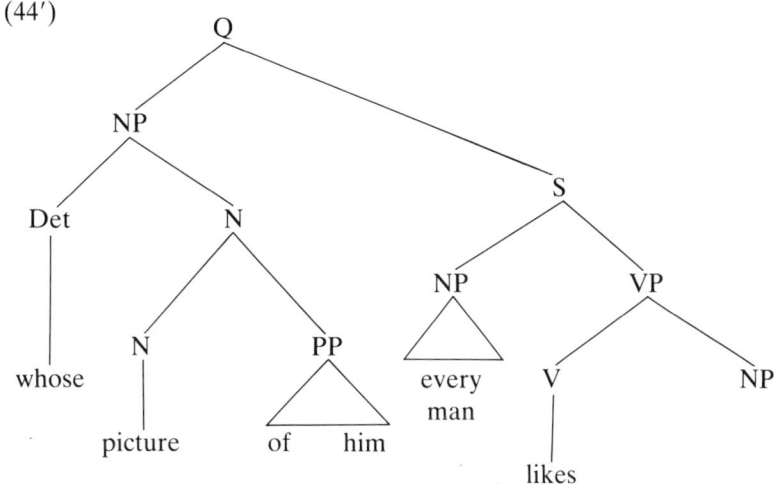

The table to tree diagram (44′) is given on p. 40.

The interpretation of the gap, [$_{NP}$], is a distinguished NP-intension, designated by *. We can now form a binding operator from *, which we represent as *i for any natural number i. The interpretation of the gap will thus be a pronoun interpretation, dependent on the ith member in the sequence of individuals with the binding operation *i in store.

Since we want *every man* to act as a binding operator for *him*, we store its interpretation, and insert a placeholding variable, [σ_8]. When we interpret the interrogative determiners *whose*, we store a WH binding operator, WH7 whose index matches the index on the variable used in the representation of the denotation, [σ_7]. In order to get the question meaning at the Q node, we perform a substitution of the interpretation of the interrogative phrase (viii) for the gap interpretation (i) in the interpretation of the sentence (iv). This permits us to recalculate the interpretation of the preposed constituent, replacing the interpretation of the gap. Since the interpretation of the preposed constituent contains a stored binding operator, WH7, this will thus become part of the interpretation of the sentence. The stored binding operator is retrieved and applied to the result of the substitution, (x). (It is important in this framework that substitution and retrieval take place at the

CHAPTER II

This table relates to tree diagram (44') on p. 39.

	STRUCTURAL DESCRIPTION	DENOTATION (Schematic)	STORE
(i)	[$_{NP}$]	[σ_7]	$*_7$
(ii)	[$_{VP}$ like [$_{NP}$]]	like ([σ_7])	$*_7$
(iii)	[$_{NP}$ every man]	[σ_8]	$\|$every man$|$8
(iv)	[$_S$ every man like [$_{NP}$]]	[σ_8]($\|$like$\|$([σ_7]))	$*_7$, $\|$every man$|$8
(v)	[$_{NP}$ him]	[σ_8]	
(vi)	[$_N$ picture of him]	$\|$picture$\|$([σ_8])	
(vii)	[$_{Det}$ whose]	GEN([σ_7])	
(viii)	[$_{NP}$ whose picture of him]	GEN([σ_7])($\|$picture$\|$([σ_8])) = $\|\sigma_7$'s picture$\|$([σ_8])	WH7
(ix)	[$_Q$ whose picture of him every man likes [$_{NP}$]]	[σ_8]($\|$like$\|$($\|\sigma_7$'s picture $\|$([σ_8])))	WH7
(x)		WH7([σ_8]($\|$like$\|$($\|\sigma_7$'s picture$\|$([σ_8]))))	$\|$every man$|$8 WH7, Substitution of (viii) for (i) in (iv)
(xi)		$\|$every man$|$8(WH7([σ_8]($|$like$|$($|\sigma_7$'s picture$|$([σ_8])))))	$\|$every man$|$8 (Retrieval of WH7) (Retrieval of $\|$every man$|$8)

same time. Otherwise it would be possible to derive interpretations where the scope of dislocated WH phrases does not correspond to their surface position.) Note that there is still an interpretation in store at this point. When we retrieve this NP, the resulting interpretation will be as in (xi), which can be paraphrased roughly as follows: for each man x, x likes y's picture of x, where y is some person.

The substitution operation thus handles the pied-piping facts correctly, i.e. only *who* (in *whose*) is interpreted as a WH binding operator which gets stored. The interpretation of the rest of the phrase, i.e. *'s picture of him*, is substituted for the gap interpretation. However, when the preposed phrase also contains an anaphoric element like *him*, this can only be bound by a NP binding operator which is retrieved after the substitution operation. Consequently, the interpretation-by-substitution technique predicts that the NP binding operator will always take wider scope than the WH binding operator, and the only reading that is assigned to (44) is the one in the step represented by (xi) in (44'). However, a main consideration in this study is that (44) is ambiguous. It also has a reading on which *every man* has narrower scope than the interrogative phrase, although this contains a pronoun, *him*, which may be interpreted as bound by *every man*. It is not obvious how the interpretation-by-substitution method should be amended to handle this reading In our account of this type of question in Chapter IV, we make a different proposal.

We end this brief exposition of Cooper's framework by noting that Cooper assumes as a condition on the substitution operation that the index on the WH binding operator and the operator associated with the gap match. He mentions that it might be possible to do without this matching requirement. However, in the types of multiple WH dependencies that we will be confronted with in Swedish, it appears that this matching is essential. It seems likely that Cooper's approach can be extended to multiple gaps since gap interpretations are distinguishable.

5. PHRASE LINKING GRAMMARS

We now turn to another non-transformational framework, Phrase Linking Grammars (PLG) which is currently being developed by S. Peters and R. W. Ritchie (cf. Peters and Ritchie (in preparation)). So far, the formal theory of PLG has not yet appeared in print, but some proofs bearing on the formal characterization of the theory as well as some applications to unbounded dependencies in English have been presented at various meetings and conferences since early 1979. The outline we are about to give here is thus based mainly on oral tradition and on conversations with S. Peters. Several of the notions in the theory that we will be discussing are still preliminary and presumably likely to be revised as the theory develops. With this caveat, we will first outline the general format of the grammar, then look at the syntactic and semantic rules, and finally compare the general approach taken in PLG to Cooper's proposal which we discussed in the previous section.

5.1. An Outline of PLG

One of the main motivations behind the PLG approach is to show how small changes in the phrase structure rules suffice to express the generalizations we want but still make the grammar more limited than a transformational grammar. Within GPSG, as we have seen, unbounded movement transformations are dispensed with by extending the set of syntactic categories with derived categories. The unbounded dependency is thus in effect encoded in the syntactic categories on the projection path from the gap to the filler. Within PLG, the same phenomenon is handled by letting the phrase structure rules generate *linked* trees. Linked trees are graphs where a node can be immediately dominated by two distinct nodes, corresponding to the fact that preposed constituents appear to play a double role in interpretation. For instance, a preposed WH-phrase both introduces a question and, in some sense, fulfills the grammatical function associated with the gap. An example of a linked tree is given in (45).

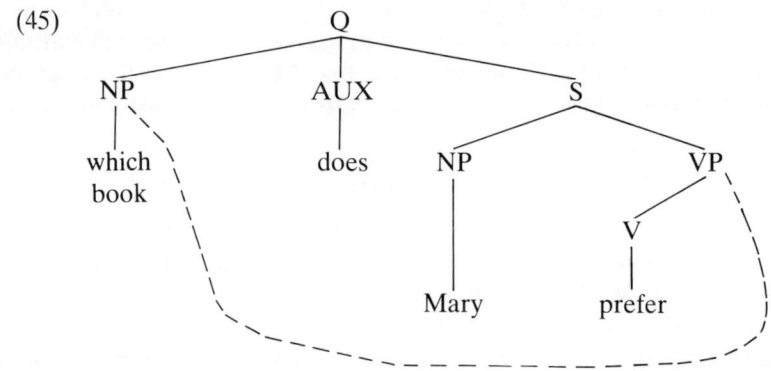

The basic idea behind PLG is that dislocated constituents syntactically and semantically act as if they were in two places simultaneously. This is represented by the link or dotted line. The dislocated constituent, in this example the NP *which book*, is referred to as the *link child* and the VP node connected by the link path is called the *link parent*.

PLG uses context-sensitive phrase structure rules which permit a more revealing description than context-free rules. The rules of the grammar are however interpreted as node admissibility conditions rather than as rewriting rules. As shown in Peters and Ritchie (1973a), this has the effect of restricting the weak generative capacity of the grammar. If we impose an upper limit on the number of links that may lead out of any one constituent, it can be proved that the language accepted is a context-free language. The proof uses the fact that if you have a context-sensitive grammar where the rules are used as admissibility conditions which admit a set of trees, then there is a way of constructing a context-free grammar for the same set of trees. This can be done by a relabeling operation which breaks down the context-sensitive information into subcategories. However, the grammar used is still a context-sensitive grammar with the facility for expressing local dependencies that this entails.

At this point it might be appropriate to compare PLG to GPSG. We recall that GPSG is able to stay within the restrictive format of context-free grammars by using a large number of distinct syntactic categories.[19] The node labels are bundles of syntactic features and virtually any grammatical or lexical dependency can be captured as a feature on nodes. We pointed out earlier that having a large number of non-terminal symbols may lead to a decrease in parsing efficiency.[20] This is an unwanted consequence for GPSG since one of the reasons for writing context-free grammars was to be able to apply certain efficient parsing algorithms. We noted above that in order to prove that a language accepted by a PLG is context-free one has to divide the categories used into subcategories. It is conceivable that the number of subcategories would approach the number of non-terminal symbols used in GPSG. However, the important difference is that whereas all these categories are actually used in a GPSG, they only play an indirect role in a PLG, viz. in the proof that enables us to show that a given PLG only admits context-free languages. As for the parsing efficiency of PLG, S. Peters in a talk at the West Coast Conference on Formal Linguistics, Stanford, January 1982, illustrated how a parser for a PLG, using a parallel processing algorithm can operate in $c \cdot n$ time where c is some constant and n is the number of words in the sentence. Apparently, c can be set as low as 3 for on-line processing and 2 for off-line.[21] We note that the parsing time is a linear function of the length of the input which is a considerable improvement over the n^3 result for context-free languages in general. It would be interesting if c, the constant for proportionality, turned out to reflect the complexity of the grammar in some definable way. However, it is not clear that this complexity metric, although it may be convenient for comparing the efficiency of various algorithms for machine parsing, has much to do with the psychological issue of what type of parsing procedure people actually use. For instance, the parallel processing procedure mentioned above requires n^2 processors working in parallel. For an attempt at defining an adequate complexity metric for human syntactic processing, see Frazier (to appear).

5.2. Linked Trees

PLG defines sets of trees, including the special type of linked tree illustrated in (45). A formal definition of linked trees is given in (46).

(46) A linked tree is a finite set N of nodes (vertices) together with binary relations I (of immediate tree domination) and L (of immediate link domination) on N, and functions P (of left-to-right precedence) and f (which labels nodes with vocabulary symbols) having domain N and ranges contained respectively in N × N and $V_T \cup V_N$ satisfying conditions (i)–(v):

  (i) *Linear Precedence Ordering of Siblings:* P(n) is a strict linear ordering of
  $\{m|\langle n, m \rangle \in I \cup L\}$ for all n in N,
  (ii) *Root:* there is an r in N such that $\langle r, n \rangle \in I^*$ for all $r \in N$,
  (iii) *Unique Tree Parent:* I^{-1} is a partial function defined just at members of $N - \{r\}$,
  (iv) *Tree Parent Dominates Link Parent(s):* if $\langle n, n' \rangle \in L$, then there are $m_0, \ldots, m_p \in N$ ($p > 0$) such that $m_1 \neq n'$, $m_p = n$, $\langle m_0 n' \rangle \in I$, and $\langle m_i, m_{i+1} \rangle \in I$ whenever $0 \leq i \leq p$, for all $n, n' \in N$,

(v) *Node Labeling:* $f(n) \in V_N$ iff there is an n' in N such that $\langle n, n' \rangle \in I \cup L$, for all n in N.

The conditions (i)–(v) are supposed to express universal properties of unbounded dependencies in natural language. For instance, condition (iv) ensures that the tree parent of a link child must always dominate its link parent, i.e., the first S node dominating the dislocated constituent must also dominate the node dominating the gap.

Peters and Ritchie also assume that link children may only occur in certain designated positions, which they refer to as 'dislocated positions'. Furthermore, every node in one of these dislocated positions must be a link child. Which positions are to be designated as dislocated positions must be stated for each language or language type, although there will presumably be a relatively small number of distinguished positions. Likely candidates are e.g., Comp, a position peripheral to S, and the so-called *Focus* position immediately preceding the finite verb in languages like Basque and Hungarian. These two assumptions, viz. that there are designated dislocation positions and that any phrase occurring in such a position must be a link child, seem motivated for the pattern of dependencies we find in so-called configurational languages,[22] i.e., languages where grammatical processes make crucial use of constituent order. It is an open issue how to interpret these assumptions in cases of non-configurational languages, supposing that the theory of PLG in principle should be able to extend to these types of languages as well.[23]

Peters and Ritchie suggest, as a reasonable first approximation, that dislocated positions in English are always leftmost siblings of an S node. This will account for topicalization, matrix constituent questions, tensed embedded questions and tensed relative clauses. However, it does not automatically cover the dislocated positions which are linked to gaps inside infinitival clauses as in the case of infinitival relatives and infinitival questions, illustrated in (47a and b).

(47) a. Here is [a book $_i$] to read $_i$.

b. John didn't know [what $_i$] to say $_i$.

If we assume with Chomsky and several others (Chomsky, 1981; Koster and May, 1982) that infinitival structures are really sentential, then the only thing we have to say for English is that dislocated positions are always left siblings of S. But if we take the position argued for by among others J. Bresnan (Bresnan, 1978) and E. Bach (Bach, 1979) that these structures involve a VP node, then it is not totally clear how we would characterize the dislocated position. Suppose we say that the set of possible dislocated positions in English are the ones indicated by X in the diagrams in (48).

(48) a.   b.

Then we also predict that only link children can occur as leftmost siblings of $\overline{\text{VP}}$. This is obviously wrong in view of examples like (49).

(49)   John [$_\text{VP}$[$_\text{V}$ tried] [$_{\overline{\text{VP}}}$ to leave]]

We might still be able to use the characterization in (48) if we add the (independently needed?) assumption for English that link children must always be dominated by a phrasal category as opposed to a lexical category. Another way would be to distinguish in some way between the two types of infinitival complements illustrated in (47) and (49), respectively, but this presumably would go against the general spirit of PLG. In languages like Swedish, which have infinitival relatives but lack infinitival questions (see Chapter III.4.4), we need to make further distinctions.

PLG allows for more than one link leading out of the same constituent. This is obviously necessary if we want to account for languages with multiple extractions. As long as one assumes that the amount of escape is bounded, i.e., that there is an upper limit on the number of links out of the same constituent, the languages recognized will still be context-free. Whether or not one would want to make this assumption raises the same issues that were discussed above in Section 3.1. There is nothing in the formal theory of PLG that prevents links from crossing. If one wanted to incorporate something like Fodor's Nested Dependency Constraint (cf. Fodor, 1978) for a language like English, then one would have to add further conditions on the permissible link-paths.

For the purpose of case marking and number and gender agreement, the link child will count as if it were in the gap position. Consequently the same rules that handle the facts in (50) and (51) will apply to the linked representations in (52) and (53).

(50)   John said his friends were/*was coming.

(51)   You can rely on me/*I.

(52)   [Which people] did John say were/*was coming?

(53)   [Me/*I,] you can rely on .

In English there appears to be one case where this generalization does not hold, brought to my attention by R. Cooper and L. Karttunen. Many speakers of English require the case marked form *whom* when the word is immediately preceded by a preposition, but allow or even prefer *who* when the preposition is stranded. Compare,

(54)   Who talked to whom/*who?

(55)   [To whom/*who] did you talk ?

(56)   [[Who/??whom] did you talk to ?

This fact together with some observations about failure of agreement in certain complex unbounded dependencies can be taken as an argument for being able to distinguish dislocated positions and gap positions and it might be considered a plus for the theory that it makes this distinction formally available.

The fact illustrated by (56) is rather exceptional, however. The general rule appears to be that dislocated constituents behave exactly as if they were in the position of the gap. The possibility of using the same agreement rules for structures with and without links reflects this generalization. In this respect, PLG has an advantage over the syntactic theory proposed by R. Cooper. Recall that Cooper freely generates trees with gaps by allowing for zero lexical insertion (cf. (42) above). He puts restrictions on the semantic interpretation rules to the effect that only structures where the number of fillers and gaps match can be interpreted. But it doesn't seem appropriate to extend the semantic restriction on interpretable structures to also handle the facts illustrated in (52) and (53). Actually, the case of number mismatch might be considered as something that should be handled by the semantic rules; a singular VP is not of the right type to be predicated of a plural NP. But it seems less plausible to account for idiosyncratic casemarking requirements this way. Furthermore, in languages where gender is assigned by the lexicon and does not correspond to any semantic distinction, it seems inappropriate to put gender agreement as a condition on interpretability. In Swedish, for instance, common nouns are either neuter or non-neuter. The choice is either morphologically conditioned or totally arbitrary in most of the cases. Adjective phrases must agree with their heads, both in attributive and predicative position. We thus get the pattern in (57).

(57) Vilket bord$_i$ målade Kalle ___$_i$ rött / *röd?
      [+NEUT]   [+NEUT] [−NEUT]
   Which table did Kalle paint red?

If we assume that the dislocated constituent **Vilket bord** also counts as a sister constituent of **rött**, we can account for this pattern quite straightforwardly without invoking a semantic distinction.[24]

5.3. Semantics

We now turn to a brief outline of the semantics associated with PLG. So far the semantic approach taken has been in line with the model theoretic semantics common in the framework of Montague Grammar, incorporating some recent work on generalized quantifiers (Barwise and Cooper, 1981). (But see Barwise *et al.* (to appear) for an approach that uses situation semantics instead of possible world semantics.) In order to account for sentences which are ambiguous with respect to quantifier scope (i.e., the free quantification phenomena we discussed earlier in Section 4.1), a NP like *some man* is either given an ordinary NP interpretation, i.e., a property of sets, or interpreted as a variable, x_n, together with a variable binding operator, *for some man x_n*, constructed from the meaning of the NP. The variable binding operator is stored and at the appropriate level, it is applied to a sentence meaning. Variable binding operators can be distinguished with respect to *valence*. The valence of a stored binding operator corresponding to a NP is $\langle\langle s, t\rangle, \langle s, t\rangle\rangle$. It applies to a proposition and yields a proposition. Interrogative phrases like *who* and *which book* have the valence $\langle\langle s, t\rangle, \langle\langle s, t\rangle, t\rangle\rangle$, that is, they apply to interpretations of sentences and yield sets of propositions. The interpretation rules apply compositionally. The meaning of a constituent is a function of the meanings of its parts, and this is where the link paths, so to speak, pay off. We said earlier that the presence of a link enables a dislocated constituent to count as an immediate constituent of the constituent dominating the gap. For the purpose of the interpretation rules, it will thus count as a daughter of the constituent dominating the gap and as contributing to the meaning of this node. We illustrate the way the interpretation rules work for a linked tree in (58).

(58)
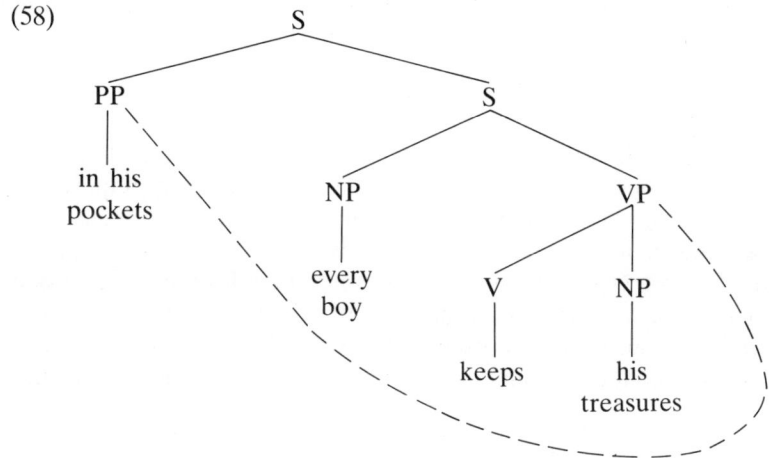

When we compose the interpretation of the VP, we take into account the interpretation of the dislocated constituent *in his pockets*, which is of the appropriate type to be an argument to the interpretation of *keeps*. At this point, the interpretation of the pronoun *his* contains a free individual variable. When we interpret *every boy* as a variable binding operator, this can bind the free individual variable in *his*. This way we get the intended reading for sentences with bound pronouns in dislocated constituents.

Consider next the case when the dislocated constituent is an interrogative phrase as in (59).

(59)   Which table did ⌐ Mary put a book [$_{PP}$ on ⌐]?

When we interpret the PP, the linkparent, we consider the meaning of the dislocated constituent *which table*. The preposition *on* requires a NP meaning, but the meaning of the dislocated phrase is a variable binding operator with the valence $\langle \langle s, t \rangle, \langle \langle s, t \rangle, t \rangle \rangle$. The only way we can interpret the PP is by storing the variable binding operator and inserting a NP variable in its place. This way, the semantic rules force *obligatory storage* of interrogative variable binding operators. Only when we interpret the constituent dominated by S do we have an interpretation of the right type so that we can apply the stored variable binding operator. Not surprisingly, it turns out that the way bound pronouns in dislocated constituents as in (58) are handled and the way interrogative variable binding operators as in (59) are handled in (59) will interact to give us the desired interpretation for a question like (60).

(60) [In which of *his* pockets ᵢ] does *every boy* keep *his* treasures ᵢ?

By letting the interpretation of the dislocated constituent contribute to the meaning of the linkparent, while simultaneously requiring that interrogative variable binding operators be stored until they can apply to a sentence interpretation, we have a way of accounting for questions like (44) and (60), without giving the antecedent for the bound pronoun wider scope than the interrogative phrase. This, then, seems to be a promising approach to accounting for Swedish examples like in (7) and (61) which contain a bound anaphor inside an interrogative constituent.

(61) [Vilken av **sina** böckerᵢ] tycker **de flesta författare** bäst om ᵢ?
          POSS
          REFL

Which of their books do most authors like best?

We noted above that the valence of the interrogative binding operator forced it to be stored. Quite generally, the semantics will filter out impossible interpretations in this way. If the root node is assigned the empty set of interpretations, it means that the sentence is semantically anomalous in some way, although it may be syntactically well formed. This means that we can account for why (62) is not a sentence of English without using special features in the syntax.

(62) *John wonders the boy ᵢ Mary likesᵢ .

wonders requires a question type meaning as argument, i.e., a set of propositions. The only way we can get that type of interpretation for the embedded sentences is if we apply an interrogative variable binding operator to the meaning of the sentence. The meaning of *the boy* is of the right valence, and hence we don't get an interpretation for this sentence.[25]

To sum up some features of PLG, we have seen that the syntax of PLG, which defines what a well-formed linked tree is, will ensure that the number of dislocated constituents matches the number of gaps. Trees with too many or too few arguments won't be admitted. The semantics will filter out syntactically well-formed structures which are uninterpretable because some constituent is of the wrong type to contribute to a sentence interpretation or question interpretation for the root tree.

6. UNBOUNDED DEPENDENCIES IN THE GOVERNMENT-BINDING FRAMEWORK

This overview over recent approaches to unbounded dependencies would be incomplete if we didn't mention the way these phenomena are handled in current versions of transformational grammar, in particular in the Government-Binding theory, henceforth GB, outlined in Chomsky (1981, 1982). GB differs from earlier versions of transformational grammar in several important repects. Here we will just bring up a few aspects which are relevant to the present discussion.

In the GB theory, the transformational component is reduced to one general scheme, Move α, where α is a constituent. Applications of Move α involve coindexing of the moved constituent and its trace. Move α is defined by the characterization in (63) (cf. Chomsky, 1982, p. 33).

(63) Move α is the relation between an antecedent and a gap where:
 a. the antecedent lacks an independent Θ-role (and is therefore in a $\bar{\Theta}$-position)
 b. the gap is properly governed (if it is trace)
 c. the relation is subject to bounding theory (Subjacency)

This characterization is intended to subsume both NP-movement and *wh*-movement. Note that subjacency is considered to be a defining property of the relation, just as it was for *wh*-movement in Chomsky (1977). For true long-distance dependencies, this means that Move α must incorporate some version of Comp-to-Comp movement which provides a means of factoring an apparent unbounded dependency into a series of bounded dependencies. Making subjacency a defining property for Move α, which in turn accounts for unbounded dependencies, is a questionable assumption from the point of view of Scandinavian languages where unbounded dependencies violate standard formulations of subjacency (see Chapter III.7 for examples and discussion. Cf.

also Engdahl, 1982c). Conceivably one could attempt to redefine subjacency in such a way that these cases wouldn't qualify as violations. I have argued elsewhere (Engdahl, 1980b) that such reformulations tend to void the notion of subjacency of its explanatory potential.

Chomsky assumes that there are three syntactic levels of representation, D-structure and S-structure, and logical form (LF). Note that LF is taken to be a syntactic level of representation and a prerequisite for semantic interpretation. Each level of representation is subject to well-formedness conditions. The levels are related by the *Projection Principle* which states that the thematically relevant arguments of each lexical item must be represented at all levels. At both S-structure and LF, the notion of coindexing plays a crucial role, both for determining syntactic well-formedness and as a necessary feature for establishing legitimate binding relations and anaphoric relations. It appears that it is this reliance on coindexing in the syntax that distinguishes current transformational approaches from non-transformational approaches.[26] In Chapters III and IV, we will develop an approach to binding and anaphora in Swedish which does not make use of coindexing of syntactic constituents, and in Chapter V we will return to a comparison with the approach taken in GB.

7. CHOOSING A FRAMEWORK

We will summarize the discussion in the preceding sections by way of comparing the frameworks and indicating the reasons behind our choice of a framework in which to develop our analysis of questions. The main focus of this study is the analysis of constructions that in English and Swedish involve what we have called unbounded dependencies. Although such dependencies have often been used as arguments for a transformational approach, we have seen that there are now a number of non-transformational accounts of these phenomena. These non-transformational approaches only use phrase structure rules in their syntax. They hence permit more restrictive grammars for which it is known that it is decidable whether or not the grammar will admit a given sentence. We consider this a main reason for choosing a non-transformational approach.

When it comes to choosing between the various non-transformational frameworks available, we have to judge how easily they can be extended to account for the wider range of extraction facts we find in Swedish. As

RECENT APPROACHES TO UNBOUNDED DEPENDENCIES 53

we have seen, GPSG handles unbounded dependencies by encoding the required information into the syntactic categories used. Extending this approach to Scandinavian data would presumably lead to an undesirable increase in the number of syntactic categories in the grammar. In this respect, PLG seems to extend more readily to multiple extractions. In this framework, multiple extractions are handled by linked trees in which one constituent may be directly dominated by two nodes, thereby reflecting the dual role a dislocated constituent plays. There are in principle no constraints in the formal theory on the number of links or on the interaction between links. This becomes relevant when we look at the availability of intersecting readings in certain languages.

The PLG approach and Cooper's approach are quite similar. They differ slightly in what phenomena are handled by the syntax. In Cooper's framework, both mismatches in the number of fillers and gaps and morphological mismatches are handled by the semantic interpretation rules (or, in the case of morphological mismatches, by rules for discourse pronominalization). In PLG, such facts are captured by the syntax in the definitions of well-formed linked trees. Since we take morphological agreement to be basically a syntactic phenomenon, we find the PLG approach more suitable in this respect.

With respect to issues like constraints on unbounded dependencies and on possible wide scope interpretations, on the other hand, Cooper's approach is more explicit. He outlines how one can look at island constraints and restrictions on wide scope interpretations as conditions on when the store must be empty and shows how certain constraints appear natural from a parsing perspective (cf. Cooper, 1983, Chapter V).

The main difference between PLG and Cooper's approach lies in the semantics. In order to handle pied-piping in initial WH phrases, Cooper develops an interpretation-by-substitution technique. Although this technique correctly handles pied-piping cases, we saw in Section 4.2 that it makes wrong predictions for questions with anaphors bound by quantifiers inside the sentence. This problem need not arise in PLG. Given the notion of linked trees in the syntax, PLG can define compositional interpretation rules which take into account the interpretation of the dislocated constituent, i.e. the link child, when the interpretation of the link parent is composed.

The framework we will propose for Swedish is a version of a PLG. The syntax conforms with Peters and Ritchie's proposal in all important respects. We will suggest some additions in order to handle unbounded dependencies with resumptive pronouns. As for the semantics, we have chosen not to adopt Peters and Ritchie's complete reliance on semantic filtering for variable binding operators. Instead we will formulate explicit quantification rules for NP and WH quantification rules for NP and WH quantification. This permits us to better illustrate certain syntactic constraints on the application of such rules. We recall that the interaction of syntactic rules and interpretation rules in the analysis of unbounded dependencies is one of the main aspects of this study.

NOTES

[1] It is slightly misleading to use the term 'gap' here since preposed constituents in Swedish are under certain conditions related to resumptive pronouns. See Chapter III for further discussion of the distribution of gaps and resumptive pronouns.

[2] For further discussion of **som**, see Andersson (1975) and Taraldsen (1978, to appear).

[3] See Chapter III for some qualifications of this general rule.

[4] This is just a brief overview. For all details the reader is referred to the authors' own presentations given in the references in the text.

[5] If phrase-structure rules are understood as node admissibility conditions rather than as rewriting instructions, it does not matter if the phrase-structure rules are context-free or context-sensitive, as shown by Peters and Ritchie (1973a). They proved that a language is context-free if there is a finite set of context-sensitive rules which analyze the sentences of the language. Note that this result only holds if both the nonterminal symbols and the rules in the grammar are finite.

[6] The idea of using syntactic features to encode information about unbounded dependencies was introduced independently in Hellan (1977, note 22).

[7] (11) follows Gazdar (1981: (23)). Several other proposals for eliminating slashed categories have been made in the literature, e.g. the Trace Introduction Metarule in Sag (1982) and the Slash Termination Metarules in Gazdar, Klein, Pullum, and Sag (1982). Whether or not gaps should be represented as empty nodes in the syntactic tree is an interesting issue with ramifications for the formulation of agreement rules, interpretation rules, and the account of parasitic gaps. Cf. Engdahl (1984a) for some relevant remarks.

[8] Ejerhed (1982) proposes, mainly for purposes of computational efficiency, a recursion-free grammar for Swedish.

[9] Bill Ladusaw, following an idea of Barbara Partee's mentioned in Engdahl (1980a, p. 48), has suggested that one way of looking at this would be to say that although the mechanism for extending the value for SLASH will in the limit lead to a grammar with an infinite number of categories, any derivation of an actual sentence will only involve a finite, actually a very small, number of SLASH values, given the inherent limitations on human processing capabilities. There may still be a problem, though, in deciding whether the grammar in question employs a finite number of categories, as Mark Johnson and Stuart Shieber have pointed out to me.

[10] See Huntley (1982) for an interesting proposal which attempts to capture the modal character of infinitival questions.

[11] One way of doing this would be to use the 'storage mechanism' developed by R. Cooper (Cooper, 1975, 1983). See Section 4 for a presentation of this technique.
[12] This problem was first brought to my attention by S. Peters at the Sloan workshop on Alternatives to Transformational Grammars at Stanford, January 1980.
[13] One way to eliminate the problem entirely would be to require that all translation rules for linking rules be of the form

$$\lambda v_{\langle XP\rangle}[(S/XP)'](XP'')$$

where XP'' is the result of replacing all occurrences of x_n in XP' by occurrences of x_m, where x_m has no occurrence in either XP' or $(S/XP)'$ (cf. Thomason's footnote (12) to PTQ). Such an approach would not be correct, however, since it would exclude any binding between an antecedent in the sentence and an anaphor in the dislocated constituent. This is clearly not adequate for sentences with preposed reflexives.
[14] To my knowledge, this proposal was never put in print. The account I give here is based on a report of what Klein suggested at the meeting. More recently, a slightly different and more general account of reflexives, including topicalized reflexives, has been proposed by Pollard and Sag (1983). A version of this approach will apparently be adopted in Gazdar, Klein, Pullum, and Sag (to appear). Although Pollard and Sag's account in some sense solves the problem for topicalized reflexives, sentences with preposed bound personal pronouns and interrogative phrases with anaphoric expressions still remain problematic.
[15] The problem generalizes even further than mentioned in the text. A full presentation and discussion of the problem and its consequences can be found in Engdahl (1982a). Here we will just note that the problem also arises in cases of rightward dependencies, such as relative clause extraposition and right-node raising, which are accounted for in GPSG by a linking schema that looks like the inverse of the topicalization schema.

(i) $\langle \alpha/\beta\ \beta,\ \lambda h_{\langle \beta\rangle}[(\alpha/\beta)'](\beta)'\rangle$ (Gazdar, 1981:(74))
(α ranges over clausal categories, β can be any phrasal or clausal category)

Of course, reflexives and bound pronouns may occur in such dependencies as well, as illustrated in (ii) and (iii), and the same problem for assigning the correct interpretations arises.

(ii)   *No man* would resign who is interested in *his* career.
(iii) *Mary* sent to her parents and gave to her boy friend, a nice picture of *herself*.

A similar problem arises in the converse case, i.e. when a displaced constituent contains a quantifier which binds a pronoun somewhere in the sentence, as in (iv):

(iv)   To *every participant in the annual spring clean up operation*, the Town Council will give a diploma with *his* or *her* name printed on it.

It thus appears that whenever a dislocated constituent contains a quantifier of a pronoun, i.e. elements that enter into anaphoric relations, then the interpretation rules of current versions of GPSG with their heavy reliance on lambda conversion will fail to provide the desired meanings.
[16] It has been noticed that when a speaker intends a reading where the order of the quantifiers doesn't mirror the order in surface structure, he/she often uses some intonational device, such as contrastive stress, to emphasize this reading. However, since this is

not a necessary condition for these readings, I think it would be wrong to build that in as a condition on the derivation.

[17] This is a simplified exposition. The reader is referred to Cooper (1983, Chapter 3) for a more complete presentation.

[18] I am grateful to Y. Kuroda for some observations related to this point.

[19] In earlier unpublished papers, Gazdar also used context-sensitive rules, interpreted as admissibility conditions. In later published papers, however, all the rules have been context-free and as far as I can tell, the issue of generation or admission is not important for the GPSG framework.

[20] R. Cooper (personal communication) has pointed out that it's not clear that having a large number of nonterminal symbols necessarily leads to a decrease in parsing efficiency. Presumably the features used in subdividing syntactic categories can also be used to cut down on the search space. This issue, as well as several others mentioned in the text, awaits further testing through implementation.

[21] The distinction between on- and off-line processing in this context has to do with the form of the input. In on-line processing, the input is presented bit by bit, whereas in off-line processing the input has been prestructured in some fashion.

[22] See Hale (1983) for a discussion of what he calls the configuration parameter.

[23] A similar problem presumably arises in the Government-Binding framework of Chomsky (1981, 1982) with respect to characterizing non-argument positions in non-configurational languages. See Huang (1982) for some discussion of covert *wh*-movement in Chinese.

[24] R. Cooper (personal communication) has suggested that this type of agreement might be accounted for by the same mechanism that is independently required in order to handle agreement between NPs and pronouns across discourse, as illustrated in (i).

(i) A.   Jag har just köpt en ny   stol
                                  [−NEUT]
    B.   *I just bought a new chair.*

          Är **den** / *__det__ bekväm?
              [−NEUT] [+NEUT]
          Is it comfortable?

E. Ejerhed has made a similar suggestion in Ejerhed (1982), namely that filler-gap association is a semantic process rather than a syntactic one, and that the type of agreement that is required is of the same type that dictates the morphological choice in the case of predication of contextually given referents, as in (i).

[25] We need to say something more about the interpetation of WH phrases in non-dislocated constituents in order to prevent a sentence like (i) from getting any interpretation, in particular from getting the interpretation normally associated with (ii).

(i)   *John wonders the boy which girl likes.
(ii)   John wonders which girl likes the boy.

See Chapter III.4.2 for a discussion of this issue.

[26] Chomsky (1982) clearly deemphasizes the notion of derivation of one level from the other. Rather he considers Move α to be a relation that holds between D-structure and S-structure. According to him (Chomsky (1982, p. 33)) '... it is immaterial ... whether

Move α is regarded as a rule forming S-structure from D-structure, or whether it is regarded as a property of S-structures that are "base-generated" ...'. This opens up for interesting comparisons with non-transformational approaches. Given that all information relevant to establishing well-formed D-structure is present also at S-structure through coindexing, it seems that the theory could directly generate indexed S-structures which have to satisfy the conditions given in the definition of Move α as well as the conditions of the Binding theory. It thus appears that what may distinguish a transformational approach like GB from non-transformational approaches like GPSG and PLG is not so much the notion of a transformational derivation (in the sense of a sequence of phrase markers) as whether or not directly generated surface structures can be admitted given recognition devices that only recognize context-free languages.

CHAPTER III

A FRAMEWORK FOR SWEDISH

1. INTRODUCTION

In this chapter we will present the framework we are adopting for our analysis of constituent questions. In order to make our proposal explicit and to facilitate an evaluation of its scope and adequacy, we will present a relatively complete grammar for a fragment of Swedish, following in the tradition of Montague (1974, esp. chapters 6, 7, 8), Thomason (1976), Cooper (1975, 1978b, 1983), McCloskey (1979), and Partee and Bach (1981).

We will concentrate on the analysis of constructions involving unbounded dependencies since our main goal is to provide a linguistically motivated syntax and semantics for constituent questions. Consequently, several grammatical phenomena will receive a very superficial analysis. When possible, we will refer the reader to relevant literature where examples of more detailed analyses can be found.

The grammar is essentially a phrase structure grammar with rules that directly admit the structures needed for e.g. passive and other local dependencies. In addition we adopt the notion of linked trees from Phrase Linking Grammars (cf. Peters and Ritchie (in preparation) to account for unbounded dependencies. Our framework differs from transformational grammars of the Extended Standard Theory (EST) of Chomsky not only in the absence of transformations but in another feature as well which has to do with the interaction of the syntax and semantics. A common feature in the models of grammar proposed in EST is the assumption that the syntax generates sentential structures which provide the input to interpretative semantic rules. A derivation of a sentence consists of a sequence of structural objects (phrase markers) related by rules in the grammar. It is commonly assumed that the different types of rules define distinct levels of representation which are sensitive to different types of well-formedness conditions. Within recent versions of transformational grammar such as the Government-Binding theory, (GB), the essential levels of linguistic representation are assumed to be D-structure, S-structure, and Logical Form (LF). It is characteristic for the approach to semantic interpretation taken in these frameworks that the semantic rules essentially apply to and interpret sentential structures, generated and annotated by the syntactic rules. We will contrast this approach with one in which syntactic and semantic rules are taken to apply in tandem during the construction of a sentence. This view has been dubbed the 'rule-to-rule' approach to syntax and semantics by E. Bach (1976). The basic assumption behind this approach is that we can derive pairs consisting of a structural description and a meaning representation for each expression of the language, not just for sentences, and that we can do this without assuming intermediate levels of representation. In this framework, we will adopt the rule-by-rule approach.

Within the Extended Standard Theory and the Government-Binding theory, relations between anaphors and antecedents, between quantifiers and elements bound by them, as well as between moved constituents and their 'traces' are indicated by means of coindexing of syntactic constituents. In the framework proposed here, we take coreference and binding relations to belong primarily to the domain of semantics. Instead of expressing these relations at some syntactic level of representation, we will explore the hypothesis that they can be shown to follow from the ways in which the semantic rules apply. We will compare the two approaches on some specific areas in Chapter V.

2. THE FORMAT OF RULES

The format of rules in the grammar will reflect the *rule-to-rule* approach to grammatical derivations that we alluded to in the preceding section. The structure of a rule of the grammar will be as in (1)

(1) $\langle [n]$ syntactic rule, interpretation rule$\rangle$

where $[n]$ is the rule number. The grammar defines recursively a set of pairs of a well-formed labeled bracketed string over the vocabulary of the language and a representation of the meaning. Lexical entries also conform to the same general structure. They are given as ordered triples consisting of an orthographic representation of a word, its syntactic category together with a feature matrix, and a representation of the meaning. The feature matrix will contain values for certain morphologically realized features such as number and gender. Since our purpose here is not to do word level semantics, we will simply indicate the meaning of lexical items of major categories by constants, represented by the primed form of the corresponding English word. A few examples of lexical entries are given in (2).

(2) a. ⟨Sven, NP: [+SG +3 pers +MASC −PRO ...], $\lambda PP\{\hat{\,}s\}$⟩
 b. ⟨hon, NP: [+SG +3 pers −MASC +PRO ...], $\lambda PP\{\hat{\,}x_i\}$⟩
  $i \in N$
 c. ⟨slår, V: [+FIN +PRES ...], hit'⟩

We assume that every non-terminal is associated with a feature matrix, similar to the ones given in the lexical entries in (2). This way we can handle agreement phenomena in the syntax. We assume that a node α, dominating a node β, where β is terminal or non-terminal, can be admitted only if α and β agree in feature values for those features which are specified in α (cf. Gazdar (1981) and Hellan (1977)).[1]

2.1. Syntax

We will give the syntactic part of the rule in the customary phrase structure rule format, A → B C. (For reasons discussed in Chapter II, it might be convenient to regard the arrow as representing node admissibility conditions.) We have chosen to present the rules as phrase structure rules in a top-down fashion mainly for expository reasons since this mode is familiar to most linguists. Nothing important hinges on this choice. We could equally well have used the categorial grammar format (cf. Montague, 1974; Bach, 1979, 1980; Dowty, 1978).[2]

A sample of the basic rules of the grammar is given in (3) together with a few examples of expressions generated (or admitted) under the dominating node.

The phrase structure rules in (3) are given in a highly schematic form.[3] We assume that they could be more adequately expanded in some version of an $\bar{X}$ theory. In rule [1] we follow Montague (1974, ch. 8) and let the subject NP take the VP as its argument. We could also have followed Keenan and Faltz (1978, 1985) and Bach and Partee (1980) and let the VP apply to the subject. This issue will have nothing to do with our discussion of questions.

Various possibilities for expanding the VP are given in [4]–[10]. In case the phrase structure rule contains an optional argument, i.e. is an abbreviation for two rules as in [4], we have indicated the interpretation for the maximal expansion (cf. Ladusaw (1979) and McCloskey (1979/

(3) *Basic rules*

⟨ [1] S → NP VP, NP'(^VP') ⟩

⟨ [2] NP → Det CN, Det'(^CN') ⟩

⟨ [3] VP → V, V' ⟩

⟨ [4] VP → V (NP), V'(^NP') ⟩

⟨ [5] VP → V NP₁ NP₂, V'(^NP₁')(^NP₂') ⟩

en pojke springer
a boy runs

en pojke
a boy

springa, andas
run breathe

äta glass, äta
eat ice cream, eat

ge Kalle en bok,
give Kalle a book
avundas Lisa hennes
envy Lisa her
utseende
looks

Continued on p. 62.

(3) continued.

⟨ [6] VP → V NP (PP)   V′(^PP′)(^NP′)⟩   ge en bok till Kalle
give a book to Kalle

lägga en bok på
put a book on

bordet
the table

⟨ [7] VP → V S̄,   V′(^S̄)⟩   säga att ...
say that

⟨ [8] VP → V Q,   V′(^Q′)⟩   fråga om ...
ask if

⟨ [9] VP → V VP,   λx[V′′(^VP′(x))(x)]⟩   försöka gå
try (to) walk

⟨[10] VP → V (NP)   VP,   (see below)⟩   övertala Lisa att komma,
persuade Lisa to come

lova   Lisa att komma
promise Lisa to come

⟨[11] S̄ → **att** S,   S′⟩
⟨[12] Q → **om** S,   λp[⌣p ∧ p = ˆS′ ∨ p = ˆ¬S′]⟩

202) for precise and economic formulations for how to interpret the different expansions).

Since not all of the rules are binary, we have to indicate the order of functional application in the interpretation rule in case the semantic types of the constituents involved are not distinct, as for instance in [5].

The VP expansion rule in [10] subsumes a variety of complement taking verbs which have different control properties. We illustrate this with a few examples in which we use number agreement to indicate the appropriate control facts.

(4) a. Vi övertalade Lisa att vara **glad**
         PL   SG   SG

   b. *Vi övertalade Lisa att vara **glada**
         PL   SG   PL

   we persuaded Lisa to be happy

(5) a. Vi lovade   Lisa att vara **glada**
         PL   SG   PL

   b. *Vi lovade   Lisa att vara **glad**
         PL   SG   SG

   we promised Lisa to be happy

There are a number of different ways to capture the difference between (4) and (5) in the grammar and this issue has been extensively discussed in the literature (cf. Bach, 1979; Brame 1976; Bresnan, 1978; Chomsky and Lasnik, 1977; and Thomason, 1976). One way would be to divide the class of VP complement taking verbs into various subclasses and let different rules admit the distinct subclasses. This is the approach taken in Gazdar (1981, 1982) and also in Engdahl (1980a). This way, identical syntactic expansions can be associated with different interpretation rules. If we follow Gazdar and let V*n indicate the set of verbs that can appear under the V node introduced by rule [n], then we can divide rule [10] into [10a] and [10b] and spell out the interpretation rules accordingly.

(6) $\langle$[10a] VP $\rightarrow$ V NP VP, $\lambda x[\text{NP}'(\lambda y[\text{V}'(\hat{\text{P}}\text{P}\{y\})(\hat{\ }[\hat{\text{P}}\text{P}\{y\}(\hat{\ }\text{VP}')])])(x)]\rangle$

$$V^*10a = \begin{Bmatrix} \text{övertala, be, befalla, } \ldots \\ \textit{persuade, ask, order,} \end{Bmatrix}$$

$\langle$[10b] VP $\to$ V NP VP, $\lambda x[V'(\hat{\ }NP')(\hat{\ }VP'(x))(x)]\rangle$

$V^*10b = \begin{Bmatrix} \text{lova,} & \text{bedyra, \dots} \\ \text{promise, vow,} & \end{Bmatrix}$

These rules will give us the following representations of the meanings of (4a) and (5a).[4]

(4a') **persuade**$'_*$ (**we**', l, $\hat{\ }$**be-happy**$'_*$ (l))

i.e. we stand in the *persuade* relation to Lisa and the proposition that Lisa be happy.

(5a') **promise**$'_*$ (**we**', l, $\hat{\ }$**be-happy**$'_*$ (**we**'))

i.e. we stand in the *promise* relation to Lisa and the proposition that we be happy. On this approach, we thus let the same syntactic configuration be interpreted in different ways depending on which lexical class of verbs is admitted by the rule.

Another approach would be to have just one rule in the grammar and let the meaning of the complement taking verb determine the order of the composition of the meanings. On this approach we can say that because we understand what *persuade* and *promise* mean, we also know what the interpretation of the complement phrase must be in each of the cases. As E. Bach puts it: '... the control properties of verbs and other elements, and the associated features of agreement, are direct reflexes of the meaning of the items in question ...' (Bach, 1979, p. 529). Because we understand what *persuade* means, we know that the meaning of this verb is a function which applies to a VP meaning to make a transitive verb meaning, i.e. a function from NP meanings to intransitive verb meanings, $V_t/VP = (V_i/NP)/VP$. *promise* on the other hand is the type of verb that denotes a function from NP meanings to a function from VP meanings to intransitive verb meanings, i.e. $(V_i/VP)/NP$. Given the meaning of the verb, reflected in its semantic type (and its functionally related syntactic category) a lot of other facts follow, for instance that only *persuade* type verbs passivize (see Bach (1979) for an overview of the predictions made).

We find this approach, which takes the meaning of words to determine how they will combine with the meanings of other constituents, to be the simplest and intuitively most appealing account and we will adopt it in this study. For good illustrations of this general approach in other areas of the grammar, the reader is referred to Bach (1979, 1980),

Dowty (1978), Jacobson (1982), and Thomason (1974, 1976). A different type of approach to control phenomena is the one that is customary taken within EST and GB. On this approach, control is indicated by coindexing at a syntactic level. See for instance Wilkins (1980) and Williams (1980) for some illustrations. Cf. also Hellan (1980a) for an approach which combines an EST type syntax with a Montague semantics.

In addition to the basic rules given in (3) we need rules that introduce linked constituents, i.e. the rules that will account for unbounded dependencies. The rules for Topicalization and Constituent questions will be as in (7), still disregarding verb inversion in main clauses.

(7) $\langle [13]\ S \rightarrow XP\ \ S,\ S' \rangle$ $\qquad$ XP = AP, NP, PP, VP, $\bar{S}$
 $\quad\ \ \langle [14]\ Q \rightarrow XP\ \ S,\ \text{(see below)} \rangle$ XP = AP, NP, PP

Topicalization is very free in Swedish, as shown by the fact that all phrasal categories except S can occur in dislocated position. Although a certain amount of pied-piping occurs in constituent questions, it is not so common in colloquial Swedish and never involves a verbal category.

The interpretation rule in [13] might superficially look as if the interpretation of the dislocated constituent is disregarded. However, this is not correct since a dislocated constituent, i.e. a link child, contributes its interpretation to the interpretation of its link parent. See Section 3.2 for an illustration.

2.2. Semantics

The semantic part of the rule format in (1) consists of a compositional interpretation rule. It gives the meaning of the dominating node as a function of the meanings of the daughter nodes. We are assuming the semantic framework of R. Montague (cf. Montague (1974), esp. chapter 8, *The Proper Treatment of Quantification in Ordinary English*, which we abbreviate PTQ). The meaning of a sentence in Montague grammar is taken to be a function from contexts to a function from possible worlds to truth values. Since contexts won't play any role in the initial discussion, we will often take the meaning of a sentence to be simply a function from possible worlds to truth values, i.e. a proposition. Knowing the meaning of a sentence enables us to distinguish those situations where the sentence is true from those where it is false. More generally, each syntactically well-formed expression is a meaningful expression whose meaning is some function. Since it is not very perspicuous to refer to these functions, we represent the meaning of an expression by its translation into Intensional Logic (IL). We follow PTQ (p. 260f) in the assignments of variables to types. In the translations into IL we assume the abbreviatory conventions defined in PTQ and explained in Partee (1975) and Dowty *et al.* (1981). For ease of reference we here give a list of the variables used in this chapter:

(8) | VARIABLE | TYPE | DENOTATION |
|---|---|---|
| u, v | e | individuals |
| $x, y, x_0 \ldots$ | $\langle s, e \rangle$ | individual concepts (i.c.) |
| p, q | $\langle s, t \rangle$ | propositions |
| P, Q | $\langle s, \langle \langle s, e \rangle, t \rangle \rangle$ | properties of i.c. |
| $\mathcal{P}$ | $\langle s, \langle \langle s, \langle \langle s, e \rangle, t \rangle \rangle, t \rangle \rangle$ | properties of properties of i.c. |

It may be worth pointing out that the use of a representation in IL serves an expository purpose only and is not a necessary level of representation in this framework. We would also have defined the meaning relation directly on expressions of the language, as Montague does in *English as a Formal Language* (chapter 6 in Montague (1974)).

3. QUANTIFICATION

In this section we will discuss how quantifiers are interpreted in this framework. We will look first at ordinary quantifiers like **var och en** (*everyone*) and **ingen** (*no one*) and then look at interrogative quantifiers like **vem** (*who*) and **vilken bok** (*which book*). This approach to quantifiers has been inspired by analyses such as Barwise and Cooper (1981), Cooper (1983), Karttunen and Peters (1980) and Peters (1982). We will show how the two types of quantifiers enter into free and controlled quantification, respectively, and what the consequences are for deriving well-formed and meaningful expressions.

3.1. Free Quantification

The syntactic form of sentences of natural languages often underdetermines their meaning. For instance, a sentence like (9) has two readings which can be distinguished by considering the possible continuations.

(9) Every Englishman admires a woman (a) namely his mother
(b) namely the Queen

In order to account for the two readings, Montague gave this kind of sentence two distinct syntactic derivations in his fragment in PTQ. On one derivation, *admire* combines directly with *a woman* which gives us the VP meaning *love-a-woman* which fits well with the continuation in (9a). On the other derivation, *admire* first combines with a subscripted pronoun, him_1. At the sentence level, we quantify in the meaning of *a woman* which thus get wider scope than the universal quantifier in the meaning of *a woman* which thus get wider scope than the universal quantifier *every Englishman*, cf. (9b). Even if (9) has two meanings, it does not seem motivated to assume that there are two distinct syntactic structures for the sentence. In addition, the use of subscripted pronouns in the syntax violates a constraint on well-formed grammars that B. Partee has suggested, and which we find to be a desirable condition on grammars. The constraint is given in (10).

(10) *The Well-formedness Constraint*

Each syntactic rule operates on well-formed expressions of specified categories to produce a well-formed expression of a specified category.

(Partee, 1979b)

This constraint rules out the use of abstract symbols in the syntactic expressions that never get realized in the actual sentences of the language. A subscript on a pronoun would be an instance of such an abstract symbol. As we briefly outlined in Chapter II.4, there is an alternative interpretation procedure for sentences with scope ambiguities, developed by R. Cooper (Cooper, 1975, 1983). On this approach, which is commonly referred to as the *storage* method, scope ambiguities are handled entirely in the semantics. Here we will spell out the technique in more detail and show how it is incorporated in our framework.

In natural languages, the elements that typically display scope ambiguities are NPs. Hence, we adopt the convention, that each time we are about to interpret a NP, i.e. to integrate the interpretation of a NP with the interpretation of some other constituent, we have the option of 'storing' this NP interpretation and inserting a variable as a placeholder for the NP interpretation. The store will contain the NP interpretation indexed with the variable used as a placeholder. For convenience we will represent a stored NP as $[NP]_i$. The store is carried along during the derivation and becomes an element of interpretations of higher constituents. At some later point in the derivation, the NP interpretation in store is retrieved and quantified in, thus getting scope over the elements composed so far. Notice that all storage and retrieval takes place in the semantics. Identical surface structures will have identical syntactic derivations, but may differ as to where a given NP is interpreted.

Given the option of storing NP meanings, every NP node will generate at least a pair of meanings. It follows that any constituent that dominates a NP somewhere will have associated with it a set of meanings, represented as expressions in IL. We let $m(\alpha)$ indicate the set of meanings associated with a node α. By $M(\alpha)$ we mean the set of reduced or complete meanings associated with α, i.e. those meanings which do not have any elements in store. We will require that a matrix node, S, S̄, or Q, be accepted only if there is a set of complete meanings, $M(S)$ or $M(Q)$, associated with it. If there is still some meaning in store, i.e. if the meaning is not complete, the sentence cannot be completely interpreted. We give a formal definition of the storage convention in (11).[5]

(11) *NP Storage Convention*

If α is a NP[-PRO] and α' is the meaning of α,
then the sequence $\langle \lambda PP\{x_i\}, [\alpha]_i \rangle \in m(\alpha)$. $i \in N$

To show how the storage convention applies, we will go through a derivation of the sentence we took as an example of a scope ambiguity. In our sample derivations, we will first give the expression with its labeled bracketing, then the interpretation which consists of an expression in IL together with one or more elements in store. In relevant cases, we will indicate the rule used in a certain step in the derivation. The subscripts on the nodes are used for expository reasons, to make references to a certain node more perspicuous.

(12) Varje engelsman beundrar en kvinna.
      Every Englishman admires a woman.

A FRAMEWORK FOR SWEDISH

(12) continued.

```
          S
         / \
       NP₁  VP
        |   / \
     varje V   NP₂
   engelsman |   |
         beundrar en kvinna
```

EXPRESSION	INTERPRETATION	STORE	RULE USED
[NP₂ en kvinna]	$\lambda P \exists x[\textbf{woman}'(x) \wedge P\{x\}]$	$[\lambda P \exists x[\textbf{woman}'(x) \wedge P\{x\}]_2 \, (=[NP]_2)$	NP storage (11)
	$\lambda PP\{x_2\}$		
[VP beundrar en kvinna]	$\begin{cases} \textbf{admire}'(\hat{P} \exists x[\textbf{woman}'(x) \wedge P\{x\}]) \\ \textbf{admire}'(\hat{P}P\{x_2\}) \end{cases}$	$[NP]_2$	[4]
[NP₁ varje engelsman]	$\begin{cases} \lambda P \forall y[\textbf{E-man}'(y) \rightarrow P\{y\}] \\ \lambda PP\{x_1\} \end{cases}$	$[\lambda P \forall y[\textbf{E-man}'(y) \rightarrow P\{y\}]]_1 \, (=[NP]_1)$	NP storage (11)
[s varje engelsman beundrar en kvinna]	$\begin{cases} \forall y[\textbf{E-man}'(y) \rightarrow \exists x[\textbf{woman}'(x) \wedge \textbf{admire}'_*(\check{}y, \check{}x)]] \\ \exists x[\textbf{woman}'(x) \wedge \textbf{admire}'_*(\check{}x_1, \check{}x)] \\ \forall y[\textbf{E-man}'(y) \rightarrow \textbf{admire}'_*(\check{}y, \check{}x_2)] \\ \textbf{admire}'_*(\check{}x_1, \check{}x_2) \end{cases}$	$\begin{array}{l} [NP]_1 \\ [NP]_2 \\ [NP]_1, [NP]_2 \end{array}$	[1]

The meaning set m(S) for the tree rooted in S contains four elements. This is not yet the set M(S) of complete meanings associated with S since there are still quantifier meanings in store. To get only the reduced meanings, we retrieve the NP meanings from store by the rule given in (13).

(13)   *NP Quantification*

If α is an S and $\langle \beta, \sigma_0, [NP]_i, \sigma_1 \rangle \in m(\alpha)$ then $\langle [NP]_i(\hat{x}_i[\beta]), \sigma_0, \sigma_1 \rangle \in m(\alpha)$.

β is an expression in IL.
σ is a sequence of elements in store.

Given the storage convention, the meaning of any expression will be represented as a sequence of a formula in IL, β, and stored quantifier meanings. What (13) says is in effect that at any S node where the meaning set for that node contains a sequence with a stored NP meaning, we have the option of quantifying in that NP meaning. As a result, that NP will have scope over the subtree rooted in S and its meaning is removed from store.[6,7]

Returning to our example, we note that there are two NP meanings in store. We can quantify them in either order. However quantifying in $[NP]_1$, the quantifier associated with **varje engelsman**, after quantifying in $[NP]_2$, the quantifier associated with **en kvinna**, will give us a formula which is equivalent to one that is already in the set. When we weed out equivalent formulas, it turns out that M(S) contains the following members:

(12')   M(S) =

$\left\{ \begin{array}{l} \forall y[\textbf{Englishman}'(y) \rightarrow \exists x[\textbf{woman}'(x) \wedge \textbf{admire}'_*(\check{}y, \check{}x)]] \\ \exists x[\textbf{woman}'(x) \wedge \forall y[\textbf{Englishman}'(y) \rightarrow \textbf{admire}'_*(\check{}y, \check{}x)]] \end{array} \right\}$

The two members of M(S) correspond to the two readings of the sentence.

To summarize briefly, using the NP storage technique, we generate sets of meanings for each expression that contains a NP. The reduced meaning set for a *n*-way ambiguous sentence should be represented by *n* distinct formulas. The NP Storage Convention insures that we get all readings for a sentence which differ with respect to the scope of quantificational NPs without having to create a disambiguated structure for each reading. This, however, is necessary in PTQ and also in the EST framework where ambiguous sentences must have distinct representations at LF (logical form) which, despite its name, is a syntactic level of representation. The fact that NPs can be interpreted *either* in place *or* in some higher position shows the *optionality* of NP storage. We will contrast this with the *obligatory* storage which applies to WH phrases and reflexives.

We have not put any restrictions on the NP Storage Convention or on the NP Quantification Rule, neither on the type of quantifiers that can be stored, nor on what constituents can have filled stores associated with them. As is well known, quantifiers differ with respect to how easily they take wide scope over other quantifiers and negation (cf. Ioup, 1975; Fodor, 1982; and Vanlehn, 1978). It would be straightforward to restrict our storage convention and quantification rule so that they conformed better to the set of meanings that people agree sentences have. This would involve splitting up the rules in (11) and (13) in a number of subcases. This could of course be done but doing so would divert us from the main focus of this section which is the distinction between free and controlled quantification.

3.2. Controlled Quantification

Our basic assumption when it comes to interpreting interrogative phrases like **vem** (*who*) or **vilken flicka** (*which girl*) is that they cannot be given an appropriate interpretation in isolation. They can only be interpreted with respect to a sentence meaning. The effect of interpreting a WH phrase in this context is to turn the sentence meaning into a question meaning. Briefly, we cannot tell what *who* means, nor what *kissed which girl* means. Only when we combine the interpretation of *who* with the interpretation of an open sentence '*John kissed ____*' do we get an expression of the language, *who did John kiss*, that is meaningful. In languages like English and Swedish, interrogative constituents in (singular) questions obligatorily occur in a presentential position, i.e. what we here call a dislocated position. It is also commonly referred to as the Comp position. When we say that a WH phrase obligatorily occurs in dislocated position, we are on purpose disregarding *echo* questions of the type illustrated in (14).

(14) a. You ordered WHAT?
   b. You said that WHO came?

To be felicitous, echo questions seem to require heavy stress on the 'unmoved' WH phrase. We take echo questions to be metalinguistic requests for clarification of some distorted part of a previous utterance and not as genuine questions (cf. Cooper, 1983, p. 148). On our account, which is basically due to S. Peters, it follows from the semantics of WH phrases that they cannot be interpreted otherwise than with respect to a sentence meaning, a proposition. Because of their semantic type, WH phrases cannot contribute directly to the meaning of an embedding VP or NP. We won't go into exactly what the meaning of an interrogative quantifier is, nor what the meaning of a question is, here, but postpone this to Chapter IV. However, we will say a few things which hopefully will help to clarify the general strategy of our approach.

We take it that the reason we cannot interpret a VP like *kissed who* is that the meaning of *who* is not of the right type to combine with the meaning of a transitive verb like *kiss*. Rather, *who* is a quantifier which necessarily takes scope over a sentence. On our approach, we can express this by saying that the meaning of *who* is *obligatorily stored* and cannot be retrieved until we reach a level in the derivation where we have a sentence meaning, i.e. a proposition. At this point, we may retrieve the stored interrogative quantifier and quantify it in. The formulation of the WH quantification rule is very similar to the rule for NP quantification in (13).

(15)   WH *Quantification*

   In a structure Q → XP S, if $\langle \alpha, \sigma_0, [WH]_i, \sigma_1 \rangle \in m(S)$ then $\langle \lambda p[[WH]_i(\hat{x}_i[\check{\ }p \wedge p = \hat{\ }S'])], \sigma_0, \sigma_1 \rangle \in m(Q)$.

Notice that the WH quantification rule applies to a sentence meaning (a proposition) and results in a question meaning (a set of propositions which we represent as $\lambda p[\ldots]$). The simplest way to see how WH quantification works is to go through a derivation comparable to the derivation involving NP quantification in (12). (In order to concentrate on WH quantification, we will use an example with proper names where the optional NP storage won't play any role. See Chapter IV.5 for discussion and illustration of the interaction between interrogative quantifiers and other quantifiers.)

(16) Kalle undrar vem Maja beundrar.[8]
Kalle wonders who Maja admires.

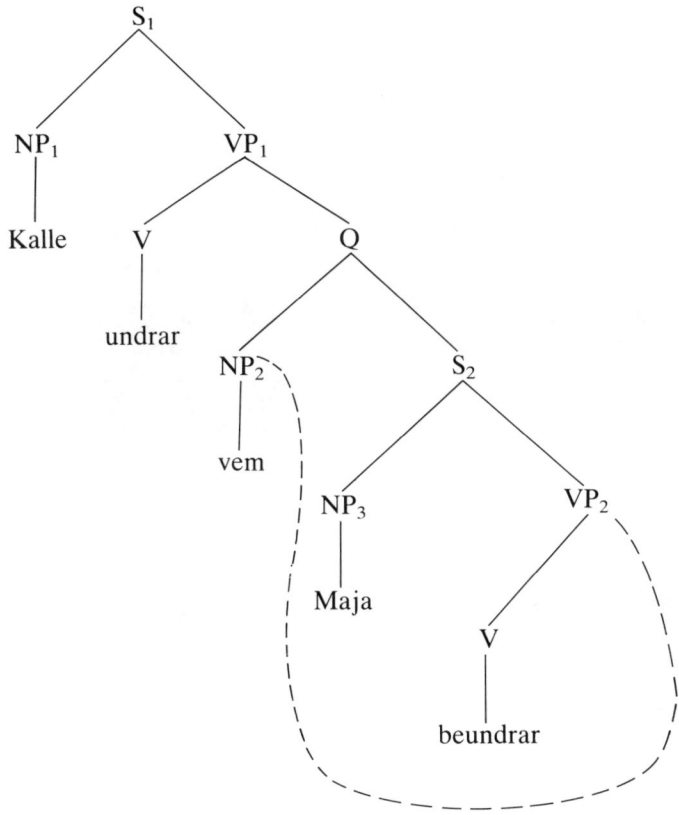

The table to tree diagram (16) is given on p. 74.

Since the stored NPs, correspond to proper names, quantifying them in won't result in any distinct readings. The linked tree in (16) is thus associated with the one meaning, represented by the proposition 'Kalle stands in the wonder-relation to the set of true propositions of the form "Maja admires x"'. We have simplified this derivation in several ways. For instance, we could have quantified in $[NP]_3$ at the S_2 level but that would not have changed the truth-conditions.

When we compare this derivation to the derivation in (12), we note that whereas the interpretation of a NP is *optionally* stored, thus giving

This table relates to tree diagram (16) on p. 73.

EXPRESSION	INTERPRETATION	STORE	RULE USED
[NP₂ vem]	$\lambda PP\{x_2\}$	$[WH]_2$	WH storage
[VP₂ beundrar]	$\mathbf{admire'}(\check{P}P\{x_2\})$	$[WH]_2$	[4] + link convention
[NP₃ Maja]	$\begin{cases} \lambda PP\{\hat{\ }m\} \\ \lambda PP\{x_3\} \end{cases}$	$[NP]_3$	NP storage (9)
[S₂ Maja beundrar]	$\begin{cases} \mathbf{admire'}(m, \check{\ }x_2) \\ \mathbf{admire'}_*(\check{\ }x_3, \check{\ }x_2) \end{cases}$	$[WH]_2$ $[WH]_2, [NP]_3$	[1]
[Q vem Maja beundrar]	$\begin{cases} \lambda p \, \exists x [\check{\ }p \wedge p = \hat{\ }\mathbf{admire'}(m, \check{\ }x)] \\ \lambda p \, \exists x [\check{\ }p \wedge p = \hat{\ }\mathbf{admire'}_*(\check{\ }x_3, \check{\ }x)] \end{cases}$		[16] WH quantification (15)
[VP₁ undrar vem Maja beundrar]	$\begin{cases} \mathbf{wonder'}(\hat{p}\ldots) \\ \mathbf{wonder'}(\hat{p}\ldots) \end{cases}$	$[NP]_3$	[8]
[NP₁ Kalle]	$\begin{cases} \lambda PP\{\hat{\ }k\} \\ \lambda PP\{x_1\} \end{cases}$	$[NP]_3$	NP storage (9)
[S₁ Kalle undrar vem Maja beundrar]	$\mathbf{wonder'}(k, \hat{p}\,\exists x[\check{\ }p \wedge p = \hat{\ }\mathbf{admire'}_*(m, \check{\ }x)])$	$[NP]_1,$	NP quantification (13)

rise to a set of meanings, the interpretation of an interrogative NP is *obligatorily* stored, thus resulting in only one interpretation for that constituent. Note that there is no interpretation where the WH phrase directly interacts with the interpretation of the embedding VP_2. This is then the fundamental difference between NP interpretation and WH interpretation. There is also an important difference in the way each quantification rule works. NP quantification is *free*, i.e. it may apply at any S node. WH quantification on the other hand is *controlled* in a sense that we will now make precise. The fact that we want to capture is that a dislocated WH phrase determines which question is being introduced by the dominating Q node. A WH phrase in dislocated position thus must be interpreted as having scope over its sentential sister constituent. This means that in a structure like (17)

(17)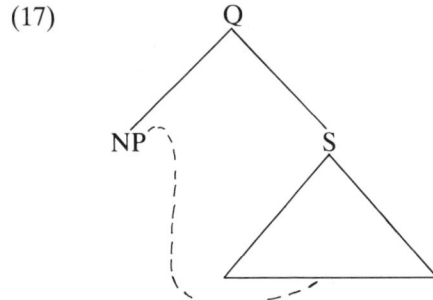

the interpretation of the NP must be or contain an interrogative quantifier which must be taken out of store and quantified in at the S level, otherwise the derivation will block. In the derivation in (16), there was only one WH phrase in store at the relevant point, so the question of a choice never arose. However, if we consider iterated questions, i.e. structures with two or more embedded questions there might be several interrogative quantifiers in store at the point when we are about to interpret the most embedded question. Consider a question like (18), conceivably uttred by a nervous organizer right before the Nobel Prize awards, and its linked tree representation in (18′)[9].

(18) Minns du vilken kunglighet det var speciellt viktigt vilken pristagare jag skulle presentera för?

Do you remember which member of royalty it was especially important which winner I introduced to?

(18')

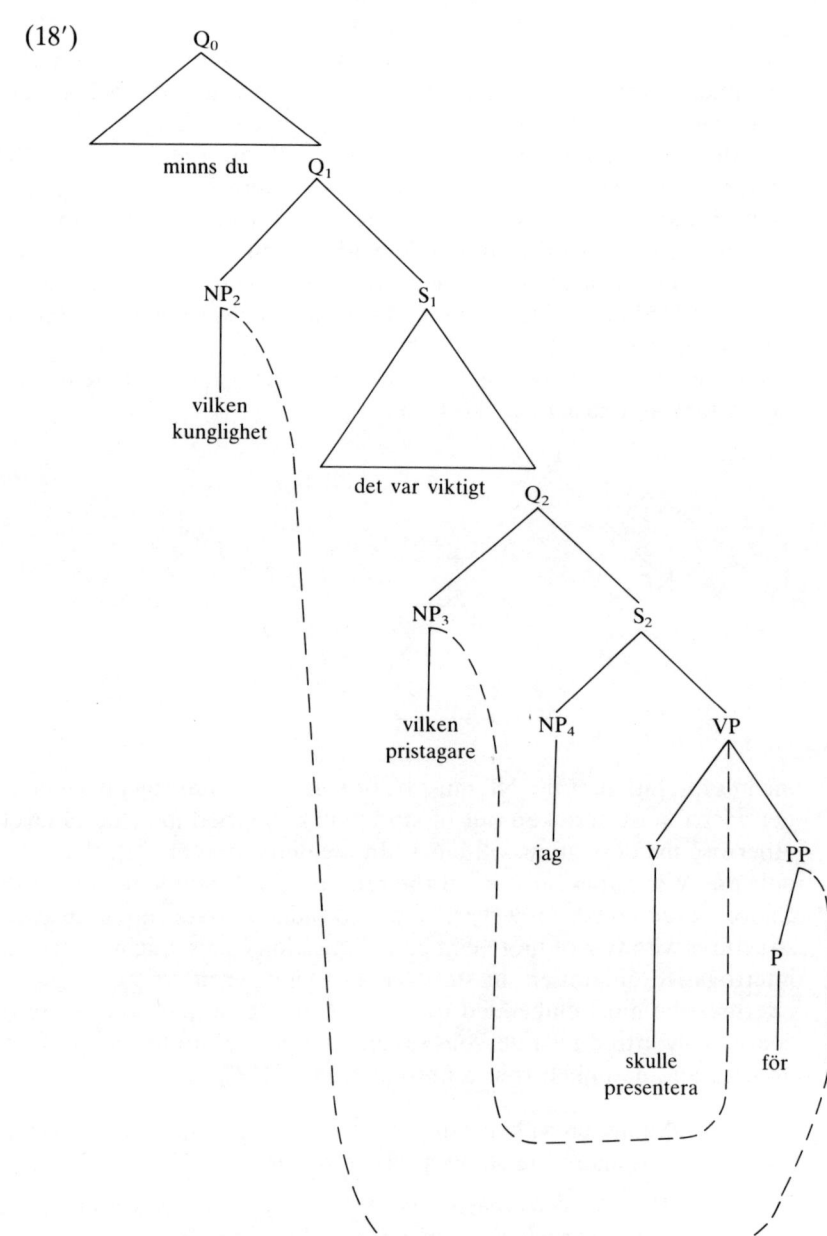

What we want to illustrate with this example is that although there will be two interrogative quantifiers in store at S_2, corresponding to the link children NP_2 and NP_3, we are not free to choose either one to quantify in at this level. Rather, we must quantify in **vilken pristagare** (*which winner*) at S_2 and **vilken kunglighet** (*which member of royalty*) at S_1. Suppose we had quantified in the opposite way around. Then we would also have ended up with a complete meaning, but a meaning that speakers of Swedish would not associate with the question in (18) but with a question like (19),

(19)   Minns du vilken pristagare det var speciellt viktigt vilken kunglighet jag skulle presentera för?

Do you remember which winner it was especially important which member of royalty I should introduce to?

which is a totally different question. In (18), the confused organizer is asking if I remember which member of royalty it was important that he did something or other to. In (19), the organizer is asking if I remember which Nobel Prize winner it was important got correct treatment. These are clearly distinct questions. Hence it's the WH phrase in the dislocated position which determines the meaning of the question introduced by the dominating Q node. We will capture this obligatory aspect of WH quantification by making sure that the rule applies to an interrogative quantifier $[WH]_i$ in the interpretation of the dislocated constituent. (See Chapter IV.7 for a formalization of this requirement.) The application of the WH quantification rule is thus *controlled* by the syntactic configuration. Whenever a dislocated constituent is admitted under a Q node, an interrogative quantifier, associated with the dislocated constituent, is quantified in[10]. In the following section, we will illustrate how obligatory storage and controlled quantification of WH phrases enter into the analysis of various types of questions.

4. QUESTIONS

In this section we will illustrate the types of constituent questions that occur in Swedish. We will first look at iterated questions and multiple questions, then discuss subject questions which have a special form, and finally turn to infinitival questions which in Swedish only occur as matrix questions.

4.1. Questions Out of Questions

In the short overview of data from Swedish in Chapter II.1, we saw that Swedish allows extractions out of embedded questions. The existence of such questions follows from the fact that we have not put any restrictions on the linked tree representations for questions, introduced by rule [14], the syntactic part of which is repeated here.

(20) $\langle [14] \quad Q \rightarrow XP \quad S, \ldots \rangle$

Q dominates trees in which the dislocated constituent, XP, is linked to some constituent inside S. Since we have not constrained these links in any way, the grammar will automatically accept a tree where an interrogative phrase is linked to some constituent inside another Q. We don't see any reason to put any structural constraints on the linked trees, but in Section 7, we will discuss certain other types of restrictions that might be relevant.

As we saw in the previous section, the interpretation of the structures admitted by [14] will involve controlled WH quantification as in the rule given in (15), i.e. quantification of an interrogative quantifier, associated with the dislocated XP, over the interpretation of the tree dominated by S. We thereby connect the acceptance of a given WH phrase in dislocated position to the retrieval of its meaning from store. However, not all WH phrases occur as link children and we now turn to a discussion of WH phrases in other positions.

4.2. Multiple Questions

Besides iterated questions like in (17) and (19), there are so-called multiple WH questions. Characteristic for a multiple question is that in addition to the intial dislocated WH phrase, there are one or more occurences of 'unmoved' WH phrases in the sentence. Such a question is often answered by providing a list of pairs (or triples ...) which supply values for the questioned phrases.

(21) Q: Vem beställde vad?   Who ordered what?
     A: Johan beställde köttbullar och Johan ordered meatballs and
        Lisa beställde ärtsoppa, ...   Lisa ordered pea soup, ...

In our grammar, interrogative phrases like **vem** and **vad** are introduced directly under NP nodes. (There is no special feature +WH in the syntax.) Consequently our grammar will accept WH phrases in all NP position. The structure for (21) is simply as in (22)[11].

(22)
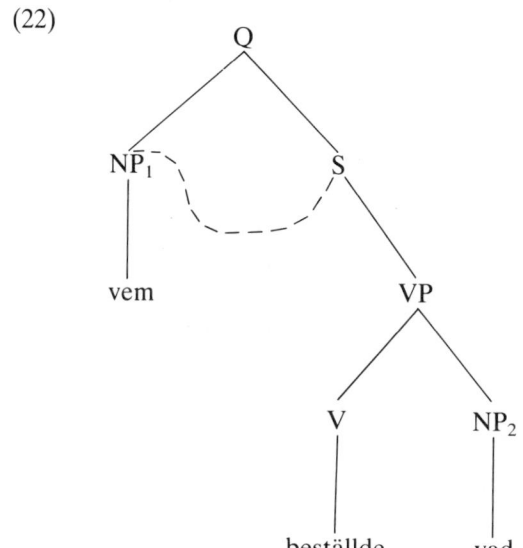

How then are structures with unmoved WH phrases interpreted? We said in Section 3.2 that WH phrases are interpreted as interrogative quantifiers which are obligatorily stored and which cannot be retrieved until we have reached a sentence interpretation. In a derivation of (21), the interpretation at the S node will thus contain two stored interrogative quantifiers, corresponding to NP_1 and NP_2, respectively. The rule for WH quantification in (15) allows us to quantify in the WH phrase associated with the link child NP_1. Using this rule we get the following interpretation for Q:

$$\langle \lambda p \ \exists x[\textbf{person}'(x) \land \ {}^\vee p \land p = {}^\wedge \textbf{order}'_*({}^\vee x, {}^\vee x_2)], \ [WH]_2 \rangle$$

This expression denotes a set of propositions, namely the set of propositions of the form 'x ordered x_2' where x is a person. It is thus of the right type to be a question meaning but there is still a WH phrase in store. Consequently this is not yet a complete meaning for (21). But we cannot reapply (15) since this rule only applies to sentence meanings. Consequently, we need a rule for multiple WH quantification, which will have roughly the form in (23).

(23) *Multiple WH Quantification*

If $\langle \alpha, [WH]_i \rangle \in m(Q)$
then $\langle \lambda q[[WH]_i(\hat{x}_i[\alpha(q)])]\rangle \in m(Q)$.

We will spell out this rule in more detail in Chapter IV.7, when we have introduced more of our semantics. Here we just note that the rule differs from the WH quantification rule in (15) in that it applies to a question meaning (a set of propositions) and yields another question meaning. This rule, then, can apply to its own output, as will be required in case there is more than one unmoved WH phrase in the sentence[12]. The fact that the interpretation of an interrogative quantifier associated with an unmoved WH phrase can only be interpreted into a question meaning accounts for why (24) is not a well-formed multiple question.

(24) Kalle beställde vad åt vem?
      Kalle ordered what for whom?

The only way (24) can be understood is as a double echo question. The questioner must have failed to grasp both what Kalle ordered and for whom. (24) cannot be understood as a multiple question, asking for a list of pairs of dishes and people. On our approach, the derivation of (24) will be blocked at the S level. There will be two interrogative quantifiers in store, corresponding to the unmoved WH phrases **vad** and **vem**. However, since none of these is in dislocated position, the WH quantification rule in (15) cannot apply. Consequently the multiple WH quantification rule in (23) cannot apply either since it is only applicable to a question meaning. By assuming that multiple questions presuppose a question interpretation, we have a straightforward explanation for why (24) cannot be interpreted as a multiple question. Incidentally, the way we have spelled out the controlled WH quantification rule and outlined the multiple WH quantification rule enables us to deal with a sentence which could be problematic for the Phrase-Linking grammar approach, as we noted in Chapter II, note 20. We mentioned there that we need to prevent a sentence like (25) from getting an interpretation, especially not the interpretation normally associated with (26).

(25) *John wonders the boy which girl likes.

(26) John wonders which girl likes the boy.

This interpretation of (25) could arise in a Phrase-linking grammar of the type outlined in Peters and Ritchie (in preparation) in the following way: The link child *the boy* is interpreted as an argument to *likes* according to the convention for interpreting link parents. The interpretation of *which girl* is stored and then quantified in at the embedded question level. Such a derivation would not be possible on the present approach since controlled quantification requires that the WH phrase quantified in be associated with a dislocated phrase at that level.

So far we have looked only at multiple questions in simple sentences. The more interesting examples involve multiple questions where the unmoved WH phrase occurs in an embedded question. Their relevance to the general theory of semantics for questions has been discussed by among others Baker (1970) and Hirschbühler (1978, 1981). Consider a multiple WH question like in (27).

(27)   Vem minns   var   Maja träffade vilken kille?
       Who remembers where Maja met   which guy?

There are two possible ways of answering (27) and we take this as an indication that the question is ambiguous. Either we can answer just the direct question and respond **Johan**. If this is a truthful answer, then Johan does in fact remember where Maja met which boy for any boy out of a contextually relevant set of boys that Maja has met. We get this reading by quantifying in the interpretation of the unmoved phrase, **vilken kille**, at the embedded question level. We can also answer with a list of pairs of 'rememberers' and boys, as in (28).

(28)   Johan vet var Maja träffade Sixten och
       Anders vet var Maja träffade Osvald, och ...

       Johan knows where Maja met Sixten and
       Anders knows where Maja met Osvald, and ...

On this reading, we interpret the unmoved WH phrase with scope over the entire question. Technically this involves storing the interpretation of **vilken kille** until we have interpreted the matrix question and quantify it in there. Notice however that (29) and (30) are not possible answers to (27), (* here means unavailable as an answer to (27).)

(29)   *Johan minns att Maja träffade vilken kille i Köpenhamn och
       ...
       Johan remembers that Maja met which guy in Copenhagen
       and ...

(30) *Johan minns att Maja träffade Rasmus i Köpenhamn och ...
Johan remembers that Maja met Rasmus in Copenhagen and
...

In (29) we have interpreted the dislocated phrase **var** as if it had scope over the matrix question and in (30) we have interpreted all WH phrases with maximal scope. This is clearly wrong. (29) and (30) show that even in multiple questions, dislocated WH phrases in embedded questions must be interpreted with the scope that corresponds to their surface position[13]. Although unmoved WH phrases optionally can take wider scope in multiple questions, this optionality does not extend to WH phrases in dislocated positions. In the present framework, this follows from the controlled quantification procedure for WH phrases in dislocated positions.

We noted above that this restriction on the interpretation possibilities for certain WH phrases is linked to the fact that languages like English and Swedish have a designated position for phrases introducing questions. In languages like Japanese where WH phrases are interpreted *in situ* we don't find this restriction. The Japanese version of (27) would be as in (31).

(31) Q: Mary-ga   dono otokonoko-ni doko-de atta-ka
Mary-SUBJ *which boy-to*   *whe̢re-in met* QUESTION
particle

dare-ga   oboeteiru-ka?
who-SUBJ *remember*-QUESTION
particle

Who remembers where Mary met which boy?

A: Tom-ga   oboeteiru.
Tom-SUBJ *remembers*

Tom does.

There is a strong preference for interpreting this question as a matrix question only, as indicated by the answer given in (31), but to the extent that speakers accept a list type of answers, all WH phrases must be instantiated in the answer[14].

4.2.1. Mixed yes/no and Constituent Questions

The possibility of interpreting unmoved WH phrases in constituent questions naturally leads us to wonder whether this is possible in yes/no questions as well[15]. At first glance, questions like in (32)–(33) seem clearly ungrammatical both in English and in Swedish.

(32) *Tycker du om vad?
 *Do you like what?

(33) *Är Lisa hur gammal?
 *Is Lisa how old?

If these questions can be interpreted at all, they are taken as direct yes/no questions with a superimposed echo question. It thus seems that we should restrict the interpretation of unmoved WH phrases to constituent questions. However, when we consider additional data, the picture changes somewhat. First, unmoved WH phrases in embedded *if* questions are possible in Swedish as shown in (34)[16].

(34) Q: Vem skulle ta reda på om Lisa tycker om vilken pojke?
 Who was supposed to find out if Lisa likes which boy?

 A: a *Maria
 b Maria skulle ta reda på om Lisa tycker om Jonas och Eva skulle ta reda på om Lisa tycker om Patrick, och

 Maria was supposed to find out if Lisa likes Jonas and Eva was supposed to find out if Lisa likes Patrik, and ...

Notice that the multiple question in (34) only allows for the list of pairs reading. This indicates that an unmoved WH phrase cannot be interpreted in its embedding question if this is an *if* question. The unmoved WH phrase can be interpreted in the higher constituent question, however. There seem to be two ways we could go about ruling out (32) and (33) and the reading represented by the answer in (34a). One would be to stipulate that WH quantification cannot apply into direct yes/no questions and embedded *if* questions. Presumably this should be a semantic constraint but it is not clear that it could be formulated in purely semantic terms if both *yes/no* questions and constituent questions denote sets of propositions.

The other way would be to allow WH quantification into all types of questions and appeal to a Gricean explanation for why (32), (33) and (34a) appear illformed. The explanation could go along the following lines: The reason (32) is not a good question is that there is a simpler and more direct way of asking the same question, namely as in (32').

(32') Vad tycker du om?
What do you like?

Similarly in (34). If the intended question is a question about *who* was supposed to find something out, then this can be more economically expressed as in (34')[17]

(34') Vem skulle ta reda på vilken pojke Lisa tycker om?
Who was supposed to find out which boy Lisa likes?

4.2.2. *Do We Need a Syntactic Category Q?*

In the previous sections we have emphasized several times that restrictions on constituent questions which in other frameworks have to be stated as syntactic restrictions naturally fall out in this framework because of the semantics we assume for interrogative quantifiers. We have dispensed with the feature [+/− WH] in the syntax altogether. At this point, one might wonder if we need to make a syntactic distinction between S̄ and Q at all, or if this too could follow from the meaning of each construction. There are several reasons why we will answer this question in the negative. One reason has to do with the general approach to syntax and semantics in the Montague framework, namely that syntactic categories and semantic types are functionally related. One and the same category cannot be mapped into distinct semantic types. Recall that S̄ denotes propositions, whereas Q denotes sets of propositions. There is a more specific reason, however, why we assume a syntactic category Q distinct from S and S̄, which has to do with the syntax of Swedish. We want to account for the fact that (35a) is a normal question, whereas (35b) is interpreted as an echo question.

(35) a. Vem gillar Kalle?
who likes Kalle
Who does Kalle like?

b. Kalle gillar vem?
   Kalle likes who

As (35) shows, *wh*-fronting is obligatory in Swedish. (It also triggers verb inversion in matrix clauses, a fact that we are not dealing with here.)

Suppose we made no distinction between S̄ and Q in the syntax. This would have as a consequence that we could not restrict the WH quantification rule in (17) to apply only in the case of syntactically interrogative clauses. Rather, the WH quantification rule could apply as soon as the semantic conditions were met, i.e. whenever we have a sentence meaning (a proposition). Then there would be no way of distinguishing (35a) and (35b). Consider the derivation of (35b) on such an approach. Having stored the interpretation of **vem**, the meaning set for the S node will contain a meaning like in (36).

(36)   m(S): $\langle \mathbf{like}'_*(k, \check{}x_3), [WH]_3\rangle$

The first member of this pair denotes a proposition, the second is an interrogative variable binding operator. Recall that on Peters and Ritchie's approach, it's the valence of the variable binding operator which determines when it may apply (cf. note 12). If we assume that interrogative variable binding operators take propositions into sets of propositions, then there is nothing to prevent the operator $[WH]_3$ in (36) from applying to the first member, turning this into a regular question meaning, indistinguishable from the interpretation for (35a). If, however, we link the application of the WH quantification rule to the presence of a particular syntactic category, Q, as we have done in (15), then this problem does not arise. Another alternative would be to dispense with Q, but instead have a feature [+WH] which identified interrogative phrases. In that case, the WH quantification rule could be formulated in a way which only made reference to a certain syntactic configuration, XP S, and to the presence of [+WH].

Note that making this distinction is only motivated for languages like Swedish which have obligatory *wh*-fronting. In a language like Japanese where WH phrases are always interpreted *in situ*, this would not be a reason for distinguishing S and S̄ from Q. Accounting for the distribution of the interrogative particle −**ka**, however, might require that some syntactic distinction is made.

4.2.3. Linked Trees and Token Indexing

It might be of some interest to compare the use of linked tree representations in the syntax to devices used in other grammatical frameworks. In the previous sections we have repeatedly argued that it is necessary to be able to determine which interrogative quantifier a dislocated phrase corresponds to when we are about to interpret a constituent question. The reason is that it is precisely the meaning of *that* dislocated WH phrase which determines the meaning of the constituent question, not any other WH meaning in store. Since there may be any number of interrogative quantifiers available in store at that level, we need some way of distinguishing the interrogative quantifier associated with the dislocated constituent. Our proposal is to account for this in the controlled quantification procedure by assuming that WH phrases are interpreted as variable binding operators and by requiring that the particular variable binding operator, $[WH]_i$ quantified in at a given point be associated with an occurrence of a free variable indexed by i in the interpretation of the dislocated constituent (see Chapter IV.7 for details). We thus make reference to the interpretation of a *syntactically identifiable* constituent in our rule.

Let us now consider some alternatives. Another approach would be to try to formulate the quantification rule with reference only to the meaning of the constituents involved. The interpretation rule corresponding to Q → NP S could then be something like in (37), omitting irrelevant details.

(37)   Quantify in the meaning of NP.

By 'the meaning of NP' we here understand the interpretation of NP minus the indexing variable, i.e. [*NP*] or [*WH*]. However, by simply referring to the meaning of a constituent, this rule cannot discriminate sufficiently between different occurrences of the same expression. Consider the two multiple questions in (38) and (39).

(38)   Who remembers [$_Q$ which student Mary talked to ____ about which student?]

(39)   Who remembers [$_Q$ which student Mary talked to which student about ____?]

When we are about to interpret the Q node, there are two interrogative meanings in store, both corresponding to the phrase *which student*.

They are presumably associated with distinct placeholding variables, but the problem is that if the quantification rule just refers to the meaning of the phrase to be quantified in, we cannot distinguish the two meanings associated with the two occurrences of *which student*. Consequently, we might get a derivation of (38) according to which it comes out with the meaning normally associated with (39), and vice versa, although these multiple questions mean different things. It thus turns out that the WH quantification rule must identify a particular variable binding operator not just in terms of its meaning but also as being associated with a particular syntactic position. We hence need some way of linking the meaning of a phrase to a particular occurrence of that phrase in a syntactic structure. The way we capture this in (15) is by linking the quantifier that is quantified in to an occurrence of a particular variable in the interpretation of a configurationally distinguished constituent.

Another way to achieve the same purpose would be to use some form of *token indexing* in the syntax (cf. Engdahl, 1980a, p. 68.f). A similar approach is proposed in Kamp (1981, p. 306f.). The point of assuming token indexing is to be able to distinguish each node in a given syntactic tree. It is straightforward to formulate an algorithm which assigns a unique index, for instance an integer, to each of the nodes in a tree. The index of a node then serves to identify the expression at that node. Given this indexing procedure, we can identify any occurrence of an expression in a tree. Kamp suggests that an occurrence of an expression be represented by an ordered pair, $\langle \alpha, n \rangle$ where α is the expression and n is the index of the dominating node. If we furthermore assume that the same index is used to uniquely identify the interpetation (or meaning) of a constituent, then a rule as in (37) will work.

Cooper (1983, chapter V) suggests that we do not require fully indexed representations in the syntax and that there is no evidence that we construct fully indexed representations in the interpretation of a sentence. Cooper argues that what is needed is some way of keeping track of the left to right order of gaps and WH phrases, since, according to him, it is only the left to right order that has to be considered in parsing and processing, as well as in the formulation of constraints.

It should be noted that the type of syntactic indexing we have brought up here is very different from the indexing procedures assumed in the Extended Standard Theory and the Government-Binding theory. The type of indexing we are talking about is used for *distinctness* in the syntax. It enables us to distinguish identical expressions at distinct nodes. The co-and-contra indexing procedures used in EST and GB serve to indicate or prohibit coreference between expressions, i.e. they are used to indicate dependence in interpretation possibilities between expressions in a tree. We return to the use of syntactic coindexing in Chapter V.

4.3. Subject Questions

When we look at subject questions in Swedish, an interesting difference shows up between matrix and embedded questions. Compare the direct questions in (40) with the set of embedded questions in (41).

(40) a. Vem kom?
    who came

   b. *Vem som kom?
    who that came

(41) a. *Jag undrar vem kom
    I wonder who came

   b. Jag undrar vem som kom.
    I wonder who that came
    I wonder who came.

   c. Jag undrar hur många (som) Kalle bjöd.
    I wonder how many (that) Kalle invited

   d. Jag undrar vem (som) Kalle tyckte skulle komma.
    I wonder who (that) Kalle thought should come

We see that embedded subject questions differ from matrix questions in that **som** obligatorily occurs adjacent to the Wh phrase. Notice that **som** is obligatory only when the subject of the adjacent S is being questioned. When a subject of a further embedded sentence, as in (41d) or an object, as in (41c), is questioned, **som** occurs optionally. **som** is also the relative marker corresponding to English *that*. Just like *that*, **som** is obligatory only in subject relatives. The distribution of **som** in Swedish questions and relatives is thus quite similar to the distribution of *that* in English relative clauses.

The phrase structure rules we have given so far will work fine for the matrix question in (40a). However, they will incorrectly admit (41a) and will not admit the grammatical (41b). We obviously need to modify our rules somewhat. Exactly how we modify the rules will to a certain extent depend on how we analyze **som**. There have been several proposals in the literature for how to analyze **som** and where to attach it. Andersson (1975) proposes that **som** is a complementizer for subordinate sentences but that it does not form a constituent with other elements that may occur in Comp. Maling and Zaenen (1981) take a similar position and generate WH phrases and **som** under distinct Comp nodes. Taraldsen (1978b) analyzes **som** as cooccurring with WH phrases in Comp and formulates a local deletion rule to account for sentences like (41c) and (41d) without **som**. In a more recent study, Taraldsen (to appear) assumes that **som** is an expletive element which does not necessarily form a constituent with the WH phrase.

Let us now consider what these approaches would look like in the present syntactic framework. A number of possible structures are given in (42).

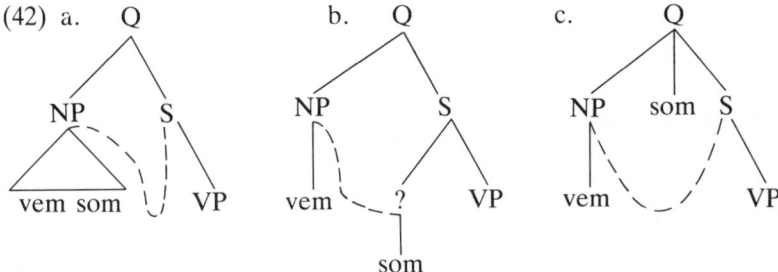

(42)

According to the structure in (42a), NP and **som** together occur in dislocated position and form a constituent, as suggested in Taraldsen (1978). This analysis thus predicts that **vem som** should always behave as a constituent. This is not correct, however, as shown by (43) which is a case of Right Node Raising of the embedded question except for the WH phrase.

(43) Jag minns   hur många pojkar, men har glömt
      I   remember how many   boys   but have forgotten

  hur många flickor som skulle komma
  how many girls   that should come

The fact that **vem** and **som** may be separated also argues against a slightly different version of (42a) which we can represent as in (42a'). On this approach, the WH phrase is not linked to the S, but is a sister of the VP.

(42) a.'

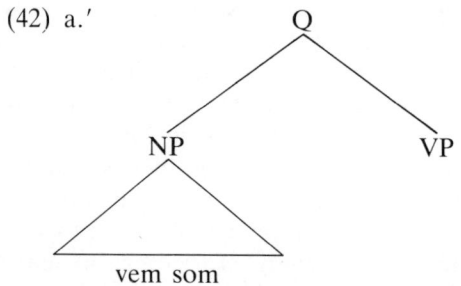

Analyzing subject questions and subject relatives as taking bare VPs has been proposed for English in Gazdar (1981) and for Swedish in Ejerhed (1982). But, as we have seen, this would run into problems with examples like (43). Furthermore, if we assume that WH phrases in subject questions don't occur as link children in dislocated position, the formulation of the WH quantification rule would have to be considerably more complex. In particular, we need to make sure that the rule can distinguish between subject WH phrases and *unmoved* WH phrases in subject position.

The second proposal, (42b) takes **som** to be a placeholder for the missing subject and as actually occurring in the subject position. On this analysis, the dislocated phrase **vem** would be linked not directly to S, but to **som**, which then might be taken to act as a resumptive pronoun. This approach could claim support from the fact that resumptive subject pronouns do occur in Swedish as shown in (44).

(44)   I går såg jag en film$_i$ som jag redan glömt hur den$_i$ slutar.
       Yesterday I saw a film that I (have) already forgotten how it ends.

Resumptive pronouns are in fact obligatory as soon as a constituent has been extracted out of a tensed sentence which is preceded by a filled 'complementizer' (see Section 5.1.1 and 6.1 for a more detailed presentation of the facts).

However, there is a clear difference between obligatory occurrences of **som** and obligatory resumptive subject pronouns. The latter are instances of the regular personal pronouns and inflect for number and gender, whereas **som** is invariant. **som** is obligatory when the extracted phrase is immediately adjacent to the gap. Resumptive subject pronouns on the other hand occur when the extracted phrase is not adjacent. Furthermore, there are good diachronic as well as synchronic arguments for analyzing **som** as a complementizer (see Andersson, 1974). Finally, this analysis would not explain the occurrences of **som** in non-subject questions as in (41c, d).

In the third structure, (42c), **som** is generated directly under Q, as a separate node. It hence does not form a constituent with **vem** and is hence not open to the objections raised against (42a)[18]. In order to introduce **som**, we could modify the rule introducing questions as in (45).

(45) $\langle [14'] \quad Q \to XP \quad (som) \quad S, \quad \ldots \rangle$

(45) optionally introduces **som** in any constituent question. However, we also have to account for the fact that **som** is obligatory in embedded subject questions and impossible in matrix questions. It turns out that in a phrase linking grammar, this restriction can be simply expressed as a prohibition against links between adjacent nodes. We can formulate this as in (46).

(46) Two adjacent nodes may be linked only if the link child is directly dominated by a root Q.

(46) will prevent **vem** in (41a) from being linked to S, but will allow **vem** in (41b) to be linked to S, since there is an intervening node, **som**. In matrix questions like (40a), adjacent links are permitted, however[19].

4.4. Infinitival Questions

In this section we will look at what kind of infinitival questions occur in Swedish. This will also give us a reason to return to the issue of characterizing the positions where dislocated constituents occur in English and Swedish. Consider the pairs of examples in (47).

(47) a. *Alla   undrade   vad   göra.
     *Everyone wondered what do.

   b. *Alla   undrade   vad   att göra.
     Everyone wondered what to do.

c. *Alla   undrade   om/huruvida åka.
   *Everyone wondered if/whether   go.

d. *Alla   undrade   om/huruvida att åka.
   Everyone wondered *if/whether   to go.

e. Vad göra?
   *What do?

f. *Vad att göra?
   What to do?

We find that whereas English allows both matrix and embedded infinitival questions, provided there is an overt infinitive marker, Swedish only allows matrix infinitival questions without an infinitive marker. One way of accounting for this difference would be to assume that English, but not Swedish, allows dislocated constituents as sisters of VP in embedded clauses. English also allows embedded questions introduced by an infinitival complementizer. Interestingly enough, only *whether* can introduce infinitival questions whereas both *if* and *whether* can introduce tensed questions. English then, has the general structure in (48a) which subsumes the two cases in (48b) and (48c). Swedish lacks (48b) altogether and allows (48c) only if the dominating node is a matrix question.

(48)   a.   C   b.   C   c.   C

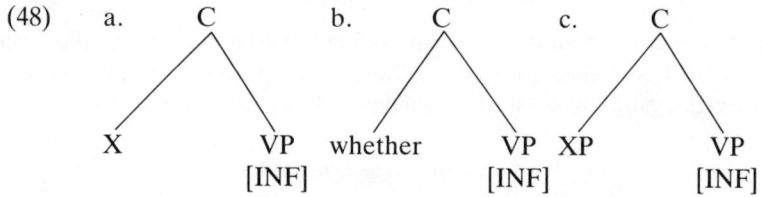

         X   VP   whether VP   XP   VP
               [INF]   [INF]   [INF]

A number of facts support the assumption that Swedish lacks (48b). First, Swedish does not allow any type of complementizer in infinitival constructions such as the English *for* NP *to* VP construction.

(49)   *Jag önskar för Kalle att vinna.
        I want for Kalle to win.

Second, although infinitival relatives occur in Swedish, they must have the form in (50a) with a bare VP complement. No lexical material can introduce an infinitival relative, as can be seen from the ungrammatical (50b).

(50) a. ett rum   att arbeta i ___
a   room to work   in

b. *ett rum   i vilket att arbeta [$_{PP}$ ___]
a   room in which to work

Pied-piping is possible in tensed relative clauses, however. Compare (50b) with the grammatical (50c).

(50) c. ett rum   i vilket jag kan arbeta ___
a   room in which I   can work

It thus appears that a dislocated constituent in a subordinate structure in Swedish must be a sister of a tensed S. Let us now turn to matrix questions. A few more examples are given in (51) together with paraphrases intended to convey how they are understood.

(51) a. Hur svara?
how answer

How is one supposed to answer?

b. När komma?
when arrive

When is one supposed to arrive?

Notice, however, that subject infinitival questions are no good. We can test the availability of such by using examples with intransitive verbs or passive VPs.

(52) a. *Vad hända?
what happen

b. *Vem komma?
who come

c. *Vem inbjudas?
who be invited

Infinitival matrix questions in Swedish are always interpreted as involving a modal element, paraphrased as 'should' or 'be supposed to', which applies to the missing subject. The same is true of English embedded infinitival questions (cf. Huntley, 1982). Notice that the embedded English counterparts to the ungrammatical questions in (52) are all bad.

(53) a. *I wonder what to happen.
 b. *I wonder who to come. /*I wonder for whom to come.
 c. *I wonder who to be invited. /*I wonder for whom to be invited.

Presumably the modal character of infinitival questions and the unavailability of subject infinitival questions are two aspects of the same fact, which will fall out once we have an appropriate semantics for infinitival questions. For now we will account for the unavailability of subject infinitival questions simply by adding a new rule to the grammar. For Swedish we can add a rule like in (54), where Q' is a new symbol, reserved for matrix questions (cf. note 3).

(54)   ⟨[15] Q' → XP VP, ...⟩

For English we would not want the rule in (54) but a rule that admits dislocated constituents in matrix and embedded questions as well as in relative clauses, which we assume will be dominated by some category R. The rules in English would be instantiations of the rule schema in (54').

(54')   ⟨[n] C → XP VP, ...⟩   C = Q, R

It thus turns out that whereas all dislocated constituents in embedded constructions in Swedish are sisters of S, dislocated constituents in matrix questions may be sisters of S or VP[20]. In English on the other hand, dislocated constituents may be sisters of S or VP in both matrix and embedded clauses.

5. PRONOUNS

In the preceding sections we have looked at how NP quantifiers and interrogative quantifiers are interpreted. We will now look at elements which can be bound by quantifiers, namely pronouns. First we will look at the dual use of personal pronouns, as deictic or as bound pronouns, including resumptive pronouns as a special case of bound pronouns. We then turn to the interpretation of reflexive pronouns which further illustrate our use of obligatory storage for elements whose interpretation cannot be determined locally. Finally we discuss certain cases where a bound interpretation for a pronoun is unavailable and introduce a convention, the Store Address Convention, to block derivations that would otherwise give rise to such readings.

5.1. Free and Bound Pronouns

First and second person pronouns in Swedish are always deictic, i.e. they denote the speaker and the addressee, respectively. This is not a necessary property of first and second person proforms. For instance, in Amharic a first person pronoun in certain embedded clauses may refer to a third person subject of the main clause (E. Bach, personal communication). Third person pronouns in Swedish, just like in English, have a dual use (cf. Partee, 1978). They can either be used deictically to pick out some individual in the context or be bound by a quantificational, non-referential, NP in the sentence. In this case, the pronoun doesn't refer to any particular individual. We will reserve using the term *bound* for the cases where the pronoun is bound by a quantifier. We will not say that a pronoun is bound if it happens to refer to the same individual as some other referring expression in the sentence. Following Montague in PTQ, we will represent the meaning of a pronoun as a NP type expression with a free individual variable, $\lambda PP\{x_i\}$, i.e. the set of properties that x_i has[21]. Whether the pronoun is interpreted as bound or not will depend on whether the free variable, x_i, gets bound by some quantifier. We can illustrate the free and bound uses of pronouns by a few examples.

(55) a. Han vinner.
He wins.

    b. Ingen tror att **han** vinner.
No one believes that he wins.

    c. Vem tror att **han** vinner?
Who believes that he wins?

d. Johan tror   att **han** vinner.
   Johan believes that he   wins.

In (55a) **han** must be interpreted as a deictic pronoun which refers to some male individual in the context of the utterance. A representation of its meaning will be as in (55a').

(55a') $\lambda PP\{x_3\}(\hat{\ }\textbf{win}') = \textbf{win}'_*(\hat{\ }x_3)$

We assume that the interpretation procedure includes an assignment function which assigns values to all free variables. In order to determine whether (55a') is true or false, we must determine which individual the assignment function assigns to x_3 and check if this individual in fact wins.

In constrast with (55a), (55b) has two readings, which we will represent as in (55b').

(55b') $\neg \exists x[\textbf{person}'(x) \wedge \textbf{believe}'_*(\check{\ }x, \hat{\ }\textbf{win}'_*(\check{\ }x_3))]$

$\neg \exists x[\textbf{person}'(x \wedge \textbf{believe}'_*(\check{\ }x, \hat{\ }\textbf{win}'_*(\check{\ }x))]$

On the first reading, where no one believes that some guy, let's say Johan, wins, the free variable in the interpretation of **han** remains free in the complete meaning and must thus be interpreted deictically, just as in (55a). On the second reading, where no one believes that he (= himself) wins, the free variable in the interpretation of **han** gets bound by the quantifier corresponding to **ingen**. The same interpretation possibilities are available for the question in (55c). It is either interpreted as a question about who believes that some contextually available person wins, or as a question about who believes that he (= himself) wins.

Consider now the interpretation possibilities for (55d). Everybody presumably agrees that (55d) can be true in two different situations, one in which Johan believes that someone, e.g. Peter, wins, and one in which Johan believes that he (= Johan) wins. However, we will not say that (55d) has two distinct meanings. The meaning of (55d) will be represented as in (55d').

(55d') $\textbf{believe}'_*(j, \hat{\ }\textbf{win}'_*(\check{\ }x_5))$

i.e. Johan stands in the believe-relation to the proposition 'x_5 wins'. Notice that x_5 is free in the proposition. Which interpretation we get depends entirely on the assignment function. In case it assigns x_5 to the individual Johan, we get one reading. In case it assigns x_5 to the individual Peter, we get the other. In a given context, the denotation of a free pronoun may thus be the same as the denotation of some other referential expression in the sentence but we won't refer to this as a case of the pronoun being bound. It is more appropriate to talk about (accidental) coreference under an assignment[22].

A different issue, raised by the interpretation possibilities of pronouns, is illustrated in (56).

(56)   Johan tror   att **hon** vinner.
Johan believes that she wins.

(56) is syntactically identical to (55d). Just like for this sentence, there will only be one meaning in the set of complete meanings, as in (55d'). However, in contrast with (55d), (56) does not normally count as true in a situation where the assignment function assigns the free variable in the interpretation of **hon** to the individual Johan, i.e. there is no reading of (56) of the form 'Johan believes that he (= himself) wins'. The issue is now whether the exclusion of this reading should be done syntactically, semantically, or by reference to presuppositions or conventional implicatures. On our approach, actually only the two latter alternatives are available. To rule out this reading in the syntax would require that we marked coreference on some syntactic representation, e.g. by coindexing of nodes. But we have chosen not to express coreference, or any semantic relation, by indexing of syntactic representations. Consequently we cannot block the unwanted reading of (56) by reference to feature clashes of coindexed syntactic nodes.

Semantically we could exclude this interpretation by using sorted variables, i.e. distinct variables for male and female individuals. Then there would be no assignment of values to the variables that assigned the free variable in the interpretation of **hon** to the individual Johan, provided that Johan is in fact a masculine entity. If we take this semantic approach, it still wouldn't be sufficient to divide up the domain according to whether the individuals are masculine or feminine. We would also need distinct variables for individuals that are denoted by neuter and non-neuter common nouns, as shown by the examples in (57).

(57) a. Stenen   var så tung   att **den**   sjönk.
        [−NEUT]   [−NEUT]
the stone was so heavy that it   sank

b. Stenen var så tung att **det** sjönk.
   [+NEUT]

Whereas (57a) is easily understood with **den** (*it*) picking out the same individual as **stenen** (*the stone*), (57b) cannot be used with the same interpretation by someone who masters the language. Since there is hardly any semantic ground for the neuter-non-neuter distinction in Swedish, it seems unmotivated to have sorted variables corresponding to this distinction. We will therefore take the third option and explain the unavailability of the coreferent readings of the examples just discussed as cases of presupposition or implicature clash. On this approach, **Johan tror att hon vinner** (*Johan believes that she wins*) can be true in a situation where **Johan** and **hon** pick out the same individual, but since **Johan** normally is a boy's name and **hon** refers to females, we get a presupposition clash. The interpretation, however, is perfectly consistent, and might well be true, as for instance in a situation where there is a girl called Johan, or in a situation where Johan is mistaken about his sex. Note that it appears to be easier to change the denotation of proper names than to change the implications associated with pronouns[23].

5.1.1. Resumptive Pronouns

In the previous section we said that personal pronouns always have a dual use, either as deictic or as bound pronouns. This is not entirely correct. In Swedish there are also resumptive pronouns which, although morphologically and phonologically identical to personal pronouns, can not refer freely. A few examples to illustrate this are given in (58)[24]. For perspicuousness, the pronoun and its antecedent are coindexed.

(58) a. Det   finns mycket$_i$ som man önskar att det$_i$ skulle
       there is a lot   that one wishes that it   should

   vara annorlunda.
   be different

   b. ett pjunket betraktelsesätt$_i$ som Bakunin skulle vrida
      a lousy view   that Bakunin would turn

   sig i sin grav om han visste att det$_i$ stundom
   around in his grave if he knew that it sometimes

   lanseras   under namnet   anarkism (Aftonbladet)
   is launched under the name of anarchism

c. Det finns ord$_i$ som man inte kan tveka om vad$_j$
    there are words that one cannot hesitate about what
    dom$_i$ betyder ___$_j$.
    they mean

d. Vilken film$_i$ kunde ingen minnas hur$_j$ den$_i$
    which film could no one remember how it
    slutade ___$_j$?
    ended

e. Olle och Johan har en hydda$_i$ som vi vet var$_j$
    Olle and Johan have a cabin that we know where
    den$_i$ ligger ___$_j$.
    it is

f. Kalle$_i$ kan man aldrig vara säker på om han$_i$ dyker upp.
    Kalle one can never be sure on if he shows up

In these examples, the indexed pronoun cannot be understood as referring to something in the context or something previously mentioned. It must be understood as controlled by the coindexed NP. We notice that the coindexed NP is either a relativized, topicalized, or questioned NP, i.e. it is a linked constituent in a dislocated position according to the present framework. The pronouns have in common that they occur in the subject position of a tensed sentence and that there is either a complementizer (**att**, **om**) present or a link child (**hur**, **vad**, **var**) which suggests that it is the type of phenomenon that Bresnan (1972) referred to as the *Fixed Subject Constraint*. We can actually show that the pronoun cannot be understood as freely referring by choosing a form that does not agree morphologically with any antecedent in the sentence, as in the primed versions below.

(58a′) *Det finns **mycket** some man önskar att **den** skulle
        [+NEUT]   [−NEUT]
        vara annorlunda.

(58f′) ***Kalle** kan man aldrig vara säker på om **hon** kommer
        [MASC]   [FEM]

Whereas native speakers have no problem understanding or producing the sentences in (58), they get very puzzled when they are presented with sentences like in (58a′) and (58f′). Most speakers say that they don't understand what you mean. Some volunteer a correction and repeat the sentence with a resumptive pronoun of the appropriate form.

The sentences in (58) would not be accepted by our grammar as currently formulated. There won't be any well-formed linked tree representations for these structures since all the nodes in the embedded S are expanded and dominate lexical material. Hence there is no attachment for the links from the dislocated constituents. However, if we try these sentences with gaps instead of resumptive pronouns, they are clearly ungrammatical in standard Swedish, although corresponding sentences are grammatical in other Scandinavian languages (see Section 6.1 and Engdahl (to appear) for further details).

(58c′) *Det finns ord$_i$ som man inte kan tveka om vad ___$_i$ betyder.

(58d′) *Vilken film$_i$ kunde ingen minnas hur ___$_i$ slutade?

The constrast in grammaticality between the primed and unprimed versions in (58) suggest that we are here dealing with a case where pronouns act as if they were syntactic gaps. The lack of a deictic interpretation of the pronoun together with the fact that gaps are impossible in these positions indicates that these pronouns need a special analysis.

One way to account for the fact that these pronouns don't have a deictic interpretation would be to use a distinct kind of *bound pronoun* variable in the semantics (cf. Janssen, 1981; Partee and Bach, 1981). In addition, we would have to mark certain occurrences in the syntax as requiring such an interpretation. However, it would not be correct to say that these resumptive subject pronouns have to be semantically bound. See for instance (58f) where a pronoun is understood as controlled by a referential expression, a proper name. We argued above that this kind of relation is not a case of semantic *binding*, reserving this term for binding by proper quantifiers. Rather than accounting for these pronouns semantically, we want to claim that the existence of examples like in (58) and the ungrammaticality of the alternatives provide evidence for extending the notion of linked representation to also include trees where the link parent is a pronoun. One condition on these links, then, would be that the link parent be adjacent to **att**, **om**, or a link child[25].

An illustration of a linked tree for (58f) is given in (58f″).

(58f″)

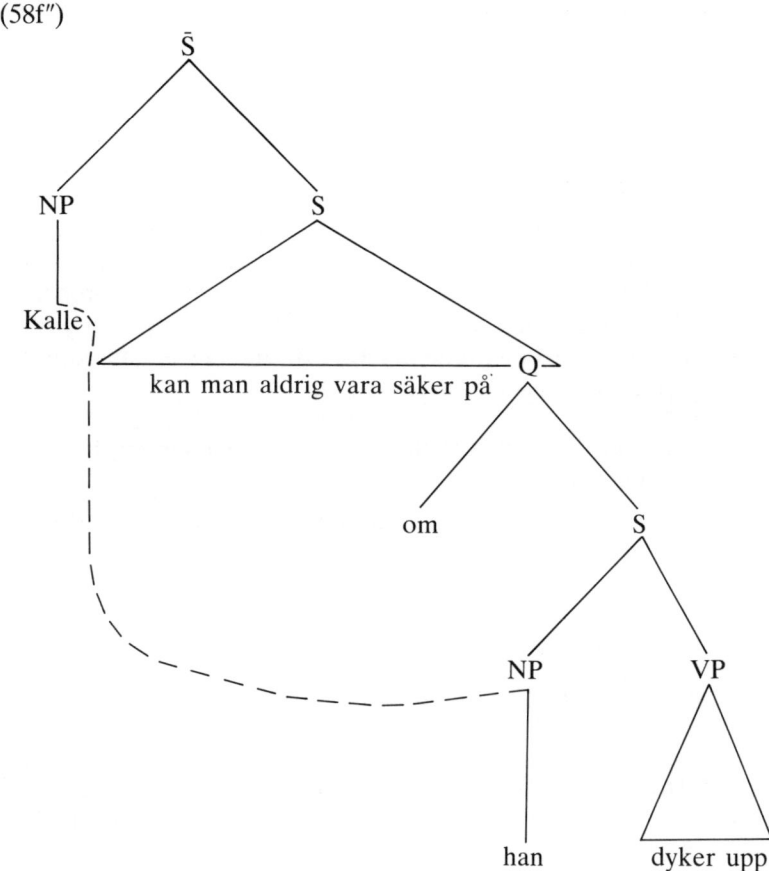

There are several advantages with accounting for the obligatory subject resumptive pronouns in Swedish by extending the use of links. By the convention for interpreting nodes dominating links, the interpretation of the link child will contribute to the meaning of the dominating S node, whereas the pronoun won't contribute any meaning. This will apply even if the dislocated constituent is a quantifier, as in (58d), or a referring expression, as in (58f). Furthermore, we said earlier that it is the same morphological rules that apply to regular trees that apply to linked trees and guarantee that the form of the dislocated constituent fits with the context of the gap. These rules can presumably be extended so that they apply also in case the tree parent is a resumptive pronoun[26].

Presumably we also need to make sure that the morphological form of the resumptive pronoun agrees with the link child.

5.1.2. Epithets

It turns out that resumptive pronouns are not the only items in the language that may occur as linked to dislocated constituents. There is also a group of so called epithets. Epithets like **den idioten** (*that idiot*), **den knölen** (*that bastard*) are often used to refer to individuals which have been introduced into the context of the discourse by a proper name or a definite description. Epithets normally occur in the demonstrative form which consists of a pronominal article and the definite form of the noun. Some examples are given in (59).

(59) a. Olle$_i$ sa att det var klockan 7 men **den dummern**$_i$ hade förstås tagit fel på tiden.

Olle said that it was at seven but the idiot was mistaken about the time, of course.

b. Q: Ska vi ta med din lillasyster$_i$?

A: Nej, **den lipsillen**$_i$ blir bara rädd.

Shall we bring your kid sister?
No, the cry baby just gets scared.

Demonstrative noun phrases like **den idioten** may of course also be used deictically, accompanied with a gesture pointing to some individual present in the situation. There is a difference, however, between epithets used as true demonstratives and epithets used anaphorically which is noticeable in spoken Swedish. When a demonstrative phrase is used deictically, the prenominal article **den** is stressed. When a demonstrative phrase is used as an anaphoric epithet, the main stress falls on the noun. The contrast is illustrated in the following examples.

(60) a. Q: Känner du de där idioterna? (pointing to some patients
       Do you know those idiots?   in a mental hospital)

A: Ja, $\begin{Bmatrix} \text{DEN idioten} \\ \text{*den IDIOTEN} \end{Bmatrix}$ känner jag väl till.

Yes, that (*the) idiot I know well.

b. Kalle kom inte hem förrän efter midnatt och
$\begin{Bmatrix} \text{den} & \text{IDIOTEN} \\ \text{*DEN} & \text{idioten} \end{Bmatrix}$ hade förstås glömt nyckeln.

Kalle didn't come home until after midnight and the (*that) idiot had of course forgotten the key.

Epithets are similar to ordinary personal pronouns in several respects[27]. In addition to referring back to some entity in the discourse, they reveal the speaker's attitude toward whom or what is being talked about. Just like personal pronouns, epithets cannot refer back to, or be bound by, a quantifier (i.e. a non-referential expression) in another sentence. Consider the following discourse.

(61) a. Ingen hjälpte till.
no one helped

b. *Den slöfocken/*de slöfockarna bara satt och latade sig.
that lazy one /those lazy ones just sat and relaxed

The quantifier **ingen** does not introduce any discourse referent to whom an epithet may refer back.

There is one interesting difference between pronouns and epithets, however. As we have seen, personal pronouns can be bound by a quantifier within the sentence. Epithets seem to resist such binding.

(62) a. Ingen alkoholist$_i$ inser hur mycket han$_i$ dricker.
no alcoholic realizes how much he drinks

b. *Ingen alkoholist$_i$ inser hur mycket den suputen$_i$
no alcoholic realizes how much that drunkard
dricker.
drinks

den suputen in (62b) can only be interpreted deictically. It might be that the lack of a bound interpretation for (62b) follows from the fact that epithets are often derogative and that bound pronouns mainly occur inside complements of propositional attitude verbs. This cannot be the whole explanation, however, since the bound reading is unavailable even if the epithet has strong positive connotations.

(63) *Varje balettdansös_i drömmer om den dag när
 every dancer dreams of the day when
 publiken jublar åt den gullungen_i.
 the audience cheers the little darling

A more likely explanation is that epithets can only refer back to *individuals* present or presupposed in the discourse. Since quantifiers like **ingen** (*no one*) and **varje** (*every*) don't introduce individuals, we would not expect epithets to be able to refer back to them.

Epithets may nevertheless occur linked to dislocated constituents in the same sentence, as can be seen in (64).

(64) a. Kalle_i undrade alla om **den slöfocken**_i för en gångs skull skulle komma i tid.
 Kalle everyone wondered if that lazy guy for once would be on time.

 b. Jag talade med några killar_i på Centralen som man inte behövde vara särskilt slug för att inse att **dom rackarna**_i hade nåt sattyg på gång.
 I talked to some guys at the Central Station that you don't have to be very clever to realize that the scoundrels had something up their sleeves.

 c. Vilket tal_i sa du att det var konstigt att **den rappakaljan**_i kunde göra intryck på folk?
 Which speech did you say that it was strange that the garbage could impress people?

In these sentences, the epithet must be interpreted as controlled by the dislocated constituent; they cannot pick their antecedents from the discourse setting. But notice that the antecedent for the epithet must be an individual or a group of individuals in the discourse. This can be seen by the fact that if we replace the existentially quantified phrase **några killar** (*some boys*) in (64b) with an expression which does not introduce any referents such as **varje kille** (*every guy*), the epithet cannot refer back.

(64) b'.*Jag talade med **varje kille**_i på Centralen som
 I talked to every guy at the Central Station that

man inte behövde vara särskilt slug för att inse
you don't have to be very clever to realize

att **den rackarn**$_i$ hade nåt sattyg på gång.
that the scoundrel had something up his sleeve.

The fact that the epithets in (64) must be interpreted as linked to the dislocated phrases thus contrasts with the unavailability of bound readings for the epithets in (52) and (63). This provides another argument against accounting for the occurrences of epithets in (64) and of resumptive pronouns in (58) by semantic binding. If we are right in saying that epithets refer to individuals in the discourse, then the example in (64c) shows that epithets may also refer to individuals presupposed in the discourse. For the question in (64c) to be felicitous, we must assume that there is a non-empty set of speeches that are somehow contextually available. Kamp's Discourse Representation Structures would conceivably be a convenient framework in which to analyze the anaphoric uses of epithets (cf. Kamp, 1981).

Whereas the personal pronouns constitute a small closed class of lexical items which presumably can be identified with some syntactic feature [PRO], it is much harder to delimit the class of epithets. For one thing, there is a lot of regional variation concerning which words are normally used as epithets. But even if it were possible to determine which words can be used anaphorically, and then somehow mark these words in the lexicon, I think this would be the wrong approach. I think it is wrong because it doesn't recognize that it is part of a native speaker's competence to understand when a demonstrative phrase is used as an epithet. It is easy to coin new epithets. Given a particular situation, just about any property in the situation can be used to create an epithet which can be used as in (60) and (64). Suppose Kalle happens to burp (**rapa**, in Swedish). Then both the following sentences are o.k.

(65) Kalle$_i$ ville komma med men **den raparn**$_i$ kan man
Kalle wanted to come along but the burper you

ju inte ha i möblerade rum.
can't have in furnished rooms (among people).

(66) Kalle$_i$ vet man aldrig vad$_j$ **den raparn**$_i$
Kalle you never know what the burper

kan ställa till me ___$_j$ härnäst.
will get himself into next.

Presumably people use both their knowledge of grammar and of conversational relevance to figure out the intended meaning. This should be contrasted with the perplexity reaction towards (58a′) and (58f′) where there was a morphological mismatch.

To sum up briefly, we have seen that whereas personal pronouns normally can be understood either deictically or as bound by a non-referential quantifier, in certain contexts, personal pronouns in Swedish can only be understood as linked to a dislocated constituent. We have argued that this link is of the same type as between a dislocated constituent and a gap. We also argued that although the semantic relation between the dislocated constituent and the resumptive pronoun may be one of binding – as in the cases of dislocated constituents in questions and relative clauses – this need not be the case, as shown by examples involving topicalization of referential expressions. Further evidence for assuming that certain occurrences of pronouns are syntactically linked to dislocated constituents was found in the distribution of epithets. Although epithets cannot normally be interpreted as bound by a quantificational antecedent, they can occur as linked to dislocated constituents in exactly the same positions where resumptive pronouns show up.

5.2. Reflexives

We now turn to the interpretation of reflexive pronouns and of constituents containing reflexive pronouns. In Swedish, special reflexive forms occur only in the third person. In the first and second person the accusative from of the personal pronoun is used. We will here concentrate our analysis on the third person reflexives[28]. As can be seen from the paradigm in (67) they have both accusative and genitive forms.

(67)   Reflexive pronouns (third person)

	sing	plur
Nominative:	–	–
Genitive:	sin	sin
Accusative:	sig	sig

Our approach to handling reflexives is basically semantic. We think that the distribution of reflexive pronouns to a certain extent is a consequence of their meaning, or, rather, of their lack of independent meaning. A reflexive pronoun in isolation does not have any denotation; it cannot be used deictically either. Hence we wouldn't expect any language of the world which has both personal and reflexive pronouns to use a reflexive form in the subject position of a discourse initial sentence. In several languages, among them English and the Scandinavian languages, reflexives are even more constrained. They must always be controlled sentence internally, that is, they cannot be understood as referring to some individual in the situation or mentioned in the previous discourse. Exactly where reflexives may occur with respect to their antecedents seems to depend largely on structural factors. Identifying the specific structural conditions appears to be a language specific task. For instance, there is a certain amount of variation among the Scandinavian languages. In Icelandic, a reflexive pronoun in a tensed subordinate clause may be understood as controlled by the subject of a higher clause under certain conditions[29]. This is impossible in Swedish. In the following examples, we indicate the possibility of an antecedent-reflexive relation by coindexing and use * to indicate ungrammatical on that reading.

(68) a. Jón$_i$ las það í blaðinu   að María hefði   komið
               SUBJUNCTIVE
       Jon read it in paper-the that Maria had   come

   till sín$_i$.
   to self
                                    (Icelandic, Thráinsson, 1976: (19b))

   b. Jon$_i$ undrade om Maria$_i$ vore   villig att hjälpa
                          SUBJUNCTIVE
       Jon wondered if Maria   were   willing to help

   sin$_{*i,j}$ mor.
   self's mother
                                    (Swedish)

In Swedish, the antecedent of a reflexive is in most cases the subject of the minimal tensed S containing the reflexive. Even within this domain there is some variation among speakers. In certain sentences, personal pronouns are preferred over reflexive pronouns although the structural conditions for reflexivization are fulfilled. We won't go into what may cause this variation here, but refer the reader to Anward (1974) and Dahl (1980) for a discussion of some factors which seem to influence the variation.

Let us now turn to the meaning of reflexives[30]. Reflexives occur in several different forms in the languages of the world, e.g. as detransitivizing morphology on verbs, as clitics, and as separate pronominal forms. A VP which contains a reflexive morphem characteristically denotes an activity or a property which involves the subject of the VP. A VP like **tvätta sig** (*wash self*) thus denotes the property of being an x such that x washes x. However, the NP **sig** can not be interpreted until we reach the level at which the VP is interpreted. We will capture this by saying that the meaning of **sig** is obligatorily stored and retrieved at the VP level. The interpretation of **sig** will be as in (69).

(69) [$_{NP}$ sig] $\langle \lambda PP\{x_i\}, [\lambda PP\{x_i\}]_i \rangle$ $i \in N$
      [PRO]

Just as in the case of WH phrases, we insert a place holding meaning in the derivation and store the reflexive meaning. The reflexive meaning is nothing but a pronoun meaning with a free individual variable, indexed by the same index as the variable. Having a reflexive meaning in store at a given level indicates that one of the expressions in the tree dominated by that node does not have independent reference but must be bound within the sentence. We assume that reflexives get bound by lambda abstraction in the formation of a property at the VP level. Evidence for this assumption can be found for instance in VP deletion cases (cf. Partee, 1975; Sag, 1976; and Williams, 1977)[31]. The reflexive thus contributes to the interpretation of the VP in a certain sense. We will link taking the reflexive meaning out of store to the application of lambda abstraction at the VP level. The rule will be as in (70).

(70) *Reflexivization*

If $\langle \alpha, \sigma_0, [\lambda PP\{x_i\}]_i, \sigma_1 \rangle \in m(VP)$
then $\langle \lambda x_i[\alpha(x_i)], \sigma_0, \sigma_1 \rangle \in m(VP)$.

This rule says that if there is a VP with a reflexive meaning in store, then there is also a VP meaning which is the result of eliminating the reflexive meaning from the store, lambda abstracting over the address variable, and supplying that variable as a subject argument. Note that the variable introduced in the interpretation of the reflexive pronoun gets bound by lambda abstraction. Consequently, infinitival clauses with reflexives can be fully interpreted as for instance in (71).

(71) Att tvätta sig är skönt
      to wash self is nice

(71) predicates 'nice' of the property of being an x such that x washes x. If there is an overt subject in the sentence, as in (72)

(72)   Maja tvättar sig.
       Maja washes self

then it follows from the rule for interpreting the S node, $(\langle[1]\ S \rightarrow NP\ VP, NP'(^{\wedge}VP')\rangle)$ that the property of being an x such that x washes x will be among the properties Maja has. By way of function argument application, Maja will appear in both argument positions of **tvätta**. We will illustrate how the reflexive rule works by going through a derivation of (72).

(72')

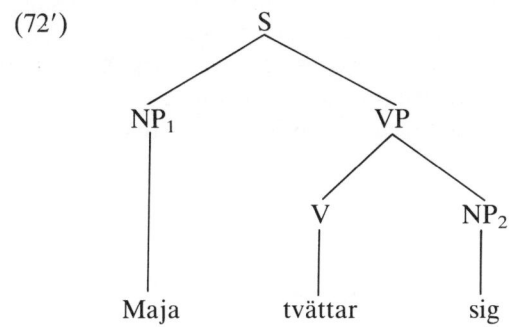

EXPRESSION	INTERPRETATION	STORE	RULE USED
[$_{NP_2}$ sig]	$\lambda PP\{x_2\}$	$[\lambda PP\{x_2\}]_2$	(69)
[$_{VP}$ tvättar sig]	**wash**$'(\hat{P}P\{x_2\}) =$ $= \lambda x_2[\textbf{wash}'(\hat{P}P\{x_2\})(x_2)]$	$[\lambda PP\{x_2\}]_2$	Reflexivization (70)
[$_{NP_1}$ Maja]	$\lambda PP\{^{\wedge}m\}$		[4]
[$_S$ Maja tvättar sig]	$\lambda PP\{^{\wedge}m\}(\hat{x}_2\ \textbf{wash}'$ $(\hat{P}P\{x_2\}))(x_2) =$ $= \textbf{wash}'_*(m, m)$		[1]

The way the reflexivization rule is formulated in (70), it will apply at any VP node, and predicts that the NP which is interpreted as the subject of the VP will control the reflexive pronoun. Consequently the rule predicts that a sentence like (73) should only have the reading on which Sven shaves himself.

(73) Morfar$_i$ [$_{VP_1}$ bad Sven$_j$ [$_{VP_2}$ raka sig$_{i,j}$]]
       grandfather   asked Sven   shave self

This is not correct, however. Although the reading where the matrix object, **Sven**, controls the embedded reflexives might be the unmarked reading, the matrix subject, **morfar** (*grandfather*), is also available as an antecedent. We can capture the ambiguity in (73) by letting the reflexivization rule apply *obligatorily* to tensed VPs containing a stored reflexive meaning, but *optionally* to untensed VPs with a reflexive meaning in store. In order to implement this, we need to distinguish in the syntax between tensed and untensed VPs. Given that we think of syntactic categories as complex features, this can be done fairly straightforwardly. We will abbreviate a VP [-TENSE] as $\overline{\text{VP}}$.

It is (at least theoretically) possible to construct examples where there are several occurrences of reflexive pronouns and where distinct occurrences are bound by different antecedents, as in (74) where the indexing indicates one of the many possible readings.

(74) Maja$_i$ [$_{VP}$ bad Lisa$_j$ [$_{\overline{VP}}$ påminna Sara$_k$ [$_{\overline{VP}}$ att
       Maja   asked Lisa   to remind Sara   to

       köra **sin**$_i$ syster hem till **sig**$_j$ i **sin**$_k$ bil]]]
       drive self's sister to self's place in self's car

We can account for such readings since each occurrence of a reflexive pronoun is associated with a distinct stored reflexive meaning and the reflexive meaning may apply at each of the VP or $\overline{\text{VP}}$ levels. We saw that (73) was ambiguous. (75), on the other hand, is not ambiguous.

(75) Kalle$_i$ bad **mig**$_j$ [$_{\overline{VP}}$ raka **sig**$_{i,*j}$]
       Kalle asked me   shave self

Because **sig** can only have a third person antecedent, only **Kalle** is a possible controller. But presumably the reflexive rule in (70) could apply at the $\overline{\text{VP}}$ level and we would get the interpretation represented in (76), assuming, that is, that deictic expressions like first and second person pronouns are interpreted like any other NPs.

(76)   **ask'$_*$**(k, **I'**, ^(**shave'$_*$**(**I'**, **I'**))

According to (76), Kalle asks me to shave myself. But this is not a possible interpretation for (75). Within the current approach, it seems natural to account for the non-availability of this reading by saying that there is a presupposition clash between the meaning of **mig** (inherently first person) and the meaning of **sig** (inherently third person). Note, however, that it is not the person of the actual referent that determines the form of the reflexive pronoun. In Swedish, definite NPs, which induce third person agreement, are sometimes used as direct address forms. In the context of a meeting it is customary to address the chairman as **ordföranden** even if you normally use **du** (*you*) or **ni** (*you*, formal). As can be seen in (77), the use of **ordföranden** triggers a third person reflexive.

(77) Får jag be ordföranden uttala sig, *dig, *er?
      *may I   ask the chairman to state himself, *yourself*

In the examples we have looked at so far, the reflexive pronouns have occurred inside a VP. Not surprisingly, reflexive pronouns also occur in dislocated constituents. A few examples with topicalized reflexives are given in (78); examples with reflexive pronouns in constituent questions will be analyzed in Chapter IV.

(78) a. **Sina**$_i$ föräldrar bör   man$_i$ lyda.
         self's parents   should one obey

     b. **Sin**$_i$ framtid tänker Lisa$_i$ ofta på.
         self's future thinks Lisa often about

On our approach, the interpretation of a dislocated constituent contributes to the interpretation of the link parent by the convention for interpreting linked trees. Hence the admittance and interpretation of such sentences does not cause any problem. Schematically, the structure will be as in (79).

(79)

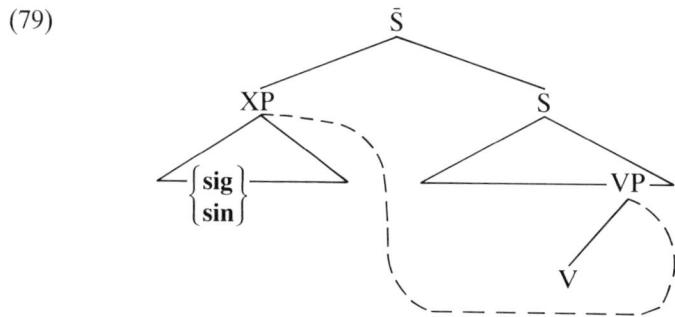

The interpretation of the dislocated constituent contains a reflexive meaning in store. This store is carried along when we interpret the tree parent, the VP node. The condition for the reflexive rule in (70) is thus met and reflexivization can take place. One consequence of this approach is that we get the same control possibilities for reflexives in dislocated positions as for reflexives inside the VP. In both of the examples in (78), there was only one available antecedent so the question which phrase the reflexive should be controlled by never arose. In more complex cases, however, where one or more third person NPs intervene between a reflexive pronoun in a dislocated constituent and the link parent, people's judgments are not always clear. Take a sentence like (80).

(80)   **Sina** föräldrar hoppades Johan att Kalle skulle vara
       self's parents   hoped   Johan that Kalle would be
       artig mot.
       polite towards

About half of the Swedish speakers presented with such a sentence tend to report that **Johan** hoped something about **Kalle's** behaviour towards his (= **Johan's**) parents, i.e. the matrix subject controls the reflexive, not the subject of the clause with the gap. The question is then if it is correct to assume that the control facts for reflexives in dislocated position are the same as for reflexives occurring inside VPs. In order to answer this question we need to look more closely at what factors might influence people's choice of antecedent. One factor is clearly a tendency towards resolving the referent of a reflexive pronoun as soon as possible. Having recognized a reflexive pronoun in a dislocated position means having an unresolved noun phrase in what is commonly referred to as short term memory. As soon as the parser recognizes a third person NP, it presumably tries the hypothesis that this is the antecedent. In a sentence like (80) there is nothing in the rest of the sentence which would cause him to revise the initial assignment. But look at (81).

(81)   **Sina** föräldrar hoppades varje lärare   att Kalle
       self's parents   hoped   every teacher that Kalle
       skulle vara artig   mot.
       would be   polite towards

(81) is structurally identical to (80). The only change is that we have replaced the name **Johan** by a quantifier **varje lärare** (*every teacher*). But speakers are noticeably less willing to report that **lärare** is the antecedent of **sina**. Presumably this has to do with the connotation of lexical items and with general knowledge of typical situations. Similarly in (82).

(82)   **Sin**   framtid tycker mamma att   Lisa tänker för
         self's future   *thinks mother that Lisa thinks too*
         litet på.
         little about

Although **mamma** (*mother*) is the first third person NP, a person hears after the reflexive, he/she might resist taking it as the antecedent, or revise an initial assignment, once he/she has heard the rest of the sentence, given the common fact that mothers tend to worry about their children rather than the other way around. If the intervening NP is non-animate, the tendency to interpret it as controlling a preposed reflexive is very low.

(83)   Sin$_{??i,j}$ framtid förelåg   ett förslag$_i$ att   varje elev$_j$
         self's future there was a proposal that every student
         skulle betänka.
         should consider

In brief, there are a number of non-structural factors which influence how people resolve antecedents of reflexives in preposed positions. However, I don't think any of them is systematic enough to motivate the assumption of a distinct rule for interpreting reflexives in preposed constituents, based on this factor. Rather I suggest that the grammar just has one rule for reflexivization but that we take into account the non-structural factors, in particular the effect of linear order, in order to explain the variation[32]. It seems highly desirable that we approach the issue how people interpret anaphors in dislocated positions experimentally, using some on-line technique. In particular, it would be interesting to find out to what extent the interpretation strategies for personal pronouns, which may always be interpreted deictically, and overt anaphors like reflexives, which must be resolved within the sentence, are different.

5.3. Restrictions on Binding of Pronouns

We mentioned in Section 5.1. that third person pronouns have a dual use, as deictic pronouns and as bound by a quantifier. We illustrated this by sentences like (84) and (85) which are ambiguous. For convenience, we will mark the possible interpretations of the pronoun by subscripts. $*i$ indicates that the pronoun can not be understood as bound by a quantifier subscripted with i.

(84) Ingen student$_i$ tror att **han**$_{i,j}$ klarar sig.   ($i \neq j$)
No student thinks that he will pass.

(85) Vilken student$_i$ tror att **han**$_{i,j}$ klarar sig?
Which student thinks that he will pass?

On our approach, which reading we get for sentences like these depends on whether the free individual variable in the interpretation of the pronoun **han** gets bound by the quantifier or not. In the first case, we get the bound interpretation. In the second case, **han** must refer outside the sentence. Without any further restrictions, however, we predict that a sentence like (86) also will be associated with two readings.

(86) Vilken student$_i$ brukade han$_{*i,j}$ säga ___$_i$ var omöjlig?
Which student did he use to say was impossible?

But, as indicated, one of the readings is excluded. Speakers' intuitions on this type of sentence are very clear. **han** in (86) cannot be interpreted as bound by the WH phrase **vilken student** (*which student*). This problem is often referred to as the Crossover constraint and has been extensively discussed in the literature (cf. Postal, 1971; Wasow, 1972; Higginbotham, 1980b).

Let us look at how the unwanted reading of (86) can arise in our grammar. The linked tree representation for (86) will be roughly as in (87).

By the convention for interpreting linked constituents, the meaning of **vilken student**, which we can represent informally as [*vilken student*]$_1$, will be a stored meaning in the meaning sets associated with S$_2$ and VP$_1$. The address variable, *1*, indicates that there is a free x_1 in the placeholding representation for the WH meaning. Suppose now we happen to pick the same individual variable when we interpret the pronoun **han**, i.e. the interpretation of NP$_2$ will be $\lambda PP\{x_1\}$. The representation of the

(87)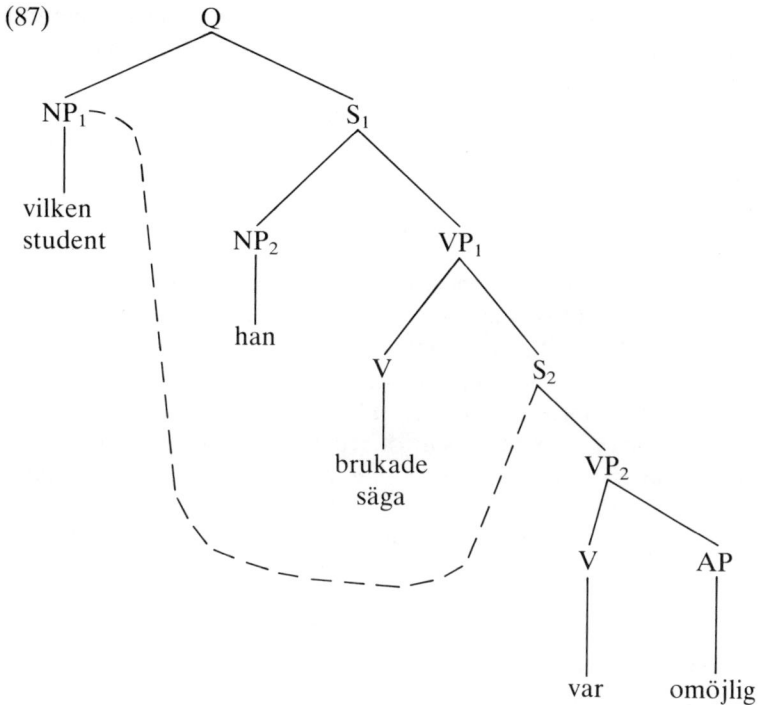

meaning S_1 will be:

$\langle$ **use-to-say'**$_*($ˇ$x_1,$ ˆ**impossible'**$_*($ˇ$x_1)), [\textit{vilken student}]_1 \rangle$

When we quantify in the stored WH quantifier, it will bind both occurrences of x_1, and we get the following interpretation:

(86') $\lambda p\ \exists x[\textbf{student}'(x) \wedge$ ˇ$p \wedge p =$ ˆ**use-to-say'**$_*($ˇ$x,$ ˆ**impossible'**$_*($ˇ$x))]$

(86') is a perfectly coherent interpretation, but unfortunately not for (86) but for (88) and (89).

(88) Vilken student$_i$ brukade säga att han$_i$ var omöjlig?
which student used to say that he was impossible

(89) Vilken student$_i$ brukade säga sig$_i$ vara omöjlig?
which student used to say himself be impossible

Since (88) and (89) do not mean the same thing as (86), we obviously have to block this derivation. What we need to do is to prevent a variable that is used as an address variable for a stored quantifier meaning from also being used in the interpretation of a pronoun to the left of the constituent whose meaning has been stored. In addition we need to prevent accidental address collisions which would occur if the same address variable were used for two distinct stored quantifiers. We can collapse these requirements into the following convention[33]:

(90)　　*Store Address Convention* (SAC)

For all rules of the form $\langle [n], \alpha \rightarrow X \beta Y, G(X' \beta' Y') \rangle$
where G is some semantic operation,
if　(i)　$\lambda PP\{x_i\} \in m(\beta)$　or
　　(ii)　$\langle \gamma, \sigma_0, [\delta]_i, \sigma_1 \rangle$ $m(\beta)$
then　$m(\alpha) = G(X' \beta'' Y')$
where β'' is the result of replacing every occurence of x_i in $m(\beta)$ with a variable that does not occur as an address variable in $m(Y)$.
α, β are syntactic categories
γ, δ are well-formed expressions of intensional logic
σ is an element in store.

The first case covers derivations where β itself is a pronoun as in the case of interpreting S_1 in (87). The choice of pronoun interpretation is totally free. Suppose we happen to pick the interpretation $\lambda PP\{x_1\}$. Since x_1 occurs as address variable for a stored meaning in the meaning set of VP_1, the SAC will apply and replace x_1 in the pronoun interpretation by some other individual variable, which will remain free in the interpretation of the matrix Q, and which hence will get a deictic interpretation. This way, the SAC insures that a dislocated quantifier can never bind a pronoun which precedes and c-commands the gap it's linked to (equivalently, a pronoun which is a left daughter of its tree parent). Since we handle NP quantification by the storage mechanism, too, the SAC will prevent a sentence like (91)

(91)　　Han introducerade var och en av studenterna.
　　　　He introduced each of the students.

from getting a reading on which each student introduced himself. SAC guarantees that (91) must be interpreted as in (91'a), not as in (91'b). **han** in (91'a) must be interpreted deictically.

(91') a. $\forall x[\textbf{student}'(x) \rightarrow \textbf{introduce}'_*(\check{}x_3, \check{}x)]$

b. $\forall x[\textbf{student}'(x) \rightarrow \textbf{introduce}'_*(\check{}x, \check{}x)]$

The second case applies when β contains a stored quantifier meaning or a stored reflexive meaning. SAC rules out the possibility of deriving an absurd reading for sentences like (92) that we otherwise could get.

(92)   Johan undrar vilken gäst alla professorer presenterade sig för.
       Johan wonders which guest all professors introduce themselves to.

Suppose we didn't have a constraint like the SAC. Then in a derivation where we happened to pick the same address variable for the reflexive **sig** as for the stored WH phrase **vilken gäst**, the reflexivization rule in (70) will give a VP meaning of the following form:

$\lambda x_3[\textbf{introduce}'_*(\check{}x_3, \check{}x_3, \textbf{to}'_*(\check{}x_3)]$

When we add the subject NP **alla professorer**, it will bind all occurrences of x_3. Consequently, the WH quantification rule will apply vacuously and the set of complete meanings for (92) will contain the formula in (92').

(92')   **wonder**$'(\check{}j, \hat{p}\ \exists x[\textbf{guest}'(x) \wedge \check{}p \wedge p =$
        $=\ \hat{}\ \forall y[\textbf{professor}'(y) \rightarrow \textbf{introduce}'_*(\check{}y, \check{}y, \textbf{to}'_*(\check{}y))]])$

If this can be at all interpreted as a question, it would mean something like Johan stands in the *wonder*-relation to the set of true propositions of the form 'if y is a professor then y introduced y to y' where x is a guest. This is clearly not a possible meaning for (92) since we lose the information that it is a question about guests.

Another way to exclude such a derivation of (92) would be to ban vacuous quantification entirely, something that has been suggested in Chomsky (1982), Cooper (1983), and Janssen (1983). However, even if such a restriction would prevent (92) from getting the unwanted reading, it still does not guarantee that the excluded reading of (86) does not get derived. Yet another way to block such readings would be to use distinct variables for deictic and bound pronouns (cf. Janssen, 1981). On such an approach, the two derivations of an ambiguous sentence like (84) would differ in that the pronoun **han** translates into an expression with a deictic variable in one case and into an expression with a bindable pronoun in the other case. However, it is not the case that **han** in structures like in (86) and (91) must be a deictic pronoun. It may well be interpreted as a bound pronoun, viz. as bound by another quantifier in the sentence which has scope over it. This is shown in the following examples.

(93) Varje lärare$_j$ minns vilken student$_i$ han$_{*i,j}$ brukade säga ___$_i$ var omöjlig.
Every teacher remembers which student he used to say was impossible.

(94) Ingen$_j$ erkände att han$_j$ introducerat var och en av studenterna$_{i,*j}$.
No one admitted that he had introduced each of the students.

The relevant restriction is rather that a pronoun cannot be interpreted as bound by a quantifier which is stored at the point of derivation when the pronoun is admitted. This is what the SAC intends to capture. We note that the SAC makes reference to the linear order of the constituents being composed. We will return to the importance of this in Chapter VI in connection with a more thorough discussion of the crossover phenomenon.

The reflexive rule in (70) in conjunction with the SAC in (90) insures that all reflexive pronouns get properly bound and that no variables used as place holders for a quantifier meaning get accidentally bound by the reflexive rule or by a quantifier in another stored meaning. However, the rules do not enforce disjoint reference. They do not rule out the case where a non-reflexive pronoun in a reflexivizable position with respect to some NP gets bound by a quantifier in the interpretation of that NP. Consider a sentence like (95).

(95) Varje man presenterade honom.
every man introduced   him

Suppose we translate **honom** with an expression that contains the free variable x_5. Nothing prevents us from picking x_5 as the address variable when we store the subject NP **varje man** (*every man*). When we retrieve that meaning from store and quantify it in, we will get a reading for (95) according to which every man introduced himself. The interpretations at the S node will be as in (95′). Recall that M(S) denotes the set of complete meanings of S, i.e. the meanings that do not have any elements in store.

(95′) m(S): ⟨**introduce**′_∗(ˇx_5, ˇx_5), [*every man*′]$_5$⟩
  M(S): $\forall x[\mathbf{man}'(x) \rightarrow \mathbf{introduce}'_*(\check{x}, \check{x})]$

This follows from the fact that we let personal pronouns be completely free in how they get interpreted. But this does not sufficiently capture the fact that in contexts where personal pronouns alternate with reflexive pronouns, the referent of a personal pronoun is required to be disjoint from whatever the referent of the subject (or the relevant controller) is. The issue of where in the grammar facts like the disjoint reference requirement and non-coreference should be handled turns out to be important for comparing and evaluating alternative frameworks. We will address this question in Chapter VI.

6. GAPS

In most instances of unbounded dependencies in Swedish that we have looked at so far, there is a one-to-one correspondence between a preposed constituent of some category α and a gap of category α in the sentence. We represent this correspondence by a link in the syntactic structure. What we are here calling a gap is just the absence of a constituent in the syntactic representation of the sentence. In this section, we will first show that gaps in Swedish cannot arise through some process which optionally deletes pronouns but that gaps must be controlled sentence internally. We will then look at two cases where gaps and pronouns alternate in Swedish. In the first case, they are in complementary distribution, in the second case, there seems to be more or less free alternation. Finally, we will look at some data involving extra gaps, which we will argue are *parasitic* on a real gap in the sense that they require its presence.

In several languages, third person pronouns may optionally be omitted if the referent of the pronoun is highly salient in the context. This phenomenon is often referred to as having optional 'pro drop'. Languages which allow pro drop are for instance Japanese, Marathi, Portuguese, Turkish, and to some extent, Italian, and Spanish. Maling and Zaenen (1980) noted that allowing pro drop is often correlated with the property of having SOV word order. There is also a tendency for there to be a correlation between allowing subject pro drop and having sufficiently rich inflectional morphology on the verb so that the sentences remain unambiguous (Taraldsen, 1978a). Old Icelandic apparently allowed pro drop for contextually salient pronouns, at least in poetry and in the sagas. Whether this was also common practise in the spoken language is unknown. In modern Icelandic, as well as in the other Scandinavian languages, Danish, Norwegian and Swedish, personal pronouns cannot be left out, even if the referent can be uniquely determined from the context. Questions often provide good examples of restrictive contexts which highlight a particular referent. Still, the pronoun may not be omitted in the answer, as shown in the following dialogues:

(96) Q: Vem är han? (pointing to a boy) Who is he?
 A: *___ är min bror. *___ is my brother.
 ᵒᵏHan är min bror. He is my brother.

(97) Q: Vad ska jag göra med din bok? What shall I do with your book?
 A: *Lägg ___ på bordet. *Put ___ on the table.
 ᵒᵏLägg den på bordet. Put it on the table.

(98) Q: Varför ramlade bordet ihop? Why did the table fall apart?
 A: *Jag ställde min ryggsäck på ___. I put my rucksack on ___.
 ᵒᵏJag ställde min ryggsäck på det. I put my rucksack on it.

The subcategorization restrictions for **lägga** and **ställa** (*put*) require both a direct object and a directional or locative adverbial phrase, hence the ungrammaticality of the answers with gaps above.

Whereas third person pronouns may never be left out in Swedish, first person pronons can be left out in writing, but only in a very special context, typically when you are writing a letter, and referring to what you are doing at the moment of writing. A phrase like in (99) is often used to start a post card.

(99) Sitter på Götaplatsen och betraktar mänskorna som
 sit at Götaplatsen and watch people that
 flanerar förbi.
 stroll by
 'I am sitting at Götaplatsen, watching people stroll by.'

(99) could also be used as a reply to the direct question in (100).

(100) Vad gör du just nu/på eftermiddagarna?
What do you do right now/in the afternoons?

Certain authors, e.g. Eyvind Johnson, have a tendency to leave out **jag** (*I*) in their novels. This type of pronoun omission, however, is more of a stylistic device than something that occurs in ordinary spoken or written language. In scientific discourse, for instance, you can not leave out **jag**. The following paragraph would be impossible in an article.

(101) Detta argument övertygade mig. *____ antar nu att ...
                                         [PRES]
                                    ᵒᵏJag antar nu att
this argument convinced me ____ assume now that

6.1. Alternation Between Gaps and Pronouns

We mentioned above in Section 5.1.1 that gaps are excluded in certain positions in Swedish. In particular, this is true for the subject position of an embedded tensed sentence which is introduced by a complementizer (**att**, **om**) or a dislocated constituent. We showed that in these cases, a personal pronoun is used instead. In view of the fact that these pronouns cannot refer freely but must be interpreted as controlled by a dislocated constituent, we used the term 'resumptive' for these pronouns and suggested that the link representation be extended to cover such pronouns as well. We emphasized in the earlier discussion that there is no optionality involved here. A sentence of this form with a gap in subject position is clearly ungrammatical in Swedish, whereas the corresponding sentence with a pronoun is fine, as we saw in the two versions of (58d) repeated here in (102).

(102) a. Vilken film$_i$ kunde ingen minnas hur **den**$_i$ slutade?
         which film could no one remember how it ended

  b. *Vilken film$_i$ kunde ingen minnas hur ____$_i$ slutade?

We want to argue that these resumptive pronouns should be analyzed as having the same syntactic properties as gaps, i.e. they are linked to a dislocated constituent and don't have any independent interpretation. Evidence for this claim comes for instance from facts about coordination (cf. Zaenen, *et al.*, 1981). It is generally assumed that extractions out of conjoined structures must apply to all conjuncts simultaneously (cf. Ross' Coordinate Structure Constraint (Ross, 1967), Williams' Across-the-board rule (Williams, 1978) and Gazdar's coordination of slashed categories (Gazdar, 1981)). In Swedish, it is possible to conjoin two embedded questions, one with a gap and one with a resumptive subject pronoun, as shown in (103).

(103) I går såg jag en film$_i$ som jag dessvärre redan
yesterday saw I a film that I unfortunately already

glömt [$_{Q_1}$ både [$_{Q_2}$ vem som regisserat ___$_i$] och
forgotten both who that directed and

[$_{Q_3}$ hur **den**$_i$ slutar]]
how it ends

Yesterday I saw a film that I have unfortunately already forgotten both who directed and how it ends.

Further evidence for assuming that resumptive subject pronouns have the same properties as gaps comes from looking at the other Scandinavian languages. It turns out that Swedish is exceptional among the Scandinavian languages in requiring resumptive pronouns in this position. In Icelandic and Norwegian, subject extractions are linked to gaps, as shown in (104) for Icelandic and in (105) for Norwegian. Most speakers of Icelandic and Norwegian don't accept resumptive pronouns in such sentences at all.

(104) Hvaða bragð$_i$ sagði hann að ___$_i$ vaeri gagnslaust?
which deed did he say that ___ was useless

(Maling and Zaenen, 1978: 221)

(105) a. Denne boken$_i$ er jag sikker på at ___$_i$ kom ut i
this book I am sure that came out in

Russland.
Russia

b. Denne boken$_i$ husker jeg ikke om ___$_i$
this book I don't remember if

er oversatt til norsk.
has been translated to Norwegian

c. Denne boken$_i$ husker jeg ikke når ____$_i$ ble oversatt
  this   book   I don't remember when   was translated
  til norsk.
  to Norwegian

d. Denne forfattaren$_i$ husker jeg ikke hva$_j$ ____$_i$
  this   author$_i$ I don't remember what
  har oversatt ____$_j$ til norsk.
  has translated   to Norwegian

In contemporary Danish, the picture is somewhat more complicated. Gaps in the subject position occur, as shown in the following Danish sentences.

(106)   Det$_i$ ved jeg ikke om ____$_i$ gaar an.
    that I don't know if   is allowed

(Diderichsen, 1966: 215)

(107)   De tjente en mann$_i$ som de ikke hviste hvem$_j$ ____$_i$
    they served a man   that they didn't know who
    var ____$_j$.   (L. Holm Olsen)
    was

However, when the subject of an **at** clause has been extracted, very often we find an occurrence of the dummy element **der**.

(108)   Hvem$_i$ tror du,   at der ____$_i$ har gjort det?
    who   do you think that there   has done it

(Diderichsen, 1966: 183)

der is not a personal pronoun but more akin to the *there* of *there*-insertion in English. The Danish strategy thus differs from the Swedish case. In a recent paper, B. Jacobsen and P. A. Jensen raise the issue of how this weakly stressed **der** should be analyzed (Jacobsen and Jensen, 1982). They discuss several examples and give the following acceptability judgments for sentences with extractions out of subject position.

(109)   Hvem troede du   han sagde ∅/*at/a(t) der/der ____
    who did you think he said

havde malet huset? (Jacobsen and Jensen (37))
had painted the house

The sequence **at der** is phonetically realized as just one word without stress. Note that **der** can appear without an **at** present, although the version with **at der** is considered more acceptable ((P. A. Jensen, personal communication). The distribution of **der** in the context of missing subjects in Danish appears to be a topic worth further investigation.

Returning to Swedish, it is actually not quite correct to say that subject gaps don't occur in these contexts at all in Swedish. In the version of Swedish spoken in Finland, so-called 'finlandssvenska', subject gaps to occur in **att** clauses but apparently not in other types of subordinate clauses. The following example was brought to my attention by Per Linell.

(110) Det är en omständighet som Bengt Loman anser att
that is a factor that Bengt Loman thinks that

      ____ ytterligare ökar
further increases

We thus find a great deal of variation as to how subject extractions are realized in the Scandinavian languages. Icelandic and Norwegian have subject gaps in all cases, Danish uses a special dummy, **der**, in certain cases, Swedish requires a personal pronoun. Despite this variation in surface forms, I think it would be wrong to assume that different syntactic rules or processes are involved in the different languages. All the Scandinavian languages permit extraction out of the subject position of embedded sentences but the surface form may be realized in a number of ways, as we have seen[34]. We have here discussed examples taken from the standard languages. However, once we start looking more closely at the individual languages, we will probably find that there is dialectal variation within the languages as well and that the pattern is not as clear cut as it might seem from this brief overview[35]. Another thing that needs to be done is to look at these facts diachronically. When, for instance, do resumptive subject pronouns appear in Swedish and in what types of texts?

These examples of systematic alternations between gaps and pronouns all involve a structurally definable position, i.e. the subject position of a tensed subordinate sentence. There are other cases where gaps alternate with pronouns, but which are less, possibly not at all, amenable to identification on a structural basis. These are cases of optional resumptive pronouns which sometimes show up if a dislocated constituent is separated from its gap by too much lexical material. For instance, if the gap is embedded several sentences down, resumptive pronouns frequently show up in Swedish. One might wonder if these occurrences of resumptive pronouns can be seen as somehow saving an extraction which would otherwise have violated an island constraint, an explanation that is sometimes suggested for resumptive pronouns in English. It turns out, however, that such resumptive pronouns may turn up even when there is no violation of any of the traditional island constraints such as the Complex NP Constraint or the *wh*-Island Constraint. It appears that whether a resumptive pronoun shows up or not depends mainly on how much lexical material intervenes between the preposed constituent, i.e. between the link child and the position to which it must be attached in the tree (see Engdahl (1982c) for additional illustration of this point). Furthermore, we note that resumptive pronouns show up in Danish and Norwegian as well under similar circumstances, although these languages don't accept resumptive pronouns in the fixed subject position, as we have seen. (For a discussion of the 'distance' requirement for resumptive pronouns in Danish, see Erteschik-Shir (1982).) The optionality of these pronouns, which contrasts with the obligatoriness or impossibility of resumptive pronouns in subject position, leads us to believe that their appearance is not governed by any grammatical principle but that they show up because they somehow facilitate the production and comprehension of long utterances. Zaenen and Maling (1982) report on an experiment carried out at Brandeis by S. Wall and L. Kaufman in which the subjects, all native speakers of English, were presented with sentences with extractions corresponding either to gaps or to resumptive pronouns. The speed of presentation was compressed to either 40%, 60%, or 80% of the normal speech rate. Subjects were asked to write down what they recalled immediately after hearing the sentence. It turned out that recall was significantly better for sentences with resumptive pronouns than for the corresponding sentences with gaps. Since this experiment was carried out on English subjects we cannot conclude anything about how Swedes use resumptive pronouns in processing. However, it seems highly probable that we would get a similar result for Swedish speakers.

6.2. Pronoun-Gap Alternation as a Disambiguating Device

In Swedish, resumptive pronouns are sometimes used to disambiguate sentences that otherwise would have been ambiguous. Consider a sentence as in (111).

(111) a.

b.

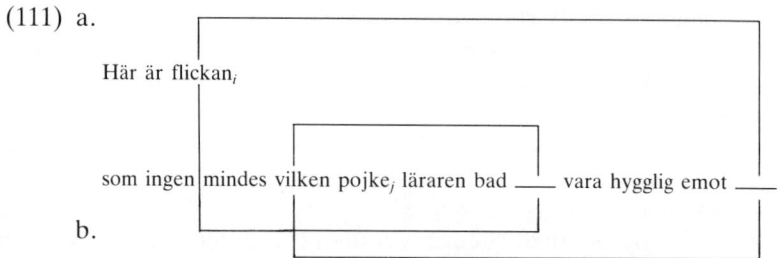

Here is the girl that no one remembered which boy the teacher told to be nice to.

Since the predicate **vara hygglig mot** (*be nice to*) is symmetric, i.e. it takes animate NPs in both subject and object positions, the selectional restrictions will not tell us which dislocated constituent to associate with which gap. There is a rather strong tendency towards interpreting the sentence with nested links, as diagrammed in (111a). However, the intersecting assignment, diagrammed in (111b) is possible, in particular in a context where it is already known that what is at stake is the behaviour of some girl towards some boy[36]. In order to enforce the intersecting reading, a resumptive pronoun is frequently inserted in the first gap position. The intersecting reading is thus expressed as in (112).

(112)

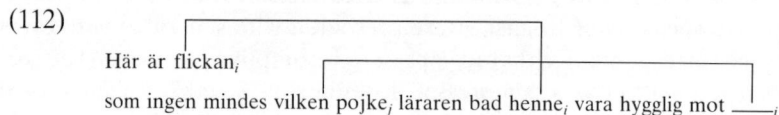

Here is the girl that no one remembered which boy the teacher asked her to be nice to.

We will use the terminology from Fodor (1978) and refer to the preposed constituents and extraction sites as *fillers* and *gaps*, respectively, abbreviated as F and G. We can then summarize the pattern of alternations as in (113) using P for pronoun.

(113)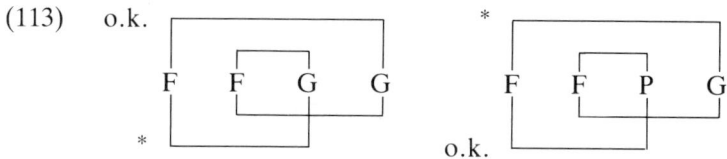

The systematic alternation diagrammed in (113) makes sense from a parsing perspective. When a listener hears a sentence like (111) and is about to interpret the gap in the clause **läraren bad** ____, he or she will presumably have two fillers in short term memory that need to be assigned, viz. the fillers corresponding to the preposed constituents **flickan** (*the girl*) and **vilken pojke** (*which boy*)[37]. If there are no restrictions on the order of gap filling in the grammar, the parser presumably has to make a choice of which filler to insert, or carry along two analyses in parallel. It seems plausible that making such a choice during the processing would increase the overall processing load of the sentence. The gap-pronoun pattern in (113) in effect allows the parser to use a very general parsing strategy which we may summarize as in (114):

(114)   Always associate a detected gap with the most recent filler.

Notice that this account of the pronoun-gap alternation makes sense in a left-to-right perspective, which presumably reflects the directionality in both perception and production. This explanation predicts that we will get a pattern as in (113) and not any other pattern of gap-pronoun constellations which would serve the disambiguating purpose. If we look solely at the structural properties, the patterns in (115) would be equally good at guaranteeing that a given string is only interpreted in one way.

(115)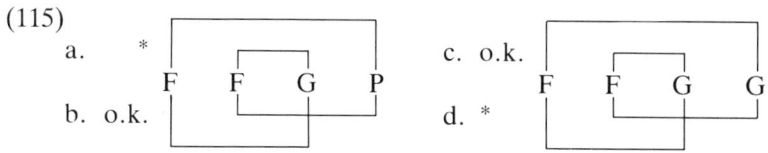

But from the point of view of an on-line parser, the pattern in (115) would not be of any help in deciding between the (b) and (c) readings at the time the gap must be interpreted. The possibility that the chosen assignment must be reanalyzed cannot be ruled out. The fact that resumptive pronouns appear in the pattern depicted in (113) supports the assumption that this is really a parsing-motivated strategy which prevents the hearer from constructing the unintended reading. When the fillers are of distinct categories and hence not interchangeable, intersecting extractions with two gaps occur, as shown in (116).

(116)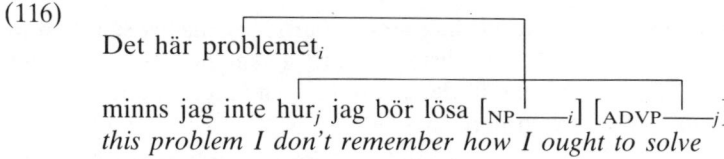
Det här problemet$_i$
minns jag inte hur$_j$ jag bör lösa [$_{NP}$——$_i$] [$_{ADVP}$——$_j$]
this problem I don't remember how I ought to solve

(116) should be compared with the similar (117) where the two fillers are of the same category due to preposition stranding and several speakers would use a resumptive pronoun.

(117)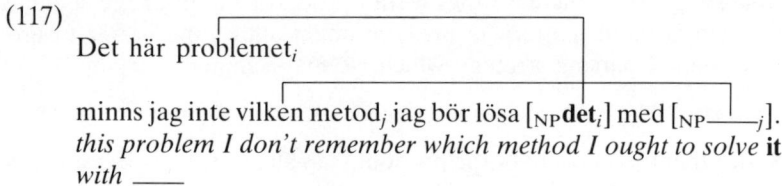
Det här problemet$_i$
minns jag inte vilken metod$_j$ jag bör lösa [$_{NP}$**det**$_i$] med [$_{NP}$——$_j$].
this problem I don't remember which method I ought to solve **it**
with ——

It should be added that the data I have discussed here to illustrate the disambiguating use of a pronoun-gap alternation reflects the facts in my own dialect, which apparently is fairly representative. However, a more extensive study of to what extent Swedish speakers use this disambiguating strategy is needed before we can conclude anything about the language in general.

One factor that clearly influences what readings people report for potentially ambiguous sentences with multiple filler-gap dependencies is pragmatic knowledge, expressed by the selectional restrictions on the verbs involved. For instance, a sentence like

a.
(118)   Strömming är den här kniven omöjlig att rensa —— med ——
b.
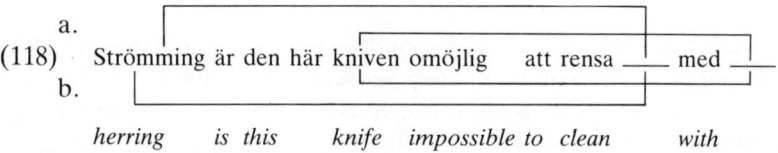
herring is this knife impossible to clean with

uniformly gets the reading associated with the intersecting assignment in (118a). Very few people notice that there is another reading, resulting from a nested association, on which one cleans knives with fish.

In order to find out to what extent people rely on pragmatic inferences due to lexical context and knowledge about the world, and to what extent structurally based strategies can explain what readings they get I have begun a series of experiments which systematically vary the amount of pragmatic information available in the sentence (cf. Engdahl (1982d) for a preliminary report). The results so far show that when a sentence is strongly pragmatically biased towards one association pattern, as in (118), people tend to report this reading, and only this reading, whereas a significant number of people report multiple readings for sentences where both assignments are possible, as in (119).

(119) Mina föräldrar$_i$ är det få personer$_j$ jag kan tänka
my   parents   are there few people   I   can think

mig att presentera ____ för ____.
me to introduce   for

My parents, there are few people I can see myself introducing to.

However, there seems to be a clear preference for the nested assignment in these cases. The experiments I have carried out so far have used the subjects' own judgments on what readings they got for the sentences, as well as in what order, and thus reflect a post-processing stage. This type of data obviously needs to be complemented with data from on-line experiments, e.g. eye movement tracking, to see if we can establish whether subjects perform the same type of analysis for sentences which they find ambiguous as for sentences which they report have only one reading.

6.3. Parasitic Gaps

We argued above that gaps in Swedish must be controlled sentence internally by a dislocated constituent, linked to the gap in an unbounded dependency such as relativization, topicalization or a constituent question. In this section, we will briefly illustrate a phenomenon which we suggest can be seen as a diagnostic for unbounded dependencies. For a fuller presentation of these facts and a discussion of their theoretical implications, see Chomsky (1982), Engdahl (1983, to appear b) and Taraldsen (1981)[38]. Consider the Swedish sentences in (112)–(114).

(112) Vilka skivor$_i$ köpte du ____$_i$ utan att lyssna på ____$_p$/dem$_i$?
       Which records did you buy without listening to them?

(113) Vem$_i$ ringde du upp ____$_i$ i stället för att skriva till ____$_p$/honom$_i$?
       Who did you call up instead of writing to him?

(114) Vem$_i$ sade du att vi skulle skicka breven från ____$_i$ tillbaka till ____$_i$?
       Who did you say that we should send the letters from back to?

The sentences all involve unbounded dependencies between an initial interrogative constituent and a gap, which we have indicated by '____'. In addition, there is an extra gap, indicated by ____$_p$, which is interpreted as controlled by the same dislocated constituent. In (114), either gap could be the real gap. (I won't discuss the methods by which one can tell which gap is the real gap here, but refer the reader to Engdahl 1983 for a fuller presentation.) In (112) and (113), these so-called parasitic gaps seem to alternate freely with a personal pronoun, which is understood as controlled by the dislocated phrase, as we have indicated. Now note that a parasitic gap is possible only if there is a filler-gap dependency in the sentence. If we remove this dependency, the parasitic gap becomes impossible, as shown in (112').

(112') Kalle köpte några skivor utan att lyssna på *____/^{ok}dem.
        Kalle bought some records without listening to *____/them.*

Furthermore, only unbounded dependencies, in our terminology, license parasitic gaps. Bounded or local dependencies such as passive don't, as shown in (115).

(115) Johan$_i$ dödades [e$_i$] av att ett träd föll på *____/^{ok}honom.
       Johan was killed by a tree falling on *____/him.*

In transformational frameworks such as EST and GB, the analysis of passive involves postulating an empty position after the verb, represented as [e] in (115), but this type of empty position cannot trigger a parasitic gap. The contrast between (112)–(114) on the one hand, where parasitic gaps are possible, and (112′) and (115) on the other hand where they are clearly excluded, motivates making a principled distinction in the grammar between bounded and unbounded dependencies. On our approach, only unbounded dependencies give rise to linked representations. The parasitic gap phenomenon then provides us with a diagnostic for unbounded dependencies. The reason we call these gaps 'parasitic' is simply that they require an unbounded filler-gap dependency in order to be felicitous. In most examples, parasitic gaps follow the real gaps, but there are also cases where they precede, as in (116). Interesting enough, in such sentences, as well as in (114), the version with a personal pronoun instead of a parasitic gap is noticeably less acceptable.

(116)   Räkna upp de filmer$_i$, som alla som sett ___$_p$/$^?$dem, tyckte om ___$_i$!
        List those movies that everyone who had seen ___$_p$, liked ___!

When we look at more data, it turns out that there is an interesting correlation between occurrences of parasitic gaps, the crossover phenomenon, and the non-coreference requirement on pronoun interpretations. We will return to this issue in Chapter VI. Here we will just show how the parasitic gap phenomenon supports our earlier claim that resumptive subject pronouns in Swedish should be analyzed as syntactic gaps. We have shown that parasitic gaps only occur where there is an unbounded dependency between a filler and a gap in the sentence. Recall that we have argued that resumptive subject pronouns act like gaps in Swedish, and that the linked representations should involve them as well. Consequently we predict that such a resumptive pronoun should trigger a parasitic gap. This prediction is borne out, as shown in the following example.

(117)   Där borta går den man$_i$ som vi fick folk att undra om **han**$_i$ var riktigt klok genom att göra narr av ___$_p$/honom offentligt.
        *Over there walks the man that we got people to wonder if **he** was quite sane by ridiculizing ___/him in public.*

han in (117) must be interpreted as being linked to the dislocated constituent. As we see, the unbounded dependency between a filler and a resumptive pronoun also licenses a parasitic gap, contrary to what is predicted in Chomsky (1982).

One way to incorporate the parasitig gap data in our framework would be to let link children dominate several links, connecting to different tree parents. This is presumably independently needed for unbounded dependencies into coordinate structures (cf. Doron (1982) for one proposal for how to treat coordination in a Phrase Linking grammar). By assuming that parasitic gaps are possible only in connection with a dislocated constituent, we automatically account for the ungrammaticality of (112′) and (115). I. Sag has proposed an elegant treatment of parasitic gaps within Generalized Phrase Structure Grammar (Sag, 1983). He introduces parasitic gaps by way of a metarule which crucially mentions a slashed category, i.e. a category of the form 'α/β' which is used to account for unbounded dependencies. This way, parasitic gaps can only be introduced if there already is an unbounded dependency, as indicated by the presence of the slashed category.

7. CONSTRAINING THE FRAMEWORK

In the previous sections we have outlined the grammatical framework that we are adopting for our analysis of unbounded dependencies and in particular constituent questions in Swedish. The syntactic part of the grammar consists of a phrase structure grammar which determines constituent structure and the possible word orders. For expository purposes, we have neglected the distinction in word order between main and subordinate clauses, but this could presumably be remedied in a straightforward fashion (see Ejerhed (1982) for one proposal). In addition to the basic phrase structure rules, we have rules which admit linked trees, i.e. the trees we need in order to directly accommodate sentences with unbounded dependencies. As the grammar is currently stated, it will admit trees with any number of links, nested and intersecting, as long as the local conditions on link parents are fulfilled. The question is now: Do we need to state further restrictions on unbounded dependencies in the grammar? We can break down this question into two. First, do we need to limit the number of links into one and the same clause? Second, do we need to restrict what type of constituents that can contain link parents? We will address these questions in turn.

7.1. How Many Extractions?

We have already encountered several examples of extractions out of embedded constituent questions, which require structures with two links into the same clause, as in (118).

(118) [NObelpriset i medicin]$_i$ ska vi snart få reda på
the Nobel Prize in medicine will we soon find out

vem$_j$ som ___$_j$ får ___$_i$.
who that gets

Such sentences show that a minimal requirement of adequacy for a language like Swedish is that it can handle sentences with two dependencies into the same clause. An obvious question at this point is whether it is sufficient to provide for two gaps in a sentence. Are there sentences with more than two dependencies? Let us try a sentence with three gaps. Such sentences naturally get quite complex since we need at least three levels of embedding to construct them. We will start off with a sentence with two extractions and a context in which it seems appropriate. Suppose there has been an epidemic at one of the hospitals in town, probably caused by a delivery of fresh produce. It is still unclear what produce or who the responsible caterer is. This might be expressed in a summary fashion as in (119).

(119) Hälsovårdsmyndigheterna håller på att undersöka
the Department of Public Health is investigating

vilka färskvaror$_j$ det var oklart vilken grossist$_k$
which produce it was unclear which caterer

som ___$_k$ levererat ___$_j$ till något
(that) had delivered to one of

sjukhus i stan.
the hospitals in town

Someone who wants to find out which hospital this whole thing occurred at might then ask:

(120) Var det Södersjukhuset$_i$ som
was it the South Hospital that

hälsovårdsmyndigheterna lät undersöka vilka
the Department of Public Health was investigating which

färskvaror$_j$ det var oklart vilken grossist$_k$ som ____$_k$
produce   it was unclear which caterer (that)

levererat ____$_j$ till ____$_i$?
had delivered   to

In an ordinary conversation, a question like (120) would sound extremely odd, mainly because it violates conversational norms on how much of the presupposed or shared information need be directly expressed in the question. Still, it seems to me that someone who is anxious to make himself perfectly clear might phrase the question in this way. Now, is (120) a 'grammatical' question in Swedish? Suppose we say it is not. Then we must explain what it is that makes (120) ungrammatical unlike (119). We cannot say that it is the question formation by itself, since we have seen that extracting out of an indirect question is permitted. In order to block (120), while admitting (119), we would have to state a condition on question formation to the effect that it cannot apply in a structure where there is already more than one gap in the smallest clause whose filler does not also occur in that clause. I don't think it is possible to formulate such a condition unless one makes reference to global properties of a derivation which presumably is something to be avoided unless it is clearly necessary. Let us instead consider why a sentence like (120) may be judged ungrammatical. Giving grammaticality judgments about sentences is very different from using sentences in ordinary conversation. Most likely the process of judging sentences for grammaticality is influenced by various factors, a fact that motivates some caution in the interpretation of such judgments. One thing that is essential when we ask for grammaticality judgments is to separate out complexity and frequency factors as far as possible in order to distinguish what constructions are genuinely ungrammatical and what constructions are merely rare. Although (120) is a highly complex sentence, each part of it is formed according to the rules of the grammar. The overall impression of complexity probably arises from the fact that three fillers must be kept available simultaneously when the parser reaches the most embedded clause. This presumably places quite a strain on the processor. Note that the parser is not incapable of detexting ungrammaticalities even in highly complex sentences. We can compare (120) with (121), which is comparable in length and structural build-up, but differs in that there is a mismatch between the number of preposed constituents and the number of gaps.

(121) *Var det Södersjukhuset$_i$ som
 was it the South Hospital that
 hälsovårdsmyndigheterna lät undersöka varför
 the Department of Public Health made inquiries why
 det var oklart vilka grossister$_j$ som ____$_j$ var
 it was unclear which caterers$_j$ that were
 ansvariga för leveransen av ____ till ____?
 responsible for the delivery of to

This mismatch is easily detected, and I doubt that any Swedish speaker would accept (121). If it were the case that speakers suspend their ability to detect ungrammaticalities when confronted with complex sentences, we would not expect any difference between (120) and (121), contrary to the facts. It might be argued that (121) doesn't prove that Swedish speakers use the same syntactic strategies they use for simple sentences when they process such complex utterances. (121) is perhaps so complicated that the listener abandons the usual parsing procedures and applies some general problem solving technique which may rely on all available knowledge, not just what is presented in the sentence. (121) then turns out to be incoherent because you cannot match up predicates and arguments. However, there is some indication that listeners do analyze such sentences as linguistic expressions, using the normal interpretation strategies. This indication comes from the detection of morphological mismatches between fillers and gaps. We have earlier shown that speakers immediately notice a discrepancy in grammatical gender between a dislocated phrase and the context of the gap, as in (122).

(122) Den där studenten var Kalle säker ____ skulle bli
 [−NEUT]
 that student was Kalle certain would be
 godkänd /*godkänt
 [−NEUT] [+NEUT]
 accepted

Similarly, in a sentence with several filler-gap dependencies, as in (123), such mismatches are detected.

(123) Den där studenten$_j$ minns jag inte   vem$_j$ som ___$_i$
      [−NEUT]   [−NEUT]
      that student,   I don't remember who   that, ___

      var säker /* säkert ___$_j$ skulle bli godkänd /*godkänt
      [−NEUT] [+NEUT]   [−NEUT] [+NEUT]
      was certain   would be accepted

Given these facts, it seems plausible to assume that listeners perform at least some grammatical analysis of the sentence, and that it is on the basis of this that the syntactic or morphological mismatch is detected.

If we assume that sentences with three extractions should be accepted by the grammar, the next question is obviously: Can we put a limit at three or should we allow for the possibility of extracting four constituents, and by induction, in principle any number of constituents? It seems that it would be exceedingly hard to establish a clear cut-off point in the grammar between grammatical and ungrammatical multi-extraction sentences. Consequently, it would be in vain to try to set a numeric limit, n, on the number of permissible extractions, such that any sentence with n extractions would be grammatical, whereas a sentence with $n + 1$ extractions would be excluded. I will argue below that the factors that influence acceptability of extractions have to do primarily with discourse requirements and may vary with the choice of lexical items, i.e. factors that have little to do with the formal capacity of the grammar as such. To illustrate the difficulty of finding a grammatical cut-off point, we can compare the sentences in (124) and (125).

(124) Jag har flera studenter$_i$ som det inte finns någon$_j$
      I have several students that there is no one

      som ___$_j$ vågar prata med ___$_i$ om politiska frågor.
      who   dares talk to   about political issues

(125) Sådana känsliga politiska frågor$_k$ har jag flera
      such touchy political issues have I several

      studenter$_i$ som det inte finns någon$_j$ som ___$_j$ vågar tala
      students   that there is   no one who   dares talk

      med ___$_i$ om ___$_k$.
      to   about

In (124), the preposed constituent **flera studenter** (*several students*) has been extracted out of a relative clause, thus creating a two-gap structure. In (125) we have topicalized **sådana känsliga politiska frågor** (*such touchy political issues*) out of the embedded relative clause, which creates three gaps in this clause. The point of these examples is that in contexts where (124) is accepted, I think (125) would also be accepted. There is no formal property of (125) that makes it clearly ungrammatical in distinction to (124), and hence no basis for putting a numeric limit on the number of extractions per clause. In actual cases, there will be a natural upper bound on the number of extractions, since the number of constituents in any actually used sentence is rather small.

Although people do not normally use sentences like (120) and (125) and may have difficulties in processing them, I think it would be in principle wrong to exclude sentences with three or more gaps by a restriction in the grammar. My argument here is reminiscent of Miller and Chomsky's claim that:

devices that incorporate competence whether or not it is realized in performance provide the only models of any psychological relevance, since only they can explain the transfer of learning that we know occurs when memory aids are in fact made available.

(Miller and Chomsky, 1963, p. 462)

Applying this argument to center-embedded relative clauses, they claimed that neither the fact that people don't spontaneously produce multiply embedded relative clauses, nor seem to process them easily should count as a reason for excluding the possibility of generating them from the grammar. I think the case for multiple extractions in Swedish is quite parallel. In English, on the other hand, the constraint against more than one gap in a tensed sentence appears to be a grammatical constraint.

7.2. *Structural Constraints*

We now turn to the second question. Do we need to formulate any constraints in the grammar on which constituents may dominate link parents, i.e. may contain gaps? In the terminology common after Ross' (1967) dissertation, the question would be: Are there any extraction islands in the language? We have seen ample evidence that the *wh*-Island Constraint is not applicable in Swedish. We will now consider the status of the Complex NP Constraint (CNPC). We note first that Ross' structural definition of the CNPC in (126) subsumes two cases, noun complements and relative clauses.

(126)
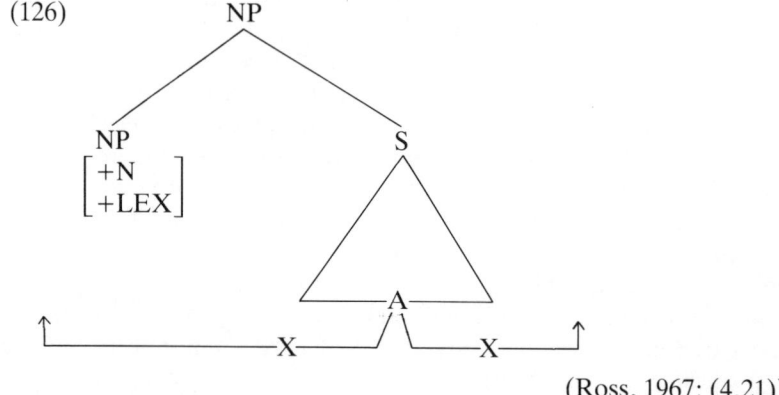

(Ross, 1967: (4.21))

Whereas some languages don't allow extractions out of either of these constructions, others allow extractions out of noun complements but not out of relative clauses. In Swedish, we can find good extractions out of both types as shown in (127) and (128).

(127) Ingen artikel som det finns [$_{NP}$den minsta risk [$_{\bar{S}}$ att
 no article that there is the least risk that

 regeringen tar anstöt av ___]] kan publiceras i
 the government is offended by ___ can be published in

 denna tidning.
 this newspaper

(128) Skaldjur är det [$_{NP}$många [$_{\bar{S}}$ som ___ inte tål ___ .]]
 shellfish, are there several who not stand

 Shellfish, there are several who can't eat.

Incidentally, we have already used a Swedish example with an extraction out of a relative clause in (124) when we discussed triple extractions. However, even if (127)–(128) are acceptable, it is also easy to find examples with extractions out of compelx NP structures which are unacceptable. Compare (127) with (129) which is also an extraction out of a noun complement but most speakers find this one highly questionable.

(129) ??Vilken fackföreningsledare var alla   upprörda över
       which union leader   was everyone   upset   over

       det faktum att bolaget   hade försökt muta ____?
       the fact   that the company had   tried   to bribe

Similarly, it is easy to find an extraction out of a relative clause which sounds impossible. For instance, extracting out of a relative clause with a definite head NP often sounds bad.

(130) ??Skaldjur känner jag mannen som inte tål ____.
       shellfish know   I   the man who can't eat

Extracting out of a relative clause where a constituent different from the subject has been relativized also seems less acceptable. Compare (128) to (131).

(131) ??Skaldjur$_j$ känner jag en man$_i$ som Lisa ofta bjuder ____$_i$
       shellfish   know   I a man   that Lisa often offers

       på ____$_j$.

The nature of the matrix verb apparently also influences the acceptability as illustrated by the contrast in (132) (cf. Allwood, 1976).

(132) a. Centerpartiet   känner jag en man som röstar på ____.
          the Center party   know   I   a man who votes for

      b. ??Centerpartiet   ringer jag upp en man som röstar
          the Center party   call   I   up a man who votes

         på ____
         for

In view of these facts, extractions out of the same structure thus can produce either fully acceptable sentences, as in (127)–(128), or questionable, to some speakers even unacceptable, sentences, as in (129)–(131b). The question is now which way to state the generalization for Swedish. Either we can say that all extractions out of complex NP structures are ungrammatical and that (127) and (128) happen to be felicitous for some unknown reason which probably lies outside the domain of syntax. Or we can assume that extractions are possible and that (129)–(132b) are infelicitous for some nongrammatical reason.

After having considered a number of cases, I have noticed that for any given unacceptable sentence, it is in general possible to construct a version that speakers will accept by systematically varying what presuppositions the sentence requires. I thus choose the second approach. I will assume that extractions out of complex NPs are not blocked by any rule in the grammar. How then can we explain that people find (129)–(132b) highly questionable or totally unacceptable? Let us first consider the case of extracting out of noun complement structures. Why is (129) unacceptable?

(129) ??Vilken fackföreningsledare var alla   upprörda över
     which union leader   was everyone upset   over

     det faktum att bolaget   hade försökt muta ___?
     the fact that the company had tried   to bribe

I think it is appropriate to appeal to the Gricean maxim of simplicity here. 'Don't use a complicated sentence if there is a simpler way to express the same message'. In the case of (129), there is a simpler way of expressing the same message, namely by just omitting **det faktum** (*the fact*).

(133) Vilken fackföreningsledare var alla   upprörda över
     which union leader   was everyone upset   over

     att bolaget   hade försökt muta ___?
     that the company had tried   to bribe

This line of explanation predicts that in contexts where a noun complement structure is the only possible one, i.e. where there is no 'simpler' way to express the message, extractions should be acceptable. Consider the noun **rykte** (*rumor*) which frequently takes a sentential complement. There is a corresponding verb **ryktas** which is mainly used in the impersonal construction **det ryktas att** . . . (*it is rumored that* . . .). However, there is no transitive (or causative) form of the verb. If we explicitly want to express that someone caused a rumor, we must use a periphrastic construction, just like in English, **sprida ut ett rykte** (*spread a rumor*). Extracting out of a complement to **rykte** when it occurs in this context is possible, which is just what we expect given that there is no simpler/shorter form without the noun complement construction.

(134) a. Vilken fackföreningsledare lät Kalle sprida ut ett rykte
   which union leader   let Kalle spread a rumor
   att bolaget   hade försökt muta ___?
   that the company had tried to bribe

 b. *Vilken fackföreningsledare ryktade Kalle att
   which union leader   rumored Kalle that
   bolaget   hade försökt muta ___?
   the company had tried to bribe

Next we will look at the alleged fact that extractions out of relative clauses with definite heads are less acceptable. In his discussion of which factors influence the acceptability of sentences with extractions in Swedish, L-G. Andersson (1982) demonstrates among other things that it is not the definiteness of the head NP per se, which is the cause for the unacceptability judgment. It is rather whether a definite NP is felicitous or not in a given sentence, and in a given discourse. Andersson's point is that if the sentence or discourse requires a definite NP, then an extraction out of a relative clause on this head will in general be possible, provided that the extraction is also motivated by the structure of the discourse etc. We can illustrate this by a pair of sentences which differ only in the uniqueness presuppositions associated with the lexical items.

(135) a. Den här tavlan känner jag faktiskt konstnären som
   this   painting know I   actually the artist who
   målat ___.
   painted

 b. ??Det här motivet känner jag faktiskt konstnären som
   this   motif   know I actually the artist who
   målat ___.
   painted

Talking about paintings, as in (135a), it is natural to assume that there is one painter who painted it and the definite NP **konstnären** (*the artist*) is appropriate. But talking about a motif, we don't have the presupposition that only one artist painted it and consequently this is a strange sentence. If instead of the definite NP **konstnären** we substitute an indefinite NP like **ingen** (*no one*), we get the opposite acceptability pattern. It is appropriate to say of a motif that you don't know any one who has painted it, but it is a strange thing to say of a painting.

(136) a. ??Den här tavlan   känner jag faktiskt ingen   som har
     this   painting know   I   actually no one who has

   målat ___.
   painted

   b. Det här motivet känner jag faktiskt ingen   som har
       this   motif   know   I   actually no one who has

   målat ___.
   painted

We conclude that the infelicity of (135b) and (136a) then is not due to the extraction but that it follows from the fact that the definiteness of the NP is inappropriate in this particular context.

We now turn to the question whether extractions out of non-subject relative clauses are significantly worse. It is probably correct that most spontaneously produced extractions out of relatives involve subject relatives, but this is in no way a requirement. (137) is a perfectly acceptable sentence although we have extracted out of a relative clause where the indirect object has been relativized.

(137)   Skaldjur$_j$ finns det   många$_i$ (som) man inte bör
        shellfish are there several (that) one shouldn't

   bjuda ___$_i$ på ___$_j$.
   offer

What then is the relevant difference between this sentence and our previous example of a similar structure, which was unacceptable?

(131) ??Skaldjur$_j$ känner jag en man$_i$ som Lisa ofta
        shellfish   know   I a man   that Lisa often

   bjuder ___$_i$ på ___$_j$.
   offers

I believe that this contrast has to do mainly with what we perceive as a relevant contribution in a normal discourse, i.e. with the 'thematic structure of a discourse', using Kuno's (1976) terminology. The fact that many people can't eat shellfish and hence shouldn't be served it is a relevant comment on the topic shellfish. But 'know a man that Lisa offers shellfish' is only very indirectly relevant to the topic shellfish, unless, of course, we are in a special context where the conversation has been about knowing people that Lisa serves various types of food to. Presumably the same type of explanation can be offered for the contrasts which depend on the choice of verb in (132). I suspect that people's expectations on normal discourses clearly influence their judgments also on sentences presented in isolation. But I don't think that how easy or difficult it is to find a suitable context for a given sentence should contribute to determining whether the sentence is ungrammatical or not. Rather, it should follow from the syntactic and semantic rules for the language whether the sentence is grammatical or not. In order to also be able to judge which sentences are 'natural' and 'useable' etc, we of course need to consider facts about sentence processing and discourse structure. See Erteschik-Shir (1973, 1982) for a discussion of pragmatic constraints on extractions. Consequently I take the view that the simplest and most revealing grammar for Swedish is one where no restrictions on the number of extractions or island constraints are formulated on the particular syntactic or semantic rules for this language, but that the limitations we in fact find follow from facts about sentence processing and discourse requirements, facts which presumably are general and which need not be specified for a particular language.

There appears to be one restriction, however, that pertains to constituents in the subject position of the sentence. It might be that this restriction also is discourse and/or processing motivated but it has been grammaticized in Swedish to a more noticeable degree than the previous examples. The following pairs provide some illustration.

(138)a. Många porträtt av Karl den tolfte hänger på
many portraits of Charles the Twelfth hang at
Gripsholm.
Gripsholm

b. *Vilken kung hänger [$_{NP}$ många porträtt av ____] på
which king hang many portraits of at
Gripsholm?
Gripsholm

(139)a. **Det** hänger många porträtt av Karl den tolfte på
there *hang many portraits of Charles the Twelfth at*
Gripsholm.
Gripsholm

b. Vilken kung hänger **det** [$_{NP}$ många porträtt av ___] på
which king hang **there** *many portraits of at*
Gripsholm?
Gripsholm

An extraction out of a subject NP as in (138) is quite bad. If the sentence has a presentational form as in (139), where the surface subject position is occupied by the dummy **det**, an extraction is possible. Although (138) and (139) have the same meaning in a truth conditional sense, they cannot be used interchangeably in a conversation. This presumably indicates that they make different types of contributions from the point of view of thematic structure of the discourse. If instead we choose a sentence with a definite subject for which there is no alternative presentational form, extractions are in general better which suggests that this restriction might be mainly a discourse level phenomenon. The following example was suggested by E. Ejerhed.

(140) Q: Har du numret till någon tandläkare?
have you the number to some dentist

A: Ja, skoltandvården$_i$ ligger [$_{NP}$ numret till ___$_i$]
yes, the school clinic lies the number to

på köksbordet.
on the kitchen table

A special case of extractions out of subjects obtains when the subject is sentential, as in (141). Such extractions generally are quite unacceptable.

(141) a. [$_S$Att domaren diskvalificerat en av spelarna]
that the judge disqualified one of the players

ledde till att AIK förlorade.
led to that AIK lost

b. ??Vilken spelare ledde [$_S$att domaren diskvalificerat ____]
   which player   did   that the judge disqualified
   till   att AIK förlorade?
   lead to that AIK lost

Lyn Frazier has recently addressed the issue why sentential subjects seem to increase the local processing load (Frazier to appear) and in Chapter V we will discuss her proposal. Here we just note that if sentential subjects as such are hard to process then we would have an explanation why extractions out of such structures are infelicitous.

The position we have taken here can be summarized roughly in the following way: Only assume that a constraint is syntactic if you have clear evidence that it is or if it is implausible that it should follow from considerations of processing complexity or discourse structure. Whether this is a good methodological strategy or not can only be determined in the light of many more analyses, in particular studies contrasting sentences which differ systematically in relative complexity. At present we refer to Anward (1981) for a discussion of functional explanations for NP movements in Swedish and to Fodor (1980) for an extensive discussion of functional explanations in general and their relevance to the actual form of constraints in the grammar. As formulated, this methodological guideline is much too static since it ignores the process by which an originally processing-motivated restriction turns into a grammatical constraint in a language. This seems to be an intriguing topic for further research. In particular, it would be interesting to compare two languages such as English and Swedish from the point of view of grammatization of constraints.

8. SUMMARY

The purpose of this chapter has been to outline a framework for Swedish, explicit enough to permit the formulation of syntactic and semantic rules for a variety of constructions, especially unbounded dependencies. The framework consists basically of a phrase structure grammar. In addition to regular trees, the grammar admits so-called 'linked trees' in which one constituent has both a tree parent and a link parent (cf. Peters and Ritchie, in preparation). Linked trees permit us to admit sentences with unbounded dependencies directly without any reordering transformations. We assume that the interpretation rules apply in tandem with the syntactic rules and interpret constituents as they are put together. Just like Peters and Ritchie, we assume a certain amount of semantic (or interpretive) filtering. Sentences that have too many or too few constituents, or constituents of the wrong category, will not be associated with a complete meaning and are hence not accepted.

Of special interest is the interaction between the structural position of a constituent and its interpretation possibilities. For instance, we have found that resumptive subject pronouns may only be interpreted as controlled by a dislocated constituent. We have discussed certain restrictions on quantificational binding of pronouns, which seem to depend on the structural positions involved and have proposed a restriction on the interpretation procedure to handle these cases (the Store Address Convention). The focus of this study is on unbounded dependencies, and in Section 6, we discussed the phenomenon of parasitic gaps which we take to be a diagnostic for unbounded dependencies.

Very few constraints have been imposed on the grammar itself. In Section 7, we discussed what types of constraints need to be expressed in the formal components, and what constraints can be seen to follow from considerations of langauge processing and the pragmatics of discourse. We have tended to leave such restrictions for which there are processing and/or discourse explanations out of the grammar. However, the issue of how an originally user-motivated constraint becomes grammaticized is intriguing and deserves further research.

NOTES

[1] We assume that this feature agreement will conform to some version of the Head Feature Convention (cf. Gazdar *et al.*, to appear, chapter 2).

[2] From the point of view of the interaction between syntax and semantics it would actually have been simpler to use a categorial grammar where every structure building operation is binary and is directly interpreted as function argument application. See Bach (1979) for a good example. However, since we want to make the exposition as approachable as possible, we have chosen the phrase structure grammar format which permits us to use standard tree diagrams with familiar constituent structure in our derivations.

[3] For instance, we have not taken into account the word order differences between matrix clauses and subordinate clauses in Swedish, nor the so-called verb second constraint. One way to do this would be to employ different symbols for matrix and embedded clauses. For instance, matrix questions could be of category Q and embedded questions of category $\bar{Q}$. See Ejerhed (1982) for additional reasons for distinguishing matrix and subordinate

clauses and for a formal implementation of this in a phrase structure grammar.
[4] The rather complex interpretation rule in [10a] is not required for this simple example but is necessary in order to get the correct interpretation for sentences with quantified NPs in object position, as in (i),

(i)   I persuaded every man to leave.

which does not mean the same as 'I persuaded every man that every man should leave'.
[5] This formulation of the quantification rule is a simplified version. For a complete and explicit formalization of Cooper's storage convention, see Ladusaw (1979).
[6] We will probably want to extend the quantification rule to allow for quantifying into VPs and CNs as well, in view of examples like

(i)   John wishes to find a unicorn and eat it. (PTQ)
(ii)   Every search for two red-haired men failed.

The second example, which shows the need for CN-quantification, was brought up by J. Higginbotham and commented upon by B. Partee, in the spring of 1980. The translation rules would be as in PTQ.
[7] The effect of the NP Quantification rule is similar to what May (1977) calls Quantifier Raising (QR). QR raises a NP from its S-structure position inside an S and adjoins it to a dominating S node. The trace left behind by QR is coindexed with the raised NP. Some rule at LF then rewrites this trace as a variable bound by the raised quantifier. Note that on the approach in the text, a NP with wider scope is never 'moved' syntactically. The relative scope facts are handled entirely in the semantics.
[8] We have chosen to illustrate controlled quantification with an embedded question in order to avoid certain syntactic complications having to do with the word order in main clauses. These are irrelevant to the present purpose.
[9] (18) is actually ambiguous. The other meaning corresponds to a tree where the links intersect and where the organizer is supposed to introduce some member of royalty to some winner. See Section 8 for a discussion of the availability of intersecting readings.
[10] Cooper (1978b) accounted for this fact by letting WH quantification be the semantic interpretation of the syntactic rule of WH fronting. Roughly the same approach was taken in Engdahl (1980a).
[11] Although there is little direct evidence from direct questions that subject WH phrases occur in dislocated position, i.e. are linked (string vacuously) to an empty position in the sentence making this assumption allows for a simpler semantics and a more uniform syntax. There is some evidence that questioned subjects in indirect questions in Swedish occur in dislocated position (cf. III.4.3).
[12] In our use of explicit quantification rules we differ from the semantic approach generally taken in Phrase Linking grammars (cf. Peters and Ritchie in preparation). In the quantification rules in (15) and (23) we have spelled out how the interpretation of a quantifier applies to the interpretation of a sentential constituent (see Chapter IV for details about what the interpretation of an interrogative quantifier is). On Peters and Ritchie's approach, quantifiers are interpreted as *variable binding operators* whose domain of application is determined by their valence, as we outlined in Chapter II.5. A variable binding operator may apply whenever the argument is of the right type, and it can't apply otherwise, thus effecting 'interpretive (or semantic) filtering'. There is one

148 CHAPTER III

complication, however, having to do with interrogative variable binding operators. We recall that WH phrases have the valence $\langle\langle s, t \rangle, \langle\langle s, t \rangle, t \rangle\rangle$, i.e. they apply to the interpretation of a sentence and yield sets of propositions. But this only holds for WH phrases in dislocated positions. Unmoved WH phrases must have the valence $\langle\langle\langle s, t \rangle, t \rangle, \langle\langle s, t \rangle, t \rangle\rangle$ i.e. take sets of propositions into sets of proposition. It will not be possible in general to determine at the point of admitting a WH phrase whether it occurs in dislocated position or not. This is because the WH phrase may be embedded inside another constituent as is the case in pied-piping. Consequently, we will either have to assume that WH phrases are ambiguous with respect to valence, or that they remain unspecified until the derivation reaches a syntactic configuration where its dislocated status can be determined. The latter, however, would violate the autonomy-of-syntax hypothesis. Cooper (1983, chapter V) defines WH binding operators so that they apply both to sentence interpretations and to question interpretations and thus resolves the problem.

[13] This point is also discussed in Engdahl (1982b).

[14] I am grateful to Yuki Kuroda and Nanako Kameshima for information about multiple questions in Japanese.

[15] Since this is mainly a study of constituent questions, we have said very little about the interpretation of *yes/no* questions. We will assume the general approach to *yes/no* questions in Karttunen (1977) but call the reader's attention to de Cornulier (1981) for some relevant distinctions.

[16] Apparently, many English speakers don't like unmoved WH phrases in *whether* and *if* questions. I believe that this is due to a correlation in extraction possibilities and interpretation possibilities for a given language (cf. Engdahl to appear a.).

[17] One occasionally hears one type of question that appears to be an instance of the type we claim in the text shouldn't exist for Gricean reasons. Consider the *yes/no* question with an unmoved WH phrase in (i), together with an answer that one might hear.

(i)   Q: Does John's mood really depend on who dances with whom?
        A: No, it depends on who dances with Mary.

However, I don't think this answer is a correct answer to the *yes/no* question. It is rather a case of what R. Manor calls a *corrective* answer (Manor, 1982). Semantically, the correct answer should be *yes*. John's mood does depend on a function which correlates dancers. The corrective answer adds the information that it is only with respect to one person that this function is relevant.

[18] Another possible structure for embedded questions which is compatible with the arguments in the text would be the structure in (i).

(i)

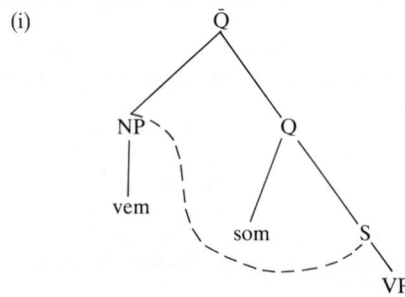

The binary branching structure in (i) would correspond more directly to the proposals in Andersson (1974), Maling and Zaenen (1981), and Taraldsen (to appear). This approach would require additional phrase structure rules but presumably no substantial changes in the phrase linking conventions or the interpretation rules.

[19] Note that (46) allows **som** in non-subject questions as in (41c, d). Apparently, this is an area where Norwegian and Swedish differ. The phrase structure grammar for Swedish proposed in Anward (1982, p. 63ff.) generates **som** in all embedded questions and relative clauses. Taraldsen (to appear) on the other hand claims that non-subject questions with an overt **som** in Norwegian are ungrammatical. It seems to me that the acceptability of **som** in non-subject questions in Swedish depends on among other things the heaviness of the WH phrase.

[20] There are no infinitival matrix declarative constructions in Swedish. However, there is one infinitival construction which is often used in narrative style.

(i)   (Och) Kalle till   att   skratta!
        (and) Kalle to   to   laugh
                       PREP INF

        And Kalle began to laugh.

[21] In Chapter IV.4.1 we will modify this interpretation slightly in order to account for relational interpretations of pronouns.

[22] See Kamp (1981) for a good illustration of the difference between proper names and quantifiers with respect to anaphora. In Kamp's Discourse Representation Structures, (DRS), the entities denoted by proper names are always entered in the highest DRS and are thus accessbile from all lower DRS.

[23] See Cooper (1983, chapter VII) for a discussion of how the presuppositions associated with gender behave with respect to quantifiers and 'plugs', 'holes', and 'filters'.

[24] These types of resumptive pronouns are quite frequent both in spoken and written Swedish as one realizes when one starts to listen and look for them. They are also described in standard grammars. (58a) is from Wessén (1965). Jan Anward provided me with (58b), Per Linell with (58c) and Lars-Gunnar Andersson with (58e).

[25] There are other occurrences of resumptive pronouns which are not in subject position. See Section 6.1 for a discussion of these pronouns, which seem to alternate freely with gaps, contrary to the present case.

[26] Stanley Peters (personal communication) agrees that it is probably correct to extend the use of links to resumptive pronouns in languages like Swedish where gaps and resumptive pronouns have the same interpretation possibilities (cf. Zaenen et al., 1981). However, in other languages resumptive pronouns may have systematically different interpretation possibilities compared with gaps and might thus call for a different analysis (cf. Chao and Sells, 1983; Doron, 1982).

[27] Heim (1979) points out some similarities in the use of pronouns and epithets which are important for the approach given here.

[28] There is also a complex reflexive pronoun of the form 'α **själv**' where α is a personal pronoun in the accusative case. In contemporary Swedish, the complex form seems to alternate freely with the simple reflexive. There is possibly a slight change in meaning. Using 'α **själv**' conveys that the agent consciously or deliberately performs the action denoted by the verb towards himself. In Norwegian, on the other hand, the choice between 'α' and 'α **selv**' is apparently governed by structural and lexical factors. See

Hellan (1980b, forthcoming a, b) for a detailed discussion of Norwegian reflexives.

[29] See Thráinsson (1976) and Maling (1984) for detailed discussions of the conditions on non-clause mate reflexives in Icelandic.

[30] The view of reflexivization expressed in this section has been inspired by Emmon Bach's approach to reflexives and reciprocals, first presented in a Linguistics Department colloquium at the University of Massachusetts/Amherst in the fall of 1978.

[31] There are also cases where it seems that **sig** and **sin** may be interpreted as referring to a specific individual, as in one of the readings of the non-sloppy reading of (i) (cf. Dahl, 1973).

(i)   Bara Kalle kände igen sin   mor.
        only Kalle recognized self's mother

Similar problems in connection with VP anaphora are discussed in Hellan (forthcoming b). Kamp (1981) notes the need to distinguish between 'true' reflexives involving property formation and 'accidental' reflexives which apepar when two expressions happen to pick out the same discourse referent. See van Eijck (1982) for an attempt to capture this dual use of reflexive (or bound) pronouns in the framework of Discourse Representation Structures.

[32] See Hellan (forthcoming b) for a different approach to reflexives in dislocated positions.

[33] Cf. Cooper (1978b, Section 2.2.3, Rules of functional application) for a similar but not equivalent restriction.

[34] For an account of the variation in terms of proper government in GB, see Engdahl (to appear b).

[35] For an indication of the variation in judgments, see Allwood (1976). This survey presumably reflects dialects from south west Sweden, i.e. the dialects spoken in the provinces close to Norway and Sweden. A large part of this territory was under Danish rule until 1658.

[36] The fact that multiple extractions are truly ambiguous was first shown for Norwegian by K. Koch Christensen in 1979 (cf. Christensen, 1982a, b).

[37] We will use 'filler' as a technical term for a constituent that the parser has not yet been able to attach into the phrase marker (cf. Frazier, 1979) or assign its grammatical function. It is an issue open for investigation in what form these constituents are represented during the processing of a complex sentence, how much of the syntactic structure that is retained etc. Cf. Engdahl (1982d) for additional observations.

[38] Chomsky (1982) argues that parasitic gaps provide empirical support for distinguishing between argument binding and non-argument binding which is central in the Government-Binding theory. Grosu (1980) discusses some cases of parasitic gaps, although he does not use this term. Rather he takes their appearance as evidence for an analogical extension of extraction rules to coordinate-like structures. However, not all occurrences of parasitic gaps can be analyzed as being in a constituent conjoined with a constituent that contains the real gap, cf. (114) and (116) in the text.

CHAPTER IV

THE INTERPRETATION OF QUESTIONS

In this chapter we will apply the syntactic and semantic framework for Swedish developed in the previous chapter to the interpretation of constituent questions. One reason that we have chosen this particular construction is that it provides a good illustration of the issue we brought up in Chapter I, namely that in order to evaluate a given account of some linguistic problem, it is not sufficient to look at the problem only from a syntactic point of view or only from a semantic point of view. One could conceivably work out syntactic or semantic approaches which are extremely elegant and simple within their own domain but which entail ad hoc solutions in other areas. It is not until we look at the interaction of the syntactic and semantic rules that we are in a position to judge their relative adequacy for a given natural language. Providing a syntax and semantics for constituent questions in Swedish turns out to be a good area in which to illustrate how semantic considerations may simplify the syntactic description.

Several of the Swedish constructions that we will be discussing are very similar to their English counterparts. In those cases, we will sometimes use English examples. Other constructions and constellations, however, don't show up in English and we will then discuss examples from Swedish.

1. SOME PREVIOUS APPROACHES TO QUESTIONS

Montague's PTQ provides an explicit syntactic and semantic account for a fragment of English with declarative sentences within a model theoretic semantics. The intension of a sentence is understood as denoting a proposition, i.e. a function from possible worlds to truth values. Hamblin (1973) extended Montague's syntactic and semantic program to certain non-declarative constructions, namely questions. He takes questions to denote sets of propositions, the set of propositions expressed by *possible* answers to the question. Karttunen (1977) provides an extension and modification of Hamblin's approach, and we will take the proposal made there as a point of departure for our discussion of constituent questions. Before going into some of the details of Karttunen's proposal, we should note one assumption that underlies this general approach to questions. By assuming that the meaning of a question is in some sense determined by what a possible answer to the question is, we are relying on a notion of answer as a criterion for individuating questions. Lest this should lead to the suspicion that there is some circularity in the argument, let me explain why I think this is a justifiable assumption. It is usually assumed in truth-conditional semantics that it is part of the semantic competence of a speaker who understands the meaning of a sentence that he or she recognizes the conditions under which the sentence would be true. I think that in the same way, it can be considered part of a speaker's semantic competence to recognize what a possible answer to a question is. This ability is for instance reflected in the fact that speakers immediately notice than none of the following question-answer pairs are well-formed.

(1) a. Q: Is John running?
        A: *Mary.

   b. Q: Who is John talking to?
       A: *Yes.

   c. Q: Where does John live?
       A: *4 p.m.

Intuitively, the reason that none of the dialogues in (1) would be accepted is that the answer is of the wrong 'type' to provide an answer to the preceding question, although it might be a perfectly good answer to another of the questions in (1).

Instead of lettting a question denote all possible answers to it, Karttunen restricts the denotation of a question to the set of propositions expressed by *true* answers to it. Karttunen's reason for limiting the range of the denotation to the set of true answers is that there is a difference in entailments between embedded questions and embedded declaratives. Consider the pair in (2).

(2) a. John told Mary that Bill and Sue passed the test.
    b. John told Mary who passed the test.

(Karttunen, 1977: (19))

THE INTERPRETATION OF QUESTIONS   153

The verb *tell* with a *that* complement as in (2a) does not entail that what is told is true. John might have told Mary a lie, or he might have a false belief about who passed the test. (2b) on the other hand seems to require that John told Mary something true. Thus it appears that only the true answers to the embedded question are relevant when we compose the meaning of the higher VP. The same fact seems to be responsible for the vapid inference in (3)[1].

(3)   John knows who passed the test.
        Bill passed the test.
        ─────────────────────────────
        John knows that Bill passed the test.

Furthermore, Karttunen argues, the semantics for non-propositional-attitude question embedding verbs like *depend on* and *determine* is simplified if we only consider true answers. I find Karttunen's reasons good and in the following analysis I will adopt his proposal and let (indirect) questions 'denote the set of true propositions that jointly constitute a true and complete answer to the question' (Karttunen, 1977, p. 10). Question embedding verbs like *wonder*, *remember*, and *investigate* will be understood to denote relations between individual concepts and properties of propositions. In most of the discussion, however, we will disregard intensions and simply talk about relations between individuals and sets of propositions. To take a simple example, we will say that the meaning of (4)

(4)   Mary wonders if John is reading

can be paraphrased roughly in the following way: Mary stands in the wonder-relation to the set of propositions which contain either the proposition that John is reading or the proposition that John isn't reading, whichever is true in the context of the question. On Karttunen's approach, (4) will translate into a formula of intensional logic as in (5).

(5)   **wonder**$'(\hat{\ }m, \hat{p}[\check{\ }p \wedge p = \hat{\ }\mathbf{read}'_*(j) \vee p = \hat{\ }\neg\mathbf{read}'_*(j)])$

Similarly, a sentence with an embedded constituent question, as in (6),

(6)   Mary doesn't know which book John is reading.

can be paraphrased as: Mary does not stand in the know-relation to the set of true propositions of the form 'John is reading x' where x is a book. The translation would be as in (7).

(7)   ¬**know**′(^m, $\hat{p}$ ∃x[**book**′(x) ∧ ˇp ∧ p = ^**read**′∗(j, ˇx)])

The use of a *which* question often seems to presuppose that there is only one true answer to the question and one might ask whether this should not somehow be expressed in the representation of the meaning of the question. However, I think there are good reasons to consider this as an implicature associated with the word *which* rather than as part of the meaning of the question. If we consider multiple *which* questions, the uniqueness presuppositions seem to disappear. Take a question like (8), uttered by a bartender who has mixed up his order slips.

(8)   Which table ordered which wine?

It seems clear that the bartender would not be satisfied if the waiter only replied *Table A ordered the Ridge Zinfandel*. Rather what he is asking for is a complete match of tables and wine orders. I don't think that a multiple question implies that there is a unique mapping involved, contrary to what has sometimes been proposed (Higginbotham and May, 1980; Belnap, 1982). To me, (8) does not exclude that some table ordered more than one kind of wine.

In the case of *who* questions, no expectation of a singular answer seems to arise. A person who asks a question like (9),

(9)   Who is coming to dinner?

would not be satisfied with *John* as an answer, if in fact both John and Mary are coming to dinner. This brings us to the issue of the completeness of answers. Notice that since Karttunen takes the meaning of the question to be the set of propositions that *jointly* constitute a complete and true answer to it, he will in fact not accept a partial answer like *John is coming to dinner* in the situation described above, but only an exhaustive list of people who are coming. However, there are other types of questions where a partial answer seems to be just what the questioner is asking for. For instance, a question like (10)

(10)   Where can I find an open gas station?

doesn't seem to be a request for an exhaustive list of places where one can buy gas. Rather, it suffices to mention one place where there is an open gas station. Belnap (1982) thinks that Karttunen is wrong in identifying the meaning of a question with the set of true answers, thus always requiring an exhaustive, and therefore unique, answer. Belnap, following Bennett (1979), takes questions to have multiple full and complete true answers. Each proposition in the set denoted by the question would on Belnap's account count as a complete answer. It seems to me that whether or not a question can be understood as requiring an exhaustive answer depends entirely on the motives behind the question. A person asking a question like (11),

(11)   Where can you buy the New York Times?

will probably often be satisfied by an answer like *at the liquor store on Main Street*. But if the inquirer is really interested in finding out something about the efficiency of the New York Times distribution, then he will want a complete list of the outlets in the relevant area. Which way a question is taken is thus largely determined by the context and need not be specified in the semantics. For this reason, I will keep to Karttunen's notion of what the meaning of a question is, and refer to the pragmatics of asking to explain why people very often expect a partial answer rather than the complete answer[2].

So far we have only given a first indication of what the meaning of an indirect question would be (see (5) and (7)), but what about direct questions? Without going into any details, we will assume that when a speaker asks a question, he thereby expresses that he stands in some 'desire-to-know' relation to the set of propositions denoted by the true answers to the question. Thus we can use in principle the same semantics for direct and indirect questions, which seems intuitively correct. We won't say anything more specific about other aspects of direct question speech acts but leave that for further development, for instance along the lines outlined within the framework of Situation Semantics (cf. Barwise, 1984). For convenience, we will represent the contribution of the direct question speech act by a constant, '?', in the representation of the meaning. One can think of '?' as an abbreviation for something like 'I wonder'.

There are a few alternatives to the slightly disguised performative approach to direct questions that we are taking here. For instance, Hausser (1978) and Hausser and Zaefferer (1979) take pairs of direct questions and their short (non-redundant) answers as basic. The representation of a short answer will contain a context variable whose type is specified by the question. The meaning of the question-answer pair is got by taking the short answer, lambda abstracting over the context variable, and applying it to the question. This approach will work for question-answer pairs like in (12), where the answer denotes an individual. However, it will not work for dialogues like in (13), where the answer consists of an expression that is bound by a quantifier in the question.

(12)   Q: Who came?
       A: John.

(13)   Q: Who did every man vote for?
       A: Himself.

If we try to correlate question-answer pairs with anaphoric relations using lambda conversion, we either do not get the correct readings or violate the principles of lambda conversion, as discussed in Chapter II[3]. Another drawback with this approach which Hirschbühler (1978) points out is that nominal questions and adverbial questions will be of different semantic types. Consequently, question embedding verbs must belong to several categories simultaneously. Multiple questions with different number of interrogative constituents will also be of distinct semantic types. It thus becomes a problem how to account for conjoined questions, both simple conjoined nominal and adverbial questions and conjoined multiple questions.

1.1. Karttunen's Treatment of Constituent Questions

On Karttunen's approach, constituent questions are derived by way of a quantification rule, quite similar to the rules of wide scope quantification in PTQ[4]. Karttunen first defines some new basic categories, P_{WH} for WH phrases, P_Q for subordinate questions, and P_{QE} for the category of question embedding verbs. In order to derive a constituent question, we first build up a sentence with a subscripted pronoun and then quantify in a WH phrase. The syntactic part of the quantification rule substitutes the WH phrase for the first occurrence of PRO_n and moves it to the front of the sentence. A short analysis tree is given in (14).

(14)   which girl John likes, Q, WHQ_3

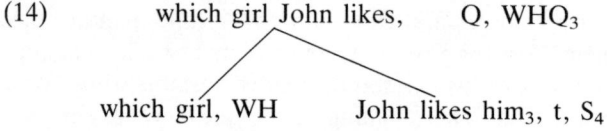

which girl, WH   John likes him_3, t, S_4

The semantic part of the WH quantification rule, WHQ, syncategorematically turns the result into a set of true propositions. The meaning of the tree rooted in Q in (14) will thus be as in (15).

(15) $\lambda p\ \exists x[\mathbf{girl}'(x) \land\ ˇp \land p =\ ˆ\mathbf{like}'_*(j,\ ˇx)]$

Just as Montague's quantification rules, the WH quantification rule makes use of subscripted pronouns in the syntax. We argued earlier against using subscripted pronouns since we are trying to avoid introducing abstract elements into the syntax, and in the following sections we will outline an alternative to Karttunen's quantification procedure. A further problem with the syntactic part of the rule is that in order to get agreement between the interrogative phrase and the syntactic environment of the 'gap', it seems that we need as many distinct sets of subscripted pronouns as there are feature constellations which are reflected by agreement in the syntax.

1.2. Some Problems for Karttunen's Approach

On Karttunen's approach, an interrogative phrase like *who*, *what*, or *which CN* gets essentially the same interpretation as the corresponding indefinite NP, *someone*, *something*, or *some CN* and it is the quantifying rule that contributes the question interpretation. This approach will be appropriate when the interrogative constituent in some sense can be interpreted 'as it stands'. When a simple question like (16) is uttered in a context,

(16)   Which girl did John invite to the party?

which girl is usually assumed to range over some more or less contextually determined set of girls. However, when the CN part of the interrogative quantifier contains a bound variable, as in (17), we cannot establish the range of the quantifier on the basis of its meaning only.

(17)   Which picture of *herself* does Mary like best?

In the case of (17) we cannot figure out which the relevant set of pictures are until we have determined who is the antecedent for the reflexive pronoun *herself*. That is, the meaning of the interrogative quantifier *which picture of herself* is in some sense dependent on what the value of *herself* turns out to be. Thus it won't be possible to quantify in the meaning of the interrogative phrase since this meaning cannot be established independently of the interpretation of the sentence into which it is supposed to be quantified.

The constituent questions we have looked at so far have been of the kind where it is appropriate to give an answer which picks out an individual. A suitable answer to (16) would be *Julie*, provided that John did invite Julie to the party. Another way of answering the question would be to say *her* or *that girl*, pointing to Julie. What these ways of answering have in common is that they supply an *individual*. However, there are other types of questions which don't seem to be asking for specific individuals, at least not on all their interpretations, and this raises a further problem for Karttunen's approach. Consider the question in (18) which has two types of plausible answers.

(18) Q: Who does every Englishman admire most?
      A: a. The Queen.
          b. His mother.

As shown by the answers, (18) can be understood either as a question about one specific individual, in which case an answer like (18a) will be appropriate, or it can be answered as in (18b), in which case the answer doesn't denote any particular individual, but rather picks out a different individual for each Englishman. Karttunen's approach will only get us one reading, the one where *Queen Elizabeth II* is a good answer. The representation of the meaning of the question on that reading will be as in (19).

(19) "?" $\hat{p}\, \exists x[\textbf{person}'(x) \wedge {\check{}}p \wedge p = {\hat{}}\, \forall y[\textbf{Englishman}'(y) \rightarrow \textbf{admire}'_*({\check{}}y, {\check{}}x)]]$

That is, the question denotes the set of true propositions of the form 'for all y, if y is an Englishman, then y admires x' where x is a person. The reason that we only get this reading for the question in (13) is that we are quantifying the interpretation of the interrogative phrase into the sentence. The existential quantifier in the interpretation of *who* will thus take wider scope than the universal quantifier in the sentence. One way to get the other reading, the one where the value of *who* varies with the choice of Englishman, would be to quantify the interpretation of *every Englishman* into the question. However, it is a problematic issue how to quantify into questions, and we will devote the next section to a discussion of some of the problems that arise.

2. QUANTIFYING INTO QUESTIONS

In his 1977 article, Karttunen assumed that quantification could not be extended to apply into questions for semantic reasons (cf. Karttunen, 1977, p. 31). If we were to quantify in *every Englishman* by a routine adjustment of the normal quantification rules we would get a formula like in (20).

(20) $\lambda p \, \forall y[\textbf{Englishman}'(y) \rightarrow \exists x[\textbf{person}'(x) \wedge \check{}p \wedge p =\,\hat{}\textbf{admire}'_*(\check{}y, \check{}x)]]$

But (20) would give wrong results for any situation where y is not an Englishman. There would be no problem to get the distributive reading for (18), the one where *every Englishman loves his mother* is a possible answer, if the question was embedded in a sentence, as in (21). Then we could simply quantify *every Englishman* into the matrix sentence. The reading we would get would be the one in (22), paraphrasable as 'for each Englishman, y, Mary wonders who y admires'.

(21) Mary wonders who every Englishman admires.

(22) $\forall y[\textbf{Englishman}'(y) \rightarrow \textbf{wonder}'(\hat{}\text{m}, \hat{p} \, \exists x[\textbf{person}'(x) \wedge \check{}p \wedge p =\,\hat{}\textbf{admire}'_*(\check{}y, \check{}x)])]$

Later we will take up the issue whether (21) doesn't also have a reading on which *every Engishman* has narrow scope with respect to *wonder*, while still having wide scope with respect to *who*. For now, we note that if we were to extend this approach to direct questions, we would have to adopt some version of the performative analysis (cf. Ross, 1970). By analyzing direct questions as always embedded inside a declarative sentence like *I wonder*, we could presumably account for questions where a quantifier inside appears to have wide scope over the question. This means that in the case of a question like *Who does every Englishman admire?*, we would have not only one direct question, but rather a set of direct questions, one for each Englishman. This is sometimes taken as an undesirable consequence. From the point of view of linking syntax and semantics together, it is a clear disadvantage to have to assume a stage of embedding in the syntax for which there is no overt evidence. But a more conclusive argument against the performative hypothesis is that it is incapable of handling all cases. There are sentences which genuinely appear to require quantificaton into questions, and which cannot be got around by postulating a higher performative sentence. For these cases, we need a different approach, and it is to be hoped that this approach can be extended to the cases that seemed to require abstract performative predicates as well.

One example that clearly illustrated the need for something besides quantifying into declarative sentences is given in (23)[5].

(23) The average grade depends on what grade each student gets.

On the most plausible reading of this sentence, *each student* has wider scope than *what grade*, i.e. we are interested in a situation where the students get different grades. However, we cannot quantify *every student* into the whole declarative sentence, because that way we would assert for *each student* that the average grade depends on what grade *he* gets, which obviously is not what (23) means. Rather *each student* has narrow scope with respect to *depend on*, but wide scope with respect to *what grade*. The problem is how to express this reading.

2.1. Karttunen and Peters' Proposal

In Karttunen and Peters (1980), a solution to this problem is suggested, which involves quantifying-in the dual of the quantifier that takes wide scope. The effect of this quantifying-in procedure can be summarized as in (24)

(24) If α is an NP which translates into α' and β is a Q (indirect question) which translates into β' with a free occurrence of pro$_i$, then the result of quantifying α into β is a Q which translates into $\lambda p[\neg \alpha'(\hat{x}_i \neg[\beta'(p)])]$.

Let us illustrate how this rule works by applying it to the indirect question embedded in (18). Taking *each student* as α and *what grade he$_0$ gets* as β, the result will be equivalent to the formula in (25).

(25) $\lambda p\, \exists x\, \exists y[\mathbf{student'}(x) \wedge \mathbf{grade'}(y) \wedge \check{}p \wedge p = \hat{}\mathbf{get'_*}(\check{}x, \check{}y)]$

According to (25), the indirect question would denote the set of true propositions of the form '*x* gets *y*' where *x* is a student and *y* is a grade. Note that the universal quantifier in the interpretation of *each student* has disappeared and that we now have two existential quantifiers inside the specification of the set of propositions. Since we are abstracting over these propositions, we will get as many propositions as there are ways of truthfully pairing students and grades they get. The set of propositions denoted by the indirect question can thus be seen as specified by an exhaustive pairing of students and grades. It turns out that (23) on this reading is indistinguishable in meaning from the sentence in (26).

(26)   The average grade depends on what grade which student gets.

Karttunen and Peters' approach amount to treating questions with wide scope universal quantifiers as if they were multiple questions. But although the treatment of multiple questions which Karttunen (1977) proposes seems quite plausible, it is not clear that it is an appropriate treatment of questions containing quantifiers with wider scope in general. For one thing, treating questions with wide scope quantifiers as multiple questions predicts that the two types of questions should have exactly the same interpretations. In Section 3, we argue that this is not the case. Here we will briefly outline how Karttunen accounts for multiple questions.

On Karttunen's approach a multiple question like (27)

(27)   Which student got what grade?

will involve quantifying the meaning of the 'unmoved' WH phrase, *what grade*, into the meaning of the question *which student got him$_0$*. Since WH phrases involve existential quantifiers on Kartunen's analysis, the quantifying in is straightforward in this case. The result will be as in (28).

(28) $\lambda p \, \exists y \, \exists x [\textbf{grade}'(y) \wedge \textbf{student}'(x) \wedge \check{\ } p \wedge p = \hat{\ } \textbf{get}'_*(\check{\ } x, \check{\ } y)]$

(28) is equivalent to the formula in (25), the one got from using the special NP quantification rule for questions. (28) seems to be an appropriate representation of the meaning of the multiple question in (28), since multiple questions typically get answers that consist of lists of pairs or triples etc., instantiating the interrogative phrases. So a typical answer to *Which student got which grade?* could be something like *John got an A, Bill got a C and Mary got a B*.

The quantification rule in (24) is rather peculiar. The way negations are inserted does not have any independent justification in some other quantification rule. Furthermore, the rule only works for universal quantifiers, i.e. quantifiers which have a natural dual involving existential quantification. It cannot be used to give an existential quantifier wide scope and it would give strange results for negative quantifiers like *no student* and quantifiers containing numerical expressions like *three students*.

2.2. *Belnap's Proposal*

In his article *Questions and Answers in Montague Grammar*, N. Belnap explicitly discusses the need for and problems with quantifying into questions. Belnap builds on an unfinished paper by M. Bennett (Bennett, 1979[6]) in which he discusses examples like (29) which are quite similar in structure to our example (23).

(29)   John wonders where two unicorns live.

Bennett argues that this sentence has three readings, depending on where the quantifier *two unicorns* is interpreted. On the narrow scope reading, John wonders which place is such that two, any two, unicorns live there. On the wide scope reading, there are two unicorns such that John wonders for each of them, where it lives. In addition there is a third, intermediate, reading which doesn't entail the existence of unicorns (narrow scope with respect to *wonder*) nor does it require that the unicorns live in the same place (wide scope with respect to *where*). If we paraphrase the meaning of *wonder* as *want to know*, then we can express the third reading as John wants to know for each of two unicorns, where it lives. It is the third, intermediate reading that requires quantification into questions, Bennett argues. Belnap accepts his arguments and develops a general approach to quantifying into questions. He breaks down the task of the quantifying-in rule into three components, as illustrated in (30). The top line illustrates the components of the rule. The second line applies this format to the example in (29), and the bottom line gives the result, what Belnap calls the 'derived question'.

(30)   QUANTIFIER   COMMON NOUN   OPEN INTERROGATIVE

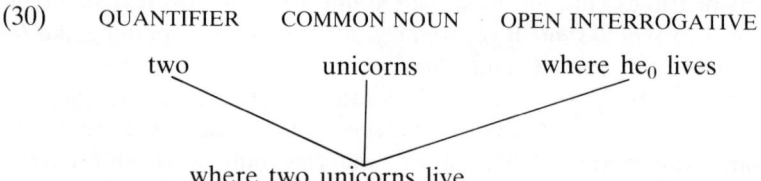

The quantifier slot can contain any quantifier. The CN phrase expresses the restriction on the quantifier. The main idea behind Belnap's proposal is that an answer to the derived question *where two unicorns live* must provide an answer to the open question *where he_0 lives* with respect to *two unicorns*, i.e. for two instantiations of he_0 by *unicorns*. Similarly, the answer to *where each unicorn lives* must tell us for *each unicorn*, where *he* lives. This way, the meaning of the derived question is determined by way of computing the meanings of a set of simple questions, one for each assignment of value to the quantifier phrase and the free variable. Working out the details of this approach requires, as Belnap says, 'a good deal of complication' such as raising the type of denotations to sets of open propositions. I won't go into the details of the solution here, mainly because I believe that there are cases where even this complicated apparatus for quantifying-in will not be sufficient to account for all possible interactions of interrogative and other quantifiers. In the light of this evidence, I will propose another method of approaching these problems which does not make use of a complicated apparatus for quantifying-in. Before developing this approach, I will give a few arguments to the effect that being able to quantify a non-interrogative quantifier into a question does not provide a full solution to the problematic cases.

3. SOME ARGUMENTS AGAINST QUANTIFYING INTO QUESTIONS

3.1. *Relational Questions Without Wide Scope Antecedents*

Let us continue the discussion of questions which can get answers which don't involve any particular individual, as in the answer given in (18b).

(18) Q: Who does every Englishman admire most?
A: b. His mother.

We will call these types of answers *relational* answers, since they essentially pick out individuals which stand in a certain relation to some other individual. The quantifying-in approaches discussed in the previous section provided for a relational reading of *who* by quantifying in *every Englishman* and letting the value of *who* depend on the value of the quantifier phrase. Consider now a slightly different example.

(31)   Who do you expect every Englishman to admire most?

I think *his mother* would count as an appropriate answer even if I only have expectations about Englishmen in general and don't know which individuals are in fact Englishmen. On this reading, it would be false to quantify in *every Englishman* since that would require that I expect certain individuals to admire certain individuals. What (31) illustrates is that we can get relational answers even in cases where the phrase that determines the relational reading (in this case *every Englishman*) has narrow scope with respect to some other scopal element in the sentence (in this case *expect*). If we quantify in *every Englishman* it will necessarily take wider scope than *expect* and we lose the desired reading. We can make the same point with an indefinite NP as in (32).

(32)   Who do you expect an Englishman to admire most?

Even in a situation where I have no particular Englishman in mind, I believe I could truthfully answer *his mother*, where *his* is understood as bound by *an Englishman*. The question in (32) can of course also be understood as a question about a certain Englishman, in which case the NP would have wide scope, i.e. be interpreted de re with respect to *expect*. In order to account for the de dicto interpretation it seems natural to interpret *an Englishman* inside the question. Nevertheless, it appears that it can induce relational answers.

Another example in which the relational reading is forced by an explicit bound pronoun inside an interrogative phrase is the following. At the end of the school year, the art teachers in the school are putting together an exhibition of the students' work. All students have done roughly the same projects and the teachers are discussing which projects are worth displaying. Given that the teachers actually agree on what projects should be represented, a possible question might be:

(33)   Which of *his paintings* did every teacher want *a student* to display?

A possible answer would be something like *his water colors* or *his still lifes*. Both in the interrogative phrase, and in the answer, *his* thus acts as a bound pronoun, bound by *a student*, although different teachers have different students in mind. It appears that the initial interrogative phrase can be interpreted as varying with the students, even though the choice of student is understood to be up to the teacher. In Swedish the bound character of the interrogative phrase is even more evident since this would be a case where a possessive reflexive pronoun would be used. The Swedish counterpart to (33) is given in (34).

THE INTERPRETATION OF QUESTIONS 165

(34) Vilka av **sina** målningar ville varje lärare att **en elev** skulle
         [REFL]
      ställa ut?

In the examples in (31)–(33), the interpretation of the interrogative phrase is taken to vary with the interpretation of some NP inside the sentence. However, as we already pointed out, these NPs can also be given wide scope over the entire question, since a NP can usually take wider scope than its surface position although, as we have seen, relational readings are possible even in cases when the antecedent NP does not take wide scope. An even more convincing example for the argument I am making here would be a sentence where the scope of the antecedent of a pronoun in an interrogative phrase can be independently determined. This would be the case if the antecedent was itself a moved WH phrase. We argued in Chapter III that WH phrases in Comp must be interpreted as having scope according to their surface position. Since the construction of such an example involves two extractions, we will discuss an example from Swedish. Suppose the art teacher asks the students in the class to rank their own paintings according to how good they think they are. During a discussion in the common room of the effects of peer pressure on the students' judgments, someone may ask the art teacher:

(35) [Vilka av **sina**   målningar]$_j$ var det förvånansvärt
       which of his-own paintings   was it   surprising

      [$\bar{s}$[Comp[**hur många elever**]$_i$ som] [___$_i$
                how many students that $_S$

      inte tyckte om ___$_j$?]]
      didn't like

The art teacher may reply **sina nakenstudier** (*his nudes*). In this case the scope of the antecedent for the bound pronoun **sina**, **hur många elever**, is determined by its surface position in Comp where it introduces the embedded question.

We can actually construct a similar example for English, using multiple questions with an unmoved WH phrase rather than an extraction out of a question. We recall from Chapter III that unmoved WH phrases in embedded questions can take scope either at the level of the embedding question or at the level of the matrix question, in which case a typical answer consists of a list of pairs. If we can get the list of pairs reading for a multiple question, where the unmoved WH phrase contains a pronoun, bound by a moved WH phrase in an intermediate Comp, then this provides further illustration of the same fact. It turns out that the list of pairs reading is indeed possible in these cases, as illustrated in (36).

(36) Q: Who remembers *which students* didn't like which of *their* paintings?

     A: a. John does.

         b. John remembers *which students* didn't like their nudes and Mary remembers *which students* didn't like *their* surrealistic paintings.

3.2. Negative Antecedents

Relational answers frequently occur when the question contains a negative quantifier. In fact, sometimes a relational answer appears to be the only possible answer. Consider a situation in which all men are married and dislike their mother-in-laws, but like their brother's mother-in-law. Suppose that all men have at least one brother and that all women have at least one son-in-law. Then every woman is liked by at least one man. Nevertheless, it seems that we can very well ask *Which woman does no man like?* and accept *his mother-in-law* as a true answer. In this case, there is no way of answering the question by supplying a singular individual, but there may be several ways of relating men and women, and a relational answer picks out one of these ways.

Quantifying into questions with negative quantifiers raises special problems. Consider the sentence in (37)

(37)   John wonders what no married man should forget.

What John probably wants to know is a proposition of the form *no married man should forget his wife's birthday*. If we were to quantify in *no married man* into the sentence, we would get something equivalent to the formula in (38).

(38) $\forall x[\textbf{married-man}'(x) \rightarrow \neg \textbf{wonder}'(\hat{\ }j, \hat{p}\ \exists y[\textbf{thing}'(y) \wedge \ ^{\vee}p \wedge p =$
     $= \ \hat{\ }\textbf{forget}'_{*}(^{\vee}x,\ ^{\vee}y)])]$

(38) says that for all married men, x, it is not the case that John wonders what x should forget, obviously not a plausible meaning for (37). If we quantified *no married man* directly into the question, using Karttunen and Peters' formula in (24), the result would fail to characterize the set of proportions denoted by the question, since that set could contain any false proposition. On Belnap's approach, the answer to the embedded question in (37) would be an answer that for *no married man* tells you what *he* should forget, which also doesn't seem to be the desired reading. Rather, what we want is a way of representing the fact that the interpretation of *what* may vary with the interpretation of *no married man*, without this phrase taking scope outside the question. Anticipating our analysis somewhat, what we will propose as the interpretation of an interrogative phrase like *what* is a function from individuals to individuals. We can think of *what* as quantifying over procedures for correlating the interpretation of the question constituent with the interpretation of one or more quantifier phrases in the sentence. Applied to the case of (37), what John then wants to know is presumably some procedure which will tell him for any man, what that man shouldn't forget.

3.3. Questions Into Opaque Contexts

As we mentioned briefly at the end of the previous paragraph, our proposal for the treatment of questions will involve quantifying over functions. The point of the following argument is that quantifying over functions permits us to express readings which cannot be expressed by taking just the extension of the function, i.e. a set of ordered pairs[7]. We will illustrate this point by the fact that the sentence in (39) does not strike us as being inconsistent.

(39)   John knows which woman every Englishman admires most, namely his mother, but he doesn't know who the women in question are.

Similarly, a question like in (40)

(40)   Which book did John believe every author would read from?

has a reading on which it is appropriate to answer *his latest book* or *his best selling book*. This reading does not necessarily imply that John knows which every author's latest book is, nor does it attribute to him direct acquaintance with every author. On Karttunen and Peters' approach, (40) would come out with the meaning in (41).

(41) "?" $\hat{p}\ \exists x\ \exists y[\textbf{author}'(x) \wedge \textbf{book}'(y) \wedge \check{\ }p \wedge p =$
  $= \hat{\ }\textbf{believe}'(\hat{\ }j,\ \hat{\ }\textbf{read-from}'_*(\check{\ }x,\ \check{\ }y))]$

According to (41), the object of John's belief are singular propositions involving individuals. John has a set of beliefs about particular authors and particular books. But on the de dicto interpretation of (40), John can believe that *every author read from his latest book* without knowing who the authors are or which books they have written. It turns out that this reading cannot be expressed in the Karttunen and Peters proposal, nor in Belnap's proposal, since both these approaches export the quantifier outside the proposition. The way we propose to account for this reading is by interpreting *every author* inside the domain of John's beliefs and by interpreting *which book* as a function-in-intension from individuals to books. Let W be such a function. Then the de dicto reading of (40) can be expressed as in (42).

(42) "?" $\hat{p}\ \exists W[\ \forall x[\textbf{book}'W(x)] \wedge \check{\ }p \wedge p =$
  $= \hat{\ }\textbf{believe}'(\hat{\ }j,\ \hat{\ }\ \forall x[\textbf{author}'(x) \to \textbf{read-from}'_*(\check{\ }x,\ \check{\ }W(x))])]$

The meaning of the question in (40) is thus taken to be the set of true propositions of the form 'John believes that if x is an author, then x reads from $W(x)$' where W is a function from individuals to books. On this interpretation, John may believe that whoever is an author reads from whatever book happens to be that author's latest book, without having any particular beliefs about author-book pairs.

3.4. Summary

In this section, we have looked at three types of questions where quantifying-in approaches fail to account for all available interpretations. The examples involve quantifiers with narrow scope of fixed scope, and negative quantifiers. We also considered questions into propositional attitude contexts which show that a representation of the meaning of a quantified question in terms of a list of ordered pairs of individuals is not sufficient. In the light of this evidence, we will develop a different approach to questions, one which does not rely on quantifying-in to get the relational readings.

4. A RELATIONAL APPROACH TO INTERROGATIVE QUANTIFIERS

One essential feature of our analysis is that we interpret interrogative phrases as potentially relational. This means that the interpretation of a word like *who* may, but need not, depend on the interpretation of some other NP in the sentence. We will capture this formally by letting the interpretation of a WH gap contain a free variable, W, over functions from individuals to individuals and letting the interpretation of the interrogative phrase include a quantifier over such functions. The intuition behind this is that interrogative phrases often do not pick out particular individuals, but rather individuals that stand in certain relations to other individuals. In this respect, interrogative phrases act in a way that is very similar to certain special uses of personal pronouns, and in the next section we will investigate these similarities a bit more closely.

4.1. Similarities Between Pronouns and Interrogatives

It is customary to talk about two distinct uses of personal pronouns, the *deictic* use and the *bound variable* use (cf. Partee, 1978). The deictic use of a pronoun is illustrated in the discourse in (43) and in the dialogue in (44).

(43)   *John* came in. *He* looked upset.

(44)   Q: Where is *John*?
A: *He* is in the kitchen.

On this use, the pronoun is taken to refer to a specific individual in the situation; which individual this is is often assumed to be specified by the function that assigns values to free individual variables. A salient reading for (43) is one where *he* picks out the same individual as *John*, and similarly in (44). The bound use of pronouns is illustrated in (45).

(45)   *Every guest* hoped *he* wouldn't be late.

The reading we have in mind here is the one where *he* doesn't refer to any specific individual, but where its interpretation varies with the interpretation of the antecedent phrase *every guest*. On this reading, what every guest hopes is that he himself won't be late. Just like deictic pronouns, bound pronouns are usually translated into expressions with free individual variables, e.g. in PTQ as $\lambda PP\{x_0\}$, which denotes the set of properties that the individual picked out by x_0 has. The bound reading then obtains when the individual variable is bound by a quantifier. Since quantifier scope does not extend across sentences or across speakers, we have an explanation why bound pronouns don't normally occur in discourses or dialogues. The * in the following examples means ungrammatical on the reading where the pronoun is bound by the italicized NP.

(46)   *Every guest* was late. **He* apologized.

(47)   Q: Why was *every guest* late?
       A: **He* missed the exit from the freeway.

In addition to these two uses of pronouns, there are some cases where pronouns seem to be neither straightforward deictic pronouns nor bound individual variables. A famous example is Karttunen's paycheck sentence.

(48)   The man who gave his paycheck to his wife was wiser than the man who gave *it* to his mistress.

                                                    (Karttunen, 1969)

On the most natural reading of this sentence, *it* is not understood as a freely referring pronoun, nor is it bound directly by any NP in the sentence. Rather, *it* seems to be short for the full NP *his paycheck*, except that *his* would now refer back to the second man. In his paper 'The Interpretation of Pronouns', R. Cooper discusses this type of pronouns, together with a variety of other cases. Actually, Cooper does not discuss the example in (48) but a similar example which does not involve a comparative construction. Cooper's example consists of the discourse in (49).

(49)   John gave his paycheck to his mistress.
       Everybody else put *it* in the bank.

(Cooper (1979: (48)))

It appears that a plausible reading for *it* in this context is again *his paycheck*, where *his* is now bound by *everybody else*. Cooper argues convincingly against a rule of discourse pronominalization. Instead he suggests that pronouns, in addition to their normal translation, should be translated into expressions containing a free property variable. The translation schema Cooper proposes is given in (50).

(50) $\lambda P \exists x \forall y[[\check{}\Pi](y) \leftrightarrow y = x] \wedge P\{x\}$
       where Π is a property-denoting
       expression containing only free
       variables and parentheses.

(cf. Cooper (1979): (53))

(50) makes the interpretation of a pronoun similar to Russell's treatment of definite descriptions. The pronoun picks out the unique entity that has a certain property. It is the context that determines what the relevant restricting property is. Π may be composed by free relational variables and free individual variables. The point is that Π allows us to have as many free individual variables as we might need in the translation of the pronoun, which may get bound by quantifiers in the sentence. On Cooper's approach, the meaning of the second sentence in (49) will be as in (51).

(51) $\forall u[\mathbf{person}'(u) \wedge \neg[u = u_0 \rightarrow \exists x \forall y[\check{}S_0(u)](y) \leftrightarrow y = x] \wedge$
       $\mathbf{put}'(\hat{}\mathbf{in\text{-}the\text{-}bank}')_*(u, \check{}x)]$

Let the value assignment function assign John to u_0, and let S_0 be a free variable over functions from individuals into properties. Its value will have to be supplied by the context. One plausible value for $S_0(u)$, given the discourse context in (49), will be the property of being u's paycheck. This way we get the reading where for every person u, distinct from John, there is a unique x that bears relation S_0 to u, and u put x in the bank.

Cooper suggests extending this approach also to occurrences of pronouns in so-called donkey sentences, as in (52), which on his approach comes out as having the meaning represented in (53).

(52)　　Every man who owns a donkey beats it.

(53)　　$\forall u[\mathbf{man}'(u) \wedge \exists v[\mathbf{donkey}'(v) \wedge \mathbf{own}'_*(u, v)] \rightarrow \exists x[\forall y[[`S_1(u)][y) \leftrightarrow y = x] \wedge \mathbf{beat}'_*(u, `x)]]$

If u is a man, and there is a donkey that u owns, then there is a unique x that bears relations S_1 to u, and u beats x. According to some contexts, $S_1(u)$ will denote the property of being the donkey u owns. In other contexts, $S_1(u)$ may pick out a totally unrelated property, and we get a non-anaphoric reading for *it*. Having a free relational variable in the translation of the pronoun gives us a way of getting the apparently bound reading for *it* without giving *a donkey* wide scope or treating it as a hidden universal and quantifying over all men and donkeys[8]. The essential feature of Cooper's proposal is to let pronouns denote entities that stand in a certain relation to other entities, where the exact nature of this relation is not specified by the sentence but is left open to be supplied by the context. The property of picking out individuals that stand in some relation to other individuals is the same property that we appealed to in the relational interpretation of interrogatives. If it is the case that ordinary pronouns occurring in sentences can be interpreted relationally, then it should not come as a surprise that interrogative phrases which are taken to be related to a position inside the sentence – be it by movement, slashed categories, or dotted lines – can get the same kind of interpretation. After all, grammars traditionally use the term *interrogative pronoun* for lexical WH phrases. What we are emphasizing here is that interrogative pronouns behave like ordinary pronouns in the ways they can be interpreted.

One quick way to illustrate the similarities between pronouns and interrogatives would be to recast Cooper's examples in the form of questions to see if they permit relational interpretations.

(54)　　　　John used his shirt to wipe his hands on.
　　　　　　Q: What did everyone else use?
　　　　　　A: *His* handkerchief.

(55)　　　　Q: Who does every man who has both a son and a daughter cherish most?

A: *His* daughter/The daughter/Her.

It turns out that both in the discourse context in (54) and in the 'donkey question' in (55) it is possible to interpret the questions relationally, as evidenced by the answers.

We saw in (50) that Cooper's translation for pronouns embeds the free relational variable inside a definite description, thus guaranteeing that the relation is functional, i.e. that there is a unique individual that stands in the appropriate relation. The proposal we will present here avoids the explicit quantification involved in a Russellian definite description. Instead our proposal captures the essential relational character of the pronoun by using variables over functions directly[9]. I think the two approaches can be shown to be equivalent in all relevant respects. For the purpose of illustration, we will show how the meaning of a donkey sentence like (52) will come out on our approach.

(56) $\forall x[\mathbf{man}'(x) \wedge \exists y[\mathbf{donkey}'(y) \wedge \mathbf{own}'_*(\check{}x, \check{}y)] \rightarrow \mathbf{beat}'_*(\check{}x, \check{}[W_0(x)])]$

W_0 in (56) is a free variable over functions from individuals to individuals. A plausible value for W_0 in this context would be a function which for any person u, gives you a donkey that u owns. The representation of the donkey question in (55) will be something like in (57).

(57) "?" $\hat{p} \exists W[\forall x[\mathbf{person}'(W(x))] \wedge \check{}p \wedge p = \hat{}\forall x[\mathbf{man}'(x) \wedge \exists y \exists x_0[\mathbf{son\text{-}of\text{-}}x'(y) \wedge \mathbf{daughter\text{-}of\text{-}}x'(x_0)] \rightarrow \mathbf{cherish}'_*(\check{}x, \check{}[W(x)])]]$

(57) denotes the set of properties of the form 'all x who have a son and a daughter cherish $W(x)$', where W is a function from individuals into persons.

To summarize briefly, we assume that the interpretation of pronouns, both personal and interrogative pronouns, will require an expression with a free relational variable. The main difference between the two types of pronouns is that in the case of personal pronouns, the relational variable remains free and gets its value from the context. In the case of interrogative pronouns, we quantify over the relational variable in the characterization of the set of true answers to the question. What the plausible values for W are, however, will still largely be a matter of the context[10].

4.2. The W Function

In this section we will present the main features of our relational approach to questions. We will first show how simple cases are handled and then show how the analysis generalizes to more complex questions. We will spell out our analysis within the general framework of Montague grammar, using the intensional logic of PTQ as a convenient way of representing the meanings of expressions of the language. However, the fact that we have chosen this particular formalism to express our proposal in is not an important issue. What is important is that the interpretation procedures for the language are such that they allow us to express the dependencies between the meanings of various expressions in a sentence, and this can presumably be done in a number of ways. One reason for working out this solution in some detail is of course that this enables us to evaluate the consequences of our assumptions and to say something reasonably explicit about the interaction between this phenomenon and other syntactic and semantic facts of the language, e.g. the effect of dislocation on scope, coreference and binding. How the general idea argued for here can be expressed for instance in the framework of Situation Semantics seems to be a promising area for research (cf. Engdahl, 1984b).

Let us return to an example discussed briefly in Section 3.3.

(40)   Which book did John believe every author would read from?

We said earlier that on the de dicto interpretation of this question, where *his latest book* would be a possible true answer, John does not have any beliefs about particular authors or particular books. Rather, what John believes appears to be that the authors did not choose books at random to read from, but that every author chose a book that was related to him in some more or less systematic fashion. We can represent this meaning on our approach because we don't quantify directly over individuals but over functions-in-intension from individuals to individuals. This enables us to characterize the set of true answers without necessarily giving NPs inside the question wide scope in the case of relational readings. We achieve this by letting the interpretation of a WH gap be essentially like the interpretation of a pronoun with a free relational variable. We will illustrate the interpretation procedure with an example. Suppose the syntactic rules admit the tree in (58).

THE INTERPRETATION OF QUESTIONS 175

(58)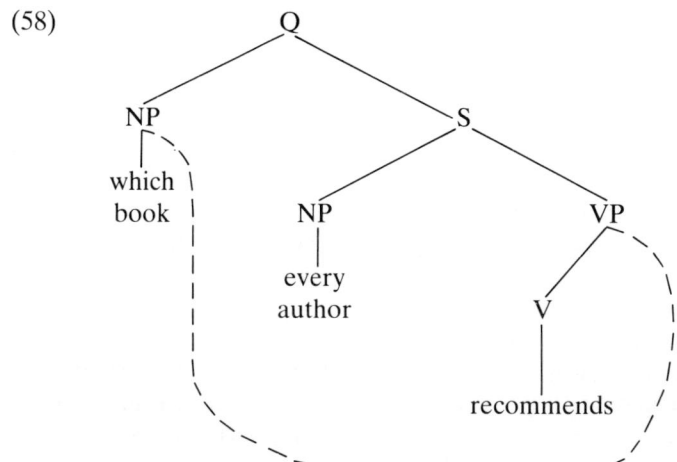

According to the interpretation procedures for linked trees introduced in Chapter II, we must take into account the interpretation of the link child when we calculate the interpretation of a link parent. In this case, the interpretation of the link child is the interpretation of *which book*, i.e. an interrogative quantifier. Since the meaning of an interrogative quantifier cannot interact with the meaning of other constituents until we get a proposition type meaning, the quantifier is obligatorily stored and the pronoun meaning enters into the composition of the VP meaning (see Chapter III, Section 3). We abbreviate the meaning of an interrogative quantifier schematically as $[WH]_i$. (The actual meaning will be given below in (59).) The meaning of the NP *which book* will then consist of the ordered pair

$$\langle \lambda PP\{W_3(x_5)\}, [WH]_3 \rangle$$

The first member of this pair is a pronoun meaning, i.e. a complex expression of NP type with a free W variable. This meaning enters into the composition of the meaning of the tree. The second member is a stored interrogative quantifier. The index on the stored quantifier encodes which free W variable is being used in the pronoun meaning. The pronoun meaning also contains a free individual variable, x_5, which is open to binding by any quantifier in the sentence, for instance *every author*. The representation of the meaning of the constituent rooted in S will be:

[$_S$ every author $\langle\ \forall x[\textbf{author}'(x) \to$
    recommends] $\textbf{recommend}'_*(\check{\ }x,\ \check{\ }W_3(x))],\ [WH]_3\rangle$

At the Q level, we apply the question interpretation rule which quantifies in the quantifier corresponding to *which book*. We should now spell out what this quantifier is and how it is constructed on the basis of the meaning of *which* and the meaning of the CN phrase *book*. The CN phrase acts as a restriction on the interrogative quantifier. In particular, it determines some properties of the value of the W function. In this case we know that the value of W must be a book. We express this restriction by a closure operation on the CN meaning, closing off the arguments of W; $\lambda x[\textbf{book}'(W(x))]$. We then quantify over W and in order for the resulting meaning to be of the appropriate type for a quantifier, i.e. denoting a set of sets, we abstract over the properties of W. Let $\mathscr{W}$ be a variable over properties of W. Then the quantifier corresponding to *which book* will be as in (59) where i represents the index of the free W used in the non-stored part of the meaning.

(59) $[\lambda \mathscr{W}\ \exists W[\ \forall x[\textbf{book}'(W(x))] \land \mathscr{W}\{W\}]]_i$

The quantification rule for questions applies the quantifier to the result of abstracting over the indexed W variable in the translation of the sentence. Schematically, we can represent the question formation rule as in (60).

(60)   WH Quantification
    In a structure Q $\to$ XP   S, if $\langle \alpha, \sigma_0, [WH]_i, \sigma_1 \rangle \in$ m(S) then $\langle \lambda p[[WH]_i(\hat{W}_i[\check{\ }p \land p = \hat{\ }S'])], \sigma_0, \sigma_1 \rangle \in$ m(Q).

    α is an expression in IL.
    σ is a sequence of elements in store.

When we apply the rule in (60) to our example in (58), we will get the formula in (61) reduces accordingly.

(61) $\lambda p[\lambda \mathscr{W}\ \exists W[\ \forall x[\textbf{book}'(W(x))] \land \mathscr{W}\{W\}](\hat{W}_3[\check{\ }p \land p =$
    $= \hat{\ }\ \forall x[\textbf{author}'(x) \to \textbf{recommend}'_*(\check{\ }x,\ \check{\ }W_3(x))]])]$ reduces to
    $\lambda p[\ \exists W[\ \forall x[\textbf{book}'(W(x))] \land \check{\ }p \land p =$
    $= \hat{\ }\ \forall x[\textbf{author}'(x) \to \textbf{recommend}'_*(\check{\ }x,\ \check{\ }W(x))]]]$

(61) denotes the set of propositions of the form 'if x is an author, then x

recommends $W(x)$', where W is a function from individuals to books.

In this question, and actually in all examples discussed so far, the interpretation of the interrogative phrase was understood to vary with the interpretation of one other quantifier in the sentence. The interpretation thus involved W functions from individuals to individuals, i.e. of type $\langle e, e \rangle$. But we need to generalize the W functions in order to account both for cases where the interpretation doesn't vary at all, i.e. where the interpretation does not depend on any other NP, and for cases where the interpretation depends on more than one NP in the sentence. The first case is illustrated by the dialogue in (62).

(62)   Q: Which boy won?
       A: John.

In this situation, a true answer amounts to naming one particular individual. The second case can be illustrated by the following dialogue:

(63)   Q: What does *every father* tell **his children** never to forget?
       A: How *he* has sacrificed himself for **them**.

Here the answer will involve a function with two arguments which are bound by *every father* and **his children**, respectively. We propose to account for this flexibility by employing a set of variables, W^n, $n \geq 0$, where W^n is of type $\langle s, \langle (e, \ldots, e), e \rangle \rangle$, i.e. W^n ranges over functions from n individuals to individuals[11]. We will sometimes omit the superscripts on W, in which case the valence of W can be read off by looking at the number of arguments. In addition, we assume that there is a corresponding set $\mathscr{W}^n$, $n \geq 0$ of variables over properties of W. A special case will be W^0 which just denotes an individual. The representation of the question in (62) will be as in (62').

(62') $\lambda p \; \exists W^0 [\textbf{boy}'(W^0) \land \;\check{}p \land p = \;\hat{}\textbf{win}'(W^0)]$

Given the flexible W functions, there will always be several ways to represent the individual type reading of a question with one or more quantifiers. Take for instance the dialogue in (64).

(64)   Q: Which book did every author recommend?
       A: War and Peace.

In this situation, a true answer consists in naming the particular book that all authors recommended. We can represent this reading by using a W^0 variable, as shown in (65').

(65') $\quad \lambda p \, \exists W^0[\textbf{book}'(W^0) \wedge \check{}p \wedge p =$
$\quad\quad\quad = \hat{} \, \forall x[\textbf{author}'(x) \rightarrow \textbf{recommend}'_*(\check{}x, \check{}W^0)]]$

But we could also have chosen a W^1 variable, in which case the representation of the meaning would be as in (65").

(65") $\quad \lambda p \, \exists W^1[\, \forall x[\textbf{book}'(W^1(x))] \wedge \check{}p \wedge p =$
$\quad\quad\quad = \hat{} \, \forall x[\textbf{author}'(x) \rightarrow \textbf{recommend}'_*(\check{}x, \check{}W^1(x))]]$

In this case, W^1 would denote a constant function which maps *every author* onto *War and Peace*. The need for such constant functions becomes apparent in the case of mixed answers as in the dialogue in (66)[12].

(66)   Q: Who does every Frenchman admire?
        A: His mother and Brigitte Bardot.

In order to be able to represent this reading, we require that W be at least of valence W^1. By including among the possible values for W^1 the constant function which maps *every Frenchman* into *Brigitte Bardot*, we can characterize the set of propositions correctly. We will assume a convention by which the lowest type of W variable necessary is chosen in any particular case. This will insure that in a simple question like (62) a W^0 variable is used, since there is no quantifier in the sentence which would motivate using a variable of a higher value.

By assuming a flexible free W variable in the interpretation of pronouns, we have a straightforward way of accounting for various relational readings of questions[13]. This follows since we use a pronoun interpretation as a placeholder for the interpretation of the quantifier, which is in accordance with the approach to quantification taken in e.g. PTQ and Cooper (1983). Since the place-holding pronoun is interpreted as if it occurred in the position of the gap, we expect its interpretation to be able to vary with the interpretation of any other NP that has scope over it. One might consider an alternative to this generalization, namely that the interpretation of a pronoun, or a WH phrase related to a gap could only depend on a preceding or c-commanding NP. In most cases, these three characterizations will make the same predictions. There is, however, some evidence which suggests that the formulation in terms of scope is the correct one. Consider the dialogue in (67), based on an example in Cooper (1978a)

(67)   Q: Who$_i$ do you think [$_S$___$_i$ should repair each TV set?]
       A: The man who built it.

In this question, the phrase *each TV set* neither precedes nor c-commands the gap corresponding to *who*. Nevertheless, the sentence is naturally understood with *each TV set* having wide scope, at least over the embedded sentence. On our approach, we derive this reading by storing the meaning of *each TV set* and quantifying it in at the embedded S level, that is after a pronoun meaning has been inserted in the empty position linked to *who*. The way we would represent this reading of (67) would be as in (67′).

(67′)   "?" $\hat{p}\ \exists W[\ \forall x[\textbf{person}'(W(x))] \land \v{p} \land p =$
       $= \hat{\ }\textbf{think}'(\hat{\ }\textbf{you}', \hat{\ }\ \forall y[\textbf{TV-set}'(y) \rightarrow \textbf{repair}'_*(\v{W}(y), \v{y})])]$

(67′) denotes the set of propositions of the form 'you think, for each TV set y, $W(y)$ should repair y', where W is a function from entities to persons. Plausible values for W would be functions from things to persons that did something to them, like the person who assembled them, or the person who inspected them.

The types of answers we have given to illustrate relational readings have all in some sense been uniform. They have involved functions that give the same type of value for the whole domain, as for instance the function that takes every man into his mother. But this is just a special case. We also get answers, characterized by functions which give different values for different subdomains. One example is given in (68).

(68) Q: Who does every man admire most?
     A: It depends, every bachelor admires his mother most, and every married man admires his wife most, except for Bill, who can't stand his wife and who admires his mistress most.

Notice that the answers partition the domain of the quantifier *every man*. An appropriate value for W in this case would be a function that maps all bachelors into their mothers, all married men except Bill into their wifes, and Bill into his mistress. In other cases the relevant way to partition the domain might be in terms of unit sets. Here there might be no other way to describe the function than to give the list of ordered pairs which is the extension of the function. One such example might be the question in (69), assuming that each car has a different owner.

(69)   Who does each car belong to?

The way we would represent (69) would be as in (70).

(70)   "?" $\hat{p}\ \exists W[\ \forall x[\textbf{person}'(W(x))] \land {}^\vee p \land p =$
$= {}^\wedge \forall y[\textbf{car}'(y) \to \textbf{belong-to}'_*({}^\vee y, {}^\vee W(y))]]$

In this case, there might not be any way of defining the function apart from giving a list of pairs of the cars and their owners, as in (71).

(71) W: $\left\{\begin{array}{l} \text{car}_1 \text{——— John} \\ \text{car}_2 \text{——— Bill} \\ \text{car}_3 \text{——— Sue} \\ \quad \cdot \qquad\quad \cdot \\ \quad \cdot \qquad\quad \cdot \\ \quad \cdot \qquad\quad \cdot \end{array}\right\}$

But then, of course, there is nothing in our approach that would require that the functions W ranges over always correspond to a simple expression in the language.

We have shown that taking pronouns, both interrogative and personal, to involve a free relational variable, and using these to characterize the meaning of relational questions, provides us with a uniform way of handling questions where the interpretation of the interrogative quantifier depends on other quantifiers in the sentence, and where this dependency can not always be expressed by quantifying in. However, one might object that this proposal is too powerful. It gives us the ability to express the meaning of certain questions, but it does so at the cost of not being able to determine exactly which set of propositions a question denotes. L. Karttunen (personal communication) has expressed some concern over this issue. We recall that on Karttunen's approach, a question denotes the set of propositions that jointly constitute a true and complete answer to it. We pointed out in this connection, that this notion of complete answer sometimes was needed, as in the case of questions like *Who is coming to dinner?* where only an exhaustive list of all the guests seems to be a sufficient answer. In case the interrogative quantifier explicitly or implicitly ranges over a finite domain, we will be able to tell exactly which propositions are in the set denoted by the question. Given that Bill, Tom, and Harry are the only boys in the class, and that Bill and Tom were late, then the question *Which of the boys in the class were late?* will have a well-defined meaning. It will denote the set consisting of the proposition that Bill was late and the proposition that Tom was late. If we quantify over functions to characterize the set of propositions that constitute the answer, then there will presumably be infinitely many propositions in the set, since there will be a potentially unlimited number of such functions. As a consequence we will not be able to specify the set of propositions by an exhaustive instantiation of these functions. However, I don't think this objection invalidates our approach. In fact, I don't think this problem is necessarily connected with the fact that we use higher order quantification. The problem arises in first order frameworks like Karttunen's as well, as soon as one tries to account for questions where one cannot assume that the quantifiers are restricted to finite domains. Consider the question in (72).

(72)   Q: Which number does every number immediately precede?
       A: Its successor.

Even if we specify the propositions in the set in terms of pairs of integers, we cannot express the meaning of (72) with a finite set of propositions. Note that on our approach we can provide a complete answer to (72), as shown in (72').

(72') $\lambda p \; \exists W [\; \forall x [\textbf{number}'(W(x))] \land \;\check{}p \land p =$
        $= \;\hat{}\; \forall y [\textbf{number}'(y) \rightarrow \textbf{immediately-precede}'_*(\check{}y, \check{}W(y))]]$

where W ranges over an infinite domain.

The reason Karttunen assumes that answers must be exhaustive is presumably that he wants to account for the intuition that a question like *Who is coming to dinner?* requires a complete enumeration of all people who are coming to dinner, i.e. it requires that for each individual who is coming to dinner, the proposition that he is coming to dinner be among the set of propositions denoted by the question[14]. Hence what is required is completeness or exhaustiveness with respect to the individuals in the domain. And this is just what a W function will provide.

A related but slightly different issue is whether there might be an infinite number of propositions in the set due to the fact that there might be an infinite number of W functions which characterize the set. I don't think this is a serious problem, however. When we say that *John knows which woman every man admires most* (on the relational reading), we mean that John knows some set of propositions expressing that every man, x, admires $W(x)$ most. We don't expect John to know or care about the entire set of propositions which are equivalent at the world of evaluation but differ only in the choice of W. Suppose the following functions

W_0: $x \rightarrow$ the mother of x
W_1: $x \rightarrow$ the woman x first smiled at
W_2: $x \rightarrow$ the woman who has worried most over x

all have the same extension in this world. Then for John to know *which woman every man admires most* it is sufficient that he knows the set of propositions got by instantiating one of these functions, since each W will provide a procedure which enables John to link up all men with the person they admire most. Speakers presumably recognize that the different values of W in this case are just different ways of providing the same answer[15], whereas mentioning just one individual or a subset of the individuals that are coming to dinner would not count as one possible way, among several, of answering the question *Who is coming to dinner*? If we want to continue talking about *the* meaning of a question, we can do this by limiting W to range over a set of contextually available functions. In our discussion, we have often tacitly assumed that the context would make certain relations more salient. The context, together with common knowledge about standard associations, will give us a way to restrict the number of plausible W functions[16]. Note that the problem of there being a number of functions picking out the same set is not one that is exclusive to this particular framework. As soon as one wants to account for NP-type answers like *someone from England*, one runs into the problem that there might be any number of descriptions which will give the right results (cf. Section 8.3).

The same observation can be made with respect to the interpretation of pronouns. Interpreting pronouns as involving occurrences of free variables which have to be contextually determined, also has the consequence that we cannot determine exactly which proposition is expressed by a given sentence, without taking into account properties given by the context, as Cooper notes (Cooper, 1979, p. 85). The same would apply to our analysis of questions. Exactly which set of propositions a given question denotes can only be determined with respect to a contextually defined set of possible *W* functions.

4.3. Questions With Bound Anaphors

Up until now we have mainly discussed questions of the form *who* ... and *which book* ... where the interrogative phrases consist either entirely of an interrogative pronoun or of the interrogative determiner *which* followed by a lexical (not derived) CN phrase. We have shown that such questions may get relational answers, although there is no overt indication of this in the question. In this section we will look at questions where the relational reading is required because the interrogative phrase contains one or more anaphors related to antecedents inside the sentence. The question is now how to establish the anaphoric relation between the pronoun in the preposed interrogative phrase and the antecedent in the sentence, since the anaphor occurs outside the scope of its antecedent, both syntactically, and, as we will argue, semantically. We will first discuss anaphoric readings involving personal pronouns, and in the next section turn to overt anaphors like reflexives.

4.3.1. Bound Personal Pronouns

The example in (73), which is a slight modification of our previous example (31), illustrates the interpretation possibilities of personal pronouns in interrogative phrases.

(73) Which relative of *his* do you expect *every Englishman* to admire most?

This question has a reading on which *his* is a bound pronoun, anaphorically related to the quantifier *every Englishman*. One way to establish this binding would be to give the antecedent wide scope over the entire question, in which case it could bind a free variable in the specification of the interrogative quantifier. This would turn (73) into a set of questions, one for each Englishman. But as we argued in Section 3.1, it turns out that we can get a relational interpretation for (73) even when *every Englishman* is understood to have narrower scope than *expect*, i.e. *his* can be understood as anaphorically related to *every Englishman* even though it appears in a position with wider scope. There seem to be two approaches one could pursue in order to make sure that *his* gets appropriately bound. One way would be to interpret the interrogative phrase, or at least the CN part of it, as if it were in the position of the gap. This way, all anaphors in the CN phrase would be exposed to binding by any antecedent with wider scope in the sentence. This was the approach I took in Engdahl (1980a). I now think that the crucial arguments that led me to adopt this approach are not valid given a more careful analysis of the interaction between tense and CN interpretations. The second approach would be to interpret the interrogative quantifier as a unit in its surface structure position and to let the interpretation of the quantifier contain a characterization of the anaphoric relation involved so that the appropriate relational reading can be computed. This is the approach taken here. In Section 9, we will compare the two approaches and discuss the reasons for preferring the second analysis.

According to the analysis of questions that we are developing here, the meaning of *which relative of his* will be a pair consisting of a pronoun interpretation with a free W variable and a stored quantifier over W, which we represent schematically as

$$\langle \text{pronoun interpretation}, [WH]_i \rangle$$

The meaning of the CN phrase in the interrogative phrase establishes a restriction on W. In case the CN meaning contains a personal pronoun, we have the option of either leaving the individual variable in its translation free or binding it in the closure operation associated with forming the interrogative quantifier. We recall that the way we form an interrogative quantifier from an interrogative determiner and an CN phrase is to close the expression over all arguments to W. The forming of the interrogative quantifier in this case would proceed as follows, presupposing certain rules which will be spelled out in Section 6.

EXPRESSION	INTERPRETATION	STORE	RULE USED
[$_{CN}$ relative of his]	$\lambda y[\textbf{relative-of-}x'(y)]$ $\forall x[\lambda y[\textbf{relative-of-}$ $\text{-}x'(y)](W(x))]$		Closure
[$_{NP}$ which relative of his]	$\langle \lambda PP\{W_2(x_4)\},$	$[\lambda \mathcal{W} \exists W[\Lambda x[\textbf{relative-of-}x'(W(x))]$ $\wedge \; \mathcal{W}\{W\}]_2\rangle$	

For convenience, we will continue to abbreviate the stored quantifier as $[WH]_i$. Note that in this case the free individual variable x in the CN translation gets bound by the closure operation. Consequently, when we quantify in the stored interrogative quantifier $[WH]_2$ at the Q level, we will get the following representation of the meaning of (73).

(74) $\text{``?''} \hat{p} \, \exists W[\, \forall x[\textbf{relative-of-}x'(W(x))] \land \, ˇp \land p =$
$= \, ˆ\textbf{expect}'(ˆ\textbf{you}', \, ˆ\forall y[\textbf{Englishman}'(y) \rightarrow$
$\textbf{admire}'_*(ˇy, \, ˇW(y))])]$

(74) denotes the set of true propositions of the form 'you expect that if y is an Englishman, then y admires $W(y)$' where W is a function which takes any individual z into a relative of z's.

We could also have taken the option of letting the individual variable in the CN translation remain free, i.e. unaffected by the closure operation. In this case, we would get the representation in (75).

(75) $\text{``?''} \hat{p} \, \exists W[\, \forall x[\textbf{relative-of-}x_0'(W(x))] \land \, ˇp \land p =$
$= \, ˆ\textbf{expect}'(ˆ\textbf{you}', \, ˆ\forall y[\textbf{Englishman}'(y) \rightarrow$
$\textbf{admire}'_*(ˇy, \, ˇW(y))])]$

On this reading, (73) is a question about which of some contextually given male individual's relatives you expect every Englishman to admire. If the conversation has turned around Prince Charles, then he might be the person referred to by *his*. Notice that even when *his* is understood deictically is it possible to interpret the entire question relationally, i.e. as varying with the Englishman. On this reading, a plausible answer might be *the one* (of Prince Charles' relatives) *that he* (the Englishman) *has been introduced to*.

(73) also has a non-relational reading where an appropriate answer would be *his mother* which in this case would pick out a specific individual, Elizabeth II. Presumably, this would be a case where we would use a zero place W function, as in (76).

(76) $\text{``?''} \hat{p} \, \exists W^0[\textbf{relative-of-}x_0'(W^0) \land \, ˇp \land p =$
$= \, ˆ\textbf{expect}'(ˆ\textbf{you}', \, ˆ\forall y[\textbf{Englishman}'(y) \rightarrow$
$\textbf{admire}'_*(ˇy, \, ˇW^0)])]$

Quantifying over zero place W functions is tantamount to quantifying over individuals (or individual concepts) and we thus get the reading where you expect every Englishman to admire one particular relative of Prince Charles'[17].

186   CHAPTER IV

We mentioned earlier that the *W* function must be flexible enough to generalize to cases where the interpretation of the interrogative phrase varies with more than one NP in the sentence. This can be seen clearly in cases with more than one anaphoric pronoun in the interrogative phrase, as for instance in (77).

(77)   Q: Which of *his* letters to **her** does **every woman** return to *her lover*?

   A: The ones where *he* asks **her** for money.

The felicity of the relational answers that we are giving as illustrations to this and other examples in this section of course depends on the existence of common assumptions about typical correspondences between women and their lovers. To account for the relational interpretation of (77), we require a *W* variable of valence two, in order to express the dependency on two antecedents reflected in the answer. The clause that restricts the value of *W* thus will contain two bound pronouns, and the pronoun interpretation used in the translation of the constituent dominating the gap will contain two free individual variables which can get bound by NPs in the sentence. To show how this works in detail, we give a sample derivation of (77) in (78). Recall that we abbreviate stored quantifiers as $[NP]_n$, which is similar to how we abbreviate stored interrogative quantifiers[18]

(78)

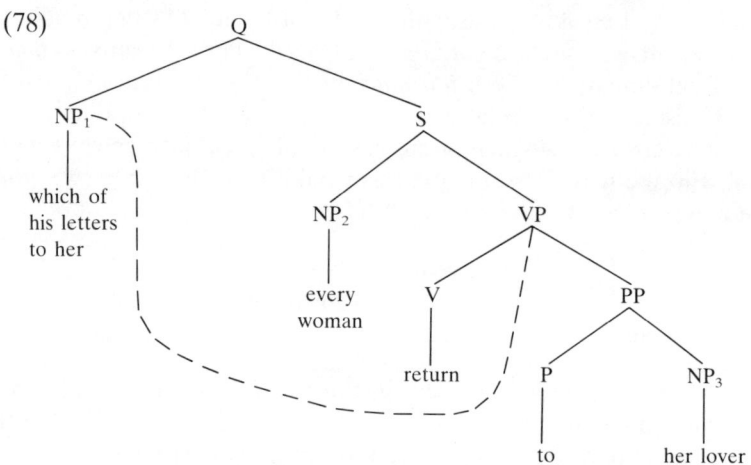

THE INTERPRETATION OF QUESTIONS

EXPRESSION	INTERPRETATION	STORE	RULE USED
[$_{NP_1}$ which of his letters to her]	$\lambda PP\{W_3(x_5, x_7)\}$	$[\lambda \mathcal{W} \mathcal{W} \mathcal{W} \wedge \mathcal{W}\{W\}]]_3 (=[WH]_3)$	WH storage
[$_{NP_3}$ her lover]	$\lambda PP\{x_5\}$	$[\lambda P \exists x [\textbf{lover-of-}x_7{'}(x) \wedge P\{x\}]]_5 (=[NP]_5)$	NP storage
[$_{VP}$ return to her lover]	$\textbf{return}{'}(\hat{P}P\{x_5\})(\hat{P}P\{W_3(x_5, x_7)\})$ $= \lambda y \exists x[\textbf{lover-of-}x_7{'}(x) \wedge$ $\textbf{return}{'}(\hat{P}P\{x\})(\hat{P}P\{W_3(x, x_7)\})(y)]$	$[WH]_3, [NP]_5$	NP quantification
[$_{NP_2}$ every woman] [$_S$ every woman returns to her lover]	$\lambda PP\{x_7\}$ $\exists x[\textbf{lover-of-}x_7{'}(x) \wedge$ $\textbf{return}_*{'}(\check{}x_7, \check{}W_3(x.x_7), \check{}x)]$ $= \forall z[\textbf{woman}{'}(z) \rightarrow \exists z[\textbf{lover-of-}z{'}(x) \wedge \textbf{return}_*{'}(\check{}z, \check{}W_3(x, z), \check{}x)]]$	$[\lambda P \forall z[\textbf{woman}{'}(z) \rightarrow P\{x\}]]_7 (=[NP]_7)$ $[WH]_3, [NP]_7$ $[WH]_3$	NP storage NP quantification
[$_Q$ which of his letters to her does every woman return to her lover]	$\lambda y[\textbf{letter-of-}x\text{-to-}y{'}(W(x,.))]] \vee \check{}p \wedge p =$ $= \forall_\wedge z[\textbf{woman}{'}(z) \rightarrow \exists z[\textbf{lover-of-}z{'}(x) \wedge \textbf{return}_*{'}(\check{}z, \check{}W(x, z), \check{}x)]]]$		WH quantification (60)

The last line of the derivation gives us as meaning for the question the set of true propositions of the form 'if z is a woman, then z returns $W(x, z)$ to z's lover x' where for any y, y_0, $W(y, y_0)$ is a letter of y's to y_0.

In a question like (77), the dependence on two antecedents is explicitly marked by the two personal pronouns. However, as we saw in the case of simple *who* questions earlier, the presence of an anaphoric pronoun is not a prerequisite for a relational reading, nor does the number of pronouns necessarily correlate with the number of potential antecedents in the sentence on which the interpretation may depend. One or more of the pronouns may be interpreted deictically or several occurrences of pronouns may be anaphorically related to the same antecedent, as in (79).

(79) Which of *his* memories from *his* childhood does *no adult* want to forget?

What determines the valence of a relational interpretation is the number of possible antecedents within the sentence, which on our approach is reflected in the number of free individual arguments to W in the pronoun interpretation that we insert as a placeholder for the meaning of the gap. So in a question containing three NPs, we expect possible answers to depend on one, two, three, or none of the antecedents, regardless of the form of the interrogative phrase. Thus we predict that all versions of the question in (80) could be given the uniform relational answer indicated.

(80) Q: a. Which letters
          b. Which of her letters
          c. Which of her letters to him
          d. Which of her letters about him
          e. Which of her letters to him about him
          f. Which letters to him
          g. Which letters about him
          h. Which letters to him about him

      does *every man* threaten **his mistress** to show to HER HUSBAND?

      A: The ones where **she** asks *him* to kill THE OLD BASTARD.

The epithet *the old bastard* is here understood anaphorically, just like the pronouns[19].

If we want to express an answer like this which depends on three antecedents, we need to quantify over a *W* function of valence three, regardless of how many possible anaphors there are in the interrogative phrase. To pick one case for illustration, the meaning of the question in (80b) would be represented as in (81).

(81) "?" $\exists W^3[\ \forall x\ \forall y\ \forall z[\textbf{letter-of-}x'(W^3(x, y, z))] \land {\check{}}p \land p =$
$= \hat{}\ \forall x[\textbf{man}'(x) \rightarrow \exists y[\textbf{mistress-of-}x'(y) \land \exists z[\textbf{husband-of-}y'(z) \land$
$\textbf{threaten}'_*(\check{}x, \check{}y, \hat{}\textbf{show}'_*(\check{}x, \check{}W^3(y, x, z), \check{}z)))]]]]$

(81) denotes the set of true propositions of the form 'if x is a man, then x has a mistress y who has a husband z and x threatens y to show $z\ W^3(y,x,z)$' where the value of this three place function must be a letter of y's. Note that which NP it is that will be understood as the antecedent for a bound pronoun in the interrogative phrase depends on which NP binds the corresponding argument to *W*. Since *her* in (80) requires a female antecedent and only one of the three NP's in the sentence is female, the only bound reading for (80) will be the one given in (81) where the existential quantifier introduced in the translation of *his mistress* binds the first coordinate of *W*. Any other binding will presumably lead to a presupposition clash and the sentence will come out as pragmatically weird. We assume that the type of gender matching required between antecedents and bound pronouns can be accounted for in the way outlined in Cooper (1983, chapter VII) which combines a presuppositional treatment of gender agreement with the use of partial functions for pronoun interpretations (cf. also Heim (1979)). The fact that there is only one potential antecedent of appropriate gender in (80) thus matters for determining the number of readings of the sentence. A question like (82), on the other hand, will have two bound readings, depending on which NP is understood as anaphorically related to *her* in the interrogative phrase *which of her letters*.

(82)   Q: Which of her letters does **every woman** hide from *her mother*?

A: The ones which **she** doesn't want *her* to open.

The two readings are given in (83) and (84).

(83) "?" $\hat{p}$ $\exists W^2[$ $\forall x$ $\forall y[$**letter-of**-$x'(W^2(x, y))] \wedge$ ˇ$p \wedge p =$
= ˆ $\forall y($**woman**$'(y) \rightarrow$ $\exists z[$**mother-of**-$y'(z) \wedge$
hide-from$'_*($ˇy, ˇ$W^2(y, z)$, ˇ$z)]]]$

(84) "?" $\hat{p}$ $\exists W^2[$ $\forall x$ $\forall y[$**letter-of**-$x'(W^2(x, y))] \wedge$ ˇ$p \wedge p =$
= ˆ $\forall y[$**woman**$'(y) \rightarrow$ $\exists z[$**mother-of**-$y'(z) \wedge$
hide-from$'_*($ˇy, ˇ$W^2(z, y)$, ˇ$z)]]]$

In these formulas, the restriction on the quantifier W^2 ensures that its value must be a letter belonging to its first argument. The difference in readings depends on which NP in the sentence binds the first argument of W in the characterization of the proposition. In (83), the quantifier corresponding to *every woman* binds this argument position, and we get the reading where *her* is anaphorically related to *every woman*. In (84), the quantifier corresponding to *her mother* binds the first argument of W[20].

Stepping back somewhat from the intricacies of these examples, the generalization that emerges is that an interrogative phrase may be interpreted as dependent on any NP in the sentence that has scope over the gap. We get the bound reading for a personal pronoun in a preposed interrogative phrase by letting the individual variable in the translation of the pronoun get bound in the closure operation which characterizes the W function in the interrogative quantifier. The free reading obtains when the individual variable remains free and thus gets interpreted as referring to a particular individual in the context. The optionality of interpretations is thus a consequence of the fact that personal pronouns are ambiguous between the deictic use and the bound use. However, in the case of overt anaphors like reflexives the situation is different. Here the anaphor must be linked to a syntactically determined antecedent. We now turn to a discussion of such cases.

4.3.2. Reflexive Pronouns

The question in (85) illustrates perhaps even more clearly than the examples with personal pronouns discussed in the previous section that interrogative quantifiers must sometimes be interpreted relationally.

(85) Which picture of *herself* did *every girl* send in to the contest?

The interpretation of *which picture of herself* will vary with the interpretation of *every girl*. It is of course possible to give wide scope to *every girl*, in which case (85) will be understood as a set of questions, one for each girl, *x*, asking which picture of *x*, *x* sent in to the contest. However, as we have argued in previous sections, (85) can also be interpreted in a way which does not require that the antecedent of the anaphor takes wide scope over the entire question. We can force this reading by embedding the antecedent under another scopal element as in (86).

(86)   Which picture of *herself* did someone say that *every girl* sent in to the contest?

On the interpretation of this question where *every girl* is interpreted in its own clause, i.e. with narrow scope with respect to *someone*, appropriate answers would be *the picture of herself in profile* or *the one where she is wearing a bathing suit*. We are going to assume that the only reading of (86) relevant to the specification of the syntactic and semantic rules of the grammar is the one where the antecedent for *herself* is *every girl*, that is, we are going to assume that the rules for interpreting reflexives in dislocated positions are essentially the same as the regular rules for reflexive interpretation. As we noted in connection with the discussion of the reflexive rule in Chapter III, judgments about the anaphoric relations in sentences with preposed reflexives sometimes vary. Some people reportedly also allow for a reading where *someone* is understood as the antecedent of *herself*. However, since the variation is always in the direction of wanting to associate a preposed reflexive pronoun with the leftmost antecedent that occurs in the sentence, we take this to be due to performance factors. It is presumably costly to keep an unresolved anaphor in processing memory which may explain why many people display a preference for reflexive resolution according to linear order in these cases.

Given that the antecedent possibilities for a reflexive pronoun in a preposed constituent should be determined with respect to the position of the gap, a proposal that accounts for the binding of a reflexive pronoun in an interrogative phrase by quantifying in the antecedent becomes very complicated. Not only must we require that the antecedent is obligatorily quantified in, we must also ensure that *only* the appropriate antecedent can be quantified in to bind the reflexive pronoun. In the case of (86), the problem amounts to preventing a derivation where *someone* is quantified in and binds *herself*. In order to guarantee that only *every girl* binds *herself* we need some way of encoding which stored NPs are appropriate antecedents for which reflexive pronouns in which dislocated positions. Given the possibility of using auxiliary devices like special stores for registering possible antecedent-anaphor relations, this can probably be done. However, it seems that putting special conditions on the quantification rules for antecedents of reflexive pronouns is an unnecessary and otherwise unmotivated complication of the interpretation procedures. A proposal that uses the same interpretation rules for reflexives in place as for reflexives in dislocated positions seems preferable and we will now illustrate how our rules for interpreting reflexives interact in the desired way with the interpretation of preposed interrogatives.

Recall that we take the choice of a reflexive pronoun to be a signal that the interpretation of that constituent cannot be established independently of the interpretation of the antecedent. We capture this fact by obligatorily storing the information about which individual variable is used in the translation of the reflexive pronoun, and which accordingly must be bound. Contrary to the case of personal pronouns, the translation of a reflexive pronoun will not contain any free relational variable. This reflects the fact that its reference can never be affected by the context. The interpretation of *herself* will thus be an ordered pair

$$[_{NP} \text{ herself}]; \quad \langle \lambda PP\{x_3\}, \quad [\lambda PP\{x_3\}]_3 \rangle$$

The first member of the ordered pair is the pronoun translation which enters into the composition of the main translation. The second member is the same meaning in store, indexed by the free variable. At each point when the phrase containing the reflexive pronoun combines with another phrase, the stored reflexive meaning will be passed up and become part of the meaning of the higher constituent according to the general interpretation rule for complex meanings (see Chapter III.3.2). At the VP level, the reflexive interpretation rule abstracts over the free individual variable, forming a property which can be picked up by the subject. The rule for reflexive interpretation, introduced and motivated in Chapter III.5.2, is repeated here in (87).

(87) *Reflexive interpretation rule*:
If $\langle \alpha, \sigma_0, [\lambda PP\{x_i\}]_i, \sigma_1 \rangle \in m(VP)$
then $\langle \lambda x_i[\alpha(x_i)], \sigma_0, \sigma_1 \rangle \in m(VP)$.
σ is a sequence of elements in store.

When a reflexive pronoun occurs as part of the meaning of a CN phrase,

THE INTERPRETATION OF QUESTIONS   193

as in the interrogative phrase in (85) and (86), the meaning of the CN phrase will have a reflexive meaning in store. Intuitively, what this means is that a certain variable in the CN phrase interpretation may not remain free in the translation of the question, since a reflexive pronoun can never be interpreted deictically. Consequently, the closure operation obligatorily applies to this variable, whereas it applies optionally to other free variables in CN translation. In addition, we need to make sure that the corresponding variable in the pronoun translation inserted in the gap gets bound by the abstraction operator at the VP level. We ensure that this information is transmitted properly by requiring that the free individual variable in the pronoun meaning matches the index on the stored reflexive meaning. The way we get the meaning of an interrogative phrase like *which picture of herself* which contains a CN meaning with a reflexive meaning in store is illustrated schematically in (88).

(88) EXPRESSION   INTERPRETATION   STORE

  $[_{CN}\ ]$ CN' $[\lambda PP\{x_i\}]_i$
  $[_{NP}\text{ which CN}]$ $\lambda PP\{W_j^n(x_1, \ldots x_i \ldots, x_n)\}$ $[\lambda PP\{x_i\}]_i, [WH]_j$

The first member is the pronoun translation, the second member is the stored interrogative quantifier, and the third stored reflexive meaning. Notice that a free individual variable in the pronoun translation matches the variable in the stored reflexive meaning. To illustrate the interaction of the reflexive rule with the interpretation procedure for interrogative quantifiers, we will give a derivation of the question in (85).

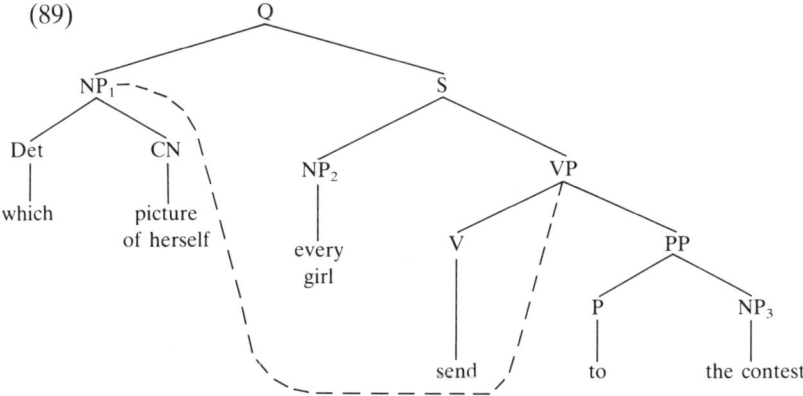

The table to tree diagram (89) is given on p. 194.

194 CHAPTER IV

This table relates to tree diagram (89) on p. 193.

EXPRESSION	INTERPRETATION	STORE	RULE USED
[$_{CN}$ picture of herself]	$\lambda y[\textbf{picture-of-}x_3'(y)]$	$[\lambda PP\{x_3\}]_3$	Obligatory storage of reflexive meaning
[$_{NP_1}$ which picture of herself]	$\lambda PP\{W_1(x_3)\}$	$[\lambda \mathcal{W}. \mathcal{W} \forall x \forall W[\textbf{picture-of-}x'(W(x))] \vee \mathcal{W}\{W\}]]_1$ $(=[WH]_1), [\lambda PP\{x_3\}]_3$	
[$_{VP}$ send to the contest]	$\textbf{send-to-the-contest}'(\hat{P}P\{W_1(x_3)\})$ $= \lambda x_3[\textbf{send-to-the-contest}'$ $(\hat{P}P\{W_1(x_3)\})](x_3)$	$[WH]_1, [\lambda PP\{x_3\}]_3$	
[$_S$ every girl send to the contest]	$\forall y[\textbf{girl}'(y) \rightarrow$ $\textbf{send-to-the-contest}'_*(^\vee y, ^\vee W_1(y))]$	$[WH]_1$	Reflexive rule (87)
[$_Q$ which picture of herself did every girl send to the contest]	"?" $\hat{p} \exists W[\exists x[\textbf{picture-of-}x'(W(x))] \wedge$ $^\vee p \wedge p = ^\wedge \forall y[\textbf{girl}'(y) \rightarrow$ $\textbf{send-to-the-contest}'_*(^\vee y, ^\vee W(y))]]$	$[WH]_1$	WH quantification (60)

The tree rooted in Q thus comes out as denoting the set of true propositions of the form 'if y is a girl, then y sent in $W(y)$ to the contest, where for all x, $W(x)$ is a picture of x'.

By making the closure operation associated with the formation of the interrogative quantifier obligatory for any variable that occurs in a stored reflexive meaning, and by using the same variable in the placeholding pronoun meaning, we make sure that a reflexive pronoun occurring in a preposed interrogative phrase (i) can not be interpreted deictically, (ii) that the range of the W function is restricted in the intended way, (iii) and that the corresponding argument of W in the sentence gets bound by the appropriate controller for the reflexive pronoun. The antecedent thus does not bind the reflexive pronoun in the preposed constituent directly, but given the characterization of the W function, we get the intended anaphoric reading. By using the regular rules for reflexive interpretation, as well as the regular rules for creating a relational interrogative quantifier, we get the correct interpretation for questions like (85) and (86) without requiring that the antecedent be obligatorily quantified in.

5. INTERACTION BETWEEN INTERROGATIVE QUANTIFIERS AND OTHER QUANTIFIERS

In this section we will look in more detail at the interaction between interrogative quantifiers and other quantifiers. We will first look at quantifiers occurring elsewhere in the sentence or the discourse. In Section 5.2 we will turn to quantifiers that are embedded in the dislocated constituent.

5.1. *Quantifiers and Pronoun Interpretation*

We looked earlier at examples like (73), repeated here,

(73)   Which relative of *his* do you expect *every Englishman* to admire most?

which we took to illustrate that the different interpretation possibilities for a pronoun in dislocated position are the same as for a pronoun occurring in the corresponding gap position inside the sentence. The pronoun can either be interpreted as referring to a particular individual, or as bound by a quantifier in the sentence. However, it cannot be understood as referring back to a quantifier expression in previous discourse. In this respect, Cooper's analysis of pronoun, which we are adopting here, makes some clear predictions. Recall that we take the interpretation of pronouns to involve expressions with a free individual variable and a free relational variable. The free individual variables are open to being interpreted deictically or as bound by a quantifier with wider scope in the sentence where the pronoun occurs. The relevant relation is determined contextually. It cannot be the case that the relation or function picked out in the interpretation of the pronoun depends on some variable bound by a quantifier in a previous sentence. To see what is at issue here, let us consider the discourse in (90) in which both (a) and (b) are possible continuations.

(90) Every student had to paint one painting of each of five motifs. The freeway motif was by far the most popular. When the art teacher came to select paintings for the art show,
(a) every student wanted to display *it*.
(b) she wasn't surprised at *which painting* every student wanted to display.

it and *which* painting can here be understood as referring to each student's painting of the freeway motif. The way we would represent this reading would be as in (91), for (90a).

(91) $\forall x[\textbf{student}'(x) \rightarrow \textbf{want-to-display}'_*(\check{}x, \check{}W_0(x))]$

In order to interpret (91) we must find a suitable value for the free function variable W_0. A likely candidate, given the previous discourse, would be a function that maps every student x into x's painting of the freeway motif. Similarly for the question in (90b). But note that we cannot interpret W_0 as a function from students to *each of five motifs*, i.e. as a function which maps for each motif y every student x into x's painting of y. Clearly this is not a possible reading for the continuations in (90). This reading cannot be generated on the present approach. The arguments of W can only be interpreted deictically or be bound by a sentence internal quantifier with wider scope than the pronoun or the gap. In case the quantifier does not take wide scope, we find that it cannot influence the interpretation possibilities for a pronoun outside its scope. The * in the following examples indicates ungrammaticality on the bound interpretation.

(92) *[$_S$[$_{\bar S}$ That *every donkey* was hungry] annoyed *it*.]

(93) *A man [$_{\bar S}$ that owns *every donkey*] beats *it*.

We assume here that *every donkey* does not have scope outside the minimal tensed clause that contains it. Even if we interpret *it* with a free individual variable and a free relational variable, e.g. as $\lambda PP\{W_1(x_3)\}$ as suggested in Section 4.2, there is still no way to get the anaphoric reading without giving *every donkey* wide scope over the whole sentence. In (93), *a man* could presumably bind the free individual variable in the interpretation of *it*. We would then get a representation like in (94).

(94) $\exists x[\mathbf{man}'(x) \wedge \forall y[\mathbf{donkey}'(y) \rightarrow \mathbf{own}'_*(^\vee x, ^\vee y)] \wedge \mathbf{beat}'_*(^\vee x, ^\vee W_1(x))]$

(94) says of some man x that owns every donkey that x beats the individual that is the value of the W_1 function applied to x. Obviously W_1 can not be a function from men into *every donkey* since the latter is not an individual.

5.2. Constituent Questions with Quantifiers

In Section 4.3.2 we looked at cases where part of the specification of the interrogative quantifier contained anaphors like reflexives or bound personal pronouns. We will next consider examples of the converse phenomenon, i.e. when the specification of the interrogative contains a quantifier. As is well known, the scope possibilities of quantifiers embedded inside tensed sentences and NPs are quite restricted (cf. e.g. May (1977) and Partee and Bach (1910). (95) illustrates that it is hard to interpret a universal quantifier inside a tensed sentence as having wide scope over the matrix subject.

(95) Some teacher thought that every student had cheated.

It is extremely hard to understand (95) as saying that for each student x there was some teacher who thought that x had cheated. Indefinites, on the other hand, can get wide scope interpretations even out of tensed sentences, as shown by (96).

(96)   Every teacher said that a student had cheated.

However, as Fodor and Sag (1982) have argued, the indefinite NP *a student* does not have all the properties of a true quantifier but acts more like a name of a specific individual. There are some cases, nevertheless, where an embedded quantifier easily takes wider scope than the embedding constituent. It appears that the ease with which a particular quantifier may take wider scope than its embedding constituent depends both on lexical properties of the quantifiers and on the availability of a 'distributive' reading for the embedding phrase (cf. Vanlehn, 1978). Some examples are given here.

(97)   [NP The phone number [PP of [NP *each student*]]] is indicated on *his/her* chart.

(98)   [NP The result [S̄ that *each student* got]] was noted on *his/her* chart.

We note that in sentences like these, the denotation of the head noun is understood to vary with *each student*. We can account for these readings on our approach by storing the quantifier phrase and quantifying it into the sentence, thus permitting it to bind a pronoun, as indicated by the italics in the example. It is somewhat more controversial whether a quantifier in a possessive determiner can take sentential scope. It is clear that it normally takes scope over the common noun, but the issue is whether it also takes scope over the embedding NP. The question amounts to whether the relation between the italicized NPs in the following examples is one of anaphoric binding or not (cf. Partee and Bach (1981), Higginbotham (1980), and Cooper (1983) for some discussion).

(99)   *Every boy*'s mother loves *him*.

(100) *Who*se mother loves *him*?

The answer to this question is not crucial for this discussion. We will analyze (99) and (100) as cases of bound pronouns, got by quantifying in the antecedent. Note that quantifiers embedded inside interrogative constituents can also take wide scope in this fashion, which amounts to taking scope over the whole question, as illustrated by the dialogue in (101).

(101) Q: Tell me which of each skater's obligatory figures you liked best.

A: I liked Peggy's 8 and Linda's 3, and ...

Since *each* normally takes as wide scope as possible, (101) is naturally interpreted as a request that for each skater x, you tell me which of x's figures you liked best. In addition to this reading, where the quantifier takes wide scope over the whole question, this structure permits for another reading where the quantifier takes scope over the embedding NP but does not take scope over the entire question. One example is given in (102).

(102) Q: Which of *every* applicant's scores did someone forget to enter on *his/her* records?

A: *His* or *her* GRE scores.

An answer like the one suggested here reflects a reading of the question on which what someone forgot to enter was the result that every applicant got on some particular test. Of course, the actual number will be different for each applicant, but it is still possible to give a functional answer. Note that on this reading the interpretation of *someone* does not vary with the interpretation of *every applicant* which it presumably would do if we interpreted *every applicant* with scope over the whole question and hence with scope over *someone*. Still, it turns out that *every applicant* can be anaphorically related to the bound pronoun *his* or *her*.

Another example which shows that we cannot always account for the bound reading of a pronoun in the sentence by raising the quantifier out of the interrogative phrase and giving it wide scope over the entire question is given in (103).

(103)   The reputation of the department depends on which of *every student*'s grades the secretary entered on *his/her* record.

It would not make sense to quantify *every student* into the sentence since that would mean that the reputation depends on each individual student, contrary to the most plausible reading for (103).

It appears that the relative scope possibilities for the universally quantified NP inside a preposed interrogative phrase are roughly the same as for the declarative counterpart. Compare (102) with (104).

(104)   Someone forgot to enter one of *every applicant*'s scores on *his/her* record.

In order to account for the bound interpretation of *his/her* in this sentence, we must store *every applicant* and quantify it in either at the VP level or at the S level, depending on how wide scope we want to give it. It turns out that we can use essentially the same procedure in the derivation of (102). The question in (102) is interesting because the interrogative quantifier clearly has scope according to its surface structure position, in particular it may take scope over any quantifier inside the sentence. But a quantifier embedded inside the interrogative quantifier can take scope as if it had occurred in the gap position or at every intervening level in the sentence where it could have been quantified in. On our approach, the derivation of (102) involves a combination of the free and controlled quantification procedures that we introduced in Chapter III. We will illustrate this by giving the derivation of just one of the readings of (102), viz. the one where *every applicant* takes narrow scope with respect to *someone* but wide scope with respect to the NP that contains it, i.e. *every applicant's scores*. On this reading, *his GRE scores* would be an appropriate answer, with *his* understood as bound by *every applicant*. This derivation illustrates the interaction of free and controlled quantification. In this derivation we presuppose the interpretation rules for partitive constructions which will be discussed in Section 6.3. The variable $\mathscr{P}$ which occurs in the interpretation of plural NPs is a variable over properties of sets of individual concepts. Note that the interpretation of the interrogative phrase *which of every applicant's score* is a complex meaning consisting of a pronoun meaning with a free W variable and a free individual variable, together with a stored WH quantifier meaning and a stored NP quantifier meaning.

THE INTERPRETATION OF QUESTIONS

(105)
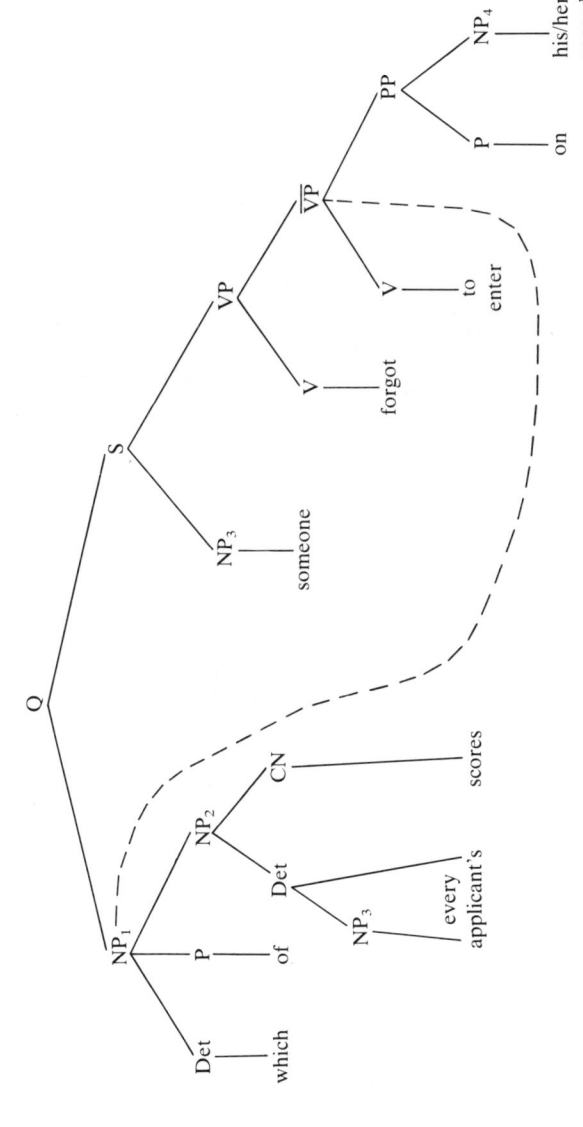

The table to tree diagram (105) is given on p. 202.

This table relates to tree diagram (105) on p. 201.

EXPRESSION	INTERPRETATION	STORE	RULE USED
[$_{NP_2}$ every applicant's scores]	$\lambda \mathscr{S}[\mathscr{S}\{\text{score-of-}x_3{'}\}]$	$[\lambda P \ \forall y[\text{applicant}'(y) \rightarrow P\{y\}]]_3 (=[NP]_3)$	NP storage (11)
[$_{NP_3}$ which of every applicant's scores]	$\lambda PP\{W_2(x_3)\}$	$[\lambda \mathscr{W} \exists W[\forall x[\text{score-of-}x'(W(x))] \land \mathscr{W}\{W\}]]_2$ $(=[WH]_2), [NP]_3$	WH quantifier formation with closure
[$_{NP_4}$ his/her record]	$\lambda P \ \exists x[\textbf{record-of-}x_3{'}(x) \land P\{x\}]$		
[$_{VP}$ forgot to enter on his/her record]	**forget-to-enter**$'(\hat{P} \ \exists x[\textbf{record-of-}x_3{'}(x) \land P\{x\}])(\hat{P}P\{W_2(x_3)\}) =$ $= \lambda z \ \forall y[\textbf{applicant}'(y) \rightarrow \exists x[\textbf{record-of-}y'(x) \land \textbf{forget-to-enter}_*('z, \ \vee W_2(y), \ \vee x)]]$	$[NP]_3, [WH]_2$	VP quantification
[$_S$ someone forgot to enter on his/her record]	$\exists x_1[\textbf{person}'(x_1) \land \forall y[\textbf{applicant}'(y) \rightarrow \exists x[\textbf{record-of-}y'(x \land \textbf{forget-to-enter}_*('x_1, \ \vee W_2(y), \ \vee x)]]]$	$[WH]_2$	
[$_Q$ which of every applicant's scores did someone forgot to enter on his/her record]	"?" $\hat{p} \ \exists W[\exists] \forall x[\textbf{score-of-}x'(W)x)]] \land$ $\check{}p \lor p = \hat{} \exists x[\textbf{person}(x) \land \forall y[\textbf{applicant}'(y) \rightarrow \exists x[\textbf{record-of-}y'(x \lor \textbf{forget-to-enter}_*('x_1, \ \vee W(y), \ \vee x]]]]$		WH quantification rule (60)

According to the derivation in (105), this question denotes the set of true propositions of the form 'there is some person x such that if y is an applicant, then x forgot to enter $W(y)$ on y's record' where $W(y)$ is a score of y's. Note the similarity with the example which contained a reflexive pronoun inside the interrogative phrase which we illustrated in (89). In both cases, the specification of the interrogative quantifier will contain a variable associated with a stored meaning. We make the closure operation involved in forming the interrogative quantifier obligatory for any variable that is associated with a stored meaning[21], just as we have done with reflexives. This way, the variable will be bound in the characterization of the W function. By using the variable associated with the stored NP meaning also in the placeholding pronoun meaning, we make sure that the variable will eventually get bound by the quantifier since we only consider interpretations of matrix nodes where there are no meanings in store.

The example in (102) is admittedly rather complex but I think intuitions about its possible interpretations are fairly clear. I have chosen to go through a derivation of it in some detail because this illustrates rather well the interaction between the syntactic and semantic approaches that we have chosen in this study. Because a dislocated constituent is so to speak directly dominated by two nodes simultaneously in virtue of the characterization of linked trees (cf. Chapter II.5.2), we can assume that its meaning contributes to the meaning of the link parent, i.e. the constituent dominating the gap. However, certain phrases such as WH quantifiers can only contribute their interpretation when there is a sentence meaning. Hence they will have to be obligatorily stored. NP quantifiers, on the other hand, can either be interpreted directly or stored[22].

Another case which shows that it is the position of the gap that determines the anaphoric possibilities of quantifiers embedded inside dislocated constituents is illustrated by the contrasts between (106) and (107).

(106) [Which of the questions that *each applicant* got] ____ upset *him/her* most?

(107) *[Which of the questions that *each applicant* got] did *he/she* refuse to answer ____?

Whereas it is possible to interpret *him/her* in (106) as bound by the quantifier *each applicant* in (106) where the gap c-commands the pronoun, this bound interpretation is excluded in (107) where the pronoun c-commands the gap[23].

5.3. Excursus on Wide Scope Interpretation of Embedded NPs

When we take a closer look at the types of examples where an NP takes wider scope than an embedding NP, it turns out that they require a special interpretation. It appears that it is only when the head NP can be interpreted as a function that varies with the embedded NP that this NP can be taken to have wide scope. This can easily be seen by looking at a few examples (* means that the reading is unavailable on the bound interpretation which involves giving the antecedent wide scope).

(108)a. *Every student*'s paper annoyed *him*.
  b. ?The paper by *every student* annoyed *him*.
  c. *A/*Any paper by *every student* annoyed *him*.

(109)a. The economic effect of *each deal* caused public concern.
  b. *An/*Any economic effect of *each deal* caused public concern.

(110)a. Massachusetts law requires that [the/*a/*any class of vehicles that *each person* may drive] should be indicated on *his* license.

The difference in acceptability shows that the possibility of giving a wide scope interpretation to an embedded quantifier, reflected in its ability to bind pronouns, varies with the choice of determiner of the embedding NP. When the head NP is interpreted as a definite description which gives a unique denotation for each choice of value for the embedded NP, then the latter can enter into anaphoric relations with other constituents in the sentence. NPs with possessive determiners are usually analyzed as definite descriptions (cf. Partee and Bach, 1981, Cooper, 1979, Barwise and Perry, 1983). Thus the subject NP in (108a), *every student's paper*, appears to denote a function from students to grades, i.e. something like the type of *W* function that we have used in our analysis of pronouns and interrogatives. A question like (111)

(111) Which of *every student*'s grades was missing from *his* record?

seems to be about which of these functions from students to grades would be relevant in giving a uniform answer. A short answer to the question, then, would simply provide a value for this function, as for instance *the last* or *the P.E. grade*. It thus doesn't seem implausible that we should be able to extend our relaitonal or functional approach also to sentences like (108)–(110). However, in order to do this we would have to modify the semantics of the fragment since functions from individuals to individuals are not of the appropriate type to take VPs like *annoy him* or *be missing* as arguments. This can probably be done by some strategy for levelling the types of NPs (cf. T. Parson's use of floating types, Parsons (1979)). One way to do this would be to generalize the type of closure operation that we have used in the formation of interrogative quantifiers. Without going into any details of how this would be done, we would have a representation of the meaning of (111) as in (112).

(112)   "?" $\hat{p}$ $\exists W[$ $\forall x[\textbf{student}'(x) \rightarrow \textbf{grade-of-}x'(W(x))] \wedge \check{}\, p \wedge p =$
$= \hat{}\; \forall y[\textbf{missing-from-record-of-}y'(W(y))]]$

i.e. the set of true propositions of the form, 'for all y, $W(y)$ is missing from y's record' where W is a function from students into grades. The condition on W, expressed in the specification of the function, restricts W to students. One aspect that might make this approach more attractive than the quantifying-in approach that we outlined in the previous section, is that it fits with the intuitions that several linguists have voiced (e.g. Partee and Bach, 1981; Cooper, 1983) that although the NP *every student* has scope over the CN phrase *grade*, it does not really have scope outside the NP. It thus seems worthwhile to try to modify the semantics of the fragment so that it can encompass functional readings of definite descriptions without wide scope quantification.

It is interesting to note that in Swedish it is possible to extract out of subject NPs just in case they have the characteristics that permit a wide scope interpretation of an embedded quantifier. Compare (113) and (114)

(113)   [Telefonnumret till **var och en av studenterna**] bör
          the number   to each   of the students   should

          stå   på **hans/hennes** kort.
          be indicated on his/her   card

(114) **Vilka studenter** står [~NP~ numret   till ____]
which students   is   the number to

inte   på **deras** kort?
not indicated on their   card

The hypothesis that scope and extraction phenomena are closely related has been proposed several times in recent years (Cooper, 1983; Postal, 1974, and Rodman, 1976). Cf. also Engdahl (to appear a) where an attempt is made to look at these parallelisms from the point of view of syntactic and semantic processing.

6. THE INTERNAL STRUCTURE OF INTERROGATIVE CONSTITUENTS

As we have seen in the previous discussion, most of the examples with anaphoric relations between the dislocated interrogative quantifier and constituents in the sentence involve constituent questions where the interrogative phrase contains a complement. The most common types are partitive questions, as in (115),

(115)a. Vilken av **sina** böcker rekommenderade **varje författare**?
b. Which of *his* books did *every author* recommend?

and questions where the CN phrase contains some kind of complement, often a prepositional complement as in (116).

(116)a. Vilken dikt om **sin** syster läste **Johan**?
b. Which poem about *his* sister did *Johan* read?

We cannot go into a detailed analysis of these structures here (cf. Selkirk, 1977), nor on the restrictions on the types of NPs that can occur in partitives (cf. Ladusaw, 1982), but will only provide some simplified rules for interpreting them and then briefly comment upon them.

6.1. *Possessives*

Several of the examples we are discussing involve NPs with possessive determiners. We therefore extend the set of NP rules in Chapter III, Section 2.1, with a rule for possessive NPs. The rule will have two subcases, depending on whether the CN is singular or plural. We don't propose any complete semantics for plurals but will simply follow

Bennett (1974) and let plural NPs denote sets of properties of sets of individual concepts. We add the following variables to the variables defined in Chapter III, Section 2.2.

(117) VARIABLE   TYPE   DENOTATION

$\mathscr{S}$ $\langle \langle s, e \rangle, t \rangle$ sets of individual concepts (i.c.)
$\mathscr{S}$ $\langle s, \langle \langle \langle s, e \rangle, t \rangle, t \rangle \rangle$ properties of sets of i.c.
Σ $\langle s, \langle f(\mathscr{S}), t \rangle \rangle$ properties of $\mathscr{S}$

The rule for prenominal possessives will be as in (118)

(118)a. $\langle 21, \text{NP}_1 \to \underset{[\text{POSS}]}{\text{NP}_2} \underset{[\text{SG}]}{\text{CN}}, \lambda P[\text{NP}_2'(\hat{y}\, \exists x[\textbf{of}'_*(\check{\,}y)\,(\text{CN}')(x) \land P\{x\}])]\rangle$
$\quad\quad\quad\;$ [SG]

b. $\langle 22, \text{NP}_1 \to \underset{[\text{POSS}]}{\text{NP}_2} \underset{[\text{PL}]}{\text{CN}}, \lambda \mathscr{S}[\text{NP}_2'(\hat{y}[\mathscr{S}\{\hat{x}[\textbf{of}'_*(\check{\,}y)$
$\quad\quad\quad\;$ [PL]
$\quad\quad\quad\quad\quad\quad\quad\quad\quad\quad (\text{CN}')(x)]\}])]\rangle$

The constant $\textbf{of}'_*$ denotes a relation which perhaps should be broken down into a number of relations that can be expressed by genitive constructions. Several of these do not imply possession, which means that the choice of $\textbf{of}'_*$ is slightly misleading[24]. The rules in (118) provide the following kinds of interpretations for some sample NPs.

(119)a. Majas bok $\lambda P\; \exists x[\textbf{of}'_*(\text{m})(\textbf{book}')(x) \land P\{x\}]$
$\quad\quad\;$ *Maja's book*

b. Majas böcker $\lambda \mathscr{S}[\mathscr{S}\{x[\textbf{of}'_*(\text{m})(\textbf{book}')(x)]\}]$
$\quad\;$ *Maja's books*

The translation of the plural (119b) denotes the set of properties of those books that stand in a certain relation to Maja. The context presumably determines what this relation is and hence determines which the relevant set of books is. A singular NP with a possessive determiner usually carries a presupposition of uniqueness, similar to the definite article. We assume that this is a presupposition or conventional implicature associated with the possessive and have chosen not to represent it explicitly in the translation. There would be no problem in including a uniqueness clause (cf. Thomason, 1976; Partee and Bach, 1981).

In the interpretations given by the rule in (118), a NP in the possessive determiner automatically takes wider scope than the CN phrase. This

208 CHAPTER IV

gives us the correct reading for sentences like (120), which will have the interpretation represented in (120').

(120) **Varje students** resultat gjorde **honom** arg.
Every student's result upset him.

(120') $\forall x[\text{student}'(x) \rightarrow \exists y[\text{of}'_*(\check{}x)(\text{result}')(y) \wedge \text{upset}'_*(\check{}y, \check{}x)]]$

6.1.1. vems (whose)

A special case of possessive determiners is the interrogative possessive **vems** (*whose*). This can also get a relational reading, as shown in the dialogue in (121).

(121) Q: Vems råd lyssnar **ingen tonåring** till?
Whose advice does no teenager listen to?

A: **Sina** föräldrars.
His/her parents.

What is particularly interesting about this type of question is that on the present approach it is only the interrogative quantifier corresponding to **vem** (*who*) that gets stored. The rest of the interrogative phrase, including the interpretation of the possessive morpheme will by the link convention be interpreted as an argument of the VP dominating the link bottom[25]. The structure of (121) will be as in (122) and a simplified derivation of the relational reading is given in (123).

(122)

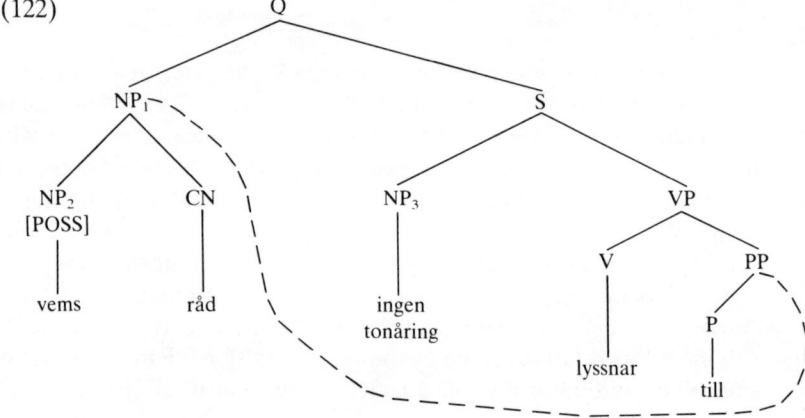

THE INTERPRETATION OF QUESTIONS 209

(123)

EXPRESSION	INTERPRETATION	STORE	RULE USED
[$_{NP_2}$ vems]	$\lambda PP\{W_3(x_5)\}$	$\lambda \mathcal{W} . \mathcal{W} \vee \lambda x[\textbf{person}'(W(x))] \vee \mathcal{W}\{W\}]]_3 (= [WH]_3)$	WH storage
[$_{NP_1}$ vems råd]	$\lambda P \exists z[\textbf{of}'_*(\check{}W_3(x))(\textbf{advice}')(z) \wedge P\{z\}]$	$[WH]_3$	
[$_{VP}$ lyssnar till]	$\textbf{listen-to}'(\hat{P} \exists z[\textbf{of}'_*(\check{}W_3(x_5))(\textbf{advice}')(z) \wedge P\{z\}])$	$[WH]_3$	
[$_{NP_3}$ ingen tonåring]	$\lambda P \neg \exists y[\textbf{teenager}'(y) \wedge P\{y\}]$		
[$_S$ ingen tonåring lyssnar till]	$\neg \exists y[\textbf{teenager}'(y) \wedge \exists z[\textbf{of}'_*(\check{}W_3(y))(\textbf{advice}')(z \wedge \textbf{listen-to}'(\check{}y, \check{}z)]]$	$[WH]_3$	
[$_Q$ vems råd lyssnar ingen tonåring till]	$= \hat{}\text{"..."} \hat{p} \wedge]\mathcal{W} \vee \lambda x[\textbf{person}'(W(x))] \vee \check{}p \vee p =$ $\hat{}\neg \exists y[\textbf{teenager}'(y) \wedge \exists z[\textbf{of}'_*(\check{}W(y))(\textbf{advice}')(z) \wedge \textbf{listen-to}'(\check{}y, \check{}z)]]]$		WH quantification (60)

On the relational interpretation, this question denotes the set of true propositions of the form 'no teenager y listens to the advice of $W(y)$ is a person.

6.2. PP Complements

Complex common noun phrases that contain prepositional phrases raise several problems having to do with where the PPs are attached as well as with their semantics that we cannot address here (cf. Lakoff, 1970; Jackendoff, 1977; Vanlehn, 1978 for some relevant observations). For the purpose of this discussion, we will assume a very rudimentary structure and we will take the argument place of the preposition to be an extensional position. The translation rule we propose in (121) performs this extensionalization (cf. meaning postulate 8 in PTQ). We extend the use of the substar notation to prepositions[26].

One rule for complex CN's will be as in (124).

(124) $\langle 23, CN_1 \rightarrow CN_2 \ P \ NP, \ \lambda y[NP'(\hat{x}[P'_*(\check{\ }x)(CN_2')(y)])]\rangle$

This rule generates the following structures and translations:

(125) brev från Johan $\quad \lambda y[\textbf{from}'_*(j)(\textbf{letter}')(y)]$
letter from Johan

dikt om Maja $\quad \lambda y[\textbf{about}'_*(m)(\textbf{poem}')(y)]$
poem about Maja

6.3. Partitive Questions

We will take partitives to have roughly the structure in (126).

(126)

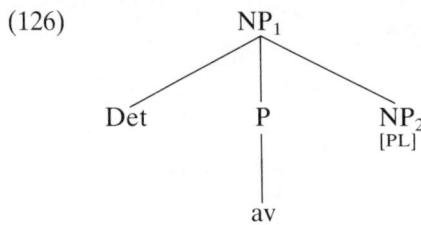

Actually, we need not even specify in the syntax that NP_2 be plural, since determiners in this position will be interpreted as applying to properties of sets of individual concepts. For example, **en** (*one*) in the context ____ **av** NP will be interpreted as in (127). We assume that **av** makes no semantic contribution besides the partitive interpretation.

(127) $\lambda\Sigma\lambda P[\Sigma\{\hat{S}[\ \exists x[S(x) \wedge P\{x\}]]\}]$

This expression is of the appropriate type to combine with the interpretation of a plural NP like **Majas böcker** (*Maja's books*) which is given in (128).

(128) $\lambda\mathscr{P}[\mathscr{P}\{\mathbf{of'_*}(\mathbf{m})(\mathbf{book'})\}]$

The result of this application, after lambda conversation, will be as in (129).

(129) $\lambda P\ \exists \mathbf{x}[\mathbf{of'_*}(\mathbf{m})(\mathbf{book'})(x)\ \&\ P\{x\}]$

The interrogative determiner **vilken** (*which*) will in the context of a partitive be interpreted as in (130).

(130) $\lambda\Sigma[\lambda\mathscr{W}[\Sigma\{\hat{S}[\ \exists W[\ \forall x[S(W(x)) \wedge \mathscr{W}\{W\}]]]\}]]$

In order to get the interpretation of the entire interrogative phrase **vilken av Majas böcker** we must apply (130) to the interpretation of (128). This is shown in (131).

(131) $\lambda\Sigma[\lambda\mathscr{W}[\Sigma\{\hat{S}[\ \exists W[\ \forall x[S(W(x))] \wedge \mathscr{W}\{W\}]]\}]]$
$(\hat{\ }\lambda\mathscr{P}[\mathscr{P}\{\mathbf{of'_*}(\mathbf{m})(\mathbf{book'})\}])$
$\lambda\mathscr{W}[\hat{\ }\lambda\mathscr{P}[\mathscr{P}\{\mathbf{of'_*}(\mathbf{m})(\mathbf{book'})\}]\{\hat{S}[\ \exists W[\ \forall x[S(W(x))] \wedge \mathscr{W}\{W\}]]\}]$
$\lambda\mathscr{W}\ \exists W[\ \forall x[\mathbf{of'_*}(\mathbf{m})(\mathbf{book'})(W(x))] \wedge \mathscr{W}\{W\}]$

Note that the interpretation in (131) is not of the type of an NP, hence it cannot immediately combine with a VP but is necessarily stored as was outlined in the discussion of the interpretation rules for interrogative quantifiers in Chapter III, Section 3.

The rules we have discussed so far will suffice to interpret both the Swedish and the English partitive questions in (115).

(115)a. Vilken av **sina** böcker rekommenderade **varje författare**?
b. Which of *his* books did *every author* recommend?

212   CHAPTER IV

The Swedish question is unambiguous. The possessive reflexive pronoun in the interrogative phrase will be obligatorily bound in the specification of the *W* variable. The English question is ambiguous, depending on if *his* is understood as a bound or a deictic pronoun. This is reflected in the derivation by the fact that the individual variable in the interpretation of *his* may or may not get affected by the closure operation. Since these two examples illustrate quite well the interaction of the closure operation with optional and obligatory quantification, we will go through the two derivations in some detail. For perspicuity we will disregard main verb inversion in the Swedish question and *do* support in the English question.

(132a)

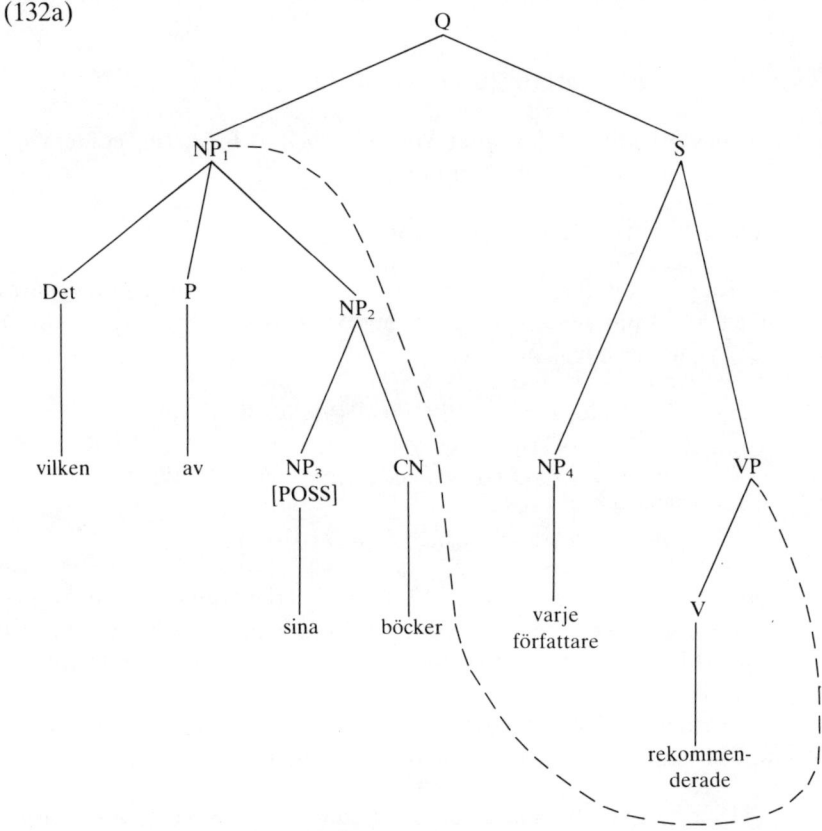

The table to tree diagram (132a) is given on p. 214.

(132b)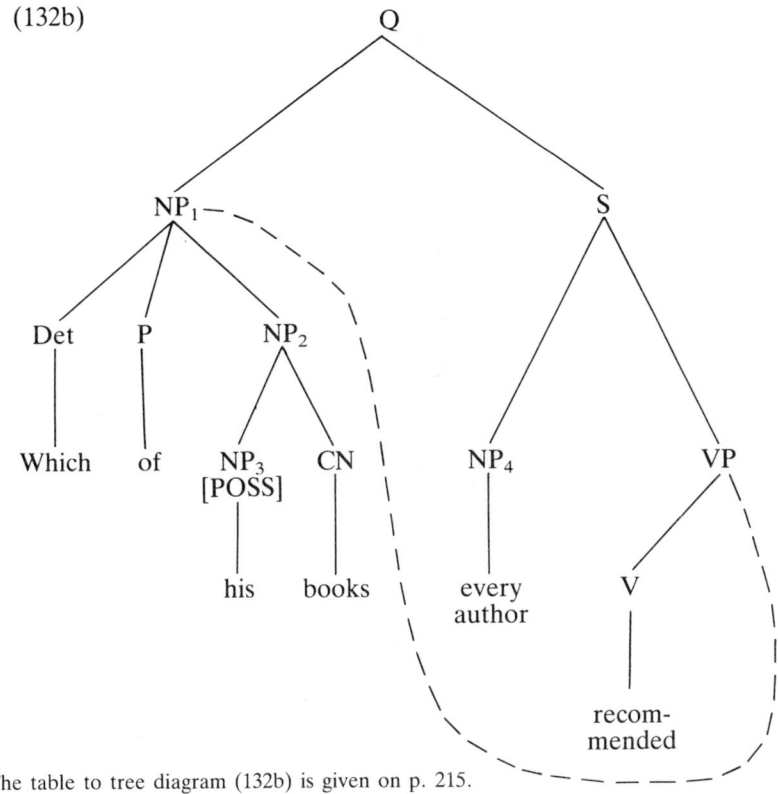

The table to tree diagram (132b) is given on p. 215.

When we compare the two derivations, we can see that the English question is indeed ambiguous. The constituent rooted in Q is associated with a set of meanings, actually four meanings. However, on closer inspection it turns out that they are not all distinct. The readings indicated by (a) and (b), express the same reading, the one on which every author recommend a particular book by some contextually given individual, referred to by the pronoun. (c) expresses the relational reading where every author recommended one of his own books. (d) also expresses a relational reading, i.e. the choice of book varies with the choice of author, but the relation involved here is less direct than in (c). According to (d) we are asked which of some given individual's books, let's say John's books, every author recommended. A possible answer on that reading would be *the one of John's books that he* (the author)

This table relates to tree diagram (132a) on p. 212.

(132)a

EXPRESSION	INTERPRETATION	STORE	RULE USED
[$_{CN}$ böcker]	$\lambda \mathscr{P}[\mathscr{P}\{\textbf{book}'\}]$		
[$_{NP_3}$ sina]	$\lambda PP\{x_3\}$	$[\lambda PP\{x_3\}]_3$	Obl. store of reflexive interpretation.
[$_{NP_2}$ sina böcker]	$\lambda \mathscr{P}[\mathscr{P}\{x[\textbf{of}'_*(\check{}x_3)(\textbf{book}')(x)]\}]$	$[\lambda PP\{x_3\}]_3$	cf (118)
[$_{NP_1}$ vilken av sina böcker]	$\lambda PP\{W_1(x_3)\}$	$[\lambda \mathscr{W} \exists W[\forall x[\textbf{of}'_*(x)(\textbf{book}\cdot(W(x)) \wedge \mathscr{W}\{W\}]]_1 (=[WH]_1) [\lambda PP\{x_3\}]_3$	WH storage, closure affects the variable in the reflexive interpretation
[$_{VP}$ rekommenderade]	$\textbf{recommend}'(PP\{W_1(x_3)\}) = $ $= \lambda x_3[\textbf{recommend}'(PP\{W_1(x_3)\})(x_3)]$	$[WH]_1$	Reflexive rule (87)
[$_{NP_4}$ varje författare]	$\begin{cases} \lambda P \ \forall x[\textbf{author}'(x) \to P\{x\}] \\ \lambda PP\{x_5\} \end{cases}$	$[\lambda P \ \forall x[\textbf{author}'(x) \to P\{x\}]]_5$ $(=[NP]_5)$	NP storage
[$_S$ varje författare rekommenderade]	$\forall y[\textbf{author}'(y) \to \textbf{recommend}\cdot(\check{}y, \ \check{}W_1(y))]$	$[WH]_1$	
[$_O$ vilken av sina böcker varje författare rekommenderade]	$\lambda p \ \exists W \ \Lambda x[\textbf{of}'_*(\check{}x)(\textbf{book}')(W(x)) \wedge \check{}p \wedge p =$ $= \forall y[\textbf{author}'(y) \to \textbf{recommend}\cdot(\check{}y, \ \check{}W(y))]]$		$[WH]_1$ applied to S' by WH quantification rule (60)

THE INTERPRETATION OF QUESTIONS

This table relates to tree diagram (132b) on p. 215.

(132b)

EXPRESSION	INTERPRETATION	STORE	RULE USED
[$_{CN}$ books]	$\lambda \mathscr{P}[\mathscr{P}\{\mathbf{book}'\}]$		
[$_{NP_3}$ his]	$\lambda PP\{x_3\}$		
[$_{NP_2}$ his books]	$\lambda \mathscr{P}[\mathscr{P}\{\hat{x}[\mathbf{of}'_*(\check{\,}x_3)(\mathbf{book}')(x)]\}]$		
[$_{NP_1}$ which of his books]	$\begin{cases} [\lambda \mathscr{W}_\in \mathbb{WE}]\lambda \mathscr{W} \mathbb{A}]\lambda x[\mathbf{of}'_*(\check{\,}x)(\mathbf{book}')(W(x))] \\ \langle\,\check{\,}\mathscr{W}\{W\}]_1 \\ [\lambda \mathscr{W}_\in \mathbb{WE}]\lambda \mathscr{W} \mathbb{A}]\lambda x[\mathbf{of}'_*(\check{\,}x_3)(\mathbf{book}')(W(x))] \\ \langle\,\check{\,}\mathscr{W}\{W\}]_2 \end{cases}$	$[WH]_1$ $[WH]_2$	cf. (118) WH quantifier formation; closure affects x_3 Closure doesn't affect x_3 WH storage WH storage
[$_{VP}$ recommend]	$\begin{cases} \mathbf{recommend}'(\hat{P}P\{W_1(x_5)\}) \\ \mathbf{recommend}'(\hat{P}P\{W_2(x_5)\}) \end{cases}$	$[WH]_1$ $[WH]_2$	
[$_{NP_4}$ every author]	$\begin{cases} \lambda P\, \forall x[\mathbf{author}'(x) \to P\{x\}] \\ \lambda PP\{x_5\} \end{cases}$	$[\lambda P\, \forall x[\mathbf{author}'(x) \to P\{x\}]]_5\ (=[NP]_5)$	NP storage
[$_S$ every author recommended]	(a) $\mathbb{A}x[\mathbf{author}'(x) \to \mathbf{recommend}'(\check{\,}x,\check{\,}W_1(x_5))]$ (b) $\mathbb{A}x[\mathbf{author}'(x) \to \mathbf{recommend}'(\check{\,}x,\check{\,}W_2(x_5))]$ (c) $\mathbf{recommend}_*(\check{\,}x_5,\check{\,}W_1(x_5)) = \\ = \forall x[\mathbf{author}'(x) \to \mathbf{recommend}_*(\check{\,}x,\check{\,}W_1(x))]$ (d) $\mathbf{recommend}'(\check{\,}x_5,\check{\,}W_2(x_5)) = \\ = \forall x[\mathbf{author}'(x) \to \mathbf{recommend}_*(\check{\,}x,\check{\,}W_2(x))]$	$[WH]_1$ $[WH]_2$ $[WH]_1, [NP]_5$ $[WH]_1, [NP]_5$ $[WH]_2, [NP]_5$ $[WH]_2$	NP quantification NP quantification
[$_Q$ which of his books every author recommended]	(a) $\lambda p\, \exists y \mathbb{A}]\lambda x[\mathbf{of}'_*(\check{\,}x_3)(\mathbf{book}')(W(x))]\mathbb{WE}]\lambda x \mathbb{A}]\lambda x\,\check{\,} . \\ \mathbb{A} x[\mathbf{author}'(y) \to \mathbf{recommend}_*(\check{\,}y,\check{\,}W(x_5))]] \land \check{\,}p \land p =$ (b) $\lambda p\, \exists y \mathbb{WE}]\lambda x[\mathbf{of}'_*(\check{\,}x_3)(\mathbf{book}')(W(x))]\mathbb{A}]\lambda x\,\check{\,} . \\ \mathbb{A} y[\mathbf{author}'(y) \to \mathbf{recommend}_*(\check{\,}y,\check{\,}W(x_5))]] \land \check{\,}p \land p =$ (c) $\lambda p\, \exists y \mathbb{WE}]\lambda x[\mathbf{of}'_*(\check{\,}x)(\mathbf{book}')(W(x))]\mathbb{A}]\lambda x\,\check{\,} . \\ \mathbb{A} y[\mathbf{author}'(y) \to \mathbf{recommend}_*(\check{\,}y,\check{\,}W(y))]] \land \check{\,}p \land p =$ (d) $\lambda p\, \exists y \mathbb{A}]\lambda x[\mathbf{of}'_*(\check{\,}x_3)(\mathbf{book}')(W(x))]\mathbb{WE}]\lambda x\,\check{\,} . \\ \mathbb{A} y[\mathbf{author}'(y) \to \mathbf{recommend}_*(\check{\,}y, W(y))]]$		$[WH]_1$ applied to S'(a) by Question rule (60) $[WH]_2$ applied to S'(b) $[WH]_1$ applied to S'(c) $[WH]_2$ applied to S'(d)

had actually read. The three meanings illustrate three ways of deriving a reading given the possibility of letting individual variables in the placeholding pronoun translation remain free, the possibility of letting individual variables in the specification of the quantifier remain unaffected by the closure operation, or both. The Swedish question, on the other hand, is unambiguous, as can be seen from the fact that there is only one meaning associated with the Q node. The difference in interpretation possibilities shows up already at the level of interpreting the interrogative quantifier. Whereas the English expression *which of his books* is associated with a set of meanings, depending on whether or not the closure operation has affected the free individual variable in the pronoun interpretation or not, the Swedish phrase **vilken av sina böcker** is only associated with one interpretation. This is because the closure operation obligatorily affects all variables associated with a stored meaning, in this case a stored reflexive meaning. Notice also that the choice of individual variable in the placeholding pronoun meaning is not free when the replaced meaning is associated with a meaning in store. This further reduces the number of interpretations in the Swedish derivation.

These are the readings we get without giving *every author* wider scope than the question. Suppose we had embedded this question as in (134),

(134)a. Maja undrar vilken av sina böcker varje författare rekommenderade.
     b. Maja wonders which of his books every author recommended.

We could then have kept the interpretation of *every author* in store until we reached the highest S level where quantifying-in would apply. We would then get the readings represented in (135), for the Swedish and the English version, respectively. We disregard equivalent readings.

(135)a. $\Big\{$ **wonder'**($^\wedge$m, $\hat{p}$ $\exists W$[$\forall x$[**of'**$_*$($^\vee x$)(**book'**)($W(x)$)] $\wedge$ $^\vee p \wedge p =$
$= {}^\wedge \forall y$[**author'**(y) $\to$ **recommend'**$_*$($^\vee y$, $^\vee W(y)$)]])
$\forall y$[**author'**(y) $\to$ **wonder'**($^\wedge$m, $\hat{p}$ $\exists W$[$\forall x$[**of'**$_*$($^\vee x$)(**book'**)
($W(x)$)] $\wedge$ $^\vee p \wedge p = {}^\wedge$**recommend'**$_*$($^\vee y$, $^\vee W(y)$)])] $\Big\}$

(135)b. $\Big\{$ (a) **wonder'**($^\wedge$m, $\hat{p}$ $\exists W$[$\forall x$[**of'**$_*$($^\vee x_3$)(**book'**)($W(x)$)]
$\wedge$ $^\vee p \wedge p = {}^\wedge$ $\forall y$[**author'**(y) $\to$
recommend'$_*$($^\vee y$, $^\vee W(y)$)]])

(b) **wonder**$'(\hat{\ }m, \hat{p}\ \exists W[\ \forall x[\textbf{of}'_*(\check{\ }x_3)(\textbf{book}')(W(x))]$
$\wedge\ \check{\ }p \wedge p = \hat{\ }\ \forall y[\textbf{author}'(y) \rightarrow$
recommend$'_*(\check{\ }y,\ \check{\ }W(y))]])$

(c) $\forall y[\textbf{author}'(y) \rightarrow \textbf{wonder}'(\hat{\ }m, \hat{p}\ \exists W[\ \forall x[\textbf{of}'_*(\check{\ }x_3)$
$(\textbf{book}')(W(x))] \wedge\ \check{\ }p \wedge p =$
$=\hat{\ }\textbf{recommend}'_*(\check{\ }y,\ \check{\ }W(y))]$

(d) $\forall y[\textbf{author}'(y) \rightarrow \textbf{wonder}'(\hat{\ }m, \hat{p}\ \exists W[\ \forall x[\textbf{of}'_*(\check{\ }x_3)$
$(\textbf{book}')(W(x))] \wedge\ \check{\ }p \wedge p =$
$=\hat{\ }\textbf{recommend}'_*(\check{\ }y,\ \check{\ }W(y))]$

As we can see from (135), the questions in both languages are ambiguous depending on whether *every author* takes wider scope than *wonder* or not. In English, the additional ambiguities arise from the choice of interpreting *his* as bound or deictic.

6.4. *More on Control of Reflexives*

So far we are able to account for reflexive pronouns which are controlled by the subject of the sentence in which they occur. The way we do this is by having the Reflexive rule (87) apply at the VP level, abstracting over the individual variable in the interpretation of the reflexive pronoun. However, reflexive pronouns can also be bound by possessive NPs as shown by the following examples. In case there is no available controller, the result is ungrammatical.

(136)a.   **Majas** kort   på **sig**   ligger på bordet[27].
         Maja's picture of (her)self is   on the table

     b.   *Ett kort   på **sig** ligger på bordet.
         a   picture of self is   on the table

(137)a.   **Majas** bok   om   **sina** föräldrar ligger på bordet.
         Maja's book about her parents   is   on the table

     b.   *Boken   om   **sina** föräldrar ligger på bordet.
         the book about self's parents   is   on the table

In this respect, possessive NPs act within their NP domains similarly to subjects of tensed sentences as has often been pointed out (cf. Chomsky, 1970). In order to account for this type of NP internal control of reflexives, we propose an additional reflexivization rule. This rule will allow the NP in a possessive determiner to bind a reflexive pronoun inside the CN phrase. Just as in the case of VP reflexivization, the effect of the rule will be to empty the reflexive meaning from store and abstract over the address variable. The rule will have two cases, depending on whether the CN is singular or plural (cf. (118)).

(138)   *NP internal reflexive rule*
   a. In a structure $NP_1 \rightarrow NP_2 \underset{[SG]}{CN}$, if

   $\langle \alpha, \sigma_0, [\lambda PP\{x_i\}]_i, \sigma_1 \rangle \in m(CN)$
   then $\langle \lambda P[NP_2'(\hat{x}_i[\ \exists x[\textbf{of}'_*(\check{}x_i)(\alpha)(x) \wedge P\{x\}]])], \sigma_0, \sigma_1 \rangle$
   $\in m(NP_1)$.

   b. In a structure $NP_1 \rightarrow NP_2 \underset{[PL]}{CN}$, if

   $\langle \alpha, \sigma_0, [\lambda PP\{x_i\}]_i, \sigma_1 \rangle \in m(CN)$
   then $\langle \lambda \mathscr{S}[NP_2'(\hat{x}_i[\mathscr{S}\{\hat{x}[\textbf{of}'_*(\check{}x_i)(\alpha)(x)]\}])], \sigma, \sigma_1 \rangle$
   $\in m(NP_1)$.

Rule (138), which gives NP internal control of reflexives, is illustrated in the derivation of the NP in (139).

(139)   Majas sång om   sig
        Maja's song about herself

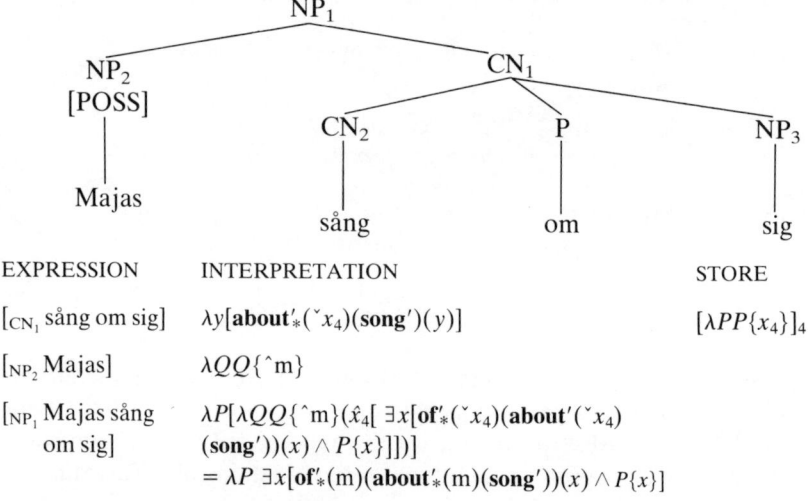

EXPRESSION	INTERPRETATION	STORE
[$_{CN_1}$ sång om sig]	$\lambda y[\textbf{about}'_*(\check{}x_4)(\textbf{song}')(y)]$	$[\lambda PP\{x_4\}]_4$
[$_{NP_2}$ Majas]	$\lambda QQ\{\hat{}m\}$	
[$_{NP_1}$ Majas sång om sig]	$\lambda P[\lambda QQ\{\hat{}m\}(\hat{x}_4[\ \exists x[\textbf{of}'_*(\check{}x_4)(\textbf{about}'(\check{}x_4)$ $(\textbf{song}'))(x) \wedge P\{x\}]])]$ $= \lambda P\ \exists x[\textbf{of}'_*(m)(\textbf{about}'_*(m)(\textbf{song}'))(x) \wedge P\{x\}]$	

THE INTERPRETATION OF QUESTIONS   219

Since there is some variation between personal and reflexive pronouns in this context, the rule in (128) is optional[28].

If the NP in the possessive determiner is not a possible antecedent for the reflexive, that is, if it is not a third person NP, the reflexive must be controlled by some other antecedent, such as the subject of the sentence.

(140)a. Maja$_i$ tycker om din sång om **sin**$_i$ syster
    Maja likes   your song about her-own sister

b. Maja$_i$ tycker om din sång om **hennes**$_{i,j}$ syster
    Maja likes   your song about her   sister

To derive (140a), the reflexive meaning must remain in store and trigger reflexivization at the VP level. The translation of the NP **din sång om sin syster** (*your song about self's sister*) will be as in (141), where there is still a reflexive meaning in store. The translation of the whole sentence is given in (140a′).

(141) $\langle \lambda P\ \exists x\ \exists y[\textbf{of}'_*(x_2)(\textbf{sister}')(x)\ \wedge$
    $\textbf{of}'_*(\textbf{you}')(\textbf{about}'_*(\check{\ }x)(\textbf{song}'))(y)\ \wedge\ P\{y\}],$
    $[\lambda PP\{x_2\}]_2\rangle$

(140a′) $\exists x\ \exists y[\textbf{of}'_*(\textbf{m})(\textbf{sister}')(x)\ \wedge$
    $\textbf{of}'_*(\textbf{you}')(\textbf{about}'_*(\check{\ }x)(\textbf{song}'))(y)\ \wedge\ \textbf{like}'_*(\textbf{m},\ \check{\ }y)]$

We conclude this section with a couple of examples where the possessive NP is a quantified NP.

(142)   **Varje flickas** sång om **sig** behagar **henne**.
    Every girl's song about herself pleases her.

(142′) $\forall x[\textbf{girl}'(x) \rightarrow \exists y[\textbf{of}'_*(\check{\ }x)(\textbf{about}'_*(\check{\ }x)(\textbf{song}'))(y)\ \wedge$
    $\textbf{please}'_*(\check{\ }y,\ \check{\ }x)]]$

In order to bind the personal pronoun **henne**, **varje flicka** must take wider scope than the NP containing it. Notice that it will also control the interpretation of the reflexive **sig**.

(143)   **Vilken flickas** sång om **sig** tycker du om?
    Which girl's song about herself do you like?

(143') "?" $\hat{p}$ $\exists W[\textbf{girl}'(W) \land \check{}p \land p =$
$= \hat{} \exists x[\textbf{of}'_*(\check{}W)(\textbf{about}'_*(\check{}W)(\textbf{song}'))(x) \land \textbf{like}'_*(\textbf{you}', \check{}x)]]$

that is, the set of true propositions of the form 'you like W's song about W' where W is a girl. Since **vilken flicka** is an interrogative quantifier, it will obligatorily be stored until we are about to interpret the sentence. The placeholding variable will then control the reflexive **sig** which will ultimately be controlled by the interrogative quantifier.

7. MULTIPLE WH QUESTIONS

The question rule in (60) will allow us to interpret single direct questions and single embedded questions as well as *iterated* embedded questions. These will have the structure outlined in (144).

(144)

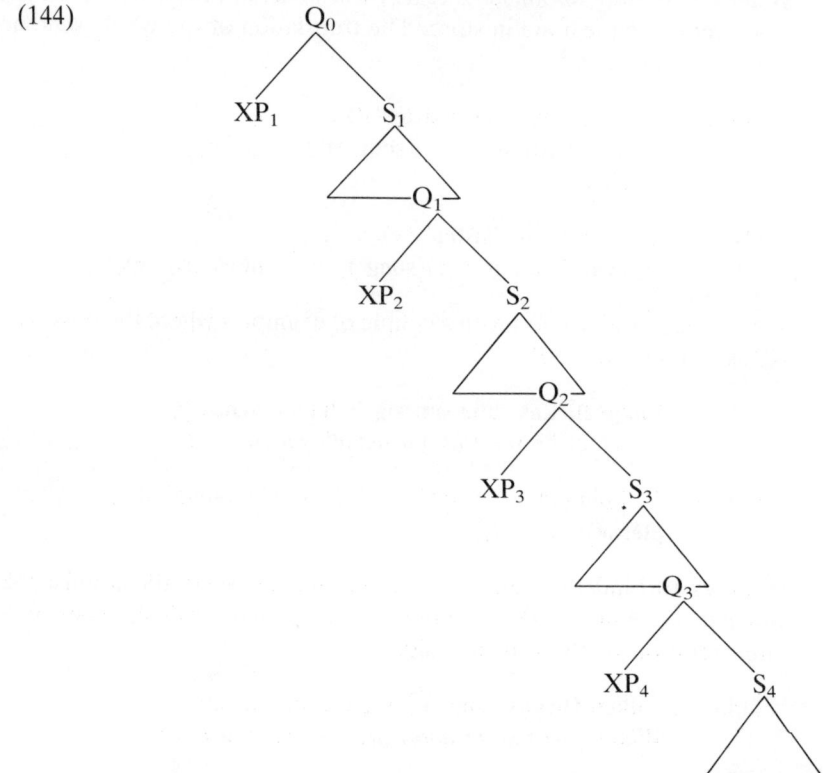

Since Swedish allows extraction out of embedded questions, the initial interrogative constituent XP_1 may be linked to a gap inside any of Q_1-Q_3, as well as in S_1, of course. An example illustrating a dependency between an initial interrogative constituent and a gap in Q_2 is given in (145)

(145)   Vilken film$_i$ mindes ingen   [$_{Q_1}$ vem$_j$ som ____$_j$
         which   movie   did no one remember   who   that

         visste [$_{Q_2}$ vem$_k$ som ____$_k$ regisserat ____$_i$]]
         knew   who   that   (had) directed

What we are here calling iterated questions should not be confused with *multiple questions*, i.e. questions where in addition to the interrogative constituents in Comp, there are one or more 'unmoved' WH phrases in the sentence. Whereas an answer to an iterated question like (145) consists of providing a value for the initial interrogative constituent, an answer to a multiple question will give a value to the initial interrogative phrase and may in addition give values to all unmoved WH phrases. By an unmoved WH phrase is usually meant an interrogative phrase that occurs in a normal argument position within a sentence, i.e. not in Comp. In languages like English and Swedish, only one constituent can occur in Comp but other languages such as Serbo-Croatian allow more than one constituent to be directly dominated by Comp (cf. Browne, 1973)[29].

In this section on multiple questions, we will first look at cases where an unmoved WH phrase occurs elsewhere in the sentence. In Section 7.2 we will look at cases where a WH phrase is embedded inside another WH phrase. This turns out to be a type of construction where the relational approach makes some interesting predictions. Finally, in Section 7.3 we will look at the special case where an unmoved WH phrase is embedded inside a WH phrase in Comp.

7.1. Simple 'Unmoved' WH Phrases

We have already mentioned one example of a multiple question, namely (8) which we briefly discussed in Section 1.

(8)   Which table ordered which wine?

Just like other questions, we take multiple questions to denote sets of propositions. In this case it would be the set of propositions of the form '*x* ordered *y*' where *x* is a table and *y* is a wine. We have argued against letting the uniqueness implicatures associated with *which* questions, and also with multiple *which* questions, become part of their meaning. We can extend our interpretation procedures for constituent questions to also apply to multiple questions quite straightforwardly. This is best seen by looking at a sample derivation. Consider (146) which is the linked tree representation of (8).

(146)

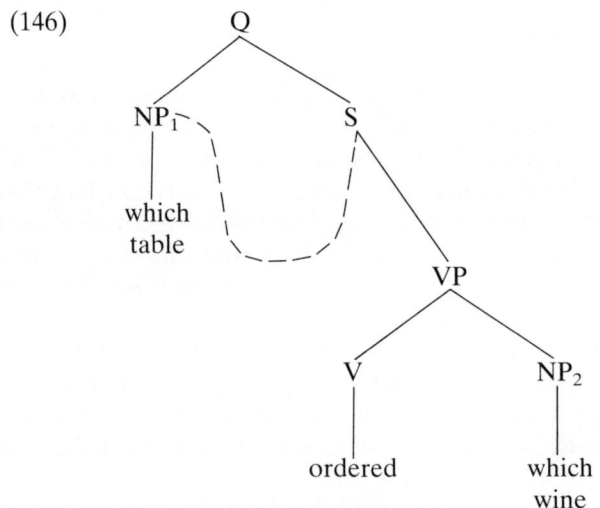

When we interpret the S node we must take into account the interpretation of the link child *which table*. Since this interpretation consists of an interrogative quantifier, it cannot immediately contribute to the interpretation of S but is stored and a placeholding pronoun meaning is inserted instead.

EXPRESSION	INTERPRETATION	STORE
$[_{NP_1}$ which table]	$\lambda PP\{W_1\}$	$[\lambda \mathcal{W} \exists W[\mathbf{table}'(W) \wedge \mathcal{W}\{W\}]]_1 \ (=[WH]_1)$

For the purpose of this example, it suffices to show an individual level derivation. The W variable used in the pronoun meaning and in the quantifier is of valence zero, hence it is equivalent to an individual variable. When we interpret NP_2, the same procedure will apply, since *which wine* is also an interrogative quantifier, i.e. not of the type of a NP which is what we need as an argument for the interpretation of *order*. The interpretation of *which wine* is thus also stored and a pronoun meaning is inserted. The interpretation of the VP will be:

[$_{VP}$ ordered which wine] **order'**$(\hat{P}P\{W_2\})$ $[\lambda \mathcal{W} \exists W[\textbf{wine'}(W) \wedge \mathcal{W}\{W\}]]_2$ $(=[WH]_2)$

The interpretation of the S node contributes the placeholding interpretation of the link child, *which table*, as given above.

[$_S$ ordered which wine]   **order'**$'_*(\check{}W_1, \check{}W_2)$ $[WH]_1, [WH]_2$

Note that we have now two interrogative quantifiers in store. At this level, our interpretation rule for questions, (60), allows us to quantify in one interrogative quantifier. Suppose we quantify in $[WH]_1$, which gives us the following representation:

[$_Q$ which table ordered which wine] $\lambda p \ \exists W[\textbf{table'}(W) \wedge \check{}p \wedge p = \hat{}\textbf{order'}'_*(\check{}W, \check{}W_2)]$ $[WH]_2$

Since there is still a meaning in store, this cannot be a reduced meaning for the multiple question in (146). We need another WH quantification rule, one which quantifies interrogative quantifiers into questions. We will assume in addition to the rule in (60), the rule in (147), which is very similar to the rule of NP quantification given in Chapter III[30].

(147) *Multiple WH Quantification Rule*
If $\langle \alpha, \sigma_0, [WH]_i, \sigma_1 \rangle \in m(Q)$
then $\langle \lambda q[[WH]_i(\hat{W}_i[\alpha(q)])], \sigma_0, \sigma_1 \rangle \in m(Q)$.
α is an expression in IL.
σ is a sequence of elements in store.

(147) applies optionally at any indirect question or matrix question level. We use (147) to quantify in the remaining WH meaning, $[WH]_2$, and get as our final representation of the meaning of (146) an expression like in (148).

(148) $\lambda p \ \exists W_1 \ \exists W[\textbf{table'}(W) \wedge \textbf{wine'}(W_1) \wedge \check{}p \wedge p =$
$= \hat{}\textbf{order'}'_*(\check{}W, \check{}W_1)]$

that is, the set of true propositions of the form 'W ordered W_1' where W is a table and W_1 is a wine.

In Chapter III we devoted some attention to the fact that multiple questions which involve embedded questions are ambiguous, as shown by the possible answers to them. Consider the question in (149) together with the two possible ways of answering it.

(149)   Q: Who knows where Mary bought which book?

   A: a. John does.
   b. John knows where Mary bought *Syntactic Structures* and Bill knows where she bought *Aspects* ...

The ambiguity depends on the fact that the unmoved WH phrase *which book* can be interpreted either at the level of the embedded question or at the level of the matrix questions (cf. Chapter III, 4.2.; Baker, 1970; Hirschbühler, 1978). On our approach, we derive the two readings for (149) by quantifying in *which book*, using the rule in (147) either at the embedded question level or at the matrix question level, again using (147). The representation of the meaning of (149) will thus consist of a set of meanings, as shown in (149'). For simplicity, we translate *where* like a prepositional phrase *in which place*.

(149') $\Big\{$ (a) "?" $\hat{q}$ $\exists W_2[\textbf{person}'(W_2) \wedge \check{} p \wedge p =$
$= \hat{} \textbf{know}'(W_2, \hat{p} \exists W_1 \exists W[\textbf{place}'(W_1) \wedge \textbf{book}'(W) \wedge$
$\check{} p \wedge p = \hat{} \textbf{in}'_*(\check{} W_1)(\textbf{buy}'_*)(m, \check{} W)])]$

(b) "?" $\hat{q}$ $\exists W_2 \exists W[\textbf{person}'(W_2) \wedge \textbf{book}'(W) \wedge \check{} p \wedge p =$
$= \hat{} \textbf{know}'(W_2, \hat{p} \exists W_1[\textbf{place}'(W_1) \wedge \check{} p \wedge p =$
$= \hat{} \textbf{in}'_*(\check{} W_1)(\textbf{buy}'_*)(m, \check{} W)])]$ $\Big\}$

On the reading indicated by (a), there is just one interrogative quantifier with matrix scope. It thus requires a singular answer like *John (does)*. On the reading in (b), there are two quantifiers, W_2 and W, at the matrix question level. Appropriate answers on this reading must instantiate both, as illustrated in (149b)[31].

The optionality of the Multiple WH Quantification rule in (147) thus allows us to derive both readings for questions like (149). However, there is one requirement on the interpretation of multiple questions that we discussed in Chapter III and that we now need to deal with formally. The scope of the WH phrase in Comp, e.g. *where* in (149), is not flexible. *where* must be interpreted at the embedded question level. Its interpretation may not remain in store and become part of the meaning of the matrix sentence or question. As we mentioned in our previous discussion, we assume that this restriction is linked to the fact that languages like English have a fixed position for interrogative phrases in constituent questions, and that this position also indicates the scope of the WH phrase. Languages like Japanese where there is no fixed position for WH phrases apparently don't have this restriction. We will enforce this requirement by making sure that any interrogative quantifier in store at an S level which corresponds to a WH phrase which occurs as a sister of that S must be quantified in at that level.

Schematically, in a structure like (50)

(150)

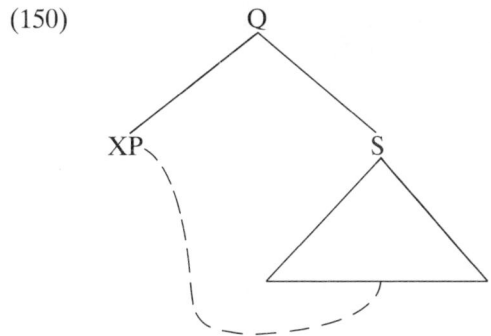

we require that there be a $[WH]_i$ in the meaning set of S which is associated with a free W_i in the meaning set of XP. By linking the occurrence of a free W_i variable to the retrieval of $[WH]_i$, we make sure that the quantifier in question, $[WH]_i$, does not take wider scope than corresponds to its surface position. We express this in a refinement of the WH quantification rule given in (60)[32].

(151)   *WH Quantification*

In a structure Q → XP   S,
if $\langle \alpha, \sigma_0, [WH]_i, \sigma_1 \rangle \in m(S)$
and $\langle \ldots W_i \ldots, \sigma_0 \rangle \in m(XP)$
then $\langle \lambda p[[WH]_i(\hat{W}[\check{}p \wedge p = \hat{}S'])], \sigma_0, \sigma_1 \rangle \in m(Q)$.

The examples of multiple questions we have discussed so far have not required making essential use of the relational W approach. We now turn to some examples where this is the case. Let us reinvoke the scenario which we briefly outlined in Section 3 of this chapter. The art teachers of some school have had their students do a series of projects. For the annual art show, they make a selection of paintings by the students. We can imagine that some art teacher encourages his/her students to suggest which of their paintings they think should be considered for the art show. In this situation, one art teacher may ask the other:

(152)   Q: **Vilken elev** föreslog **vilken av sina målningar**?
Which student suggested which of his paintings?

A: Kalle föreslog sitt skogslandskap och
Pelle föreslog sitt stilleben.

*Kalle suggested his forest landscape and
Pelle suggested his still life.*

Both interrogative phrases, **vilken elev** and **vilken av sina målningar**, are here quantified into the question at the same level. They thus in some sense have the same scope. Nevertheless, **vilken av sina målningar** contains a reflexive pronoun, apparently bound by the other quantifier **vilken elev**. Contrary to what one might assume, we need not invoke any ordering of the quantifying-in rules. We can use exactly the same approach as we have suggested for relational questions in general, namely to let a bound anaphor in an interrogative constituent be bound not directly by its antecedent, but *indirectly* in the characterization of the interrogative quantifier. The use of relational variables in the interpretation of gaps together with the convention for storing and retrieving reflexive meanings will guarantee that we get the intended interpretation for the question. The interrogative quantifier associated with **vilken av sina målningar** will be

$$\lambda \mathcal{W} \; \exists W [\, \forall x[\mathbf{of}'_*(\check{\ }x)(\mathbf{painting}')(W(x))] \wedge \mathcal{W}\{W\}]$$

i.e. the value of W must, for any x, be one of x's paintings. The meaning of (152) can be represented as in (152').

(152') $\lambda p \; \exists W^0 \; \exists W^1[\mathbf{student}'(W^0) \wedge \forall x[\mathbf{of}'_*(\check{\ }x)(\mathbf{painting}')(W^1(x))] \wedge$
$\check{\ }p \wedge p = \hat{\ }\mathbf{suggest}'_*(\check{\ }W^0, \check{\ }W^1(W^0))]$

that is, the set of true propositions of the form 'W^0 suggested $W^1(W^0)$' where W^0 is a student and for all x, $W^1(x)$ is one of x's paintings.

The relational approach to interrogative quantifiers also enables us to account for the two readings of a multiple question like (153) (cf. (36)).

(153) Q: Vem minns vilken elev som inte tyckte om vilken av sina målningar?

Who remembers which student didn't like which of his paintings?

A: a. Johan.

b. Johan minns vilken elev som inte tyckte om sin nakenstudie och Maja minns vilken elev som inte tyckte om sin surrealistiska målning.

Johan remembers which student didn't like his nude study, and Maja remembers which student didn't like his surrealistic painting.

We argued above that an answer like (153b) shows that the unmoved WH phrase has scope at the matrix question level. Nevertheless, **vilken av sina målningar** contains an anaphor, related to the WH phrase in Comp **vilken elev** whose scope is arguably fixed to be the embedded question. We can handle this apparent scope conflict, again by making use of indirect binding of anaphors in the characterization of the interrogative quantifier. The meaning of (153) then comes out as in (153').

(153')   (a) "?" $\hat{p}$ $\exists W[\textbf{person}'(W) \wedge \check{}p \wedge p =$
$= \hat{}\textbf{remember}'(W, \hat{q}$ $\exists W_1$ $\exists W_2[\textbf{student}'(W_1) \wedge$
$\forall x[\textbf{of}'_*(\check{}x)(\textbf{painting}')(W_2(x))] \wedge \check{}q \wedge q =$
$= \hat{}\neg\textbf{like}'_*(\check{}W_1, \check{}[W_2(W_1)])])]$

(b) "?" $\hat{p}$ $\exists W$ $\exists W_1[\textbf{person}'(W) \wedge$
$\forall x[\textbf{of}'_*(\check{}x)(\textbf{painting}')(W_1(x))] \wedge \check{}p \wedge p =$
$= \hat{}\textbf{remember}'(W, \hat{q}$ $\exists W_2[\textbf{student}'(W_2) \wedge \check{}q \wedge q =$
$= \hat{}\neg\textbf{like}'_*(\check{}W_2, \check{}[W_1(W_2)])])]$

The interpretation associated with (153) consists of a set of meanings, one where **vilken av sina målningar** is interpreted inside the embedded question, (a), and one reading where it is interpreted as part of the matrix question, (b).

7.2. *Embedded WH Phrases*

WH phrases may also occur as constituents embedded inside other WH phrases. Depending on the availability of possible antecedents within the question, such complex WH phrases may require a relational interpretation, as for instance in (154).

(154)　Q: *Which actress* was upset by [which review of [which of her films?]]
　　　　　　　　　　　　　　　　NP　　　　　　　　NP

　　　　A: Greta Garbo was upset by *Dagens Nyheter's* review of 'Ninotschka' and Liz Taylor was upset by the *Times'* review of 'Cleopatra', and ...

In order to represent the reading where the choice of film depends on the choice of actress, we need a relational *W* variable in the representation of the interrogative quantifier *which of her films* as well as in the placeholding pronoun interpretation. Since there is only one possible antecedent, *which actress*, which can bind an argument of *W*, the valence of *W* will be one. Had there been more than one quantifier with scope over the unmoved WH phrase, we would have needed a *W* variable of higher valence. The interesting cases turn out to be the ones where a relational interrogative phrase is embedded inside another relational interrogative phrase and where the anaphors are bound by different antecedents, as for instance in the following elaboration of the previous example:

(155)　*Which actress* thanked **which critic** for which of **his** articles about which of *her* films?

On the bound interpretation of this multiple question, a complex WH phrase which consists of a relational interrogative quantifier *which of her films* with *her* bound by *which actress* is embedded inside another WH quantifier *which of his articles about* ___ where *his* is understood as bound by *which critic*. It is instructive to look at some of the steps in the derivation of (155) because they illustrate what the consequences of syntactic embedding are for the interpretation possibilities of embedded WH phrases. Let us first look at the interpretation of the most embedded interrogative quantifier *which of her films* which will be:

$$\langle \lambda PP\{W_6(x_3)\}, [\lambda \mathcal{W} \ \exists W^1[\ \forall x[\textbf{of}'_*(\check{\ }x)(\textbf{film}')(W^1(x))] \wedge \mathcal{W}\{W^1\}]]_6 \rangle$$

The interpretation of the quantifier is stored and a pronoun interpretation with a free *W* variable as well as a free individual variable, x_3, is

THE INTERPRETATION OF QUESTIONS

(156)

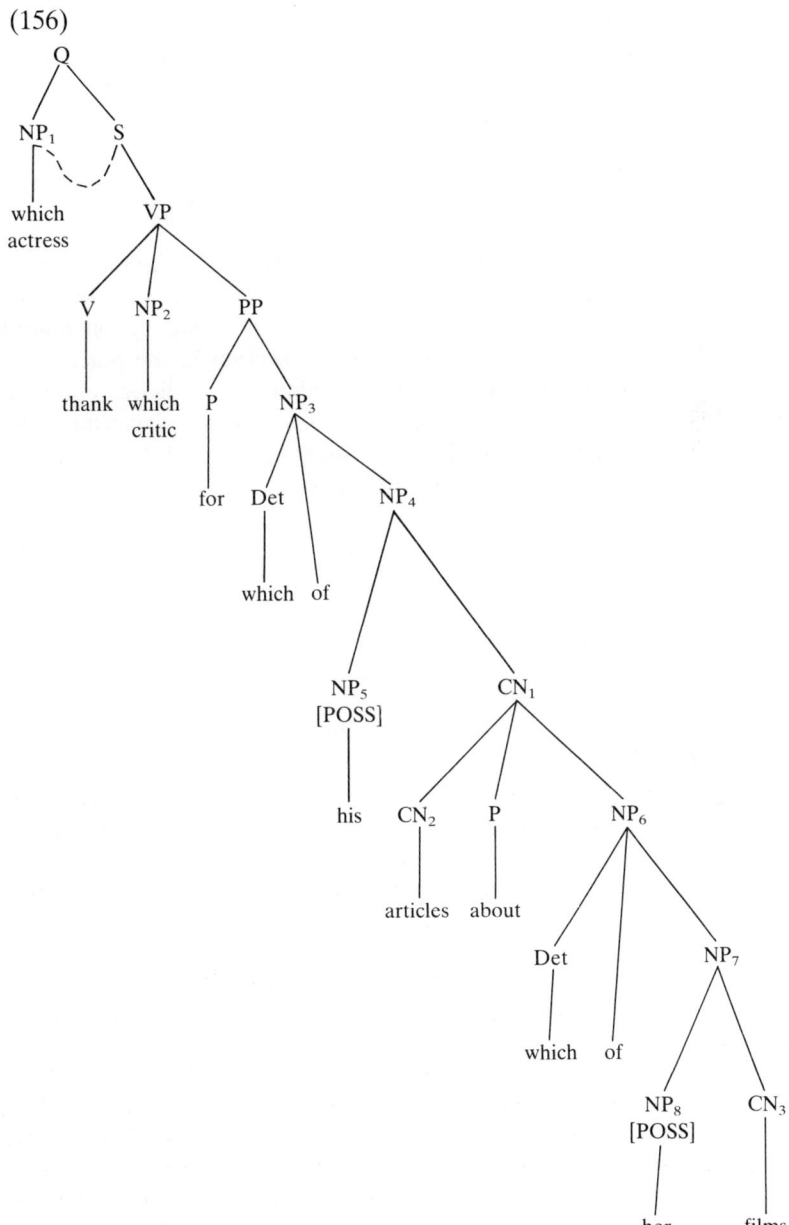

inserted. Since we are interested in the bound interpretation, we let the free individual variable in the interpretation of *her* be affected by the closure operation in the formation of $[WH]_6$. When we reach NP_3, we get the following representation of the meaning:

$$\langle \lambda PP\{W_3(W_3, W_2)\}, [\lambda \mathcal{W} \exists W^2[\forall x \ \forall y[\mathbf{of}'_*(\check{\ }y) \\ (\mathbf{about}'_*(\check{\ }W_6(x))(\mathbf{article}')(W^2(x, y))] \wedge \mathcal{W}\{W^2\}]]_3 \rangle$$

Note that the pronoun interpretation inserted as a placeholder for *which of her films* now occurs as an argument of *about* in the specification of $[WH]_3$ but that the free individual variable now has become bound by the closure operation. The individual variables in the placeholding meaning for $[WH]_3$ are W variables of valence zero, hence equivalent to individual variables. The interpretations of *which critic* and *which actress*, both being interrogative quantifiers, are stored. We assume for simplicity that these phrases are independent of each other and hence only require individual level quantifiers, viz. W^0 variables. The representation for the interpretation of S will be as follows, taking *thank for* to be a complex extensional verb.

$$\langle \mathbf{thank\text{-}for}'_*(\check{\ }W_1, \check{\ }W_2, \check{\ }W_3(W_1, W_2)), [WH]_6, [WH]_3, \\ [WH]_2, [WH]_1 \rangle$$

We note that there are four interrogative quantifiers in store but that only three distinct W variables occur in the representation of the meaning. This follows from the fact that NP_6 is embedded inside NP_3 and that it is only the placeholding meaning for $[WH]_3$ which shows up at this level. Finally, at the Q level, we quantify in the stored interpretations using the rules in (60) and (147). After having quantified in $[WH]_1$ and $[WH]_2$, we get the following representation:

$$\langle \lambda p \ \exists W^0 \ \exists W_1^0[\mathbf{actress}'(W^0) \wedge \mathbf{critic}'(W_1^0) \wedge \check{\ }p \wedge p = \\ = \hat{\ }\mathbf{thank\text{-}for}'_*(\check{\ }W^0, \check{\ }W_1^0, \check{\ }W_3(W^0, W_1^0))], [WH]_6, [WH]_3 \rangle$$

When it comes to quantifying in the interrogative quantifiers associated with the embedding and embedded WH phrases, $[WH]_3$ and $[WH]_6$, respectively, we note that only if we first quantify in $[WH]_3$ (corresponding to the embedding NP_3) and then $[WH]_6$ (corresponding to the embedded NP_6) do we get a final representation for the meaning of (155) where all occurrences of W variables are bound.

(155') $\lambda p \; \exists W^1[\; \forall x[\mathbf{of}'_*(\check{}x)(\mathbf{film}')(W^1(x))] \wedge$
$\exists W^2[\; \forall y \; \forall z[\mathbf{of}'_*(\check{}z)(\mathbf{about}'_*(\check{}W^1(y))(\mathbf{article}'))(W^2(y,z))] \wedge$
$\exists W^0 \; \exists W^0_1[\mathbf{actress}'(W^0) \wedge \mathbf{critic}'(W^0_1) \wedge \check{}p \wedge p =$
$= \; \hat{}\mathbf{thank\text{-}for}'_*(\check{}W^0, \; \check{}W^0_1, \; \check{}W^2(W^0, W^0_1))]]]$

that is, the set of true propositions of the form

'W^0 thanked W^0_1 for $W^2(W^0, W^0_1)$'
where W^0 is an actress, W^0_1 is a critic and
for all y, z, $W^3(y, z)$ is an article of z about $W^1(y)$,
where for all x, $W^1(x)$ is a film of x's.

If we had applied the final quantifications in the other order, i.e. quantified in $[WH]_6$, the interpretation associated with the embedded NP_6 first, (which would have been an instance of vacuous quantification, since at the point of quantification, there is no free W_6 variable in the representation), we would have got a representation where the W_1 variable remains free in the specification of W^2 and it is not clear what this question would mean.

$\lambda p \; \exists W^2[\; \forall y \; \forall z[\mathbf{of}'_*(\check{}z)(\mathbf{about}'_*(\check{}W_1(x))(\mathbf{article}'))$
$(W^2(y, z))] \wedge \ldots$

If we make the assumption that controlled quantification, as in the case of WH quantification, can never be vacuous, then we will automatically get the reading where the order of the quantifiers inversely reflects the embedding order in the syntax. We get this result without having to postulate any extrinsic ordering of the quantification rules or any embedding of stored interpretations[33]. This also has consequences for predicting which readings we get when embedded WH phrases occur in Comp, a case to which we now turn.

7.3. Embedded WH Phrases in Comp

It is interesting to look at the interpretation possibilities for WH phrases which are embedded inside another WH phrase which in turn occurs in Comp, or, as we would say within the present framework, in a linked constituent. Take a multiple question like (157).

(157)   Q: Who remembers [$_Q$[$_{NP}$whose recording of [$_{NP}$which Beethoven symphony]][$_S$Mary prefers?]]

A: a. John does.

b. John remembers whose recording of the fifth symphony Mary prefers and Bill remembers whose recording of the ninth symphony Mary prefers and ...

c. *John remembers that Mary prefers Karajan's recording of the fifth symphony.

As shown by the two possible types of answers, the embedded WH phrase *which Beethoven symphony* can be interpreted either as part of the embedded question, (a), or at the matrix question level, (b). *which Beethoven symphony* occurs in Comp and we have previously argued that the scope of a WH phrase in Comp is fixed to that position (equivalently that the scope of a WH phrase in a linked constituent is fixed to that position). Nevertheless, if a WH phrase is embedded inside another WH phrase, it can apparently take wider scope than indicated by its surface position. An embedded WH phrase in Comp thus acts as if it were 'unmoved'. We derived the two readings for (157) by using the rule of Multiple WH Quantification given in (147) either at the embedded question level or at the matrix question level.

Another thing worth noticing is that a WH phrase that is embedded inside a WH constituent in Comp can never have narrower scope than its embedding constituent, i.e. than the Comp where it occurs. Suppose a complex WH phrase were linked to a gap inside an embedded question, as in (158), a Swedish elaboration of (157).

(158) [$_Q$Vem minns   [$_{Q_1}$[vilken inspelning av vilken
       who remembers   which recording of which
       symfony] [$_S$$_1$Maja ville   veta [$_{Q_2}$vem som
       symphony   Maja wanted know   who that
       hade ___?]]]]
       had

The scope of **vilken symfoni** can be either the matrix question, Q, or the embedded question, Q_1. However, **vilken symfoni** cannot be interpreted (= have scope at) the most embedded question, Q_2. This follows directly from the way we interpret the complex WH constituent and from the requirement that WH quantification cannot be vacuous. Although the interrogative quantifier corresponding to **vilken symfoni**, which we can abbreviate as $[WH]_7$, will be in store at the Q_2 level through the interpretation of the linked constituent, and thus in some sense part of the meaning of Q_2, there is no occurrence of W_7 in the representation of the meaning of Q_2. Consequently, WH quantification cannot take place.

We conclude this discussion of multiple WH questions by looking at a case of an embedded WH phrase in Comp where a relational analysis is called for. Someone might object that as we have proceeded, the examples have become very complicated and less and less like questions that one might actually hear and use. Still, it is often only by looking at rather complex data that we can determine exactly what the scope of a certain theory is, as well as the predictions it makes[34]. With this as our motivation, let us look at (159), cf. (155) above).

(159)   Which of **his** articles about which of *her* films does *every actress* thank **her favorite critic** for?

In order to make the intended bound reading fully explicit, we have included two bound pronouns in the interrogative phrases, each bound by a different antecedent. This admittedly further decreases the naturalness of the question. On our analysis, the pronouns *her* and *his*, which are taken as bound by *every actress* and *her favorite critic*, respectively, are not bound directly by quantifiers in the interpretation of these constituents. Rather they are bound indirectly in the characterization of the interrogative quantifier in which they appear. Our representation of the meaning of (159) will be something like (159′).

(159′) $\lambda p \; \exists W^1 [\; \forall x [\mathbf{of'_*}(\check{x})(\mathbf{film'})(W^1(x))] \land$
$\exists W^2 [\; \forall y \; \forall z [\mathbf{of'_*}(\check{z})(\mathbf{about'_*}(\check{W^1}(y))(\mathbf{article'}))(W^2(y,z))] \land$
$\check{p} \land p = \;\hat{} \; \forall y [\mathbf{actress'}(y) \to \exists z [\mathbf{of'_*}(\check{y})$
$(\mathbf{favorite\text{-}critic'})(z) \land \mathbf{thank\text{-}for'_*}(\check{y}, \check{z}, \check{W^2}(y,z))]]]]$

that is, the set of true propositions of the form

'y thanks z for $W^2(y, z)$'
where y is an actress and z is y's favorite critic and for all x, x_0, $W^2(x, x_0)$ is an article by x_0 about $W_1(x)$, where for all x, $W^1(x)$ is a film of x.

To get this representation of the meaning, we first quantify in the interrogative quantifier corresponding to the embedding WH phrase *which of his articles about* and then the interrogative quantifier corresponding to the embedded WH phrase *which of her films*. Had we attempted to quantify in in the opposite order, this would have led to vacuous quantification of *which of her films*, just as in the similar case in (157).

The interpretation possibilities for embedded WH constituents, whether in a linked constituent (in Comp) or within the sentence, thus fall out from our basic assumption that WH phrases can only be interpreted at a sentential level, i.e. that WH phrases cannot contribute to the meaning of a dominating NP or VP directly, but must be stored until the derivation reaches a point where it can be quantified into a sentence or question meaning. The ordering of interpreting embedded and embedding interrogative quantifiers follows from this assumption, together with the assumption that controlled quantification (WH quantification) may not be vacuous.

8. QUESTIONS INVOLVING OTHER CATEGORIES

Up until now we have basically looked at constituent questions that contain interrogative NPs. In this section we will look at questions of other categories and outline how the approach taken here can be extended. We will first look in some detail at questions involving pied-piping, then in Section 8.2 look at adjectival, adverbial and predicate nominal questions. We have proposed to account for relational readings of questions by introducing functions from individuals to individuals. In Section 8.3. we will discuss whether this is sufficient or whether we need functions which yield NP type interpretations.

8.1. Pied-Piping

Both in English and Swedish, constituent questions may involve what Ross (1967) called *pied-piping*. This shows up in questions like (160)

(160   I vilket land föddes du?
In which country were you born?

where not only the interrogative phrase **vilket land** (*which country*) occurs in initial position, i.e. as a linked constituent, but also the preposition **i** (*in*). There have been several accounts of this phenomenon in the literature (e.g. Chomsky, 1977; Bresnan and Grimshaw, 1978; Gazdar, 1981). Most of these approaches treat it as mainly a syntactic problem. In this section, we will illustrate how the pied-piping facts fall out quite naturally given the assumptions we make about the interpretation of interrogative quantifiers[35].

Let us first look at a linked tree repesentation for (160).

(161)

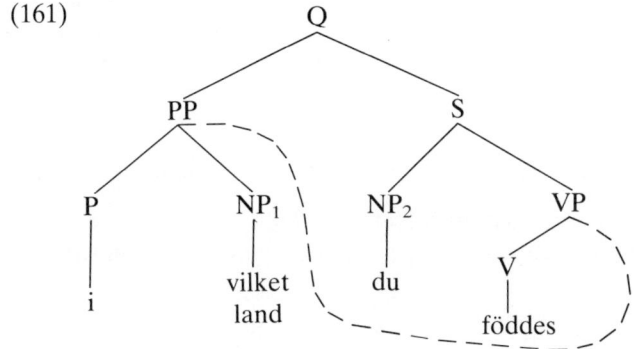

The link child [$_{PP}$**i vilket land**] matches the subcategorization restrictions on **föddes** which we assume belongs to a class of verbs that require some kind of adverbial or prepositional modifier. When we interpret the VP node we must, according to the convention for interpreting link parents take into account the interpretation of the constituent connected to the VP by a link, i.e. **i vilket land**. The interpretation of this phrase will be:

$$\langle \mathbf{in}'(\hat{P}P\{W_1\}) = \mathbf{in}'_*(\check{\ }W_1), [\lambda \mathcal{W}\ \exists W[\mathbf{country}'(W) \wedge \mathcal{W}\{W\}]]_1, \rangle$$

i.e. a pair of a preposition meaning with a pronoun meaning as argument and a stored interrogative quantifier, $[WH]_1$. The link child will thus contribute the interpretation of the preposition together with its argument to the interpretation of the VP, leaving the quantifier in store.

$$\langle \mathbf{in}'_*(W_1)(\mathbf{was\text{-}born}'), [WH]_1 \rangle$$

At the S level, we quantify in $[WH]_1$ and get the following representation for the meaning of (160).

(160') $\lambda p\ \exists W[\mathbf{country}'(W) \wedge \check{\ }p \wedge p =$
    $= \hat{\ }\mathbf{in}'_*(\check{\ }W)(\mathbf{was\text{-}born}')(\hat{\ }\mathbf{you}')]$

that is, the set of true proportions of the form 'you have the property of being born in W', where W denotes a country.

The meaning of the preposition **i** (*in*) in the PP correctly occurs inside the specification of the proposition. Notice that this is a direct consequence of our semantics for constituent questions. Since it is only the interrogative quantifier proper which gets stored, the rest of the PP will be interpreted as contributing to the meaning of the VP and hence to the S that determines the proposition. We thus get the desired account for the pied-piping facts without having to assume any 'reconstruction' at the level of interpretation[36].

8.2. Adverbial, Adjectival, and Predicate Nominal Questions

Not surprising, questions of these categories also permit relational interpretations. We will first look at adverbial questions as illustrated in (162)–(164).

(162)   Q: How did *every student* do on the exam?
A: Better than *he* expected.

(163)   Q: Where do you suppose *most people* want to settle?
A: Close to where *they* grew up.

(164)   Q: When is *every driver* suppose to renew his driver's license?
A: On *his* birthday.

We see that this type of questions permits answers where the value of the questioned phrase varies with the interpretation of some quantifier in the sentence, without this quantifier necessarily having wide scope over the entire question. Using the same type of arguments as earlier, we can show this by embedding the quantifier under the scope of another quantifier or an intensional verb, as for instance in (163). For a general discussion of the possibilities of interpreting interrogative adverbs as modifying embedded clauses, see Larson (1983). Corresponding to the temporal and locative interrogatives we have *then* and *there* as proforms. English apparently lacks a proform for manner adverbs and the expression (*in*) *that way* is often used for this purpose. We have argued that in order to express various relational readings of personal and interrogative pronouns, they should be interpreted as containing a free W variable over functions from individuals to individuals. It turns out that adverbial proforms display the same kind of relational readings as illustrated in (162)–(164). In (165) we give a Swedish example with the manner proform **så**.

(165)   Alla pojkarna åt som om de inte sett mat på 14
        all the boys ate as if they hadn't seen food in 14
        dagar, men ingen av flickorna åt så.
        days, but none of the girls ate so

så in the second conjunct is presumably interpreted 'as if *they* hadn't seen food in 14 days' with *they* bound by *none of the girls*. (166) illustrates the availability of locative and temporal proforms.

(166)   It is said that elephants return to their birthplace when they are about to die. Some people also long to go *there then*.

We propose to handle these cases analogously with the way we interpret pronouns. In PTQ, manner and locative adverbs are interpreted as VP modifiers. i.e. of the type $\langle s, \langle\langle s, f(\text{IV})\rangle, f(\text{IV})\rangle\rangle$. We will consequently analyze the corresponding proforms as involving n-ary functions-in-intensions from individuals to adverbs. Let M be a variable over functions-in-intensions from individuals to VP modifiers, i.e. of type $\langle s, \langle e, \langle\langle s, f(\text{IV})\rangle, f(\text{IV})\rangle\rangle\rangle$. We can now represent the question in (162) as in (167)[37]

(167)   "?" $\hat{p}$ $\exists M[\check{~}p \wedge p =$ ^ $\forall x[\textbf{student}'(x) \rightarrow$
        $\check{~}M(x)(\hat{~}\textbf{do-on-the-exam}')(x)]]$

(167) denotes the set of true propositions of the form 'if x is a student then x performed on the exam in a $M(x)$ way'.

Adjectival questions like *How are you?* and *How was the concert?* seem to be asking for properties. They freely permit relational interpretations as shown in (168).

(168)   Q: How was *every patient*?
        A: Better than *he/she* was yesterday.

In Swedish the interrogative proform for adjectival questions is **hurdan**, which is distinct from **hur** used for adverbial questions.

(169)   Q: Hurdan will **ingen man** bli?
           how does no man want to become?

        A: Alltför lik **sin** far.
           too like his father

In the case of adjectival questions, we actually have two ways of accounting for the relational reading. We could either take the same approach as we have done earlier and analyze adjectival questions as involving functions-in-intension from individuals to properties, thus getting a uniform approach to relational questions across categories. Or we would take adjectival questions to involve quantification over properties directly. Let A be a variable over functions-in-intensions from individuals to properties and P be a variable over properties. Then we can represent the meaning of (168) as in (170) or in (171).

(170)   "?" $\hat{p}$ $\exists A[\check{\ }p \wedge p = \hat{\ } \forall x[\textbf{patient}'(x) \rightarrow [\check{\ }A(x)](x)]]$

(170) denotes the set of true propositions of the form 'if x is a patient, then x is $A(x)$', where A is a function from individuals to properties. One instance of such a function would be a function from x to the property of being better than x was yesterday.

(171)   "?" $\hat{p}$ $\exists P[\check{\ }p \wedge p = \hat{\ } \forall x[\textbf{patient}'(x) \rightarrow \check{\ }P(x)]]$

(171) denotes the set of true propositions of the form 'if x is a patient, then x has P, where P is for instance the property of being an y such that y is better than y was yesterday.

As far as I can tell, (170) and (171) are equivalent. Given that lambda abstraction forms properties, it is straightforward to capture the relational nature of the intended readings without explicitly introducing functions from individuals to properties.

The same option to quantify over properties directly is available for relational VP questions and predicate nominal questions, as in (172) and (173).

(172)   Q: What must *every boy* do before dinner?
A: Wash *his* hands.

(173)   Q: What should *every woman* learn to become?
A: *Her* own legal advisor.

In Swedish, a predicate nominal is realized syntactically either as a CN or as an NP. However, predicate nominal questions are always introduced by **vad** (*what*), not by **vem** (*who*) or **vilken** (*which*), as shown by the following examples.

(174)   Q: Vad vill Maja bli?
What does Maja want to become?

A: a. Hon vill bli [_CN_lärare]/*[_NP_en lärare]
   teacher/ *a teacher

b. Hon vill bli [_NP_den snabbaste störtloppsåkerskan i
   the fastest downhill skier in
   Sverige]
   Sweden

(175) Q: Vad utnämndes Johan till?
   What was Johan appointed to?

A: a. [_CN_professor i musikvetenskap]
   professor of musicology

b. [_NP_sitt lands första professor i musikvetenskap]
   his country's first professor of musicology

Several linguists e.g. Lees (1960), Bach (1976) and Williams (1980) argue that although predicate nominals may be NPs, they are interpreted semantically as predicates, i.e. as CNs. In Swedish and English it is easy to determine whether a given NP has a predicate nominal interpretation or not by looking at the corresponding question since distinct question words are used for NP questions and predicate nominal questions. Other languages may use the same question form, for NP questions and predicate nominal questions, but use word order to signal the difference in meaning. Finnish is apparently such a case (L. Karttunen, personal communication). Consider the two questions in (176) and (177).

(176) Kuka on Jussi?
       who is Jussi

(177) Kuka Jussi on?
       who Jussi is

According to L. Karttunen, when you ask a question like (176) you are interested in finding out which of the people is Jussi. An appropriate answer would be **tuo mies tuolla nurkassa** (*that man over there in the corner*) or an appropriate gesture. (177), on the other hand, asks for the content of the predicate nominal and could be answered by **professori** (*professor*).

8.3. Questions with Quantifier Type Answers

In the earlier sections, we have analyzed NP questions as involving functions from individuals to individuals (or to be more precise, from individual concepts to individual concepts). The question is now whether this is sufficient or whether we also need to consider functions which yield values of higher type, e.g. NP type values. Some examples that bear on this issue are given here.

(178) Q: What is John looking for?
A: A unicorn

(179) Q: Who would you like to talk to?
A: Someone who speaks English.

(180) Q: Who did *everyone* hope would come for dinner?
A: Someone *he/she* knew.

(178) and (179) show that when the interrogative phrase is linked to a position inside an intensional context we get answers that don't require the existence of any particular individual. (180) shows in addition that these answers may be systematically related to some quantifier in the sentence[38]. It seems to me that there are two ways of approaching these types of questions. We could use the same approach as earlier but change the type of W so that it yields NP type interpretations as values. If we adopt this approach, W should presumably always have the higher type, for reasons for uniformity and simplicity. Individual level readings could be got by meaning postulates, just like in PTQ. The second approach would be to say that *what* and *who* are ambiguous between asking for individuals and asking for kinds of individuals, i.e. that *what* can be used instead of *what kind of thing* etc. So the question in (178)–(180) are really kind level questions, not individual level questions, using the distinction G. Carlson has argued for in connection with bare plurals (Carlson, 1977). If we accept Carlson's arguments that we need to enrich the ontology with kinds and stages, then the second approach seems to permit a straightforward implementation of these distinctions for questions. One indication that this might be the right approach to take comes from the fact that a question like (181)

(181) Q: What do you want to study?

A: a. The subject that gets me the best job.
b. Something that will get me a job.

appears to be ambiguous between a reading where an intensional answer at the individual level as in (a) is appropriate, and a reading where an intensional answer at the kind level as in (b) is appropriate[39]. Which answer to choose presumably depends on what degree of completeness of answers is expected in the context of the question.

9. AN ALTERNATIVE APPROACH

In earlier sections, we have mentioned an alternative way of accounting for the type of scope conflict illustrated by examples like (182).

(182)   Which picture of *herself* did you expect *every girl* to send in to the contest?

On our approach, outlined in Section 4.2, we take it that the interrogative phrase should be analyzed as a constituent, both syntactically and semantically, and that its scope is determined by its surface structure position. Consequently, the anaphor *herself* cannot be directly bound by the antecedent *every girl*. Instead the relation is expressed as a restriction on the W function, quantified over in the question interpretation rule. However, there is another approach which permits anaphors in preposed constituents to be bound directly by their antecedents. This approach was the one I developed in Engdahl (1980a). In this section, I will briefly outline the main motivations behind this approach and then provide the reasons why I no longer think this approach is to be preferred.

9.1. Analyzing Which as a Quantifier

The pattern that emerges when one looks at constituent questions with complex interrogative phrases, i.e. phrases like *which picture of herself*, *which relative of his*, *which of every student's grades*, *which of the questions that he/she was asked*, where the derived CN phrase contains either an anaphor or a quantifier, is that not only the morphological form of the preposed constituent but also the interpretation possibilities for the anaphor or the quantifier are determined by the position of the gap to which the preposed constituent is linked. It is by looking at the link parent and the nodes dominating it that we can decide what the appropriate antecedent for a reflexive or bound pronoun is, as well as what the scope possibilities for a quantifier in dislocated position are. It thus lies close at hand to suggest that dislocated constituents should be interpreted in the gap position or – to use transformational terminology – previous to movement. However, as we have seen, there are strong arguments for giving an interrogative phrase scope according to its surface position, arguments having to do with multiple questions and distinguishing the meanings of iterated questions. One way to reconcile these two, apparently contrary, requirements would be to split up the interrogative phrase into its determiner, *which*, and the CN phrase, and interpret them separately. What we need to do is to devise a compositional interpretation procedure that allows us to interpret *which* with scope according to the dislocated position, and interpret the CN part according to the gap position. In Engdahl (1980a), I developed such an approach, using a syntax with movement transformations.

We have seen that when *which* applies to a CN phrase with a bound anaphor, we get a relational interpretation. *Which picture of herself* in (182) does not pick out an individual directly. Rather it seems to identify an individual by means of a relation that it bears to an antecedent. My 1980 proposal amounted to saying that *which* is a determiner whose meaning involves a function which applies to sets, the denotation of the CN phrase, and yields subsets of these sets. If we think of determiners as defining relations between sets (cf. Barwise and Cooper, 1981) then this is not such a strange assumption. The translation of *which* will thus contain a variable, let us say F, over functions which pick out a subset of the hostset, i.e. the set denoted by the CN phrase to which the determiner *which* applies. The free variable F in the translation will get bound when the stored meaning of the determiner is quantified in. The syntax generates WH phrases in their deep structure position, but since WH phrases cannot be interpreted until they move into Comp, the meaning of *which* is obligatorily stored. The translation of the interrogative determiner *which* thus consists of an ordered pair of a determiner meaning, essentially like the meaning for *every*, with a free F variable and a stored quantifier meaning, i.e. a set of properties of F. This is illustrated in (183) where the translation of *every* is also given for comparison.

(183)   every' $\lambda Q\, \lambda P\ \forall x[Q\{x\} \to P\{x\}]$
         which' $\langle \lambda Q\, \lambda P\ \forall x[F_i\{Q\}\{x\} \to P\{x\}], [\lambda \mathscr{F} \mathrm{E} F[\mathscr{F}\{F\}]]_i \rangle$

F is a function of type $\langle s, \langle \langle \langle s, e \rangle, t \rangle, \langle \langle s, e \rangle, t \rangle \rangle \rangle$ over intensions of functions from sets of individual concepts to sets of individual concepts. $\mathscr{F}$ is a variable over properties of F^{40}.

THE INTERPRETATION OF QUESTIONS 243

(184)

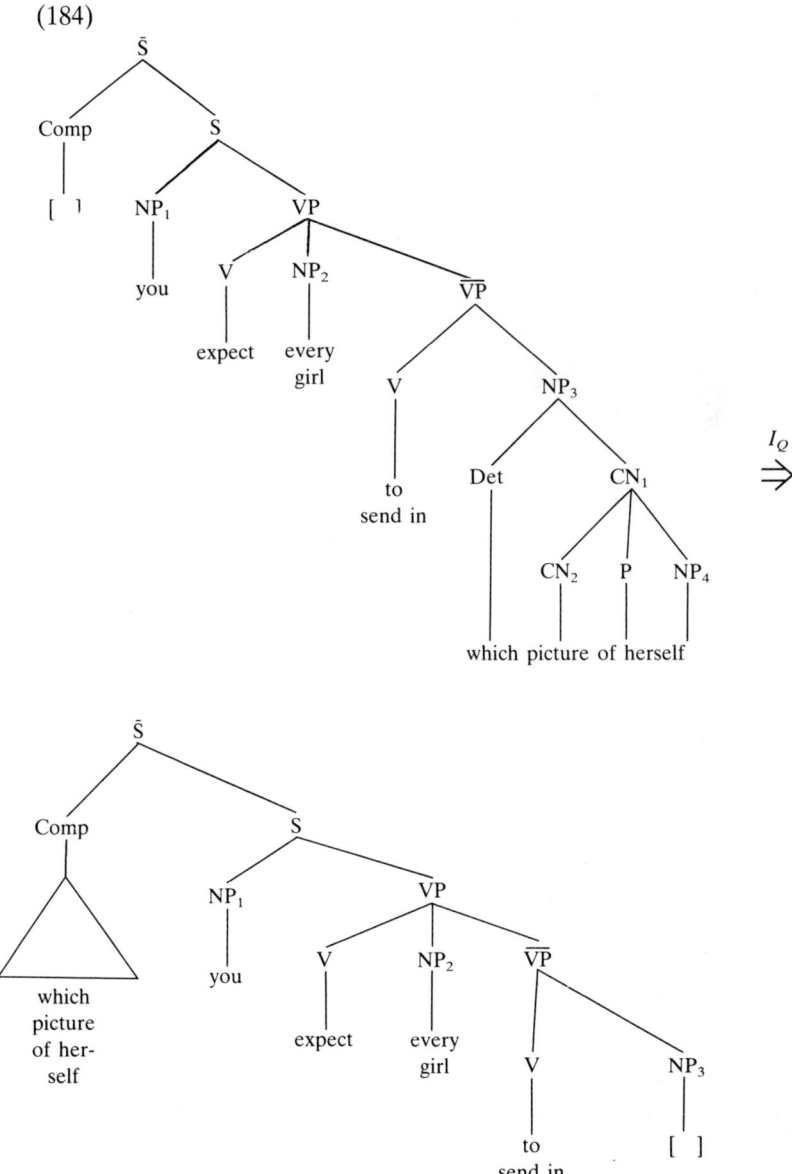

$\Rightarrow$ I_Q

The table to tree diagram (184) is given on p. 244.

244   CHAPTER IV

This table relates to tree diagram (184) on p. 243.

EXPRESSION	INTERPRETATION	STORE	RULE USED
[$_{Det}$which]	$\lambda Q \lambda P \, \forall x [\check{}\, F_4(Q)(x) \to P\{x\}]$	$[\lambda \mathscr{F} \, \exists F [\mathscr{F}\{F\}]_4 (=[WH]_4)$	*which* storage
[$_{CN_2}$picture of herself]	**picture-of-**x_2'	$[\lambda PP\{x_2\}]_2$	Reflexive storage
[$_{NP_2}$which picture of herself]	$\lambda P \, \forall x [\check{}\, F_4(\textbf{picture-of-}x_2')(x) \to P\{x\}]$	$[WH]_4, [\lambda PP\{x_2\}]_2$	
[$_{VP}$to send in which picture of herself]	**send-in'**$(\hat{P} \, \forall x [\check{}\, F_4(\textbf{picture-of-}x_2')(x) \to P\{x\}]) =$ $\lambda y [\forall x [\check{}\, F_4(\textbf{picture-of-}y')(x) \to \textbf{send-in'}_*(\check{}\, y, \check{}\, x)]]$	$[WH]_4, [\lambda PP\{x_2\}]_2$	Reflexive rule
[$_{VP}$expect every every girl to send in which picture of herself]	**expect'**$(\check{}\, \forall z [\textbf{girl'}(z) \to \forall x [\check{}\, F_4(\textbf{picture-of-}z')(x) \to \textbf{send-in'}_*(\check{}\, z, \check{}\, x)]])$	$[WH]_4$	
[$_{S}$you expect every girl to send in which picture of herself]	**expect'**$(\check{}\, \textbf{you'}, \check{}\, \forall z [\textbf{girl'}(z) \to \forall x [\check{}\, F_4(\textbf{picture-of-}z')(x) \to \textbf{send-in'}_*(\check{}\, z, \check{}\, x)]])$	$[WH]_4$	
[$_{S}$which picture of herself do you expect every girl to send in]	"?", $\exists F [\check{}\, p \land p = \check{}\, \textbf{expect'}(\check{}\, \textbf{you'}, \check{}\, \forall z [\textbf{girl'}(z) \to \forall x [\check{}\, F(\textbf{picture-of-}z')(x) \to \textbf{send-in'}_*(\check{}\, z, \check{}\, x)]])]$		T_Q and question interpretation rule

Since this approach involves storing of the determiner part only, the interpretation of the CN phrase will enter into the composition of the interpretation of the tree; in particular, anaphors and pronouns inside the CN phrase are free to be bound by antecedents higher up. In order to transform a sentence with a WH phrase as one of the constituents into a question, a syntactic rule moves the entire WH phrase into Comp. The semantic rule corresponding to the application of the movement transformation, retrieves the stored WH meaning and quantifies it in. Since it is only the determiner meaning that has been stored, the meaning of the CN phrase will be part of the specification of the proposition. To illustrate how this approach works we will look at a derivation of (182). We first give the two trees related by the transformational rule T_Q, and then the stepwise composition of the interpretation.

So the question in (182) will denote the set of true propositions of the form 'you expect that every girl, z, sent in x if x is an element of a certain subset of pictures of z'. The subset in question is picked out by the F function. In this example, appropriate instantiations of F would be functions dentoed by CN modifying expressions like *in profile*, *in color*, etc. Supplying a particular value for F in the translation of (182), we get the formula in (185).

(185)   **expect'**($^{\wedge}$**you'**, $^{\wedge}\forall z$[**girl'**$(z) \rightarrow$
               $\forall x$[**in-color'**(**picture-of-z'**)$(x) \rightarrow$ **send-in'**$_{*}(^{\vee}z, ^{\vee}x)$]])

That is, you expect that every girl z sends in all x that have the property of being a picture of z in color.

In ordinary discourse, an answer to a question seldom repeats material expressed in the question. Instead one provides a short answer, corresponding to the questioned constituent. The F function does not correspond directly to any syntactic constituent which is why answers like *in color* don't occur in isolation. Typical answers pick up on the implicature of uniqueness associated with the question and take the form of definite descriptions. The value for F provides part of the restricting property, for the description.

9.2. Temporally Ambiguous Questions

Besides wanting to account for bound anaphors in a simple way, there appears to be another reason for interpreting the CN phrase inside the specification of the proposition. This reason has to do with when the CN phrase should be evaluated. Take a simple question like (186), which on Karttunen's approach will have the representation in (187).

(186)   Which girl dates John?

(187)   "?" $\hat{p}$ $\exists x[\mathbf{girl}'(x) \wedge \check{}p \wedge p = \hat{}\mathbf{date}'_*(\check{}x, j)]$

(187) denotes the set of true propositions of the form 'x dates John' where x is a girl. By quantifying in the WH phrase *which girl*, Karttunen will get a formula where the existential quantifier ranges over individuals that are girls at the time of evaluation. The whole question is in the present tense and no problem arises. Consider now sentences like (188) and (189) where the question is under the scope of a temporal operator:

(188)   Which third year students took the Tense and Aspect seminar last year?

(189)   Which fourth year students will start writing their dissertations next year?

(188) and (189) are genuinely ambiguous. (188) is *either* a question about which current third year students took a particular seminar last year *or* a questions about which of last year's students took this seminar. Similarly, (189) is *either* a question about which students who are currently in their foruth year will begin their dissertations next year *or* a question about which students will be fourth year students next year and start their dissertations then. In Karttunen's system we get the following, somewhat simplified, translations for (188) and (189) respectively. We use H for the past tense operator and G for the future tense operator.

(188')   "?" $\hat{p}$ $\exists u[\mathbf{third\text{-}year\text{-}student}'_*(u) \wedge \check{}p \wedge p =$
         $= \hat{}H \exists x[\mathbf{seminar}'(x) \wedge \mathbf{take}'_*(u, \check{}x)]]$

(189')   "?" $\hat{p}$ $\exists u[\mathbf{fourth\text{-}year\text{-}student}'_*(u) \wedge \check{}p \wedge p =$
         $= \hat{}G[\mathbf{start\text{-}dissertation}'_*(u)]]$

The meaning of the question in (188) thus comes out to denote the set of true propositions of the form 'it has been the case that u take a seminar' where u is a third year student (now). (189) denotes the set of true propositions of the form 'it will be the case that u start dissertation-writing' where u is a fourth year student (now). The translations we get on

Karttunen's approach only express one of the readings, the one where we are asking about current third or fourth year students. The other reading cannot be expressed given the way the quantification rule is formulated.

Karttunen takes the whole WH phrase to constitute the interrogative quantifier which takes scope over the whole question. Hamblin takes the opposite view. He considers just the *which* part of the WH phrase to be the quantifier and lets all the descriptive material of the CN phrase be expressed inside the proposition where it becomes part of the content. Hamblin's primary motivation does not come from temporally ambiguous questions, but from the fact that common nouns are not rigid designators. Their extension may vary from world to world. Hamblin therefore takes the CN phrase as part of the assertion. He notes that if we distinguish between asserted and presupposed material, we might take another approach, but he does not undertake the pragmatic treatment that this would involve (cf. Hamblin, 1976, p. 257).

On Hamblin's approach, we would get translations of the form in (188″) and (189″), disregarding the difference arising from letting questions denote only their true answers.

(188″) "?" $\hat{p}$ $\exists u[\check{~}p \wedge p = \hat{~}H$ $\exists x[\text{seminar}'(x) \wedge$ **third-year-student**$'_*(u) \wedge$ **take**$'_*(u, \check{~}x)]]$

(189″) "?" $\hat{p}$ $\exists u[\check{~}p \wedge p = \hat{~}G[\textbf{fourth-year-student}'_*(u) \wedge$ **start-dissertation**$'_*(u)]]$

(188″) denotes the set of true propositions that pick out a set of worlds w such that it has been the case that u be a third year student in w and u take the seminar in w. Similarly, (189″) denotes the set of propositions true in those worlds w where it will be the case that u be a fourth year student in w and u start dissertation writing in w. We note that Hamblin only gets the reading where (188) is a question about individuals who were third year students at the time they took the seminar, and where (189) asks about future fourth year students.

The temporal ambiguities noted in (188) and (189) are of course not exclusive to questions. Declarative sentences show the same kind of ambiguities (cf. Bach, 1968; Fodor, 1970) as can be seen in (190), a declarative counterpart to (188).

(188) Two third year students took the Tense and Aspect seminar last year.

When the ambiguity is tied to a NP, these facts can be handled in Montague grammar by interpreting the NP either in place, inside the scope of the temporal operator in the sentence, or by quantifying it in. In this respect the temporal opeators act just like modals and intensional verbs in creating intensional contexts (cf. Ejerhed, 1981). The particular problem raised by the questions is that whereas quantification is optional for NPs, (a NP can always be interpreted 'in place') it is obligatory for WH phrases. We cannot represent the 'true-at-event-time-reading' of the questions by interpreting the WH phrase in place and simultaneously interpret it as an interrogative quantifier which makes a sentence into a question and has scope over that question.

For the examples in (188) and (189), it seems relatively clear when the CN phrase applies, *third year student* may hold either at the event time, the time when the students took the seminar, or at utterance time. The question is, though, if the interpretation possibilities of CN phrases are limited by the moment of utterance and the times introduced by tense operators and adverbs in the sentence. Consider a question like (191).

(191)   Which U.S. presidents have attended Amherst college?

Our knowledge of the world tells us that they were not presidents at the time they went to college, and that at most one of them is a president now. Nevertheless, (191) is a plausible question which seems to range over both past and present presidents.

In her dissertation, M. Enç (1981) argues convincingly that the denotation of a common noun need not depend on tense operators and temporal adverbs in the sentence but is determined by the context. She argues furthermore that there are cases of scope conflict which cannot be resolved if we require that the interpretation of a noun always depends on what quantifiers and tense operators have scope over it. As an illustration, we will look at an example from Enç (1981, p. 60).

(192)   Every member of our investment club will buy a house.

(192) can easily be understood as saying something about every person who is a member of the club now or will become one in the future, namely that he or she will buy a house. (192) does not require that the people still be members at the time of the house buying. The problem is that we cannot express this reading on a standard analysis of tense like in PTQ. On a PTQ approach, we will get two interpretations for (192),

depending on whether the subject NP is under the scope of the future tense or not. The two readings are given in (193) and (194).

(193) $G \ \forall x[\textbf{member}'(x) \rightarrow \textbf{buy-a-house}'_*(\check{\ }x)]$

(194) $\forall x[\textbf{member}'(x) \rightarrow G[\textbf{buy-a-house}'_*(\check{\ }x)]]$

(193), where the future operator has scope over the whole sentence, is true if at some time in the future, everyone who is a member at that time buys a house then. (194), in which *every member* has been quantified into the open sentence *he$_0$ will buy a house*, is true if all present members will buy a house at some future time. Thus, on a standard analysis of tense operators and universal quantifiers, there is no way of representing the reading where some people buy houses while they are members and others buy houses after they have left the club. As Enç concludes, what we want is to be able to quantify over present and future members simulatneously, without making any claims about whether they are members at the time of buying a house. Enç takes examples like (192) to show that when we use a common noun like *president* or *member of our investment club* we can use it to refer to any set of individuals we please. Which set of individuals we have in mind is determined by the discourse, i.e. it is determined pragmatically. Enç suggests that nouns be evaluated with respect to an interval, *T*, which is relevant to the discourse[41]. The interval may be identical to the utterance time, or be the same as the interval in which the tensed verb in the sentence is evaluated, but it may also be distinct from both, as shown by (191), or overlapping both, as in (192). The fact that there appears to be two ways of interpreting questions like (188) and (189) is thus not an argument for treating them as semantically ambiguous. The two readings depend on which interval we choose to evaluate *third year student* at. Enç's analysis furthermore predicts that the two readings discussed above should not be the only possible readings for these examples and this seems correct. If the conversation is about a particular year in the history of the deparment, let us say 1980, then it seems to me that one could ask the question in (195) in 1982, having in mind the people who were third year students in 1980[42].

(195)   Which third year students didn't finish their qualifying papers until last year?

Given Enç's arguments for the independence of noun interpretations from tense operators, it appears that the argument that we need to be able to evaluate CN phrases inside the proposition in order to express the reading where the CN holds at the time of the event in the question, not the time of asking the question, is no longer a conclusive argument. In the next section we will look at some further arguments against the alternative approach.

9.3. Arguments Against Splitting up the Interpretation of Interrogative Quantifiers

One general argument that can be raised against the alternative approach outlined in 9.1 and that I believe should be taken seriously is that it involves semantically splitting up a constituent which syntactically behaves like a unit. Since we would like our syntactic and semantic rules to work in parallel as much as possible given a compositional semantics, this is not a particularly attractive feature. We have seen that the alternative approach allows anaphors and pronouns in preposed constituents to get bound directly by their antecedent by interpreting the CN constituent as if it were a constituent of the sentence and thus contributing to the specification of the proposition. This, however, is also one of the disadvantages of the analysis since there seem to be good reasons not to let the descriptive content of the WH phrase be asserted as part of the content of the proposition, but rather take it to be presupposed, as is done for instance in Karttunen (1977). One argument for separating the material in the interrogative quantifier from what is actually part of propositional content comes from questions like (196).

(196)   John wondered which of the students were students.

(196) does not necessarily mean that John was wondering about a tautology, which would be the case if *of the students* was evaluated inside the proposition. Rather, *which of the students* is taken as the speaker's contribution and does not imply that John knows that the people under consideration actually are students. Groenendijk and Stokhof (1982) have argued that there is actually a *de dicto-de re* ambiguity in constituent questions depending on whether the CN phrase is evaluated inside or outside the proposition. They account for the ambiguity by having both Term and CN quantification in their fragment. However, it seems to me that it is not clear that distinctions having to do with where a CN is evaluated (or who is responsible for the

description) should be captured by a scope analysis (see Hellan (1981b) for a detailed analysis of similar problems for declarative sentences and Enç (1981, chapter V) for an argument that a scope analysis leads to scope clashes in the case of modal contexts).

A further shortcoming of the alternative approach is that it is not clear how to extend it so that it can account also for relational readings of questions without overt anaphors in the CN phrase, as for instance in (197)[43]. On the alternative approach, the meaning of this question would be represented as in (197').

(197)   Which woman does *every Englishman* admire most? *His* mother.

(197')   "?" $\hat{p}$ $\exists F[\check{}p \wedge p = \hat{}\ \forall x[\textbf{Englishman}'(x) \rightarrow \forall y[\check{}F(\textbf{woman}')(y) \rightarrow \textbf{admire}'_*(\check{}x, \check{}y)]]]$

(197') denotes the set of true propositions of the form 'if x is an Englishman, then x admires every y that is a member of a certain subset of women'. However, since the interpretation of the CN phrase *woman* doesn't contain any variable that can be bound by *every Englishman*, it will presumably denote a fixed set of women. Thus, F will pick out a subset of these women but this will not get us the relational reading. One way to get around this problem would be to treat all common nouns as inherently relational, containing one or more free individual variables, but I see no independent motivation for this move[44].

10. CONCLUSION

In this chapter, we have developed an explicit semantics for constituent questions. We have argued that in order to be able to handle interesting questions such as questions where the interpretation of the interrogative quantifier interacts with the interpretation of other quantifiers in the sentence and vice versa we need a relational approach to interrogative quantifiers. Our analysis takes off from the semantics of questions proposed in Karttunen (1977). But whereas Karttunen assimilates the interpretation of *who* and *which girl* to the interpretation of the corresponding indefinite, *someone* and *some girl*, we assimilate the interpretation of interrogative phrases to the interpretation of personal pronouns. Following Cooper (1979), we assume that pronoun interpretations sometimes require a relational variable in order to express all available readings. Similarly we take the interpretation of interrogative pronouns like *who* to involve relational variables. On a given interpretation of a constituent question these relational variables will be quantified over. The interpretation of an interrogative quantifier like *which film* or *which or her films* will involve a function whose value may be explicitly restricted in various ways depending on whether the CN part of the quantifier contains bound anaphors or not. This allows us to give a complete characterization of the meaning of an interrogative quantifier in its surface position, even if it contains one or more bound anaphors.

In our discussion so far, the emphasis has been on expressive power and syntactic adequacy. We have tried to provide a semantics which is both powerful enough to express all the readings and can be naturally fitted onto an independently motivated syntax. Besides this purely theoretical motivation, I believe that there are a few practical considerations which support this approach. First, the relational approach fits very well with the type of short answers that people usually give. This is also the type of answer that people expect and are quick both at assessing and at integrating with previous knowledge. Second, I think this approach could become quite useful in computationally based question-answering systems. It seems to be quite efficient to store and express certain information relationally, or functionally. For example, it would be straightforward to find the answer to a question like (198)

(198)   Where is every book filed?

provided that the data base contained information of the form represented in (199).

(199) $\forall x[\mathbf{book}'(x) \rightarrow \mathbf{under}'_*(\check{\ }W(x))(\mathbf{be\text{-}filed}')(x)]$

On particular instance of W could be *name of author of* which would provide the answer *under its author's name* to (199).

NOTES

[1] See Groenendijk and Stokhof (1982) where this argument is spelled out in more detail.
[2] The example Belnap gives to illustrate that a question can have more than one full true answer is *What's an example of a prime number between 10 and 20?* (Belnap, 1982, p. 174). I think the phrase *What is an example of* serves as an explicit metalinguistic signal that an exhaustive answer is not called for. Karttunen (1977, fn. 4) makes the same point with respect to 'for instance'. Cf. also Åqvist (1965) who distinguishes 'complete-list-what questions' from 'at-least-what questions'.

[3] See also Manor (1982) for an approach which takes pairs of questions and answers as basic. Manor's proposal is not open to the criticism raised against Hausser and Zaefferer in the text.

[4] This is a simplified exposition. For details, see Karttunen (1977) and Karttunen and Peters (1980). In Karttunen (1977), the WH quantification rule applied to a proto-question, but nothing of importance for the present discussion hinges on this.

[5] Cf. Belnap (1982, p. 178) where a similar example is discussed.

[6] *Questions in Montague Grammar* was originally planned to be a joint paper by Bennett and Belnap. Bennett died before it reached final form and the version published by IULC was edited by Belnap.

[7] The argument in this section was initially worked out during a discussion with J. Groenendijk and M. Stokhof in the fall of 1981. See also Groenendijk and Stokhof (1982) for a similar argument to the effect that knowing a function does not imply knowing its value as a set of ordered pairs of individuals.

[8] The anaphora problems raised by so-called donkey sentences have been the subject of several studies recently. Besides Cooper (1979), we refer to Evans (1980), Heim (1982) and Kamp (1981).

[9] This approach is similar to an idea developed by Irene Heim in the spring of 1979. She suggested letting the translations of pronouns and definite descriptions involve what she called 'completion functions'. Her approach was presented in a paper given in Bielefeld in June 1979 under the title 'The Semantics and Pragmatics of Definite NPs'.

[10] A brief remark about how this approach developed might be in place. I first started to investigate the possibility of taking a relational approach to questions during 1979–80 when I was writing my dissertation (Engdahl, 1980). Together with L. Hellan I worked out an analysis along these lines. For reasons having to do with the temporal interpretation of common nouns, I abandoned this analysis in favor of an alternative analysis which will be briefly discussed in Section 9. As will become clear there, I no longer think that the arguments against the relational approach are valid. During the fall of 1981 I had several fruitful discussions with J. Groenendijk and M. Stokhof who have independently developed an approach to this type of question using Skolem functions (Groenendijk and Stokhof, 1983a). However, I think there are good reasons not to think of the relational variables as variables over Skolem functions (cf. Dahl (1983) and Schiebe (1982)) as will become clear in subsequent sections.

[11] Actually we want W to be a function from individual concepts to individual concepts. In order to simplify the exposition we have just talked about functions from individuals to individuals. However, in the formulas, we conform to the types of variables used in PTQ, and the arguments of W are variables over individual concepts. R. Cooper (personal communication) has suggested that there are some cases where we actually need functions involving individual concepts and not plain individuals, if we assume with Cresswell (1973) and Löbner (1976) that NPs like *the mayor* crucially involve individual concepts. Consider the following examples:

(i)   The Mayor of Boston keeps the city revenue under his mattress.
        Every other mayor puts *it* in the bank.

(ii)   The Mayor of Boston used the city revenue to gamble.
        What did every other mayor use?

On the most natural interpretation, *it* in (i) refers to the revenue of the city where the mayor in question presides. Similarly, *what* in (ii) is understood to vary with the mayors and towns.

[12] The existence of these kinds of mixed answers was brought to my attention independently by Östen Dahl, Alice ter Meulen, and Barbara Partee.

[13] Readers familiar with Belnap 1982 might recall that Belnap quantifies over functions-in-intensions from individuals into open propositions. This gives him the set of answers which vary with respect to the value of the phrase quantified in. Intuitively, what Belnap does is to relativize the interpretation of what he calls an open interrogative to the individuals that are values of the quantifier, which thus necessarily has wider scope than the question. We argued in Section 3 that approaches that account for relational readings by giving the antecedent wide scope only can handle a subset of the interesting cases, namely those where the quantifier phrase clearly takes wide scope over the question. However, it is hard to see how Belnap's proposal, given its reliance on quantifying in, can be extended to other cases of relational readings which don't require wide scope quantification.

[14] It is not quite correct to require that the answer be a full specification at the level of individuals, since an answer like *a philosopher and a linguist* would also count as a complete answer, provided that two people were coming to dinner. We return to NP type answers in Section 8.

[15] We are again touching on the complex issue of how to interpret definite descriptions inside opaque and epistemic contexts which came up in the discussion of (40). We return to this question in Section 9.

[16] See Hawkins (1978) and Heim (1982) for further illustrations of how definite descriptions presuppose standard associations.

[17] This reading can also be expressed by (75), viz. if we let W be a constant function from Englishmen into one specific individual. We refer back to the discussion of this issue in Section 4.2.

[18] To simplify the derivation, we disregard *do* support and treat *to* essentially as case-marking on the indirect object of *return*. Note that we quantify in *her lover* at the VP level to enable it to bind a free variable in the translation of the direct object.

[19] See Chapter III, Section 5.1.2, for an outline of how epithets can act as bound expressions.

[20] Note that it seems considerably easier to get the reading where *her mother* binds the pronoun in *her letters* when this phrase occurs in dislocated position than when it occurs *in situ* as in (i).

(i)   Every woman hides her letters from her mother.

Cf. our discussion of weak crossover in chapter IV.

[21] Cf. the discussion in Chapter III.5, where we argued that the meaning of a reflexive constituent can not be determined until one has reached a VP level. Analogously, the meaning of a constituent containing a bound pronoun cannot be determined until one has reached the appropriate antecedent.

[22] It's not totally clear how an example like (105) would be derived on an approach using QR. Presumably, *wh*-movement would first move NP, to Comp, then at LF, everything but *which* would have to be lowered into the trace position. The QR would have to raise NP_3 and adjoin it to VP (or an intermediate S). But note that in order to get the relational reading, *which* could not be an individual level quantifier (cf. Chapter V.5.3).

²³ Structures like (107) provides another case where speakers' judgments are not so clear, cf. the cases of preposed reflexives discussed above. For instance, some speakers apparently accept bound readings in quiz-questions of the type in (i), suggested by R. Cooper.

(i) [Which right that *every American* is entitled to] should *he* be informed about ____ when he is arrested?

²⁴ The translation rules here are not well suited to represent the meaning of relational CN's, which is a shortcoming. In the translations given here, PP complements and possessives act as CN modifiers. We could also have interpreted them as relations between individuals according to the following rules, where $\mathbf{P}_{1*}'$ abbreviates the relation in question:

(118a') $\ldots \lambda P[\text{NP}_2'(\hat{y}\ \exists x[\text{CN}'(x) \wedge \mathbf{P}_{1*}'(\check{}y, \check{}x) \wedge P\{x\}])]$

(118b') $\ldots \lambda \mathscr{S}[\text{NP}_2'(\hat{y}[\mathscr{S}\{\hat{x}[\text{CN}'(x) \wedge \mathbf{P}_{1*}'(\check{}y, \check{}x)]\}])]$

The two approaches are equivalent, as long as PP modifiers are being viewed as extensional.

²⁵ Essentially the same approach to possessive interrogatives but in different syntactic frameworks has been suggested by Karttunen (1978) and Cooper (1983, chapter V). In both English and Swedish, the form of a short answer to these questions conforms to the form of the interrogative phrase, i.e. is given in the possessive case, although the genitive marking is really redundant. I have no other explanation for this than that it is a case of adaptation to the surface form of the question (cf. Levelt and Kelter (1982) for some evidence that speakers retain the actual form of a question, not only its meaning, and make use of this in the composition of the answer).

²⁶ If $\delta \in \text{ME}_{\text{IAV/T}}$ then δ_* is to be the expression $u[\delta(\hat{P}P\{\hat{\ }u\})]$. Just like in PTQ we can let δ translate only a subset of $B_{\text{IAV/T}}$ in order to preserve the intensional character of certain prepositions.

²⁷ Some speakers might prefer **Majas kort på sig själv**. See Hellan (forthcoming a,b) for detailed discussion of the domain for **själv**-reflexives in Norwegian. Whereas the distinction between **sig** reflexives and **sig själv** appears reasonably clear in Norwegian, it is not observed by many speakers of Swedish, the present writer included.

²⁸ Compare the optional application of the reflexive rule at infinitival VPs discussed in Chapter III.5.2). One factor that seems to influence the choice of pronoun is the animacy of the antecedent. Reflexive pronouns tend to occur with animate antecedents. See Anward (1974) and Dahl (1980) for further illustration of the variation.

²⁹ The fact that only one constituent can occur under the Comp node in Swedish makes attempts to account for multiple extractins in this language by postulating two or more excape positions in Comp appear lacking in empirical support (cf. Engdahl, 1980b).

³⁰ This rule is similar to Karttunen's rule for multiple WH quantification (1977: (47B)).

³¹ The question in (149) has two readings due to the fact that there are two scope possibilities for *which book*. We consequently expect multiple questions where the unmoved WH phrase occurs embedded inside a sequence of *n* indirect questions to be *n* + 1 times ambiguous, since the multiple WH quantification rule in (147) can apply at each of the embedded questions as well as to the matrix question. For instance, a question like (i) should have four readings depending on whether *which prize* is interpreted in Q_0, Q_1, Q_2, or Q_3.

(i) $[_{Q_0}$ Who would know
      $[_{Q_1}$ where I can find out
        $[_{Q_2}$ which dean decides
          $[_{Q_3}$ which student gets which prize?]]]

Not surprisingly, the readings where *which prize* takes narrowest scope (i.e. in Q_3) or widest scope (i.e. in Q_0) are the easiest to get, just like with other quantifiers (cf. Fodor and Sag, 1982). These readings correspond to the two types of answers in (ii) and (iii). For ease of exposition, we will use x, y, z, w, as variables of type W^0 in the representation of the meanings.

(ii)   *which prize* interpreted in Q_3
     a.   John would.
     b. Q_0: $\lambda p_0 \; \exists x[\textbf{person}'(x) \wedge \;\check{}p_0 \wedge p_0 = \;\hat{}\textbf{know}'(x,$
           Q_1: $\hat{p}_1 \; \exists y[\textbf{place}'(y) \wedge \;\check{}p_1 \wedge p_1 = \;\hat{}\textbf{find-out}'(\hat{}I', \textbf{at}'_*(\check{}y),$
           Q_2: $\hat{p}_2 \; \exists z[\textbf{dean}'(z) \wedge \;\check{}p_2 \wedge p_2 = \;\hat{}\textbf{decide}'(z,$
           Q_3: $\hat{p}_3 \; \exists w[\textbf{prize}'(w) \wedge \; \exists x_3[\textbf{student}'(x_3) \wedge \;\check{}p_3 \wedge p_3 =$
              $= \;\hat{}\textbf{get}'_*(\check{}x_3, \;\check{}w)]])])])]$

(iii)   *which prize* interpreted in Q_0
     a.   John probably knows where I can find out which dean decides which student gets the Teaching Award,
         and Bill would know where I can find out which student gets the Travel Grant, . . .
     b. Q_0: $\lambda p_0 \; \exists w[\textbf{prize}'(w) \wedge \; \exists x[\textbf{person}'(x) \wedge \;\check{}p_0 \wedge p_0 = \;\hat{}\textbf{know}'(x,$
           Q_1: as in (ii)
           Q_2: as in (ii)
           Q_3: $\hat{p}_3 \; \exists x_3[\textbf{student}'(x_3) \wedge \;\check{}p_3 \wedge p_3 = \;\hat{}\textbf{get}'_*(\check{}x_3, \;\check{}w)]])])])]]$

The two intermediate readings are harder to establish, but I believe they can be distinguished, although they most likely hardly ever are intended.

(iv)   *which prize* interpreted in Q_1
     a.   John would know the 'place-prize' correlation
     b. Q_0: as in (ii)
           Q_1: $\hat{p}_1 \; \exists w[\textbf{prize}'(w) \wedge \; \exists y[\textbf{place}'(y) \wedge \;\check{}p_1 \wedge p_1 = \;\hat{}\textbf{find-out}'(\hat{}I', \textbf{at}'_*(\check{}y),$
           Q_2: as in (ii)
           Q_3: as in (iii)

(v)   *which prize* interpreted in Q_2
     a.   John would know where I can find out the 'dean-prize' correlation.
     b. Q_0: as in (ii)
           Q_1: as in (ii)
           Q_2: $\hat{p}_2 \; \exists w[\textbf{prize}'(w) \wedge \; \exists z[\textbf{dean}'(z) \wedge \;\check{}p_2 \wedge p_2 = \;\hat{}\textbf{decide}'(z,$
           Q_3: as in (iii)

It thus apears that we don't have to constrain the rule for multiple WH quantification but that it can apply at any Q node. So far we have assume that NP quantification (free quantification) is totally unconstrained, that it may apply arbitrarily high up in the derivation. The reason we have taken over this assumption from PTQ is that it enables us to account for *de dicto-de re* ambiguities with indefinites. However, this assumption predicts that we should get a large number of scope distinctions, distinctions that most speaker don't agree to. Many people (e.g. May, 1977; Heim, 1982) have noted that genuine quantifiers such as universal quantifiers rarely take scope outside the tensed clause where they occur. The clearest exceptions seem to involve relative clauses where the head NP is interpreted as varying functionally with the interpretation on some constituent inside the relative clause, as in Karttunen's example *The grade that every student gets will be recorded in the computer*. We suggested in Section 5 that such readings are maybe more appropriately handled by a relational or functional approach to quantifiers. Robin Cooper (personal communication) has suggested that if we give up the assumption that *de dicto-de re* distinctions should be expressed by means of quantification, and instead take care of such distinctions by e.g. *value loading* as in Situation Semantics (Barwise and Perry, 1983) then it might be that NP quantification is always limited to tensed S domains. The relevant distinction between NP quantification and WH quantification would then be that the latter is not limited to the immediate question where the WH phrase occurs but that it may percolate up through Q nodes. Exactly how one would account for the WH quantification facts and different scope possibilities within Situation Semantics thus emerges as an interesting area for research.

[32] (151) will get the desired effect for the structures we have discussed so far. However, in order to get the correct result also for more complex structures such as questions with embedded WH phrases in Comp, which will be discussed in Section 7.3, we will probably need to refine (151) somewhat. Following Ladusaw (1979), we will refer to the non-stored part of a meaning as the *head* of the meaning (head (m(X)) for any constituent X). We will refer to the stored part of the meaning as the *tail* of the meaning. With these distinctions, we can reformulate the relevant clause as

(151')   and head (m(XP)) = ... W_i ...

[33] In this respect, the present analysis represents a theoretical simplification compared to the one proposed in Engdahl (1980a) where it was necessary to assume embedding of stores in order to get the correct interpretation.

[34] Compare e.g. Higginbotham (1980a) for an illustration of 'inversely linked' quantifiers which uses an indexing approach.

[35] This approach is very similar to Karttunen's (1978) suggestions for how to account for pied-piping in questions.

[36] See Chapter V for a discussion of and comparison with approaches within EST and GB that make use of reconstruction at logical form. The treatment of constituent questions proposed in Groenendijk and Stokhof (1982, 1983) also relies on some form of reconstruction, but as shown here, this does not appear to be necessary.

[37] This is just a sketch of an approach to manner questions. For a more detailed analysis of *how* questions, see Bayer (1981).

[38] B. Partee has objected that the relational reading apparently does not survive embedding very well. She finds the relational reading harder to get in a sentence like (i).

(i)   I know who everyone hoped would come for dinner.

After having looked at examples with various quantifiers and various embedding contexts, I don't think this is in general true. It seems to me that (ii) easily permits a relational interpretation.

(ii)   It is well known who *no woman* would like to have in her kitchen, namely, *her* mother-in-law.

[39] This distinction was brought to my attention by B. Partee.

[40] This is actually a simplified version. The definition used in Engdahl (1980a, p. 134) contained a restriction on F functions in the specification of the interrogative quantifier, as in (i).

(i) $\lambda \mathcal{F} \exists F[\forall Q[F\{Q\} \subseteq Q] \wedge \mathcal{F}\{F\}]$

This restriction served to capture the intuition that the interrogative determiner is subsective, i.e. that the result of applying F to some set must always be a subset of the original set. This is probably not correct in view of the possibilities of dialogues like in (ii), suggested by R. Cooper.

(ii)   Q: Which citizens are most important to a country?
              A: The future ones.

Furthermore, requiring that F be extensional like in (i) will sometimes have the wrong consequences as Mats Rooth and Robin Cooper independently brought to my attention. Consider a situation where there are three authors who have co-authored three books. The extension of the set *his books* with *his* bound by *every author* will thus be the same, nevertheless we want to be able to have the exchange in (iii)

(iii)   Q: Which of *his* books did *every author* recommend?
             A: *His* favorite book

and understand the answer in a way which permits F to pick out different books for different authors.

[41] Identifying a temporal interval is just one side of establishing the relevant context. We also need information about place and salient properties. See Enç (1981) for a full presentation of the theory.

[42] Irene Heim and Edwin Williams have both pointed out the existence of this reading to me. Some people find it easier to get this reading if a partitive question with a definite description is used as in *which of the third year students*.

[43] I believe it was Angelika Kratzer who first raised this objection to me.

[44] A further argument against the technical solution in Engdahl (1981a) has been brought to my attention by Jeroen Groenendijk and Martin Stokhof (1981). They claim that in a question like (i)

(i)   Which picture of *herself* did *no girl* send in?

the analysis proposed in Engdahl (1980b) gets a wrong result, due to the interaction of the negation in the antecedent and the universal quantifier supplied in the interpretation of *which*. It seems to me that the answers I predict are technically correct but misleading in the Gricean sense. The issue depends to a large extent on what kind of analysis one assumes for plural questions. Since I no longer advocate this approach, and since the problem does not arise in the relational approach proposed here, I won't try to give any counter-arguments here.

CHAPTER V

A COMPARISON WITH EST-GB

1. INTRODUCTION

In connection with our analysis of syntactic and semantic aspects of constituent questions in the preceding chapters, we have often alluded to how these phenomena would be handled within current transformational grammar as developed in Chomsky (1981, 1982), but have not gone into any detailed comparison. The purpose of this chapter is to provide a more coherent and systematic comparison in terms of a discussion of how the syntactic and semantic facts that are central to our investigation can be handled within a transformational framework. We will first look at the role and place of semantic interpretation within transformational grammars, then look at to what extent Chomsky's syntactic characterization of *wh*-movement is applicable to the Swedish facts. We then turn to the rule which interprets questions in this framework and find that the rule, as currently formulated, does not give the desired results, in particular, it does not allow for relational interpretations of questions. A more flexible interpretation rule is apparently needed. The main moral of this comparison is that the rather complex interpretation for interrogative quantifiers that we propose in Chapter IV is not the result of our choosing a non-transformational syntax. Exactly the same type of semantic analysis is needed in a transformational grammar as well. The choice of syntactic framework is thus independent of the question of semantic adequacy.

The most specific account of the semantics of questions within transformational grammar up to date is probably the proposal made by Higginbotham and May (1980). In the final section we take up some of their main claims.

2. SEMANTIC INTERPRETATION IN TRANSFORMATIONAL GRAMMAR

In transformational grammar, the derivation of a sentence is seen as the mapping structures from one level of representation to another. In current versions of transformational grammar such as in Chomsky

(1981, 1982) it is assumed that there are (at least) three essential levels of linguistic representation, D-structure, S-structure, and logical form, often abbreviated LF. During the development of transformational grammar there has been a shift with respect to which level of interpretation provides the input to the rules of semantic interpretation. In the Aspects model, (Chomsky, 1965), it was assumed to be deep structure. In later versions, such as the ones assumed in Chomsky (1975, 1976, 1977, 1980) and May (1977), semantic interpretation takes place off S-structure, a representation enriched by traces, coindexed with moved constituents. These traces make the thematic roles of moved constituents recoverable. The semantic interpretation rules which map S-structure into a LF representation consist of operations like Quantifier Raising (QR) which leaves a coindexed variable, and various co-and-contra-indexing operations, intended to capture notions like reflexive and reciprocal interpretation, disjoint reference, and control. QR is supposed to provide an intuitive interpretation for quantifiers, including interrogatives, and handle quantifier scope. The resulting level, LF, is essentially a syntactic representation in the sense that syntactic category information is preserved. Different types of NPs, e.g. traces, PRO, and lexical anaphors are replaced by variables, coindexed with antecedents or quantifiers. The LF representation thus is not an interpretation for the language, in the sense of an interpretation which determines the meaning of sentences. It is assumed that LF in turn provides the input to further interpretive rules which might be sensitive to other cognitive factors as well. There have been suggestions that these rules should include a model theoretical semantics of the type familiar from the Montague tradition, but so far very little work has been done on these types of interpretation rules.

It is a controversial issue whether LF is an essential level of linguistic representation or not. Chomsky seems to take the main motivation for assuming LF as a distinct level to be that it reflects people's intuitions about coreference, bound anaphora, and quantifier scope.[1] However, although it's uncontroversial that people do have intuitions about such issues, the step from recognizing the existence of such intuitions to asserting the existence of a separate level of representation is quite controversial. Other linguists have argued explicitly that the status of LF is an empirical issue, that there are in fact linguistic phenomena which require a level like LF for their explanation. For instance, facts pertaining to VP deletion (or VP anaphora) in English have been brought forward in this context (cf. Cormack, 1982; Partee and Bach, 1981; Sag, 1976; Williams, 1977).

In the development of GB theory, the focus of interest has shifted somewhat. Instead of looking specifically at what properties of grammar are expressed at which level of representations, these levels are seen as derivative of the modular approach to grammar. Chomsky (1981, 1982) assumes that there exist independent subsystems of general principles which regulate phenomena within certain domains. For instance, phenomena like coreference and disjoint reference are handled by a certain set of principles referred to as the Binding Theory (see Section 5.2). These principles permit a deductive approach to the establishment of what the possible readings are for a given sentence. Before discussing this approach in more detail, we will briefly look at how the facts that we have been concerned with in this study can be accounted for within the EST/GB frameworks. We will first investigate what consequences the unbounded dependencies in Swedish will have for a universal characterization of *wh*-movement, then discuss what modifications are required in order to handle bound anaphors in moved constituents, and finally raise the question if the rule of *wh* interpretation, as currently formulated, is adequate.

3. CHARACTERIZING *wh*-MOVEMENT

In his article 'On *wh*-movement', Chomsky points to a cluster of properties which he suggests can be taken as a diagnostic for the rule of *wh*-movement. (In later versions of the theory, this rule is seen as an instance of the more general rule 'move α' (cf. Chomsky, 1982, p. 33).) The characteristic properties of *wh*-movement are:

(1) (i) it leaves a gap
    (ii) where there is a bridge, there is an apparent violation of subjacency, the Propositional Island Constraint, and the Specified Subject Constraint
    (iii) it observes the Complex NP Constraint
    (iv) it observes the *wh*-Island Constraint

(cf. Chomsky, 1977:49)

Question formation in Swedish, however, does not conform to this characterization. For instance a sentence like (2) shows that a moved constituent does not always leave a gap but may require a resumptive pronoun (cf. Chapter III.5.1.1).

(2)   Det finns ord$_i$ som man inte kan tveka om   vad
       there are   words that one cannot   doubt about what

       dom$_i$/*___$_i$ betyder.
       they   mean

In the previous chapters, we have discussed several examples involving extractions out of indirect questions, which consequently violate the fourth criterion in (1). In Chapter III.7 we took up the issue what factors determine the acceptability of multiple extractions out of indirect questions and extractions out of Complex NP structures. We argued there that neither the *wh*-Island Constraint nor the Complex NP Constraint should be invoked as structural constraints which need to be explicitly formulated in a grammar for Swedish. Instead we suggested that apparent restrictions on extraction processes are due to limitations of processing capacity and to discourse requirements, i.e. to factors which presumably hold for speakers of all languages and which need not be explicitly incorporated in the syntax of a particular language. Consequently, we don't take subjacency to be relevant to the characterization of when a constituent may be moved in Swedish[2]. Since none of the diagnostic features in (1) seem to be applicable to Swedish, the issue is raised whether it is the characterization in (1) which fails to provide a universally valid description of movement rules, or if the Swedish facts are the result of some other grammatical process, very similar to *wh*-movement, but not to be identified with this rule. The characterization in (1) represents a way of thinking about language universals that was common in the seventies and which was partly a result of looking mainly at English. Since then, though, careful syntactic analyses of a number of other languages and language families have been performed and a much more varied pattern is emerging (cf. for example for Celtic, McCloskey (1979), and Harlow (1981), for Chinese, Huang (1982), for Romance, Rizzi (1982), for Semitic, Borer and Aoun (1981), Doron (1982), and Reinhart (1982a), and for Scandinavian, Engdahl and Ejerhed (1982) and references therein).

What in 1977 were taken more or less as absolute notions are now conceived of as parameters which can be set at different values in different languages. Indeed, much of the current syntactic research is aimed at studying the parametric variation between languages. The goal is to show how a slight difference in the choice of parameters will have far-reaching but systematic consequences in the individual languages. (For some illustrations of this approach, see Rizzi (1978) who discusses the choice of bounding nodes in English and Italian, and Taraldsen (1982) who suggests that the Romance and Germanic languages differ in whether S is the maximal expansion of V or INFL.) Even with this parametric approach to the formulation of restrictions on movement rules, however, Swedish unbounded dependencies do not fall under the pattern we would expect if they were the result of a syntactic movement rule. In view of this fact, certain linguists, N. Chomsky, H. van Riemsdijk, and E. Williams (personal communications) have suggested that there is no *syntactic* rule of *wh*-movement in Swedish. Instead these facts arise from the application of *interpretive* rules which coindex an initial constituent with a pronoun in the sentence. Since interpretive rules are not subject to subjacency, we would not have any violation of the constraints[3]. However, since these pronouns normally don't show up on the surface, we also need to devise a rule that deletes the pronouns in all but a few contexts. A first approximation of this deletion rule could be as in (3).

(3)   Delete a pronoun everywhere except where it serves a disambiguating role in the language (and in specific contexts).

This explanation might seem simple and appealing. However, it leaves several facts unexplained. Although the principle in (3) would fit in well with the kind of pronoun-gap alternation that some Swedish speakers use to disambiguate intersecting and nested interpretations of multiple filler-gap sentences, which we discussed in Chapter III.6.2, it would not fit with the lack of such an alternation for speakers who don't use it, nor for Norwegian which displays the same range of unbounded dependencies. There is also the systematic contrast between the two languages with respect to subject extractions from the position adjacent to a filled Comp. Whereas standard Swedish requires pronouns in these positions, as can be seen e.g. in (2), standard Norwegian requires gaps. However, it would not make sense to say that the Swedish sentences are ambiguous and hence the pronoun is not deleted, but the Norwegian sentences are not ambiguous. The characterization in (3) also fails to explain why pronouns cannot be deleted in general in Swedish whenever there is no doubt about the intended referent. However, this is not the case as we showed in Chapter III.6.1.

The account that takes *wh*-movement to be an interpretive rule in Swedish in essence amounts to saying that all long distance phenomena in this language are like Left Dislocations. A base generated initial constituent is interpreted as necessarily coreferent with a pronoun inside the sentence, as in (4)[4].

(4) Eva$_i$, jag tror de flesta killar tycker bra om henne$_i$.
     Eva, I   think most   guys   like   her

On this account, however, we have no explanation for why there is in fact a clear difference between Left Dislocations and sentences with other unbounded dependencies in this language. In Swedish, topicalization and matrix constituent questions trigger verb second adjustment, Left Dislocation does not. Topicalized and questioned constituents in most cases leave a gap whereas the pronoun in a sentence with a left dislocation may not be deleted. The left dislocation in (4) should be compared with the topicalized sentence in (5).

(5) Eva$_i$ tror jag de flesta killar tycker bra om ___$_i$/*henne$_i$.
     Eva   think I   most   guys   like   her

If we assimilate all long distance dependencies in Swedish to left dislocations, we have no explanation for why the pronoun must delete in (5) but must not delete in (4). It seems that (4) and (5) can be used pretty much interchangeably in discourse. Consequently, if the conditions for pronoun deletion are some form of an avoid ambiguity strategy, then (4) and (5) would seem to fall under the same conditions and we would not expect any syntactic difference.

Let us return briefly to the issue of resumptive pronouns. One might argue that the fact that Swedish uses both gaps and resumptive pronouns provides support for the position that unbounded dependencies in this language do not involve syntactic movement, but are better accounted for by a combination of a interpretive rules and obligatory deletion rules, assuming that a better formulation of the latter can be given than in (3). In the case of Norwegian, however, this kind of reasoning is much less plausible. We noted earlier that resumptive pronouns are used much less (if at all) in most Norwegian dialects and are in general perceived as unacceptable. Hence, to say that unbounded dependencies in Norwegian arise from a rule that interprets a pronoun as coreferent with an initial constituent lacks any empirical support. N. Chomsky and E. Williams (personal communications) have suggested that languages like Norwegian and Swedish in fact have zero resumptive pronouns, i.e. phonologically unrealized pronouns, and that interpretive principles coindex a base generated initial constituent with such zero pronouns. There are in fact languages where the notion zero resumptive pronoun seems to play a role. Italian, for instance, allows pronominals lacking phonological content in the subject position of tensed sentences as in (6) (see Rizzi (1982) and Chomsky (1982)).

(6) e parla
         speak-3sg
         He/she is speaking.

Since there is clearly no extraction in this sentence, and furthermore, since the sentence is interpreted with the missing subject referring to a specific, contextually recoverable, individual, it seems natural to assume that the empty category e is a zero pronominal. Given the existence of these zero pronouns in the language, Taraldsen (1978a) and Chomsky (1981) argue that they are also involved in the derivation of sentences with long subject extractions as in (7), adapted from Taraldsen (1978).

(7)   Ecco la ragazza$_i$ [che mi domando [chi$_j$ [e_j crede
         this is the girl   that me ask-1s   who   thinks
         [che e_i possa cantare]]]]
         that   may   sing
         Here is the girl that I wonder who thinks may sing.

Note that the relation between **ragazza** and e_i would violate subjacency if (7) was derived by *wh*-movement. But if e_i is a zero pronoun, then (7) would just be an instance of a relative clause derived through predication. The question then arises if we can extend the account given for the Italian long subject extractions to the cases in Norwegian and Swedish. First we note that the primary motivation for assuming zero pronominals in Italian, viz. the existence of sentences like (6), is lacking in the modern Scandinavian languages.

(8) a.   *e har åkt
         has gone

b. Han har åkt
   he has gone

(9) a. *Jag talade med e
   I   spoke with

b. Jag talade med henne
   I   spoke with her

A third person pronoun cannot be omitted even if the referent is contextually determined, as shown by the minimal pairs in (8) and (9). Given that there hence is no language internal support for assuming zero resumptive pronominals, the proposal that sentences with unbounded dependencies don't involve syntactic extraction but some interpretive rule involving predication at LF appears lacking in both empirical motivation and explanatory potential. A more promising approach seems to be to assume that the unbounded dependency constructions in Swedish that we are dealing with are in fact syntactic dependencies of the same type that is characterized by Move α in GB. This means that the characterization in (1) is too narrow to be a truly universal characterization of possible syntactic dependencies.

It seems plausible that when we look at a wider range of languages from different types, it will turn out that a universal characterization of *wh*-movement, i.e. of unbounded dependencies, will not make reference to any of the specific properties mentioned in (1). Instead the appropriate type of characterizations might be statements of the level of generality illustrated in (10).

(10) Unbounded dependencies in natural languages are always binary.

Such a generalization would rule out unbounded dependencies or instances of *wh*-movement which involve three distinct positions. Whereas there is a lot of variation in the realization of unbounded dependencies in different languages; there is to my knowledge no attested case of ternary relations. In view of this, I would like to put forward the hypothesis that (10) is not just a stipulation but a characteristic property of human languages[5]. Incidentally, if this hypothesis is correct, it would have as a consequence that a grammar which generates languages of the $a^n b^n c^n$ type is not adequate for natural languages.

4. wh-INTERPRETATION AND RECONSTRUCTION AT LF

Having looked briefly at the syntactic properties of *wh*-movement, we will now turn to how structures arising from *wh*-movement are interpreted. We will first look at the role of *wh*-interpretation in an EST model of grammar. The model of grammar assumed in EST can be represented schematically as in (11).

(11)

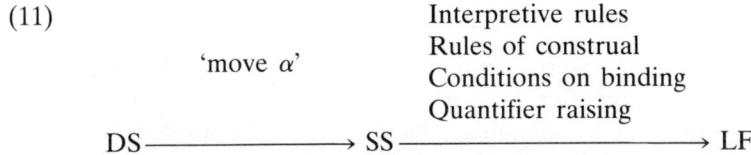

'Move α' is the syntactic rule which moves any constituent, in particular NPs and WH phrases, leaving behind a trace, coindexed with the moved constituent. Construal rules relate anaphors to antecedents, also by coindexing. The interpretive rules include rules for quantifier construal (cf. May, 1977). WH phrases are taken to be a special kind of quantifier whose meaning can be given roughly by the paraphrase 'for which x, ...'. In 'On *wh*-movement', Chomsky gives the following interpretation rule for constituent questions.

(12)   Given an $\bar{S}$ of the form: $[[_{Comp} - WH\text{-}\bar{N} - +WH][_S ... t ...]]$
where t is the trace of WH-$\bar{N}$, rewrite it as:

$[_{Comp}$ for which x, x an $\bar{N}]$, $[_S ... - x - ...]$.

(Chomsky, 1977: (38))

The effect of (12) is to insert a variable, x, bound by the WH quantifier in the position of the trace. Notice that the rule explicitly states that the position where the variable is inserted is the trace of *that* WH phrase, i.e., the required correspondence between syntactic constituents and variables used in the semantics is explicitly built into the rule.

(12) construes a surface structure like in (13) as the logical form (13b).

(13) a. $[_{\bar{S}}[_{Comp}$ Which student$]$ $[_S$ did John see $t]]$
     b. $[_{Comp}$ for which x, x a student$]$, John saw x

$\bar{N}$ is the level we have referred to as CN. The material in $\bar{N}$ thus serves as a restriction on the variable x. This leads to certain problems when the restriction contains an anaphor, as we will see.

The interpretation rule in (12) applies quite straightforwardly when the phrase in Comp consists of a simple NP of the form [$_{NP}$ *which* N̄]. But since *wh*-movement can apply to other constituents than NPs, there will be cases where additional syntactic material has been moved along ('pied-piped') with the *wh*-phrase into Comp, as in (14) and (15).

(14)   From which book did Mary read?

(15)   Whose book did Mary read?

The rule of WH interpretation rewrites the phrase as an expression prefixed by a quantifier *for which x*. But pied-piped material such as prepositions and containing NPs cannot be interpreted in Comp. It must somehow be 'lowered' back into the position of the trace where it can be interpreted. Chomsky (1977) refers to this process as *reconstruction* since part of a moved structure must be reconstructed inside the sentence for semantic interpretation. Presumably the dash, –, in (12) is intended to cover such material and would allow sentences like (14) and (15) to be rewritten as below.

(14′) a. [$_{\bar{S}}$[$_{Comp}$ From which book][$_S$ did Mary read t]]
       b. [$_{Comp}$ for which x, x, a book] Mary read from x

(15′) a. [$_{\bar{S}}$[$_{Comp}$ Whose book][$_S$ did Mary read t]]
       b. [$_{Comp}$ for which x, x a person] Mary read x's book

As stated, the rule in (12) is not quite correct. The correspondence clause requires that 't is the trace of WH-N̄'. Actually, t must be the trace of '– WH-N̄ –' and the effect of the rule should be to insert '– x –' in the position of t, provided that this can be made more precise than in the present formulation.

We note that although (12) is supposedly an interpretive rule, it performs a movement of syntactic material, much like the syntactic rule 'move α'. The movement performed by the interpretive rule (12) in effect undoes the pied-piping and puts material back into its pre-*wh*-movement position. Since an interpretive rule must thus perform the inverse of a syntactic rule, it might seem like the distribution of tasks between the syntactic and the semantic components in EST is not optimal. We recall that on our approach to pied-piping, which we illustrated in Chapter IV.8.1, this phenomenon does not raise any problem. It follows from our general semantic approach, namely that storage only applies to quantifiers, that the pied-piped material will be interpreted as contributing to the interpretation of its link parent, that is to the constituent dominating the gap, and thus indirectly to the characterization of the true propositions in the set denoted by the question. In the EST model, the semantic rule lowers everything but the *wh*-quantifier down into the pre-*wh*-movement position. Which of the models one prefers will presumably depend on one's metatheoretical stand on what processes belong to the domain of syntactic and semantic rules, respectively. I think it is an advantage of the present proposal that we get the desired interpretations following the straightforward principle that storage only applies to quantifiers, i.e. those constituents whose actual scope might be different from their syntactic position. There is no need to express any reconstruction of syntactic material in the interpretation rules.

5. BOUND ANAPHORS IN MOVED CONSTITUENTS

In this section we will look at the problem of bound anaphors inside *wh*-moved constituents. We will first outline a possible account within a version of EST and then discuss what changes in the Binding Theory of the GB framework are required in order to account for these phenomena.

5.1. Anaphora Interpretation in EST

We recall that in the EST model of grammar as outlined in (11), the rules which relate anaphors to their antecedents apply at S-structure, after *wh*-movement. The relevant principle for antecedent-anaphor relations is taken to be the structurally defined notion of *c-command*, formulated e.g. in Reinhart (1976, 1981b) and given here in (16).

(16)   A node α c(onstituent)-commands a node β if and only if neither α nor β dominates the other and the first branching node which dominates α also dominates β.

Common to all anaphora rules is the requirement that the antecedent c-command the anaphor, equivalently, the anaphor must be in the *syntactic domain* of the antecedent, i.e. within its c-command domain. Since anaphora rules apply at S-structure, we will run into problems when an appication of *wh*-movement removes an anaphor from the syntactic domain of its antecedent. We have already encountered several examples where this is the case, such as in (17).

(17) [Which picture of herself$_i$]$_j$ do you think Mary$_i$ likes t_j best?

At S-structure, the reflexive anaphor *herself* is no longer c-commanded by its antecedent *Mary*. Consequently, if we want to express the anaphoric relation between reflexives and their antecedents by coindexing constituents in a structure, we need to modify the rules. Given the possibility of referring to traces of moved constituents, this can be done rather straightforwardly. We note that although the antecedent in (17) does not c-command the anaphor, it c-commands the trace of a constituent that contains the anaphor. One way of formulating the rule would be as in (18).

(18) *Reflexive interpretation*
(i) if α is an anaphor that occurs in S, then α must be coindexed with some NP in S which c-commands α.

(ii) If α is an anaphor that does not occur in S, but either α is coindexed with an empty category, e_i, in S or α is *contained* in a phrase β coindexed with an empty category, e_i, in S, then α must be coindexed with some NP in S which c-commands e_i. S must be minimal.

The first case in (18ii) would apply to sentences like in (19).

(19) Himself$_i$, John$_i$ despises e_i.

The second case is intended to cover examples like (17). We note that this case uses the term *contained*. This term of course must be defined properly in order for (18) to make the correct distinctions (cf. Higginbotham (1980a) for one proposal). Assuming that such a definition has been given, clause (ii) will allow *herself* in (17) to be coindexed with the antecedent *Mary*. The structure would be as in (20). Presumably we would have to invoke similar conditions on anaphoric interpretation in a model which base-generates empty categories and preposed constituents in their surface positions and connect them to empty nodes by some linking device (cf. Koster, 1978).

Since information about the pre-*wh*-movement position of the moved constituent is recorded by the indexed trace, it will always be possible to write rules like in (18). The question is whether this two-pronged

(20)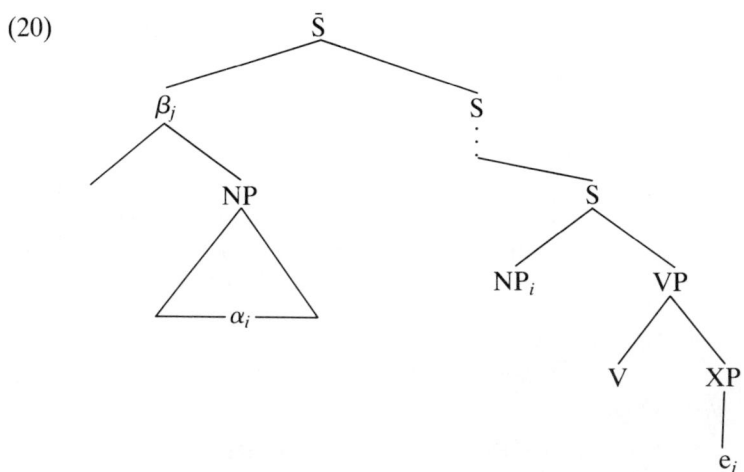

approach is independently motivated or if there is a simpler account. We noted above that it is the pre-*wh*-movement position of the anaphor with respect to the antecedent that determines the coindexing possibilities. It thus seems plausible that anaphoric relations should be assigned at some stage in the derivation that precedes *wh*-movement. We could assume that the relevant level for coindexing is after the application of cyclic (bounded) rules like NP movement, but before post-cyclic (unbounded) rules like *wh*-movement, using Postal's (1971) distinction. Such considerations has led some linguists to the conclusion that there is a theoretical advantage in not collapsing NP movement and *wh*-movement under the common rule schema 'move α' which is commonly assumed in Chomsky's writings (cf. Hellan 1980b, van Riemsdijk & Williams 1982). On such an approach, the model of the grammar could look like in (21). We will refer to the intermediate level as *shallow structure*, abbreviated Sh S)[6]

(21)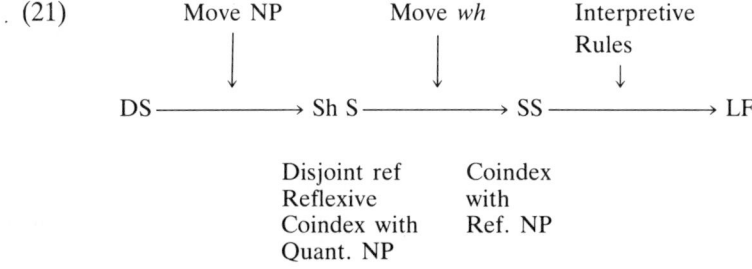

In this model, reflexive interpretation and disjoint reference assignment would take place at shallow structure. After the indexing operations at this level, *wh*-movement applies and moves entire WH phrases, but note that the reflexive or personal pronoun inside a WH phrase will now carry the same index as its antecedent. It is clear that reflexive and reciprocal coindexing must take place after NP movement since this rule may alter coindexing possibilities. For example, the subject of a passive sentence, presumably moved by NP movement may control a reflexive pronoun in the agentive phrase, as illustrated in (22).

(22) a. *Sina$_i$ kolleger kritiserar ofta Sven$_i$
   colleagues criticize often Sven
   POSS
   REFL

   b. Sven$_i$ kritiseras ofta t_i av sina$_i$ kolleger
   Sven is often criticized by his (own) colleagues

If we separate the application of NP movement and *wh*-movement and let the anaphoric rules apply at the intermediate level, shallow structure, the rules that coindex antecedents and anaphors can operate quite generally. In addition, we can express permissible anaphoric relations between quantificational NPs and personal pronouns at this level. The condition for coindexing in this case would be that any personal pronoun may be coindexed with a dominating WH phrase or quantificational NP to its left. This condition will exclude violations of cross-over without further restrictions. We can contrast this with the model given in (11). In this model, all co- or reindexing takes place at surface structure and special conditions must be formulated in order to prevent cross-over violations. We return to this topic in greater detail in Chapter VI. The model grammar depicted in (21) thus appears to be a preferable model from the point of view of anaphora interpretation. It involves postulating one additional level of representation in the grammar, which needs independent justification. Van Riemsdijk and Williams, in fact, argue that there is a cluster of properties which characterize this intermediate level[7].

Another consequence of adopting the model in (21) is that there is no longer one structural level in the grammar which provides the whole input to semantic interpretation. Certain relations which are relevant to semantic interpretation will be determined at shallow structure, whereas others, such as the scope of WH phrases, will be determined by rules that apply to surface structure. A still more radical approach would be to say that shallow structure is really the output of the base component. NP movement rules are essentially structure preserving, and only move NPs into positions where they could have been generated by the base rules alone. If we assume that the base rules allow for direct generation of sentences involving passive and raising subjects, we could say that deep structure equals shallow structure. For instance J. Bresnan (1978) assumes that passive structures are generated directly and interpreted via lexical rules, and Bach (1980) argues that there is a special syntactic category Passive VP. Proposals that let active and passive sentences both be generated by the base rules would of course have to be evaluated from the point of view of overall complexity and theoretical adequacy (cf. Hellan (1980a) who argues that both Bach's and Bresnan's approach lead to more complex grammars overall).

The revised model in (21) overcomes the problem of how bound anaphors in moved constituents can be coindexed with their respective antecedents. However, merely coindexing two constituents is not sufficient to determine how they are to be interpreted as we will show after having looked at the way anaphors are handled in the GB theory.

5.2. *The Binding Theory in the Government-Binding Framework*

Within the framework of the GB theory, as presented in Chomsky (1981, 1982), the conditions on coreference and disjoint reference, which in earlier versions of the theory were stated as independent principles, have been consolidated to a set of three postulates, the so-called Binding Theory. These three postulates reflect Chomsky's idea that NPs in natural languages can be partitioned into three types, each subject to its own binding principle. The binding principles are expressed using the terms *bound* and *free* which in turn are structurally defined (see below). In addition, the binding principles refer to a certain domain or *governing category* of a particular item (see Chomsky (1981) for details).

Binding is defined in terms of c-command. Chomsky distinguishes two types of binding, argument binding (A-binding) and non-argument binding ($\bar{A}$-binding). The distinction has to do with whether the binder occurs in an argument position, i.e. a position that receives a grammatical function at D-structure, or in a non-argument position such as Comp[8]. If we let X range over A and $\bar{A}$, we can define binding as in (23).

(23) α is X-bound by β if and only if
     (i) α and β are coindexed
     (ii) β c-commands α
     (iii) β is in an X-position
    α is X-free if and only if α is not X-bound

By and large, A-binding corresponds to relations established by NP movement and Ā-binding to relations established by *wh*-movement and QR. Following Chomsky (1982) we can formulate the Binding Theory as in (24).

(24)   Binding Theory
     A.   An anaphor is bound in its governing category.
     B.   A pronominal is free in its governing category.
     C.   i.   An R-expression is free.
        ii.   A variable is free in the domain of the operator that binds it.

Anaphors comprise lexical anaphors such as reflexives and reciprocals as well as traces left behind by NP movement. Pronominals include pronouns and PRO. R-expressions refer to referential NPs and quantifiers and variables are the empty categories left behind in *wh*-movement[9].

Since the traces left behind by NP movement and *wh*-movement are distinguishable and subject to different binding conditions, the distinctions that led Hellan and van Riemsdijk and Williams to postulate a separate level of representation can still be made.

The Binding Theory summarized in (24) will correctly mark as ungrammatical our previous example (22a).

(22) a. *Sina$_i$ kolleger   kritiserar ofta Sven$_i$.
    his-own colleagues criticize   often Sven

(22a) is ruled out because the lexical anaphor **sina** is free in its governing category since it's not c-commanded by any coindexed binder. This is in violation of principle A.

The principles in (24) suffice to account for occurrences of anaphors in argument positions. However, just like in the EST approach, examples where anaphors occur in non-argument position such as Comp will still be problematic. Consider our earlier example in (17).

(17) [s̄[Comp Which picture of herself$_i$][S do you think Mary$_i$ likes best?]]

The anaphor *herself* is not c-commanded by any coindexed element. In order to handle this and similar cases it seems that we would have to complicate principle A somewhat. One way would be to distinguish cases where an anaphor occurs in A-position from cases where an anaphor occurs in an Ā-position. It seems that we have to distinguish two cases of the Binding Theory for anaphors. We could revise principle A as in (25).

(25) A' (i) If α is an anaphor in an A-position, then α is bound in its governing category
    (ii) If α is an anaphor in an Ā-position and either α is coindexed with an empty category, e_i, in an A-position or α is *contained* in a phrase β coindexed with an empty category, e_i, in an A-position and there is some γ, coindexed with α, in the governing category for e_i, then α is bound by γ.

The second clause is very similar to our earlier attempt at formulating the coindexing requirement in (18). It is subject to the same proviso, i.e. it needs a formal definition of *containment* in order to be useable. Alternatively we could have tried to define *binding* so that it applies to chains of anaphors and empty categories.

By thus distinguishing anaphors in A- and Ā-positions we can make sure that anaphors in Comp get coindexed with the appropriate antecedent. While this revision of principle A will make approximately the right predictions, it is far from an optimal statement given its complexity. A more general solution to the interaction of *wh*-movement and the Binding Theory seems called for[10].

5.3. wh-Interpretation Reconsidered

Whichever approach we take – allowing anaphora coindexing to take place at shallow structure or distinguishing two cases in the Binding Theory for anaphors – we have a way of making sure that lexical anaphors in moved constituents end up coindexed with the appropriate antecedents. As we foreshadowed in a previous section, however, this is not the same as saying that they can be appropriately interpreted. Recall that WH interpretation, the rule that construes a WH phrase in Comp as an interrogative quantifier, applies at S-structure. In the case of a question like (26a), WH interpretation will construe the S-structure in (26b) as the LF representation of (26c).

(26) a. Which picture of herself does Mary prefer?
b. [$\bar{s}$[Comp[which picture of herself$_i$]$_j$][$_S$ does Mary$_i$ prefer t_j]]
c. [for which x, x a picture of x_i], [for x_i = Mary], x_i prefers x

Note that although *Mary* and *herself* are coindexed at S-structure, the variable inside the interrogative quantifier at LF is still free. The natural way to interpret (26c) would be to let x_i pick out some individual in the context. The interrogative quantifier *which picture of herself* thus would come out with the same meaning as *which picture of her*, where *her* is understood deictically. In the case of coreference between individuals, as in (26) it is conceivable that we could design further interpretive principles to the effect that the value assignment function assigns *herself$_i$* to the individual picked put by *Mary$_i$*, although such a move would presumably require that the interpretation rules have access to global information. In case the antecedent is a non-referential, quantificational NP as in (27), not even this move would be sufficient.

(27) a. Which picture of *herself* do you think *every girl* prefers?
b. [$\bar{s}$[Comp[which picture of herself$_i$]$_j$][$_{S_1}$ do you think
[$_{S_2}$ every girl$_i$ prefers t_j]]]

If we follow May (1977) in assuming that the rule that interprets NP quantifiers Chomsky-adjoins a quantifier to S or $\bar{S}$, we have a choice where to adjoin *every girl*. If we adjoin it to the top, we get the LF in (28).

(28)   [for each y, y a girl] [for which x, x a picture of y], you think y prefers x

(28) represents the reading where *every girl* has wider scope than the interrogative phrase, a reading which we could paraphrase 'for each girl y, tell me which picture of y you think y prefers'. On this reading, (27) is equivalent to asking a set of questions, one for each girl, and an appropriate way to answer would be as in (29).

(29)   Mary, I think prefers the picture I took of her in France,
       Sue, I think prefers the studio portrait,
       Ellen, I think prefers the snapshot from last summer ...
       (etc. until all girls have been mentioned)

(29) represents one reading of (27), but this is not the only one. As we showed in Chapter III, this type of question often get relational answers which are compatible with a reading where *every girl*, the antecedent for the anaphor in the interrogative quantifier, is understood to have narrow scope with respect to the propositional attitude verb *think*. Typical answers on this reading would be *the one where she is laughing* or *the one her boyfriend took*. We could try to express this reading by raising *every girl* only to the embedded S_2, leaving it within the scope of *think*. We then get the LF representation in (30).

(30)   [for which x, x a picture of x_i] [you think for each y, y a girl] y prefers x]

But note that x_i, the variable inserted for the anaphor *herself* in the specification of the interrogative quantifier, is still free. There is thus nothing that connects x_i with the interpretation of *every girl*. To interpret x_i deictically would clearly be false. It turns out that *wh*-interpretation as currently formulated is unable to express the relational reading of questions like in (27).

In this and the preceding section, we have discussed various ways of making sure that anaphors in moved constituents are coindexed with their respective antecedents. As we have seen, this would meet the requirement of principle A of the Binding Theory. Nevertheless, this type of coindexing does not guarantee that these anaphors, or bound pronouns in general, can be appropriately interpreted, if, that is, we construe WH phrases as interrogative quantifiers which range over individuals only. In our discussion of the interpretation possibilities of WH phrases in Chapter IV (especailly Sections 4 and 5), we argued that the interpretation of a WH phrase can be understood to vary with the interpretation of any NP in the sentence which has scope over the empty position that the WH phrase is linked to. We showed that such *relational* readings are possible regardless of whether the WH phrase contains explicit anaphors. In order to capture this relational character of consituent questions, we have suggested that interrogatives involve quantification over n place functions, where n corresonds to the number of

NPs with which the interpretation of the WH phrase may vary. In case $n = 0$ the result will be equivalent to quantification over individuals directly. We have showed how this analysis of interrogative quantifiers permits us to take a unified approach to a variety of questions, to account for questions into opaque contexts, etc. Here, in the context of discussing a transformational approach to these structures, we want to emphasize that the issue of what type of interpretation to assume for interrogative quantifiers is independent of the particular syntactic framework one chooses. It is thus not the case that it is our choice of a non-transformational syntax that forces us to adopt what might be seen as a more complex interpretation for interrogative quantifiers. As we have seen in this section, even if we adopt a syntax with movement transformations, it will not be possible to account for relational readings of questions as long as we assume that interrogative quantifiers always involve quantification over individuals. This is shown by the failure of the LF in (30) to express one of the readings of the question in (27). However, there is nothing to prevent us from combining a syntax with *wh*-movement with the type of semantic interpretation we have suggested in Chapter IV. This would enable us to express relational reading within for instance a GB framework. The conclusion we can draw is thus that a more flexible approach to the interpretation of interrogative quantifiers is needed regardless of what type of syntactic framework one assumes, and that we cannot, at least not in this area, use arguments of the type 'theory x enables us to have a simpler semantics than theory Y' to choose between alternative syntactic approaches.

6. HIGGINBOTHAM AND MAY'S THEORY OF QUESTIONS

We noted earlier that although a LF representation containing an expression like *for which x, x a Ñ,* ... gives an intuitive paraphrase of the meaning of an interrogative quantifier, it does not provide an *interpretation* for the question in which the quantifier occurs. By interpretation we understand a procedure through which you can tell what the denotation of an expression is. In the case of questions, this can amount to determining what the possible answers to the question are. It is clear that we need something more than the rule for *wh*-construal given in (12) to be able to determine whether the LF representation associated with a given S-structure is a correct representation of the meaning of that question. Within the EST framework,

J. Higginbotham and R. May have outlined a theory of questions that promises to provide exactly such a general semantic background for Chomsky's rule of WH interpretation. The theory also addresses the semantics of other complicated questions and we will here discuss certain points of their analysis which bear directly on the types of questions we are investigating here.

In their paper, 'Questions, Quantifiers, and Crossing', Higginbotham and May outline a theory of questions according to which a question corresponds to a partitioning of the possible states of affairs into a set of mutually exclusive and jointly exhaustive alternatives. An appropriate answer to a question is a sentence that eliminates one or more of the possible states of affairs. If we assume that the relevant domain of individuals only contains two members, John and Mary, then a question like in (31a) will correspond to the partitioning in (31b).

(31) a. Which students came?
b. $\{j \& m, j \& \neg m, \neg \& m, \neg j \& \neg m\}$

A sentence like (32) will count as an answer

(32)   John came.

since it eliminates the possibiity that John didn't come. However, Higginbotham and May maintain that (32) is only a partial answer to (31) since it leaves us in ignorance about whether Mary came or not. A complete answer would be as in (33).

(33)   John came, but Mary didn't.
Only John came.

It seems to me that in a speech community where Grice's maxim of quantity is respected, (32) would also count as a complete answer, since the listener would infer that if the speaker knew that someone else besides John came, he would have said so (cf. Grice, 1975).

Higginbotham and May's approach is very similar to the ones presented by Hamblin (1973) and Karttunen (1977). Hamblin takes a question to set up choice-situations between a set of propositions, viz. those propositions that count as answers to it. Karttunen differs slightly from Hamblin in that he takes the meaning of a question to be the set of propositions that jointly constitute a *true* and complete answer to it. To characterize the set of true and complete answers is of course nothing different from what Higginbotham and May call 'acquiring a complete relief of ignorance as to what states are compatible with the real world'. One point where Higginbotham and May's approach differs from the one presented by Karttunen and further developed in Karttunen and Peters (1976) is in the treatment of presuppositions of questions. It is generally agreed that a question like (34)

(34)   Which girl came?

is associated with a presupposition of uniqueness, that only one girl came. Karttunen and Peters do not express this uniqueness requirement as part of the meaning of the question, but say that it is conventionally implicated, and forms part of the implicature expression associated with the representation of the meaning of question. Higginbotham and May make the uniqueness requirement part of the interpretation of the WH quantifier. However, this will not be appropriate for the interpretation of multiple questions like (35).

(35)   Which man saw which woman?

In their theory, the question expressed in (35) will carry the presupposition that exactly one man saw one woman. But, as Higginbotham and May note, this is clearly not correct since appropriate answers to (35) could be either one single pair or a list of ordered pairs, as in (36).

(36)   John saw Mary and Bill saw Sally.

(Higginbotham and May, 1.13)

Instead they claim that (36) always presupposes that no man saw more than one woman, and that no woman was seen by more than one man[11]. To get the list of paris reading, (36), Higginbotham and May propose to augment the set of quantifiers for natural languages by n-ary quantifiers which are, in effect, n-place operators. For this purpose they define a rule called *absorption*, which generates representations containing n-ary WH quantifiers ($n \geq 2$) from adjacent pairs of quantifiers, as in (37).

(37) $[(\text{WH } x: \bar{N}(x)] [\text{WH } y: \bar{N}(y)] \rightarrow [\text{WH } x, \text{WH } y: \bar{N}(x) \wedge \bar{N}(y)]$

(Higginbotham and May, 1.30)

Absorption can apply to the question in (35) but, interestingly enough, not to a question like (38), on the reading where *his* is construed as bound by *which boy*.

(38)   Which boy admires which one of *his* sisters?

(Higginbotham and May, 1.32)

This is so, Higginbotham and May say, because Absorption cannot apply to pairs of WH quantifiers whose second member contains a variable bound by the first. (38), on this bound reading, of course corresponds to the Swedish sentence in (39), where **sina** is a reflexive pronoun.

(39)   **Vilken pojke** beundrar vilken av **sina** systrar?
       which boy *admires* *which of* POSS *sisters*
                                           REFL

Since Absorption is blocked, Higginbotham and May predict that (38) only has the reading which presupposes that there is a unique boy which admires one of his sisters and that only a singular answer like in (40) will be correct.

(40)   John admires his sister Mary.

In support of the correctness of this prediction, they note that (41) is not a good answer to (38).

(41)   John admires (his sister) Mary, and Fred admires (his sister) Sally.

Judgments vary on the appropriateness of (41), but nevertheless it does not seem to justify the claim that (38) only has the singular interpretation. For instance, an answer like (42) seems quite appropriate.

(42)   *John* admires *his* oldest sister, and *Fred his* youngest sister.

(42) gives a list of pairs where the second instantiation is given as a function of the answer to the first. Not surprisingly, it turns out that this is exactly the type of answer we frequently get in relational questions. The denotation of *which of his sisters* will vary with the choice of antecedent for *his*. It is also clear that we cannot express this depen-

dency by quantifying over individuals directly. This type of data, in fact, provides part of the motivation for our proposal to let interrogative quantifiers involve quantification over functions. The interpretation our grammar would give to (38) and (39) can be represented as in (43).

(43)   "?" $\hat{p}$ $\exists W$ $\exists W_1[\textbf{boy}'(W) \wedge \forall x[\textbf{of}'_*(\check{}x)(\textbf{sister}')(W_1(x))] \wedge$
        $\check{}p \wedge p = \hat{}\textbf{admire}'_*(\check{}W, \check{}(W_1(W)))]$

(43) denotes the set of true propositions of the form 'W admires $W_1(W)$' where W is a boy and for all x, $W_1(x)$ is a sister of x's.

To summarize, we find that Higginbotham and May's analysis for multiple questions is not sufficient to account for all possible answers to questions like (38) and (39) where there is a dependency between the two WH phrases. Higginbotham and May's approach involves the introduction of n-ary quantifiers in the respresentation of natural language. The motivation for n-ary quantifiers depends to a large extent on the assumption that the uniqueness presupposition associated with the occurrence of a WH phrase should be explicitly represented as part of the meaning of the quantifier. We have seen that there is an alternative to this assumption, namely that uniqueness presuppositions arise as conventional implicatures of a question and need not be expressed as part of the meaning of the quantifier (cf. Karttunen and Peters, 1976). Additional evidence for introducing n-ary quantifiers comes, Higginbotham and May argue, from considering Bach-Peters sentences (cf. also Thomason (1977) for similar considerations). We have no analysis of Bach-Peters sentences to offer at present and leave the issue whether their interpretation requires n-ary quantifiers open. Here we just note that multiple questions do not provide evidence that we need such quantifiers.

NOTES

[1] For instance in a lecture at the Sixth Scandinavian Conference of Linguistics, Røros, Norway, June 1981.

[2] In Engdahl (1980b) I discuss various proposals for modifying the *wh*-Island Constraint so that multiple extractions could be handled without violation of subjacency. I argue there that Swedish can be shown to obey subjacency only if this principle is substantially redefined, in which case it looses most of the explanatory potential which motivated its introduction in the grammar of English.

[3] Chomsky has recently suggested that relative clauses in English be derived by a rule involving a kind of predication (Chomsky (1982), fn. 11). Chomsky's motivation is partly

to account for certain contrasts in weak cross-over between relative clauses and questions in English. Presumably the same type of predication could be appealed to in the Swedish cases. This approach involves several assumptions, among others the postulation of additional levels of LF, LF', which we won't discuss here. We just note that there does not appear to be any contrast between constituent questions, relative clauses, and topicalizations in this respect in Swedish.

[4] Such Left Dislocations are actually rather rare in Swedish. Much more frequent are sentences like (i) where the dislocated constituent is doubled by an agreeing pronoun which is case marked with the case appropriate to the gap context.

(i) Eva$_i$, henne$_i$ tycker de flesta killar bra om ____$_i$.
     Eva, her   most guys like

Andersson (1974) analyzes structures like (i) as a combination of dislocation and topic movement. See also Zaenen (1980, 1982) for a discussion of such *contrastive dislocations* in Dutch and Icelandic.

[5] A statement like (10) would of course not have any independent status in the theory. Ideally, what we would want is to have something like (10) fall out as a consequence of general principles of universal grammar.

[6] I believe this term was first introduced by Lakoff (1971) in a discussion of Postal (1971).

[7] See van Riemsdijk and Williams (1982) for a full exposition of the argument. In their model, all interpretation rules apply at the intermediate level, which they refer to as *NP structure*. The rules of quantifier interpretation coindex quantifier phrases and S nodes that dominate them in order to indicate their scope. This indexed representation supposedly provides input to LF. However, it is not clear what the rules that map indexed NP structures into LF look like.

[8] This distinction is not essential to the problems we are discussing here. But cf. Aoun (1981) who claims that there are two types of anaphorization processes, A-anaphorization and Ā-anaphorization.

[9] The particular reasons for assigning one type of NP to one category rather than to another have to do with how these subclasses behave with respect to other phenomena. For instance, lumping WH traces together with R-expressions allows us to deduce the cross-over facts without further assumptions. It will not be possible to go into details here. The reader is referred to Chomsky (1981, esp. chapter 3; 1982, esp. chapter 5) and Aoun (1981) for further elaborations.

[10] Similar revisions would have to be made of principles B and C in (24) in order to get the disjoint reference and cross-over facts right for sentences with preposed constituents.

[11] I believe that this claim is actually too strong, judging from my intuitions on corresponding Swedish sentences, but I will not pursue this point further here.

CHAPTER VI

RESTRICTING THE INTERPRETATION OF PRONOUNS

1. INTRODUCTION

We will devote the final chapter to a discussion of what types of restrictions on pronoun interpretations we should capture in our grammar, thereby taking up some issues that were left open in the previous chapters. We will first look at the so-called disjoint reference and non-coreference facts. We find that although such facts can be represented syntactically by a contra-indexing procedure, this does not solve the problem of how they can be interpreted. We will then discuss an alternative approach, advanced by T. Reinhart (Reinhart, 1983). According to Reinhart, the only sentence grammar restriction on pronoun interpretation that we need to consider is the condition on what she calls 'bound anaphora'. Both the disjoint reference and the non-coreference effect, she argues, follow from general pragmatic principles. Interestingly enough, some rather strong support for Reinhart's line of argumentation comes from the distribution of parasitic gaps, which we discuss in Section 2.2.

Finally in Section 3, we will compare two approaches to the so-called 'cross-over' phenomenon. Higginbotham's (1980b) approach which crucially refers to an indexed syntactic representation is representative for the way such facts have been handled in the EST-GB frameworks. We will contrast this approach with the one proposed here according to which the cross-over facts follow from the way the interpretation rules work. We point out that Higginbotham's and our approaches make different predictions for weak cross-over constructions and end with a few remarks on the general approach to binding in GB. We suggest that it would be worthwhile to investigate what the correlation is between the primitive types of NPs assumed in the GB theory and the types of interpretation procedures that we have associated with different types of NPs.

2. DISJOINT REFERENCE AND NON-COREFERENCE

In Chapter III.5, we discussed the interpretation possibilities for pronouns. We distinguished there between *deictic* interpretations and *bound* interpretations of pronouns, where the two types of interpretations follow from whether the individual variable in the pronoun interpretation was bound by a quantifier or not. We there introduced one constraint on pronoun interpretation, the Store Address Convention (SAC III: (90)), the purpose of which, we recall, was to prevent a pronoun which c-commands a quantifier (NP or WH phrase) from being bound by it. In addition, our rule for reflexive interpretation (III: (70)) guarantees that reflexive pronouns are bound by the interpretation of the closest subject NP. However, our rules do not exclude that a personal pronoun is interpreted as coreferent with the subject of the same clause, although this is a context which is assumed to require what has been called 'disjoint reference'. This is illustrated in (1).

(1) a.   **Kalle** tycker om **sin**   syster
         Kalle likes   *POSS* *sister*
                               REFL

    b.   **Kalle** tycker om **hans**   syster
         Kalle likes   *POSS* *sister*
                               PERS

There is nothing in the way our interpretation procedures are stated which prevents a reading of (1b) where **han** picks out the individual denoted by **Kalle**. This could happen if the assignment function that assigns values to free values assigned **Kalle** to the free variable in the interpretation of **hans**. Furthermore, in so-called 'non-coreference' contexts, as in (2)[1],

(2)   **Hon** hälsade på **Ulla**
         She greeted   Ulla

where it is commonly assumed that **hon** must refer to an individual distinct from Ulla, this interpretation is not ruled out by our grammar. It would arise in the same way as the coreferent interpretation for (1b). Since a deictic pronoun is free to refer to any individual, we will also get the readings where it happens to pick out an individual which is also picked out by some other referring expression in the sentence. We will now take up the issue whether we should restrict our interpretation rules to prevent accidental coreference in disjoint reference and non-coreference contexts.

The usual way to account for the disjoint reference facts illustrated in (1) has been to assume that personal and reflexive pronouns are in complemantary distribution, to define the domain for reflexive pronouns, and to exclude personal pronouns on a coreferent reading in that same domain. One way of doing this is to use some kind of contra-indexing device (cf. Chomsky, 1980, 1981)[2]. There have also been several attempts in the literature to account for the non-coreference facts by referring to structural properties. One example is Lasnik's (1976) non-coreference rule which excludes coreference between two definite NPs, NP_1 and NP_2, if NP_1 commands NP_2 and NP_2 is not a pronoun. Similarly, Reinhart (1976, 1981b) assumes that a NP must be interpreted as non-coreferent with any non-pronominal NP it c-commands.

An interesting proposal for capturing these restrictions semantically is made in Bach and Partee (1980) and Partee and Bach (1981). Their grammar simultaneously defines sets of pairs of well-formed expressions and interpretations. In addition they give a recursive definition of the properties of being a *free* and a *locally free* variable in a translation. *Free* means free in the whole expression and *locally free* means free within the translation of some constituent, α. α may be the cyclic nodes of the language, for instance. This recursive definition works together with a condition on the application of function-argument rules in the semantics. Two variables that are locally free may not have the same subscript within an expression. Presumably some kind of reindexing will be invoked in case of unpermitted variable clashes (cf. the formulation of the Store Address Convention in Chapter III: (90)). Bach and Partee enforce this condition by storing the information which variables are free or locally free, respectively, in a special store which is accessible all through the derivation. (Storing information like this is, as far as I can tell, very similar to the way Thomason uses 'analysis trees' as a parameter in the formulation of the rules (Thomason 1976)).

2.1. A Pragmatic Account for Non-Coreference

In an interesting paper, 'Coreference and Bound Anaphora: A restatement of the Anaphora Question', T. Reinhart (1983) points out several problems with those accounts that impose non-coreference by some kind of contra-indexing. She suggests that the whole contra-indexing machinery can be dispensed with. The only sentence grammar restrictions that need to be stated are the conditions on 'bound anaphora', she argues. The disjoint reference and non-coreference facts can be shown to follow from pragmatic principles, outside the domain of sentence grammar[3]. Reinhart argues that it is unclear in the first place how the contra-indexing device should be interpreted semantically. She points out that it would not be semantically correct to take contra-indexing to involve some kind of disjoin operation in the semantics which had the effect that two contra-indexed NPs necessarily denote distinct individuals, since it may very well be the case that a sentence with two contra-indexed NPs nevertheless is true in a situation where the two NPs happen to pick out the same individual. Reinhart calls this 'the problem of accidental coreference' in non-coreference contexts. It has been noted by several people, e.g. Postal (1971), Lasnik (1976), Evans (1980) and Higginbotham (1980a). One example of such accidental coreference can be found in (3).

(3)   *He* put on *Johns*'s coat.

As Higginbotham (1980a, fn. 1) notes, (3) can be used in a situation where *he* happens to pick out the person normally referred to as John. One might object that if the speaker had known that it was John who put on the coat in question, he wouldn't have expressed himself in this manner. This kind of reaction, I think, actually provides an argument for saying that the rule of non-coreference falls outside the grammar proper, since it shows that the non-coreference rule would have to be sensitive to speaker's beliefs and presuppositions. This is generally not the case for grammatical rules. For instance, the non-coreference rule only applies in contexts where the speakers of the sentence purports to confer the information that *he* and *John* are distinct individuals. Non-coreference does not apply in contexts where identity is asserted, as in (4), nor when a sentence is used to express uncertainty about identity as in (5), suggested by Higginbotham (1980a).

(4) A: Who is that man over there?
    B: *He* is *John*.

(5) A: Was John the man in the brown hat?

B: I don't know, but *he* put on John's coat before leaving, so it may well have been.

Furthermore, (3) may be used to provide the reasons for an identity statement, as pointed out by B. Partee (personal communication).

(6) A: That man in the brown hat is John.
B: How do you know?
A: Because *he* put on *John*'s coat ...

The clearest examples where non-coreference seems mandatory are in sentences like (7)

(7)   *He* is kicking *John*.

where our knowledge of what it is to 'kick' someone forces us to postulate two distinct individuals. In this respect, Higginbotham's example (5) is well chosen. Although *he* is necessarily distinct from anything *he* puts on, our knowledge of the world does not tell us that *he* may not be the owner of the thing *he* puts on. Thus, we expect it to be easier to find examples where the non-coreference rule doesn't seem applicable, when the verbs involved don't require the physical presence of two distinct individuals. Compare (7) to (8).

(8)   *He* looks like *John* (in fact, he may very well be John).

Reinhart takes examples like these to show that merely having a contra-indexing device in the grammar misses something important about how non-coreferent statements can be interpreted. Instead of having rules that are sensitive to contra-indexing, she defines a notion of bound anaphora and proceeds to show how the non-coreference facts can be seen as pragmatic consequences of the way a speaker uses the bound anaphora options available in the grammar.

Central to Reinhart's approach is the identification of those contexts where a pronoun can be interpreted as a bound variable. She argues that there is a systematic correlation between those contexts where a pronoun can be interpreted as bound (by a quanifier) and those contexts where it can get a sloppy identity interpretation under deletion. This correlation is illustrated in (9) and (10) (cf. Reinhart, 1983, p. 63f.).

(9) a. Los Angeles is adored by its residents and so is New York.
    b. *Each of the western cities* is adored by *its* residents.

(10) a. People from Los Angeles adore it and so do people from New York.
  b. *People from *each of the western cities* adore *it*.

A sloppy identity interpretation is possible in (9a) – New York is adored by the New Yorkers – whereas it is excluded in (10a). (10a) claims that New Yorkers also adore Los Angeles. Similarly, in (9b), *its* can be interpreted as bound by *each of the western cities*, but the bound interpretation is not available in (10b). Reinhart argues that the relevant distinction between these examples is that the antecedent in both (9a) and (9b) c-commands the pronoun, but this is not the case in (10). Reinhart takes the fact that the anaphor is c-commanded by the antecedent to be the licensing factor for bound anaphora. We can summarize her position as in (11).

(11) Bound anaphora between a NP and a pronoun is possible just in case the antecedent NP c-commands the pronoun.

A pronoun can thus be interpreted as bound by some other expression only if the latter c-commands the pronoun. The effect of being interpreted as 'bound' is realized both in sloppy identity readings in deletion contexts, in quantifier binding, and in the appearance of special anaphors. Exactly in what way bound anaphora is realized will depend on the immediate syntactic context. If the language has lexical anaphors such as reflexives, we can expect them to occur within a certain systactic domain.

Looking at the possibilities for sloppy identity interpretations as in (9a), bound readings of pronouns as in (9b) and reflexives as in (1a), Reinhart comes to the conclusion that it is not the nature of the antecedent NP, whether it is a quantified NP, a name, or a pronoun, which determines the availability of bound anaphora. Rather, she claims, it is the structural configuration between antecedent and anaphor defined by c-command. The anaphor has to be within the *syntactic domain* of the antecedent, i.e. be c-commanded by the antecedent, in order for their relation to be affected by a grammatical rule (cf. also Reinhart (1981b) where this generalization is spelled out and illustrated further). Nevertheless, the nature of the antecedent NP will enter into determining what readings are possible in contexts where bound anaphora is excluded, as we will see below.

Reinhart emphasizes that what is important to her argument is not the actual judgments on any particular example, but the correspondence between the availability of bound readings for pronouns. Reinhart also notes that there are certain cases where c-command fails to characterize the right domain but maintains that c-command is the best approximation available[4].

Reinhart's main point is that whenever it is possible to express a bound anaphora relation between two NPs, we will get the disjoint reference or the non-coreference effect if we don't use this option which is provided by the grammar. For instance, in a structure like (12)

(12)   [$_S$ NP$_1$ V NP$_2$]

where it is possible to express bound anaphora between NP$_1$ and NP$_2$ by using a reflexive pronoun, we will get non-coreference if we don't use this option.

(13) a. John dislikes himself.
     b. John dislikes him.

Similarly, in environments where a pronoun may be interpreted as a bound variable, we will get the non-coreferent effect if we use a non-pronoun instead.

(14) a. He thinks that he is smart.
     b. He thinks that John is smart.

In case neither of the expressions c-commands the other, we will get different predictions depending on whether there is a quantifier or a proper name involved, as Reinhart points out. Consider the contrast in how the pronoun *her* may be interpreted in the following example (Reinhart's (61) and (62)).

(15) a. Those who know *her* respect Zelda.
     b. Those who know *her* respect no president's wife.

Zelda and *no president's wife* do not c-command *her*, consequently there is no bound anaphora relation involved. This rules out the reading of (15b) according to which *her* is bound by *no president's wife*. The pronoun must be interpreted deictically, as picking out a particular female person. Similarly, in (15a), the pronoun must be interpreted referentially, but here there is nothing to exclude that *her* refers to the person denoted by *Zelda* since the pronoun does not c-command the name. Having illustrated what the interpretation possibilities for the pronouns in (13)–(15) are, Reinhart concludes:

> There is no reason, however, to assume that these mirror-image non-coreference results require special rules of the grammar to be captured, since they just follow from Gricean requirements on rational use of the language, for communication ...: In a rational linguistic exchange we would expect that if a speaker has the means to express a certain idea clearly and directly, he would not choose, arbitrarily, a less clear way to express it. So if a rational speaker intends two of his expressions to corefer, and the grammar provides him at no extra cost with the means to signal their coreference by use of bound anaphora, he would not, intentionally, avoid this option.
>
> (Reinhart, 1983:75)

Reinhart then proposes two pragmatic strategies, intended to approximate the strategies involved in encoding and decoding coreference.

(16) a. *Speaker's strategy:* When a syntactic structure you are using allows bound anaphora interpretation, then use it if you intend your expressions to corefer, unless you have some reason to avoid bound-anaphora.

b. *Hearer's strategy:* If the speaker avoids the bound anaphora option provided by the structure he is using, then, unless he has reasons to avoid bound-anaphora, he didn't intend his expressions to corefer.

(Reinhart, 1983:(67))

A similar approach is taken by D. Dowty in his discussion of Bach and Partee's (1980) proposal for encoding notions like 'locally free' for the purpose of disjoint reference and disjoint reference. Dowty there raises the question whether such constraints actually need to be stated as part of the grammar at all, or whether these constraints could be attributed entirely to conversational principles. Several people, e.g. McCawley (1978), have alluded to some kind of Gricean conversational principle which would govern the distribution of pronouns. Dowty suggests (17) as one way of formulating such a principle.

(17) *A neo-Gricean conversational principle:*

If a language has two (equally simple) types of syntactic structures *A* and *B*, such that *A* is ambiguous between meanings X and Y while B has only meaning X, speakers of the language should reserve the structure A for communicating meaning Y (since B would have been available for communicating X unambiguously and would have been chosen if X is what was intended).

(Dowty, 1980:(2))

Dowty is very cautions about the status of (17). It is not clear that it is universal, nor that all kinds of syntactic variation follows it, presumably because it is not self-evident how one would make Dowty's notion 'equally simple' or Reinhart's 'at no extra cost' precise in general. But the choice of reflexive and non-reflexive pronouns fits the principle, Dowty notes. Since a reflexive pronoun in a certain context unambiguously refers to the subject whereas a non-reflexive pronoun in the same context would have a range of possible referents, it makes sense to reserve the non-reflexive pronoun for the cases where the referent is not intended to be the same as the subject.

Should principles like (16) and (17) be thought of as part of the grammar? Reinhart and Dowty seem to agree that they shouldn't be but differ slightly in what role they assign to them. Dowty suggests that such principles could supply the functional explanation for the existence of restrictions on coindexing, even though the restrictions are actually part of the grammar. Reinhart, as we have seen, maintains that the only kind of sentence grammar restriction that is required is the condition on bound anaphora. The non-coreference effect follows from a failure to exploit the bound anaphora options available through the grammar. The non-coreference interpretations thus arise as conversational implicatures in Grice's sense. To take an earlier example:

(13) b. John dislikes him.

In this case, the assumed reasoning could be: Since the speaker is obviously flouting one of the conversational super maxims 'Be perspicuous!' (i.e. the speaker uses an ambiguous expression *him* where a non-ambiguous expression *himself* is available) and the speaker knows that the listener can calculate this, the intended implicature must be that John is not the intended referent of *him*. If the non-coreferent interpretation is due to a conversational implicature, which arises through a particular wording, we would expect that it could be cancelled in any particular case. This appears to be the case. Suppose we embed (13b) in a context where the coreferent reading is intended.

> Q: Is it really true that no one likes John?
> A: Yes, I am afraid so. Mary dislikes him, Sue dislikes him, Fred dislikes him and John dislikes him, that is, John actually dislikes himself.

The implicature that John dislikes someone distinct from himself is immediately cancelled by the 'that is ...' clause but this doesn't seem to give rise to a contradiction.

Both Dowty and Reinhart thus attribute the disjoint reference and the non-coreference effects to the fact that the *choice* between a personal pronoun and a reflexive pronoun, or between a pronoun and a non-pronoun, is significant in the speech community. Their argumentation provides an illustration of how the central linguistic notion of 'opposition' can be used at a discourse level to explain restrictions on interpretations. Whether such a move is sufficient in all cases remains to be shown. In the next section we will look at some facts about the distribution of parasitic gaps which seems to show that speakers are, in some sense, aware of the bound anaphora options in the language.

2.2. *Bound Anaphora and Parasitic Gaps*

In Chapter III.6.3 we saw that when there is an unbounded dependency between a filler and a gap (or a resumptive pronoun) in a sentence, we might get one (or more) additional gap which is, so to speak, parasitic on the first gap. The gap is parasitic in the sense that if there is no 'real gap', i.e. if there is no unbounded dependency in the sentence, then a parasitic gap is impossible. We pointed out that the parasitic gap phenomenon is to be distinguished from the kind of pronoun omission that occurs in languages with optional pro drop such as Japanese and Turkish. In languages like English and Swedish, parasitic gaps only occur in the context of an unbounded dependency[5]. A few English examples with parasitic gaps are given below.

(18) a. Which articles did John file ___ without reading ___$_p$?
b. John filed some articles without reading *___/$^{o.k.}$ them.

(19) A formal analysis of methaphor is something we need ____ as much as we lack ____$_p$. (Cresswell, 1978, fn. 14))

(20) Who did John's talking to ____$_p$ bother ____ most?

(21) ... a dislike, which, never wanting to give way to ____$_p$, he had refused to acknowledge ____.⁶

We note in passing that several speakers find a contrast between parasitic gaps which follow the real gap, as in (18) and (19) where the parasitic gaps seems to alternate more or less freely with a personal pronoun, and parasitic gaps which occur between the filler and the real gap, as in (20) and (21). These occurrences of parasitic gaps cannot be replaced by personal pronouns without a noticeable loss of acceptability. (20) and (21) with pronouns would be cases of weak cross-over violations. We return to these cases in Section 3.

When we look at the examples in (18)–(21), we see that the parasitic gaps, just like the real gaps, would fall under Reinhart's condition for bound anaphora. Since a filler, or a dislocated constituent, always occur as sister to the S that contains the gap, the gap will automatically be c-commanded by the filler. It turns out, however, that parasitic gaps are subject to additional constraints. Consider the sentences in (22)–(25).

(22) Which articles ____ got filed by John without him reading *____$_p$/$^{o.k.}$ them?

(23) Which articles did you say ____ got filed by John without him reading *____$_p$/$^{o.k.}$ them?

(24) Who ____ took a picture of *____$_p$/$^{o.k.}$ himself?

(25) Who ____ remembered talking to *____$_p$/$^{o.k.}$ himself?

I think most everyone would agree that parasitic gaps are impossible here, although there is a filler-gap dependency and thus a real gap in these sentences. This then, cannot be the only licensing condition for a parasitic gap. It is interesting that people do not hesitate about the unavailability of parasitic gaps in (22)–(25). Swedish counterparts to these sentences are clearly impossible as well. The clear judgments show that, even if the acceptability range for parasitic gap varies a lot, the phenomenon is not random. People have quite strong intuitions about where parasitic gaps are excluded. These intuitions taken together with the overlap in intuitions about where parasitic gaps may occur suggest that we are here dealing with a systematic grammatical phenomenon.

What is it then that prevents parasitic gaps in structures like (22)–(25) while allowing them in (18)–(21)? A first observation is that the real gap in (22)–(25) is always in subject position. One hypothesis would be that subject gaps don't license parasitic gaps. This cannot be the correct generalization, however, since we can find good examples with parasitic gaps where the real gap is a subject gap, as in (26), suggested by A. Prince.

(26) Which caesar did Brutus imply ––––– was no good by ostensibly praising –––––$_p$?

We note that the relation between the parasitic gap and the filler is the same in both sets of examples; in both cases the filler c-commands the gap. There is a difference, however, in the structural relation between the parasitic gap and the real gap. In (22)–(25) the real gap c-commands the parasitic gap, but this is not the case in (18)–(21) and (26). Compare for instance (23′) with (26′) where we have circled the nodes c-commanded by the real gap.

(23′)

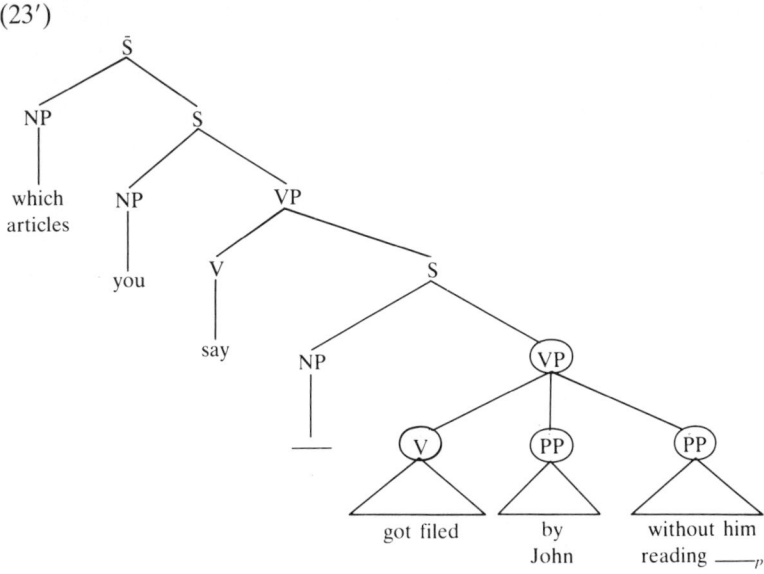

(26')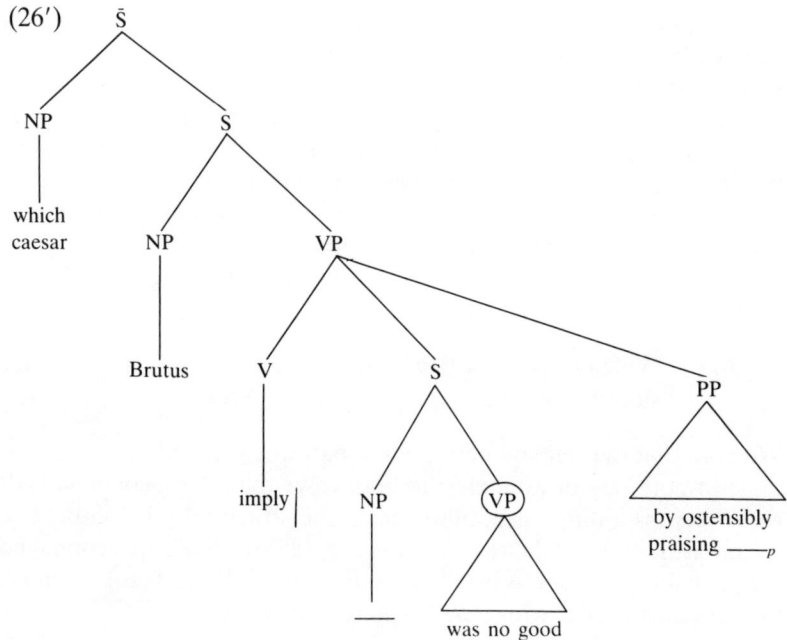

In (23′) the adverbial clause '*without him reading* ___$_p$' modifies the VP of the embedded sentence and is consequently within the c-command domain of the subject position. In (26′), on the other hand, '*by ostensibly praising* ___$_p$', modifies the VP in the embedding sentence and is outside the c-command domain of the embedded subject. Why should it make a difference whether the real gap c-commands the parasitic gap or not? We recall from the previous section that c-command plays a crucial role in Reinhart's definition of bound anaphora. If we consider the relation between the real gap and the parasitic gap in (22)–(25), it appears that parasitic gaps are impossible in just those positions where bound anaphors would be possible. Within the c-command domain of the real gap, parasitic gaps and bound anaphors, controlled by the real gap, are thus in complementary distribution. We can summarize the relation between bound anaphora and parasitic gaps as in (27).

(27) Whenever bound anaphora is possible, a parasitic gap is impossible.

We saw earlier that bound anaphora is realized as a reflexive or personal pronoun, and that not taking this option leads to a disjoint reference or non-coreference interpretation. In languages like Swedish and English, bound anaphora, in the technical sense defined by Reinhart, can apparently not be realized by a gap. Consider the pair of sentences in (28).

(28) a. Johan stod och tvättade sig.
   Johan was washing   himself

   b. Johan stod och tvättade.
   Johan was washing (clothes)

(29) a. Ingen   trodde att vi skulle   föreslå honom.
   No one thought that we were going to suggest him

   b. *Ingen   trodde att vi skulle   föreslå Ø.
   No one thought that we were going to suggest Ø

If we leave out a reflexive pronoun as in (28b) we get a reading where Johan is washing something distinct from himself[7]. Leaving out a bound personal pronoun is completely impossible, as shown by (29b). Consequently it is not surprising that a parasitic gap cannot be interpreted as anaphorically related to the antecedent. What (22)–(25) then show is that this restriction holds also in the case the antecedent is a gap. Parasitic gaps in the c-command domain of a real gap can not be interpreted as bound by, or coreferent with, the real gap (or with the phrase linked to the real gap). But they cannot be interpreted deictically either, and this would explain why (22)–(25) are ungrammatical with parasitic gaps. In all these examples, the impossible parasitic gaps occur in a position that is within the bound anaphora sphere, i.e. within the c-command domain, of the real gap. Following Reinhart's line of argumentation, we can say: Since the language provides the means to express a bound or coreferent reading in this position, not using this option will get a non-coreferent effect.

We noted above that there are certain cases where the c-command condition is not sufficient to characterize bound anaphora. For instance, the condition that the antecedent c-command the anaphor is too strong in cases like (30) and (31) where the antecedent occurs inside a PP.

(30)   I talked [to John$_i$] about himself$_i$.
             PP

(31)　　I talked to every boy$_i$ about his$_i$ results.

If there is in fact an inverse correlation between bound anaphora to the effect that parasitic gaps are excluded whenever bound anaphora is possible, we should expected parasitic gaps to be impossible here. This turns out to be correct.

(30′)　　Who did you talk to ____ about *____$_p$?

If we embedded the PP containing the antecedent inside a NP, bound anaphora, as reflected by the occurrence of a reflexive pronoun, is again not possible.

(32)　　I sent [$_{NP}$ all the letters [$_{PP}$ from Mary$_i$]] back to her$_i$/*herself$_i$.

Since bound anaphora is impossible, a parasitic gap should be possible in case we extract the antecedent.

(32′)　　Which girl did you send [$_{NP}$all the letters [$_{PP}$from ____]] back to ____$_p$?

Not everyone likes examples like (32′) but everyone perceives a contrast between examples like (24), where a parasitic gap is totally excluded, and (32′) where it is marginal. This contrast, I think, provides further illustration that people recognize contexts where bound anaphora is possible and reject parasitic gaps in exactly those contexts. It is interesting to note that in Swedish, where object control of reflexives is more limited than in English, parasitic gaps are allowed in the contexts illustrated in (29).

(33)　　Jag talade med Johan$_i$ om　　*sig$_i$/honom
　　　　I　*talked with Johan about* *SELF/him*

(33′)　　Vem brukar du sällan　prata med ____ om ____$_p$?
　　　　Who do you　　seldom talk　to ____ about ____?

There are cases in Swedish, however, where a direct object may control a reflexive pronoun. This occurs in particular when the reflexive pronoun appears in a constituent that can be construed as a predicate of the object NP (cf. Hellan (1980b) for a characterization of the conditions for object control in Norwegian). For instance, a reflexive pronoun in a locative phrase may be controlled by the direct object theme, and in those cases we would not expect a parasitic gap to be possible.

(34)   Jag såg dig bära Johan$_i$ hem till sig$_i$
       I   saw you carry Johan home to SELF

(34') Johan$_i$ har jag ofta sett dig bära ___$_i$ hem till
       Johan I have often seen you carry ___ home to
       *___$_p$/sig
       *___ /SELF

The pattern that emerges from looking at the examples in (22)–(34') is that there is an inverse correlation between parasitic gaps and bound anaphora in Reinhart's sense. Whenever bound anaphora between two NPs is possible, a real gap – parasitic gap relation is impossible. We found that this correlation apparently holds even when the c-command restriction fails to identify the bound anaphora context. Assuming that parasitic gaps are understood as non-anaphors, their distribution thus appears to support Reinhart's distinction between domains where bound anaphora is possible and domains where it is not. The consistency and sharpness of people's judgments on cases where parasitic gaps are excluded lends support to Reinhart's assumption that people are in fact aware of the contexts where the grammar provides means for expressing bound anaphora but the correlation by itself of course does not force us to adopt Reinhart's pragmatic explanation for non-coreference effects. Whether or not one also wants to take the position that the non-coreference facts should be handled pragmatically is independent of the inverse correlation between bound anaphors and parasitic gaps.

In the discussion so far the match between bound anaphora contexts and impossible parasitic gaps has been close to perfect. However, when we take into account a wider array of data we find that the correlation is not total and that the principle in (27) needs to be qualified. It seems that we, contrary to Reinhart's claim, need to make a distinction between morphologically marked bound anaphors such as reflexives and personal pronouns, interpreted as bound by an antecedent. The need for making this distinction shows itself in cases where morphological anaphors are excluded but bound personal pronouns are allowed. We saw earlier that object control of a reflexive is not possible in the

Swedish sentence (33), repeated here as (35a). A bound personal pronoun may occur in that position, though, as shown in (35b).

(35) a. Jag talade med Johan$_i$ om   *sig$_i$/honom$_i$
     I   talked with Johan about *SELF/him.

  b. Jag talade med varje flicka$_i$ om   henne$_i$/hennes$_i$ framtid
     I   talked to   every girl   about her   /her   future

  c. Jag talade med pojkarna$_i$ om   deras$_i$ uppförande, men
     I   talked to   the boys about their   conduct,   but
    inte med flickorna.
    not to   the girls.

  d. Vem brukar du   sällan prata med ___ om   ___$_p$?
     Who do   you seldom talk   to   ___ about ___?

The fact that we can get a bound interpretation of the pronoun in (35b) as well as a sloppy reading in (34c), I didn't talk to *the girls* about *their* conduct, means, according to Reinhart, that we have a bound anaphora context. Nevertheless, parasitic gaps are allowed, as shown in (35d). Reinhart's condition for bound anaphora is thus not sufficient to discriminate between these cases. Whereas her principle that anaphors must be bound by a c-commanding NP might be correct for morphologically marked anaphors (modulo some revision to allow for cases like (30)) it seems to be too strong for bound personal pronouns (cf. Reinhart 1983 Appendix where she discusses some problematic cases). For instance, I believe a bound interpretation is possible in cases like (36) where the antecedent is embedded inside a NP, and hence does not c-command the pronoun.

(36)   I sent the papers from *each of the applicants* back to *him/her*.

If the relation between *each of the applicants* and *him/her* here is one of bound anaphora, it still does not excluded a parasitic gap, as we have already seen.

(37)   Which applicants did you send the papers from ___ back to ___$_p$?

In view of examples like (35c) and (37), it appears that the crucial factor with respect to predicting the distribution of parasitic gaps in a particular context is whether a morphologically marked anaphor would appear in that context or not. However, this characterization is still not sufficient to account for the contrast between (23) and (26), repeated here.

(23)   Which article did you say ____ got filed by John without him reading *____$_p$/$^{o.k.}$ them?

(26)   Which caesar did Brutus imply ____ was no good by ostensibly praising ____$_p$?

Although reflexive pronouns are excluded in both these sentences, a parasitic gap is possible only in (26). In (23), where the real gap c-commands the position of the parasitic gap, a gap is impossible. But it is not the case that a parasitic gap is excluded whenever the real gap c-commands it. Consider the examples in (38) and (39) where parasitic gaps are quite acceptable although they are c-commanded by the real gaps in the direct object positions, assuming that the structure of the VP is [$_{VP}$ V NP S̄].

(38)   Det var dom politikerna som vi kritiserade ____ för att
       it was those politicians that we criticized   because
       vi fick vänta så länge på ____$_p$.
       we had to wait for ____$_p$ so long

(39)   Vilka fångar   varnade du   ____ att man tänkte
       which prisoners did you warn   that one was going to
       föra bort ____$_p$?
       take ____ away

We can compare these sentences with (40), where the real gap does not c-command the parasitic gap, and (41), where a subject real gap c-commands the parasitic gap.

(40)   Vilka fångar   förde man bort ____ för att avrätta ____$_p$?
       which prisoners did one take away   for to execute ____

(41)   Vilka fångar   sade du   ____ begärde att vi skulle
       which prisoners did you say ____ required that we should
       förflytta *____$_p$/$^{o.k.}$ dem?
       move   *____$_p$/ them

Although most people find the parasitic gaps in (38) and (39) somewhat less acceptable than in (40), everyone I have consulted gets a clear contrast between (38) and (39) on the one hand and (41) on the other hand. (41) with a parasitic gap is clearly impossible, whereas the responses to (38) vary between 'pretty good' and 'pretty bad'. There could be several reasons for these mixed responses. It might be that a VP containing both a direct object NP and a sentential complement has some internal structure, e.g. as in (42), in which case the real gap would not c-command the parasitic gap[8].

(42)

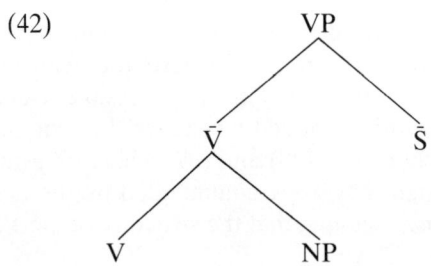

It might also be the case that factors beside the c-command condition are relevant in order to distinguish between possible and impossible parasitic gaps. It is an open issue whether these 'other factors' are primarily of a semantic-pragmatic nature or primarily structural[9]. However, we cannot go into all the ramifications of the distribution of parasitic gaps here (cf. Engdahl (1984a) for some additional considerations).

3. CROSS-OVER

3.1. Background

In Chapter III, we discussed one restriction that seems to apply to the interpretation of constituent questions, namely that a WH phrase may not bind a pronoun which occurs between the surface position of the WH phrase and its associated gap. This phenomenon is commonly referred to as *cross-over* (Postal 1971) or *the leftmost constraint* (Jacobson, 1977). It arises not only in constituent questions but in all types of unbounded dependencies. A few examples are given here.

(43)   *Who$_i$ did he$_i$ think ____$_i$ was sick?

(44) *I met the man who$_i$ Mary told him$_i$ ___$_i$ was sick.

(45) *John$_i$, he$_i$ said ___$_i$ was sick.

The same restriction seems to apply in cases with quantificational NPs. That is, a quantifier cannot be construed as binding a pronoun to its left.

(46) *He$_i$ hoped each applicant$_i$ would be admitted.

The cross-over facts have often been cited in debates about where in the grammar generalizations about possible coreference should be formulated. For instance, Postal (1971) noted that *wh*-movement may affect the coreference possibilities, as shown by contrasts such as in (47) and argued that this motivated making a distinction between cyclic and postcyclic rules.

(47) a. *She$_i$ liked some of the men Sally$_i$ dated.

b. Which of the men Sally$_i$ dated did she$_i$ like?

In current versions of transformational grammar, the notions cyclic and postcyclic have no independent status. Rather, the effect captured by this distinction should follow from general principles such as the Binding Theory. All approaches to these facts within the EST-GB framework that I'm aware of have in common that they try to express restrictions such as cross-over by means of binding relations holding on indexed syntactic representations. We will here look in some detail at one such approach, viz. the one worked out in Higginbotham (1980a, b) which is representative for this line of research. We will then contrast this approach with the one taken here where these facts are handled without recourse to indexed syntactic representations.

3.2. *Higginbotham's Approach*

Higginbotham assumes a model of grammar in which all NP's are indexed at S-structure, subject to the constraint that no non-anaphors may be coindexed. S-structures are mapped into logical forms (LF) by interpretive rules, among them the rule of Quantifier Raising (QR, cf. May, 1977). QR applies to quantificational NPs and Chomsky-adjoins them to some higher node. In May's original proposal this node was always S. Higginbotham suggests that quantifiers may adjoin to S, N̄, Ā, P̄ to account for additional scope variations. Just like the syntactic rule, 'move α', QR leaves behind indexed empty categories. The assumed model of grammar can be represented schematically as in (48):

(48)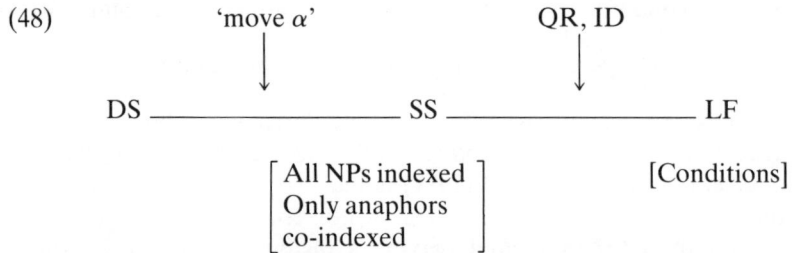

At S-structure, the NPs in sentences like (49) and (50) will consequently have distinct indices since they are non-anaphors.

(49) Who$_i$ ___$_i$ thought he$_i$ was sick?

(50) Each applicant$_i$ hoped he$_j$ would be accepted.

In order to get LF's corresponding to the bound readings for the pronouns in such structures, Higginbotham assumes that there is a reindexing rule, *ID*, which substitutes the index of some quantificational NP for the index of some pronoun. ID is defined as in (51), where *K* is some LF.

(51) *ID, etc.*

> If *i* is a quantificational index in *K*, and *B* is a pronoun with index *j*, then *id*(*i, j*) applies to *K* only if there is an empty category e_i to the left of *B* in *K*.

(Higginbotham, 1980a:(17))

We note that this condition on LFs makes reference to lexical information (*B* is a pronoun) and to left-to-right ordering. Furthermore, the condition is essentially non-local. For the sentences discussed so far, the condition in (51) will correctly allow reindexing to apply to the LF in (52b), yielding the LF in (52c).

(52) a. Who   thought he was sick?

RESTRICTING THE INTERPRETATION OF PRONOUNS 305

    b. (who)$_i$ e_i thought *he$_i$* was sick
    c. (who)$_i$ e_i thought *he$_j$* was sick

he$_j$ may reindex to *he$_i$* since there is an empty category to the left of *he$_j$*. Similarly, reindexing may apply in (53), given that QR has produced the LF in (53b).

(53) a. Each candidate   hoped that he would be accepted
     b. (each candidate)$_i$ e_i hoped that *he$_j$* would be accepted
     c. (each candidate)$_i$ e_i hoped that *he$_i$* would be accepted

But the condition in (51) prevents reindexing from applying to (43)–(45). The LF for (43) would be as in (54).

(54)   (who)$_i$ *he$_j$* think e_i was sick

There is no empty category exposed to the left of e_i. Reindexing would be blocked for (44) and (45) for the same reason.

There is however a problem with the reindexing convention in (51), as Higginbotham notes. Applications of QR may create structures which satisfy the conditions for reindexing, and thus allow bound readings although the surface structure requires distinctness.

(55)   *Which picture of *which man* does he like ____?

QR may apply to *which man*, giving the LF in (56).

(56)   (which man)$_i$ (which picture of e_i)$_h$ does *he$_j$* like e_h

In (56) there is an occurrence of the empty category e_i to the left of *he$_j$*, but reindexing should not be allowed. Higginbotham (1980a) proposes the following constraint on the reindexing operation, which would apply to (56).

(57)   The Crossing Constraint

        A pronoun *j* cannot reindex to *i* in a configuration of the form:
        ... (... e_i ...)$_k$ ... pro$_j$ ...e_k ...

That is, reindexing is prohibited in case the empty category, e_i, occurs inside a constituent that is coindexed with an empty category to the right of the pronoun. Although (57) prevents the unwanted reindexing in the case of (56), it is not sufficient to block reindexing in cases where a quantificational NP has been raised from yet another level of embedding. Compare (58) and (59).

(58) Which picture of which daughter of *which man* ___ pleases him?

(59) *Which picture of which daughter of *which man* does *he* like ___?

We want to allow reindexing in (58) but block it in (59). A solution that amounts to modifying (57) so that it applies to twice embedded NPs will not be general enough, as Higginbotham points out. The links between an empty category and the source position of the NP binding it can be arbitrarily long. Higginbotham suggests a way of getting around this problem by defining a notion of *accessibility* between pronouns and empty categories (Higginbotham, 1980a:(39)). Essentially, what this notion does is to say that if NP_i is accessible for reindexing, then this property is inherited by every NP contained in NP_i. We can illustrate the principle of accessibility by looking at the LF for (58).

(58′)

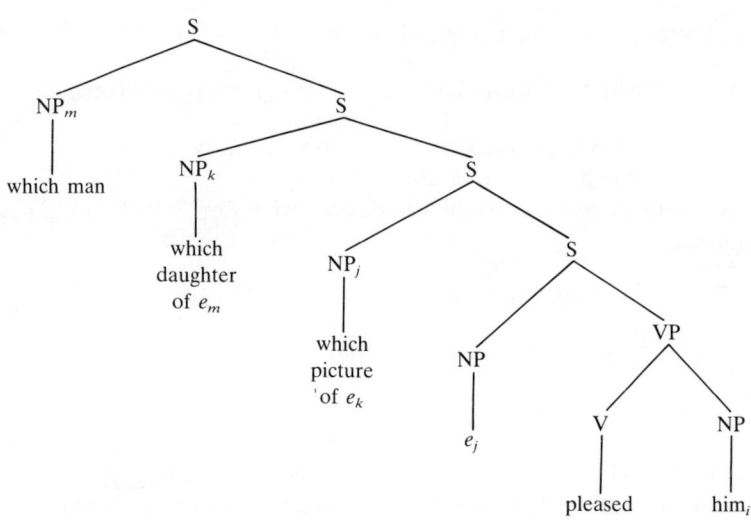

him_i may reindex to him_m. The empty category, e_m, is contained in an NP which is contained in an NP that is coindexed with e_j which is to the left of him_i.

It appears that the reindexing operation, constrained by the accessibility requirement, is just another way of saying that what determines the possibilities for binding is the position of the pronoun with respect to the WH phrase or a quantificational phrase before *wh*-movement and QR, respectively. Let us therefore reexamine the reasons for not doing reindexing at some structure preceding *wh*-movement. Postal (1971) argued that *wh*-movement changes pronominalization possibilities and used pairs of sentences like in (59) as evidence.

(59) a. *He attacked some of the men who hated *Charley*.

(Postal (10.22b))

b. Which of the men who hated *Charley* did *he* attack?

(Postal (10.19a))

The relation between *he* and *Charley* that is blocked in (a) but allowed in (b) is a relation between two *referring* expressions, a pronoun and a proper name. Both of these expressions denote individuals; let's say that the two italicized expressions in (59b) corefer. The occurrence of *Charley* and the occurrence of *he* in (59b) are interpreted as picking out the same individual. Apparently, *wh*-movement changes the possibilities for coreference, as shown by the contrast with (59a). But note that if we substitute a quantificational NP for the proper name, there is no distinction between pre- and post-WH moved structures.

(60) a. *She attacked some of the men who hated *every woman*.
b. *Which of the men who hated *every woman* did *she* attack?

Postal's conclusion that pronominalization must follow *wh*-movement has been taken over in the Extended Standard Theory in the assumption that anaphoric indexing must take place at S-structure. But his conclusion is based primarily on cases that involve anaphoric relations between referring expressions. It overlooks the evidence from relations between quantificational NPs and pronouns bound by them. In the case of NP movement, on the other hand, referential NPs and quantificational NPs behave the same. That is, anaphoric relations are equally affected in for instance passives.

(61) a. *He$_i$ despised John$_i$.
  b. *John$_i$ is despised by himself$_i$

(62) a. *He$_i$ despised nobody$_i$.
  b. Nobody$_i$ is despised by himself$_i$

These facts have led certain linguists to suggest that anaphoric relations should be determined at an intermediate level of representation, a level which follows NP movement but precedes *wh*-movement. In Chapter V, we briefly mentioned two proposals which fall within the main frame of EST but differ from it precisely on this point, namely Hellan (1980b) and van Riemsdijk and Williams (1982). Given such an intermediate level of representation, which we referred to as *shallow structure*, we can state the cross-over condition on reindexing at this level as in (63).

(63) At shallow structure, a non-anaphoric pronoun may assume the index of a quantificational NP that precedes and c-commands it.

(63) will guarantee that (43)–(45) in the text cannot be generated on the bound interpretations, but that (52)–(53) can. Notice that the rule makes reference to types of NPs. In order to get the allowed coreferential readings for sentences like (59b) we need to assume that there is a distinct reindexing rule for referential NPs which applies at S-structure.

(64) At S-structure, a non-anaphoric pronoun may assume the index of a referential NP (subject to the conditions of the non-coreference rule).

(64) will allow reindexing in the shallow structure representation of (59b).

On this approach we can thus rule out the unwanted sentences without making reference to several stages of derivation in the reindexing rule, as in the case of (51). However, formulating the reindexing conditions this way requires assuming another significant level of representation between the application of cyclical and post-cyclical rules (cf. Postal, 1972). Furthermore, the reindexing rules in (63) and (64) require that we distinguish in the syntax between quantificational NPs and referential NPs. This might not be the correct place to express this distinction, as we will argue in the next section.

3.3. Accounting for Cross-over without Indexing of Syntactic Structures

Higginbotham, Hellan, and van Riemsdijk and Williams have in common that they refer to indexed syntactic structures in order to express bound readings of pronouns. Restrictions on binding are handled by conditions on the coindexing or reindexing procedures, as we have just seen. We will now contrast these approaches, where coindexing of syntactic constituents is an essential ingredient, with the approach taken in this study. We consider binding and coreference to be essentially a *semantic* phenomena. Consequently they should be handled by the rules for semantic interpretation, or, ideally, simply fall out from the way the evaluation procedures work.

We note first that we don't need to say anything special in order to get the coreferent reading of sentences like (59b). On our approach, the interpretation of this question can be represented as in (59b′), where W is a variable of valence 0, i.e. a variable over individual concepts.

(59) b. Which of the men who hated Charley did he attack?

b′. $\lambda p\ \exists W[\mathbf{man}'(W) \land \mathbf{hate}'_*(\check{\,}W, c) \land \check{\,}p \land p =$
$= {}^\wedge\mathbf{attack}'_*(\check{\,}x_4, \check{\,}W)]$

that is, (59b) denotes the set of true propositions of the form 'x_4 attacked W' where W is a man who hated Charley. Who x_4 is depends on the assignment function which assigns free variables to individual in the domain. The proper name *Charley* translates into some constant, e.g. c, which will denote a particular individual in the domain, let us say **a**. On some assignments, the assignment function will assign x_4 to **a**, the individual denoted by c. We then get the coreferential reading. We don't want to say that there is any relation of binding between *Charley* and *he*, rather there is a relation of coreference between individuals under an assignment.

The question is now, how do we prevent a bound reading in the structurally similar question in (60b)?

(60) b. Which of the men who hated every woman did she attack?

It might be instructive at this point to look at the relevant points in the derivation. (The reader is referred back to III.5.3 and IV.6.3 for details concerning the interpretation process.) In order to facilitate the discussion, we give a simplified structure for (60b) in (65).

(65)

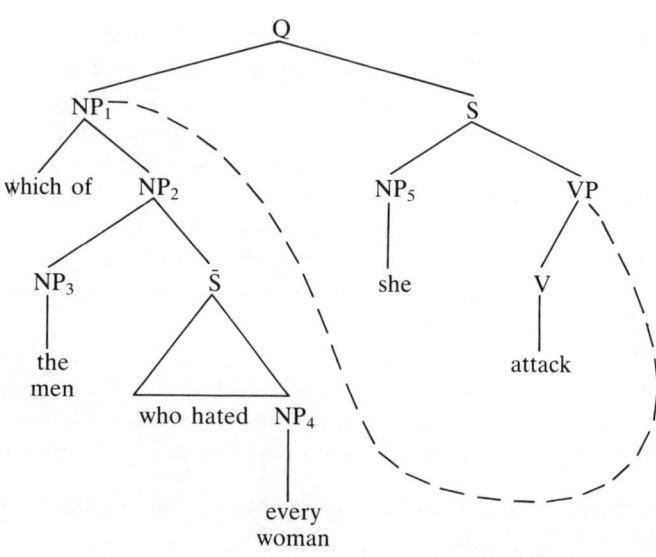

We recall that in order to get a bound interpretation of a pronoun, we must store a NP and quantify it into a formula where we abstract over the individual variable in the interpretation of the pronoun to be bound. When we interpret NP_4, *every woman*, we may choose to store the interpretation and insert a pronoun in its place, e.g. $\lambda PP\{x_6\}$. The stored interpretation is passed up the tree and will also be a component of the interpretation of the entire dislocated constituent, i.e. the interrogative phrase *which of the men who hated every woman*. By the link convention, the dislocated WH phrase will be interpreted as a constituent of the VP. However, since it is an interrogative quantifier, it cannot contribute directly to the interpretation of the VP at this point, but is obligatorily stored and a placeholding pronoun is inserted. The interpretation of NP_1 will be:

$$\langle \lambda PP\{W_2\}, [\lambda \mathcal{W} \, \exists W[\mathbf{man}'(W) \wedge \mathbf{hate}'_*(\check{}W, \check{}x_6) \wedge \mathcal{W}\{W\}]_2 \, (=[WH]_2),$$
$$[\lambda P \, \forall x[\mathbf{woman}'(x) \to P\{x\}]_6 \qquad (=[NP]_6) \rangle$$

The interpretation of this NP thus has two elements in store: the stored interrogative quantifier $[WH]_2$ and the stored interpretation of *every woman* $[NP]_6$. The interpretation of the VP will be:

⟨**attack**$'_*(\hat{P}P\{W_2\})$⟩, $[WH]_2$, $[NP]_6$⟩

When we interpret NP$_4$, *she*, we are free to choose any individual variable in the pronoun interpretation. Suppose we choose $\lambda PP\{x_6\}$. When we combine the interpretation of this subject NP with the interpretation of the VP, the Store Address Convention (SAC, defined in III: (90)) will apply since the individual variable in the interpretation of the subject pronoun is the same as the address variable on one of the stored interpretations. What this means intuitively is that the choice of variable is not free at this point, although the choice of individual is. The SAC forces a change from x_6 to some other individual variable. The purpose of the SAC, we recall, was to prevent any pronoun from being bound by a quantifier whose interpretation was stored at the point in the derivation when the pronoun interpretation is integrated. The SAC in effect guarantees that a pronoun that c-commands the link parent of a dislocated constituent may not be bound by it, nor by any quantifier contained in it. Consequently, *she* in (60b) can only be interpreted deictically, picking out some particular female person, as seen in the representation of the interpretation in (60b').

(60) b'. $\lambda p \; \exists W[\mathbf{man}'(W) \wedge \forall x[\mathbf{woman}'(x) \rightarrow \mathbf{hate}'_*(\check{}W, \check{}x)] \wedge$
$\check{}p \wedge p = \hat{}\mathbf{attack}'_*(\check{}x_6, \check{}W)]$

This denotes the set of true propositions of the form 'x_6 attacked W' where W is a man that hates every woman.

The contrast between the pair in (59) with a proper name and the pair in (60) with a quantifier shows that possible coreference between referring expressions is a necessary but not a sufficient condition for pronominal binding by a quantificational NP. On our approach, the difference in possible anaphoric relations between referring and non-referring expressions follows from the way they are handled by the interpretation rules. There is no need to mark features like [+Referential] on syntactic constituents. The fact that the types of anaphoric relations we have considered here are subject to different constraints follows from the fact that referring expressions and quantifiers play different roles in the evaluation of a sentence[10]. It should be clear that what we are proposing here is merely a way of handling the cross-over facts semantically. We do not claim that we have provided a semantic *explanation* for the existence of a restriction like cross-over. In fact, I doubt that such an explanation could be given in purely semantic (or syntactic) terms. Most likely, a satisfactory explanation for the existence of something like the cross-over constraint would have to take into account facts about language processing and what goes on in the mind of speakers and hearers when they produce and comprehend utterances (see Johnson-Laird and Garnham (1980) and Johnson-Laird (1982) for an attempt at bridging this gap). However, I believe that any such account will show that language users process referring and quantificational expressions differently and that this difference will be one of the factors underlying the cross-over restriction. Another relevant factor will presumably be order of presentation.

Before we end this section, we want to point to an important difference between the structurally based indexing approach taken by Higginbotham and the semantically based approach taken here. We note that Higginbotham makes use of a reindexing rule in (51) which maps LF representations into LF representations. Within EST-GB, the level of LF, logical form, is taken to be an essential linguistic level of representation and is considered a necessary prerequisite for semantic interpretation in the model theoretic sense (cf. Higginbotham, 1980a). The assumption that LF is a necessary level of representation contrasts with the hypothesis about the relationship between syntax and semantics in natural languages put forward in the framework of Montague grammar. On this hypothesis, syntactic expressions can be directly interpreted without going through a disambiguated representation. To my knowledge, the first explicit discussion of this co-called *direct interpretation* approach appeared in Cooper (1975). The discussion has continued in e.g. McCloskey (1979), Ladusaw (1979), Partee and Bach (1981), and Dowty, Wall and Peters (1981, esp. chapter 8). In order to justify the claim that logical form is an essential linguistic level, it seems incumbent on its proponents to show that there are facts about meanings that cannot be captured without such a disambiguated representation. In this section, we have seen that the cross-over restriction can be handled without making reference to LF.

3.4. Weak Cross-over

We now turn to an area where Higginbotham's and our approaches make different predictions. We recall that Higginbotham permits reindexing of a pronoun only in case there is an empty category left behind by *wh*-movement or quantifier raising (QR), to the left of the pronoun. This holds regardless of where the pronoun occurs. The following configuration is thus ruled out:

(66) *NP_i X pro_i Y e_i Z

On our approach, on the other hand, only a pronoun that is entered directly as an argument to the verb is prevented from being bound by a quantifier that it c-commands or by a dislocated constituent whose link parent it c-commands. The two approaches thus make different predictions in cases where the pronoun is embedded inside another constituent. These cases are commonly referred to as 'weak cross-over' (cf. Wasow, 1972). Higginbotham predicts that such instances of cross-over should be as bad as the cases given above in (43)–(45), whereas we predict that such examples should be possible. Consider the examples in (67)–(69).

(67) I fjärde klass går en $pojke_i$ som [$_{NP}$ingen [$_{\bar{S}}$ som någonsin träffat $hans_i$ far]] kan ta miste på ___$_i$.

In fourth grade there is a boy who no one who has ever met his father can fail to recognize.

(68) Vilka $studenter_i$ hade din hotelse att kontakta $deras_i$ föräldrar ringa effekt på ___$_i$?

Which students did your threat to contact their parents have little effect on?

(69) $Kalles_i$ historier brukar alla som känner till $hans_i$ livliga fantasi ta ___$_i$ med en smula salt.

Kalle's stories, everyone who is acquainted with his lively fantasy usually takes with a pinch of salt.

Most speakers who reject (43)–(45) as outright impossible on the bound interpretation find these examples acceptable. The difference in acceptability thus supports making a distinction between cases where a crossed-over pronoun c-commands the gap and cases where it doesn't. (This could presumably be incorporated rather straightforwardly in Higginbotham's approach.) We recall Reinhart's proposal that non-anaphors within the c-command domain of some NP are interpreted as non-coreferent with that NP, since, if the speaker had intended a coreferent reading, he/she would have used an anaphor. Judging from the cross-over cases in (43)-(45), the empty position linked to a dislocated constituent counts as a non-anaphor for the purpose of establishing non-coreference. In the weak cross-over cases, however, bound anaphora isn't possible and hence a coreferent reading is not excluded (cf. also the discussion of Reinhart's example (15) in Section 2.1 above).

Some readers might have noticed that all our examples of weak cross-over in (67)-(69) involve possessive pronouns and wondered if there is a reason behind this. The answer is yes. When I was checking people's intuitions on weak cross-over with sentences with regular personal pronouns, I found that a significant number of people preferred parasitic gaps in these positions. This is illustrated in (70)-(72).

(70) Olle är en pojke$_i$ som ingen som träffat $^{??}$honom$_i$/____$_p$ kan ta miste på ____$_i$.

Olle is a boy that no one who has met him/____$_p$ can fail to recognize ____.

(71) Vilka studenter$_i$ verkade ditt löfte att tala med $^?$dem$_i$/____$_p$, inte särskilt lockande för ____$_i$?

Which students did your promise to talk to them/____$_p$ not seem very appealing to ____?

(72) Kalle$_i$ brukar alla som känner $^{??}$honom$_i$/____$_p$ tycka bra om ____$_i$.

Kalle, everyone who knows him/____$_p$ usually is fond of ____.

By using possessive pronouns instead, the possibilities for parasitic gaps disappeared and pronouns were judged acceptable. The tendency for parasitic gaps to occur in weak cross-over contexts is not particular to Swedish. Several English speakers seem to prefer parasitic gaps in such contexts too, as shown for instance in our earlier example (20), repeated here in (73).

(73) a. Who$_i$ did [John's talking to ____$_p$] bother ____$_i$ most?
b. $^{??}$Who$_i$ did [John's talking to him$_i$] bother ____$_i$ most?

The question arises why parasitic gaps should be better than pronouns in these contexts. I believe that the answer has to do with how people ordinarily interpret pronouns. Let us assume that understanding a sentence in some sense involves constructing a discourse model of the situation described by the sentence (cf. Dahl, 1977; Johnson-Laird, 1982; Webber, 1978). When a person hears a third person pronoun, he/she always has the option of either interpreting it deictically and introducing a new referent into the model or identifying it with some referent already present in the discourse model. A doubtless gap, on the other hand, must be interpreted as controlled by some constituent in the sentence, at least in languages like English and Swedish where optional pro-drop does not occur i.e. it must be identified with something already present in the discourse model. By not pronouncing an anaphoric (non-deictic) pronoun, the speaker in effect disambiguates a potentially ambiguous sentence so that the listener will never consider the unintended reading and introduce a new referent.

Although Higginbotham's approach and the approach taken in the present framework are quite different, there is one respect in which they are similar. Both approaches in a certain sense assimilate the *wh*-movement facts and the wide scope facts in that they handle them by similar procedures. On Higginbotham's approach, this assimilation is due to the fact that both *wh*-traces and empty categories left by QR count for the reindexing rule (51). On our approach, the assimilation results from the fact that we treat both WH phenomena and wide scope phenomena by storage. Both approaches thus predict that there should be a covariation with respect to binding possibilities between WH extractions and wide scope interpretations. As far as real cross-over goes, the prediction seems correct, as shown by the parallelism in judgments on sentences like (74) and (75), both in Swedish and English.

(74) a. *Hon$_i$ föreslog   var och en av kvinnorna$_i$
   b. *She$_i$ suggested each woman$_i$.

(75) a. *Vilken kvinna$_i$ föreslog hon$_i$?
   b. *Which woman$_i$ did she$_i$ suggest?

However, in weak cross-over cases, there seems to be a difference between WH extractions and wide scope interpretations. We saw that weak cross-over was permitted in the case of linked constituents as in (67)–(69). The corresponding sentences with wide scope interpretations of unmoved quantifiers, reflected in the binding of the pronoun, seem notably less acceptable.

(76) a. *Ingen som träffat **hans**$_i$ far kan låta bli att känna igen **var och en av pojkarna**$_i$.
b. *No one who has met *his* father can fail to recognize *each boy*.

(77) a. *Min hotelse att kontakta **hans**$_i$ föräldrar hade ringa effekt på **var och en av studenterna**$_i$.
b. *My threat to contact *his* parents had little effect on *each student*.

(78) a. *Ingen som träffat **hennes**$_i$ syster kan ta miste på **var och en av flickorna**$_i$.
b. *No one who has met *her* sister can make a mistake about *each girl*.

The contrast between (67)–(69) on the one hand, and (76)–(78) on the other hand may be due to several factors, one of which might be the reluctance of quantifiers in object position to take wide scope. In order to account for these contrasts it seems that we need to refer to the processing of the sentence and in particular to the order in which the information in various constituents is integrated. So far we have been assuming that such considerations fall outside the scope of semantics proper. But the contrasts in binding possibilities between (67)–(69) on the one hand and (76)–(78) on the other hand suggest that they can't be disregarded. One way of incorporating such processing considerations into the actual formulation of the interpretation rules appears to be available in Kamp's Discourse Representation theory (Kamp, 1981) in which the interpretation of sentences is given by rules which build discourse structures. These are then mapped onto a model under certain conditions. In Kamp's framework, the interpretation of the head of a relative clause, e.g. **en pojke** (*a boy*) in (67), involves introducing a discourse referent into the discourse model. The same approach could presumably be taken for interrogative phrases like **vilka studenter** (*which students*) in (68). When we get to the pronouns, **hans** and **deras**, respectively, they also introduce discourse referents but these, and this is the important part, may be identified with entities already entered in the discourse model. We now look at the corresponding wide scope sentences, (76) and (77). At the point in the interpretation when the pronouns are encountered, there is no discourse referent in the discourse model which they may be identified with. Thus the fact that dislocated constituents always precede the occurrences of the pronouns for the listener seems to be the crucial factor which distinguishes the acceptable weak cross-over cases from the unacceptable wide scope cases.

There are other factors that seem to affect speakers' willingness to interpret a pronoun as bound by a quantifier which occurs later in the sentence. For instance the so-called *psych*-movement verbs where the direct object is understood as the experiencer, weak cross-over violations seem much more acceptable.

(79) a. **Hennes** barns välfärd ligger **varje mor** varmt om hjärtat.
b. *Her* children's welfare concern *every woman*.

Note, incidentally, that *psych*-movement constructions often involve predicates which have no passive form, i.e. there is no simple way of making the understood experiencer the surface subject of the sentence. Examples like in (79) suggest that people may keep the referential status of a pronoun subject NP (i.e. whether it is deictic or anaphoric) open until at least part of the VP has been interpreted.

3.5. Cross-over and the Binding Theory in GB

We will end our discussion of the cross-over phenomenon by a few remarks about how these facts are handled within the GB theory. We noted earlier that one feature that marks the development from the theory expressed for instance in 'On Binding' (Chomsky, 1980) to the Government-binding framework in Chomsky (1981, 1982) is the explicit effort to subsume the various coindexing conditions under a small set of general principles, the so-called Binding Theory. The Binding Theory as presented in *Lectures on Government and Binding* consists of three axioms which state the binding conditions for the three categories of NPs that are assumed to partition the types of NPs in natural language.

(80) Binding Theory

(A) An anaphor is bound in its governing category

(B) A pronominal is free in its governing category
(C) An R-expression is free

(Chomsky, 1981:188)

The category R-expression in Principle C includes referential NPs (proper names) as well as *variables*, i.e. traces left behind by *wh*-movement. The reason for assimilating *wh*-traces to R is the parallelism between the non-coreference facts and the cross-over facts, as illustrated in (81).

(81) a. *He$_i$ thought that John$_i$ was sick.
    b. *Who$_i$ did he$_i$ think t$_i$ was sick?

Recall that *binding* is defined in terms of being c-commanded by a coindexed element. Since *free* is defined as *not bound*, Principle C excludes all cases where a coindexed pronoun c-commands a proper name or a *wh*-trace. In the case of (81b), the *wh*-trace is clearly not *free* in the absolute sense; it must be bound by the moved *wh*-phrase. What needs to be excluded is that there is a coindexed c-commanding NP in an argument position that intervenes between the *wh*-phrase in Comp and the trace. Various reformulations of Principle C which makes this explicit have been suggested. One possible reformulation is given in (82) (cf. Chomsky, 1982, p. 31).

(82) (C) (i) A name is free.
          (ii) A variable is free in the domain of the operator that binds it.

Notice that we had to split Principle C into two subcases, one for referential expressions proper and one for traces[11].

Recently D. Sportiche (quoted in Chomsky, 1982) has argued that Principle C has no independent status in the theory and that its effects can be dervied from Principles A and B, together with the definition of PRO. The argument assumes the so-called functional definition of empty categories (cf. Chomsky, 1982, chapter 3) according to which it's possible to determine the status of any given empty category on the basis of whether it occurs in an A-position, whether it's A-bound, and whether it has an antecedent with an independent Θ-role. For instance, if an empty category is A-bound by an element with an independent

Θ-role, then it must be PRO. Suppose we have the following S-structure.

(83)   Who$_i$ did he$_i$ say Mary loved t_i?

t_i is locally A-bound by *he*, consequently t_i must be PRO. But t_i is governed by the verb, hence it cannot be PRO and the sentence must be ruled out. This is an interesting proposal which raises the issue whether the axioms of the Binding Theory are independent[12]. This is not the right place to enter into a discussion of this question but I will make a few comments on the general strategy in GB which is reflected in the structure of the Binding Theory.

Chomsky assumes that once we have the correct characterization of the types of NPs into which all NPs, both overt and empty, can be partitioned, their distinction will be predicted by the Binding Theory. This partitioning of NPs can be done either functionally, as described above, or in terms of inherent features of NPs, viz. the features [+/− pronominal], [+/− anaphoric], and [+/− phonetic content]. The decompositon of NPs into feature constellations together with the Binding Theory then provides both the necessary and the sufficient conditions to account for the distribution of NPs. This approach remains basically syntactic. The central notions of the Binding Theory, *bound* and *free*, are given purely structural definitions. The features *anaphoric* and *pronominal* are presumbably provided in the lexicon but don't affect the interpretation directly. In brief then, this theory provides an essentially syntactic account for the distribution of NPs in natural languages[13]. In the present analysis, we have explored a different hypothesis, namely that the ways different types of NPs are interpreted predict where they can occur as well as the range of meanings of sentences in which they occur and the ungrammaticality of sentences where they cannot be interpreted. For instance, we have distinguished between NPs whose interpretations directly combine with the interpretation of other constituents and NPs such as reflexives and interrogatives which can only contribute their interpretation at certain syntactic configurations, VP for reflexives and S for interrogatives. It might be possible, however, to establish a systematic correlation between the distinct types of NPs in GB and different interpretation procedures for NPs, as suggested here and in much current work in semantics, e.g. Barwise and Perry (1983), Cooper (1984), and Engdahl (1984b).

NOTES

[1] The terms *disjoint reference* and *non-coreference* are frequently used in the literature on these phenomena, cf. Lasnik (1976), Chomsky (1980, 1981), Reinhart (1976, 1981b, 1983).

[2] Actually, there is some overlap in the distribution of reflexive and personal pronouns, as pointed out e.g. by E. Bach in a colloquium on 'Reflexives and Reciprocals' at the University of Massachusetts, December 1978. Presumably the factors that determine which type of pronoun is appropriate in which sentential context are not entirely structural in nature.

[3] Reinhart's account of the non-coreference facts and her conclusions are quite similar to what I tried to say in chapter VI.2.1 of my dissertation (Engdahl, 1980a) entitled 'A Pragmatic Account for Non-coreference'. In the present chapter, I will intergrate some of Reinhart's points into my discussion of these phenomena.

[4] Sven Platzack has pointed out to me that in those cases where c-command fails to hold we can make the right predictions by invoking a notion of *predication*. Such a notion is presumably also needed in order to make the right predictions in cases where two constituents c-command each other as for instance in double object constructions (cf. Bílý, 1981; Hellan, 1980b; Herslund, to appear).

[5] Chomsky (1982) argues that the relevant property that licenses a parasitic gap is that the real gap is Ā-bound. The distinction is irrelevant for the present discussion. See Engdahl (to appear b) for a discussion of this and other issues taken up in Chomsky (1982).

[6] I am grateful to Charles Kirkpatrick for bringing this example, quoted in Visser, to my attention.

[7] The situation in English is somewhat blurred by the fact that verbs like *wash* and *shave* often are used intransitively with a medial-reflexive meaning. This is not the case in Swedish.

[8] From the point of view of parsing, it might be that the first subcategorization frame that is accessed for these verbs is [___ NP], since most of them also occur with simple direct objects. In case the parser doesn't revise this choice but attaches the incoming S̄ higher up, a parasitic gap in S̄ would not be within the c-command domain of a detected gap in the direct object position.

[9] The examples in (38) and (39) might be taken as an indication that Kayne's (1981) notion *unambiguous path* provides a better characterization for parasitic gaps than c-command.

[10] The pairs in (59) and (60) involve a proper name on the one hand and a universal quantifier on the other. These two types of NPs provide the clearest contrast between referential and non-referential expressions. In addition, we need to consider indefinite NPs and definite descriptions where the use of the expression seems to determine what anaphoric relations it may enter into. When a definite description or indefinite NP is used referentially to pick out a specific individual, it acts like a proper name with respect to possible anaphoric relations. When the same expression is used generically or attributively, it acts like a quantifier. This shows that it is not sufficient to attribute the differences in anaphoric relations to semantic factors only. We also need to take pragmatic factors into account. See also the discussion in Heim (1982), Hellan (1981b), Partee (1978), Reinhart (1976, 1981b), and Webber (1978).

[11] We have here followed the common practice in GB and talked about *wh*-traces and

variables interchangeably, although this betrays a certain conceptual sliding as Godard (1983) notes. The Binding Theory is supposed to apply at S-structure. However, it is not clear how to make sense of the notion *variable* at this, presumably syntactic, level of representation. In earlier writings (e.g. Chomsky, 1977) the transitions from *wh*-traces (a syntactic notion) to variables (a logical notion) took place between surface structure and logical form. Intuitively, talking about variables only makes sense at the level of LF where the notion *operator* is also available. However, the choice of terminology might just be a way of facilitating the exposition. What Chomsky wants to capture is presumably the parallelism between traces coindexed with a *wh*-phrase at S-structure and variables bound by quantifiers or operators at LF. One could have formulated two versions of Principle C, one for S-structure and one for LF, but that would have made the similarity in binding conditions accidental.

[12] One thing that is left unclear if Principle C is dispensed with is how to account for the non-coreference facts illustrated by (81a). Sportiche's account will take care of cross-over violations, i.e. violations involving an empty category but it doesn't say anything about referential expressions.

[13] This characterization is not entirely correct. Notice, for instance, that the second condition in (82) refers both to *variable* and *operator*. Although it's conceivable that these notions could be defined syntactically, Taraldsen (to appear) argues that the notion operator must be semantically defined in order to account for certain contrasts between expletives and referential expressions.

CHAPTER VII

THEORETICAL POSTSCRIPT

In this final chapter, I would like to briefly return to some of the central notions and devices that I have chosen to employ in this study. Against the background provided by the type of syntactic and semantic constructions we have been concerned with here, I want to look once more at the motivation behind some theoretical notions.

1. LINKED TREES

In Chapter II, I mentioned that one of the motivating forces behind this investigation was the question whether it would be possible to write a non-transformational grammar for a substantial fragment of Swedish, a fragment that includes such unbounded dependencies as constituent questions. In the general interest of investigating exactly how powerful a grammar needs to be in order to capture these kinds of dependencies in a natural language, I found it worth trying to do this using only a phrase structure grammar, without assuming that the grammar needs to recognize several levels of syntactic representations, related by transformations. As we saw in Chapter II, there are several non-transformational frameworks available. Among these I chose Peters and Ritchie's Phrase Linking grammar. The main reason behind this choice is that their definition of linked trees permits us to view a constituent as simultaneously having a syntactic relation to two distinct nodes in the tree, i.e. a dislocated constituent is at the same time directly dominated by an S or Q node and by the node that dominates the missing constituent. What is particularly attractive about Phrase Linking grammars is that they permit a syntactic characterization of this kind of dependency that does not exceed the formal apparatus of a phrase structure grammar. There are of course various other ways of accounting for the dependencies such as the transformation of *wh*-movement, or base-generating the interrogative constituent in two places with subsequent deletion under identity. Operations like *wh*-movement and unbounded deletions, however, are structure mapping devices and hence entail the existence of a syntactic derivation involving more than one level of representation. A grammar of this kind is thus formally more powerful. But if it can be shown, as I have tried to do in this study, that unbounded dependencies don't require a transformational syntax, then someone who wants to claim that transformations are an essential part of the grammar of natural languages would have to do so on the basis of other arguments.

In a Phrase Linking grammar, a dislocated cosntituent thus counts as an immediate constituent of two distinct nodes. It then seems natural that it will contribute to the interpretation of each of the dominating nodes. Constituent questions provide an illustration of this. We have been assuming that they have roughly the structure in (1).

(1)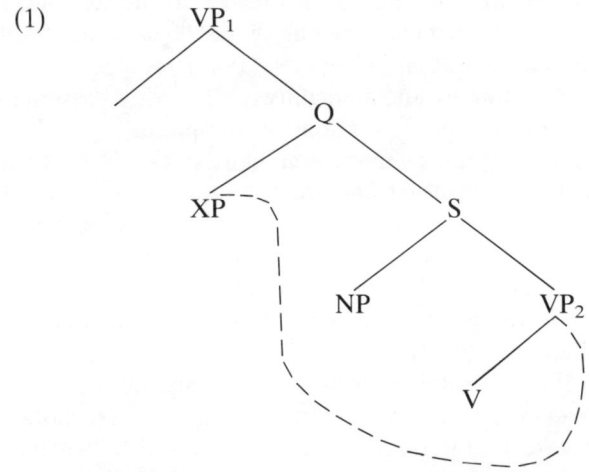

At the Q level, the dislocated phrase XP contributes the information that this clause should be interpreted as a question with the interrogative quantifier in XP taking scope at that level, i.e. in some sense identifying the question. But XP also contributes to the interpretation of VP_2 in providing a placeholding argument which is interpreted as the argument of the verb. The interrogative quantifier is obligatorily stored until it can be quantified in at the S level. Furthermore, given that only the interrogative quantifier is stored, all other material in XP will contribute directly to the interpretation of VP_2. Consequently pied-piping constructions are handled quite straightforwardly and there is no need to assume a separate process of reconstruction at LF which so to speak undoes part of the effect of syntactic *wh*-movement.

2. STORAGE

If the main motivation for adopting a linked tree representation in the syntax is that it allows us to assume a grammar with a single syntactic level of representation, then basically the same motivation lies behind my choice of using storage in the semantics. We want to be able for instance to account for the fact that a sentence like (2) is ambiguous.

(2) John didn't read a book.

On one reading, John read no book whatsoever. On the other reading he might have read other books as long as there was one particular book he didn't read. Nevertheless, we don't want to say that the sentence is syntactically ambiguous, i.e. that each reading should be associated with a distinct syntactic representation. Cooper's (1983) storage method provides a way of accounting for the ambiguity in (2) without assuming two disambiguated syntactic representations at any point.

Another way of handling the semantic ambiguity in (2) would be to use a rule like May's (1977) rule of Quantifier Raising (QR). On this approach, an S-structure like (2) would be associated with two distinct LF representations depending on to what elements and in what order QR applies. These two distinct LF representations can then be semantically interpreted and will presumably give us the two readings we associate with the sentence in (2).

The example in (2) involves the interpretation possibilities of an NP, which on our approach is handled by optional storage. We use storage obligatorily in the case of interrogative quantifiers which, we have argued, can only be interpreted at a sentential level. This permits us to account also for the varying scope possibilities of interrogative quantifiers without assuming any disambiguated syntactic representation.

The main difference between the approach taken here and approaches using QR is the following. On our approach, scope ambiguities are handled entirely by the way the semantic rules interpret the single syntactic representation, whereas an approach using QR will involve a syntactic rule which moves a syntactic constituent in a mapping between two levels of representation. Which way one chooses to take depends, I believe, mainly on where in the grammar one wants to account for semantic facts. In the EST-GB framework, it is customary to assume that the grammar needs to contain a syntactic level of LF which among other things serves to disambiguate semantically ambiguous sentence and to determine the scope of quantifiers. On the present approach, I have explored the assumption that we can write a grammar which correlates expressions and interpretations directly, without a disambiguated level of representation. As far as the facts investigated here go, I don't find any evidence that we need a level of LF. The interpretation rules, however, do need recourse to information about the syntactic structure of the sentence, not just the meanings of the constituents, as shown e.g. by some cases involving the interpretation possibilities for multiple questions (cf. Chapter IV.7).

In the main part of the semantic analysis given here, I have limited myself to working out the formal aspects of the semantic rules, i.e. what kind of input they take and what the results will be. I have not made any systematic attempt to adapt the semantic rules to procedures that people might actually be applying when they figure out what a given sentence can mean. Although this is an extremely interesting area, I think that given our present lack of knowledge in this area as well as lack of reliable techniques for increasing this knowledge, it would be premature at this point to argue for any specific semantic processing rules. Nevertheless, I believe that there are certain issues having to do with the interpretation of pronouns which can be accounted for most straightforwardly in terms of semantic processing strategies (cf. Chapter VI).

3. RELATIONAL READINGS

Maybe one of the most interesting results of this study is the number of contexts in which we find relational readings. We find them both in questions and declarative sentences as in (3) and (4).

(3)   Q: Which woman does *no man* love?
         A: *His* mother-in-law.

(4)   John gave his paycheck to his mistress.
         Everyone else put *it* in the bank.

In order to account for the most natural readings of (3) and (4), we need a way of assigning relational interpretations to pronouns and interrogative quantifiers. We saw in Chapter V that the need to account for relational readings is independent of which syntactic framework one chooses to work in. A theory that uses a transformational grammar with movement transformations would need a way of interpreting occurrences of pronouns and interrogative quantifiers relationally just as the present non-transformational framework does.

I have worked out one way of assigning relational interpretations in some detail. This way involves introducing relational variables in the interpretations of these expressions. I think what is important in this study is above all the establishment of a body of facts pertaining to relational readings, facts that any adequate syntactic and semantic theory should be able to handle, not so much the particulars of the technical solution developed here. In retrospect, I believe that the main interest in actually working out an analysis within a framework like Montague grammar is that it provides an explicit and understandable description of what the theory should account for. Assuming that there is a relational variable in the interpretation of certain phrases in no way explains why relational readings are so widespread, nor which way people process them. In order to address these questions, I believe we must turn to a semantic theory which places more emphasis on the users of the language. One promising direction seems to me to be to investigate relational readings within the framework of Situation Semantics (cf. Barwise and Perry, 1983; Cooper, 1984). In this framework, sentences are taken to describe situations which can be characterized by the facts they contain. This framework does not make use of a representation like intensional logical but tries to relate expressions directly to described situations. One natural way of thinking about relational readings in this framework would be to assume that they arise as a function of how people figure out what the facts may be in a situation described by a given sentence, and in particular, how certain facts are related to other facts. For a preliminary investigation in this direction, cf. Engdahl (1984b).

BIBLIOGRAPHY

Allwood, Jens: 1976, 'The Complex NP Constraint as a Non-universal Rule and Some Semantic Factors Influencing the Acceptability of Swedish Sentences which Violate the CNPC', in J. Stillings (ed.), *University of Massachusetts Occasional Papers in Linguistics*, **II**, reprinted in E. Engdahl and E. Ejerhed (eds.), *Readings on Unbounded Dependencies in Scandinavian Languages*, Almqvist and Wiksell International, Stockholm, pp. 15–32.

Andersson, Lars-Gunnar: 1974, 'Topicalization and Relative Clause Formation', *Gothenburg Papers in Theoretical Linguistics*, Göteborg.

———: 1975, *Form and Function of Subordinate Clauses*, Gothenburg Monographs in Linguistics, **I**, Göteborg.

———: 1982, 'What is Swedish an Exception To?', in E. Engdahl and E. Ejerhed (eds.), *Readings on Unbounded Dependencies in Scandinavian Languages*, Almqvist and Wiksell International, Stockholm, pp. 33–46.

Anward, Jan: 1974, 'Swedish Reflexivization', in Ö. Dahl (ed.), *Papers from the First Scandinavian Conference of Linguistics*, Gothenburg, pp. 17–36.

———: 1981, *Functions of Passive and Impersonal Constructions*, unpublished doctoral dissertation, Uppsala University.

———: 1982, 'Basic Swedish', in E. Engdahl and E. Ejerhed (eds.), *Readings on Unbounded Dependencies in Scandinavian Languages*, Almqvist and Wilksell International, Stockholm, pp. 47–76.

Aoun, Joseph: 1981, *The Formal Nature of Anaphoric Relations*, unpublished Ph.D. dissertation, MIT.

Åquist, Lennart: 1965, *A New Approach to the Logical Theory of Interrogatives*, Philosophical Studies 3, Uppsala.

Bach, Emmon: 1968, 'Nouns and Noun Phrases', in E. Bach and R. Harms (eds.), *Universals in Linguistic Theory*, Holt, Rinehart and Winston, New York, pp. 91–124.

———: 1976, 'An Extension of Classical Transformation Grammar', in R. Saenz (ed.), *Problems in Linguistic Metatheory*, Michigan State University.

———: 1979, 'Control in Montague Grammar', *Linguistic Inquiry* **10**, 515–531.

———: 1980, 'In Defense of Passive', *Linguistics and Philosophy* **3**, 297–342.

——— and Barbara Partee: 1980, 'Anaphora and Semantic Structure', *CLS Parasession on Anaphora*.

Baker, Carl: 1968, *Indirect Questions in English*, unpublished Ph.D. dissertation, University of Illinois, Urbana.

———: 1970, 'Notes on the Description of English Questions: The Role of an Abstract Question Morpheme', *Foundations of Language* **6**, 197–219.

Barlow, Michael, Daniel Flickinger and Ivan A. Sag (eds.): 1982, *Developments in Generalized Phrase Structure Grammar*, Indiana University Linguistics Club, Bloomington.

Barwise, Jon: 1984, 'Lectures on Situation Semantics', Winter Quarter, Stanford University. To appear in Center for the Study of Language and Information Working Papers, Stanford.

——— and Robin Cooper: 1981, 'Generalized Quantifiers and Natural Language', *Linguistics and Philosophy* **4**, 159–219.

———, Johan van Benthem, Robin Cooper, Hans Kamp, Lauri Karttunen and Stanley Peters: to appear, 'Situations in Discourse', Center for the Study of Language and Information Working Papers, Stanford.

——— and John Perry: 1983, *Situations and Attitudes*, MIT Press, Cambridge, MA.

Bayer, Joseph: 1981, *Zur Syntax and Semantik von* **wie** *Sätzen und Dialogen mit* **wie**-*Fragen*, unpublished doctoral dissertation, Konstanz.

Belnap, Nuel: 1982, 'Questions and Answers in Montague Grammar', in S. Peters and E. Saarinen (eds.), *Processes, Beliefs, and Questions*, D. Reidel, Dordrecht.

Bennett, Michael: 1974, *Some Extensions of a Montague Fragment of English*, unpublished Ph.D. dissertation, U.C.L.A., CA.

———: 1979, *Questions in Montague Grammar*, Indiana University Linguistics Club, Bloomington.

Berwick, Robert and Amy Weinberg: 1982, 'Parsing Efficiency and the Evaluation of Grammatical Theories', *Linguistic Inquiry* **13**, 165–191.

Bílý, Milan: 1981, *Intrasentential Pronominalization and Functional Sentence Perspective*, Lund Slavonic Monographs.

Borer Hagit and Joseph Aoun: 1981, *Theoretical Issues in the Grammar of Semitic Languages, MIT Working Papers in Linguistics* **III**.

Brame, Michael: 1976 *Conjectures and Refutations in Syntax and Semantics*, North-Holland, Amsterdam.

———: 1978, 'Binding and Discourse without Transformations', *Linguistic Analysis* **4**, 365–404.

Bresnan, Joan: 1972, *Theory of Complementation in English Syntax*, Ph.D. dissertation, MIT.

———: 1976, 'On the Form and Functioning of Transformations', *Linguistic Inquiry* **7**, 3–40.

———: 1977, 'Variables in the Theory of Transformations', in P. Culicover, T. Wasow and A. Akmajian (eds.), *Formal Syntax*, Academic Press, New York.

———: 1978, 'A Realistic Transformational Grammar', in M. Halle, J. Bresnan and G. Miller (eds.), *Linguistic Theory and Psychological Reality*, MIT Press, Cambridge, MA.

——— (ed.): 1982, *The Mental Representation of Grammatical Relations*, MIT Press.

——— and Jane Grimshaw: 1978, 'The Syntax of Free Relatives in English', *Linguistic Inquiry* **3**.

Brown, Wayles: 1973, 'Conjoined Questions and Conjoined Relative Clauses in Serbo-Croatian', in S. R. Anderson and P. Kiparsky (eds.), *A Festschrift for Morris Halle*, Holt, Rinehart and Winston, New York, pp. 227–231.

Carlson, Grey: 1977, *Reference to Kinds in English*, unpublished Ph.D. dissertation, University of Massachusetts.

Chao, Wynn and Peter Sells; 1983, 'On the Interpretation of Resumptive Pronouns', in P. Sells and C. Jones (eds.), *Proceedings of NELS 13*, GLSA, University of Massachusetts.

Chomsky, Noam: 1957, *Syntactic Structures*, Mouton, The Hague.

——: 1965, *Aspects of the Theory of Syntax*, MIT Press, Cambridge, MA.
——: 1970, 'Remarks on Nominalization', in R. Jacobs and P. Rosenbaum (eds.), *Readings in English Transformational Grammar*, Ginn, Waltham, MA.
——: 1973, 'Conditions on Transformations', in S. R. Anderson and P. Kiparsky (eds.), *A Festschrift for Morris Halle*, Holt, Rinehart and Winston, New York.
——: 1975, *Reflections on Language*, Pantheon, New York.
——: 1976, 'Conditions on Rules of Grammar', *Linguistic Analysis* **2**, 303–51.
——: 1977, 'On *wh*-Movement', in P. Culicover, T. Wasow and A. Akmajian (eds.), *Formal Syntax*, Academic Press, New York.
——: 1980, 'On Binding', *Linguistic Inquiry* **11**, 1–46.
——: 1981, *Lectures on Government and Binding*, Foris, Dordrecht.
——: 1982, *Some Concepts and Consequences of the Theory of Government and Binding*, MIT Press, Cambridge, MA.
—— and Howard Lasnik: 1977, 'Filters and Control', *Linguistic Inquiry* **8**, 425–504.
Christensen, Kirsti K.: 1982a, 'On Filler-Gap Dependencies in Norwegian', in T. Fretheim and L. Hellan (eds.), *Papers from the Sixth Scandinavian Conference of Linguistics*, Trondheim.
——: 1982b, 'On Multiple Filler-Gap Dependencies in Norwegian', in E. Engdahl and E. Ejerhed (eds.), *Readings on Unbounded Dependencies in Scandinavian Languages*, Almqvist and Wiksell International, Stockholm, pp. 77–98.
Church, Alonzo: 1940, 'A Formulation of the Simple Theory of Types', *Journal of Symbolic Logic* **5**.
Cooper, Robin: 1975, *Montague's Semantic Theory and Transformational Syntax*, unpublished Ph.D. dissertation, University of Massachusetts, Amherst.
——: 1977, 'Towards a Semantic Account of Constraints on Movement Rules', paper presented at the Montague Grammar Symposium, LSA, Chicago, December 1977.
——: 1978a, 'Variable Binding and Relative Clauses', in F. Guenthner and S. J. Schmidt (eds.), *Formal Semantics for Natural Languages*, D. Reidel, Dordrecht.
——: 1978b, 'A Fragment of English with Questions and Relative Clauses', unpublished, University of Wisconsin, Madison.
——: 1979, 'The Interpretation of Pronouns', in F. Heny and H. Schnelle (eds.), *Syntax and Semantics* **10**, Academic Press, New York, pp. 61–92.
——: 1983, *Quantification and Syntactic Theory*, D. Reidel, Dordrecht.
——: 1984, 'Lecture on Preliminary *ELIUSS*', Center for the Study of Language and Information Working Papers, Stanford.
Cormack, Annabel: 1982, 'Variables and VP Anaphora', paper presented at the Fourth Amsterdam Colloquium on Formal Methods in the Study of Language.
de Cornulier, Benoît: 1981, 'Yes-No Questions and Alternative Questions in French', *Papers in Romance* **3**, University of Washington, pp. 75–82.
Cresswell, Max: 1973, *Logics and Languages*, Methuen, London.
——: 1978, 'Semantic Competence', in F. Guenthner-Reutter and F. Guenthner (eds.) *Meaning and Translation*, Duckworth, London.
Dahl, Östen: 1973, 'On So-called 'Sloppy Identity'', *Synthese* **26**, 81–112.
——: 1977, 'Games and Models', in Ö. Dahl (ed.), *Logic, Pragmatics and Grammar*, University of Gothenburg.
——: 1980, 'Über *sin* und *hans*', in J. Allwood and M. Ljung (eds.), *ALVAR*, Stockholm Papers in English Language and Literature, Stockholm.

———: 1983, 'On the Nature of Bound Pronouns', Papers from the Institute of Linguistics, University of Stockholm, **48**.
Diderichsen, Poul: 1966, *Elementaer Dansk Grammatik*, Gyldendal, København.
Doron, Edit: 1982, 'On The Syntax and Semantics of Resumptive Pronouns', *Texas Linguistic Forum* **19**, 1–48.
Dowty, David: 1978, 'Lexically Governed Transformations as Lexical Rules in a Montague Grammar', *Linguistic Inquiry* **9**, 393–426.
———: 1980, 'Comments on Bach and Partee's Paper', *CLS Parasession on Pronouns and Anaphora*, Chicago.
———, Robert Wall, and Stanley Peters: 1981, *Introduction to Montague Semantics*, D. Reidel, Dordrecht.
Earley, J.: 1970, 'An Efficient Context-free Parsing Algorithm', *Communications of the ACM* **13**, 94–102.
van Eijck, Jan: 1982, 'Discourse Representation, Anaphora, and Scope', paper presented at the 4th Amsterdam Colloquium.
Ejerhed, Eva: 1981, 'Tense in Intensional Contexts' in F. Heny (ed.), *Ambiguities in Intensional Contexts*, D. Reidel, Dordrecht.
———: 1982, 'The Processing of Unbounded Dependencies in Swedish', in E. Engdahl and E. Ejerhed (eds.), *Readings on Unbounded Dependencies in Scandinavian Languages*, Almqvist and Wiksell International, Stockholm, pp. 99–150.
Enç, Mürvet: 1981, *Tense Without Scope: An Analysis of Nouns as Indexicals*, unpublished Ph.D. dissertation, University of Wisconsin, Madison.
Engdahl, Elisabet: 1980a, *The Syntax and Semantics of Questions in Swedish*, unpublished Ph.D. dissertation, University of Massachusetts, Amherst.
———: 1980b, 'WH Constructions in Swedish and the Relevance of Subjacency', NELS X, *Cahiers Linguistiques d'Ottawa* **9**, 98–108.
———: 1982a, 'A Note on the Use of Lambda Conversion in Generalized Phrase Structure Grammars', *Linguistics and Philosophy* **4**, 505–515.
———: 1982b, 'Constituent Questions, Topicalization, and Surface Structure Interpretation', in D. Flickinger, M. Macken and N. Wiegand (eds.), *Proceedings of the West Coast Conference on Formal Linguistics*, Vol. **1**, Stanford, pp. 256–267.
———: 1982c, 'Restrictions on Unbounded Dependencies in Swedish', in E. Engdahl and E. Ejerhed (eds.), *Readings on Unbounded Dependencies in Scandinavian Languages*, Almqvist and Wiksell International, Stockholm, pp. 151–174.
———: 1982d, 'Interpreting Sentences with Multiple Filler-Gap Dependencies', Working Papers in Linguistics **24**, Lund University.
———: 1983, 'Parasitic Gaps', *Linguistics and Philosophy* **6**, 5–34.
———: 1984a, 'Why Some Empty Subjects Don't License Parasitic Gaps', in M. Cobler, S. Mackaye and M. Wescoat (eds.), *Proceedings of the West Coast Conference on Formal Linguistics*, Vol. **3**, Stanford University, pp. 91–104.
———: 1984b, 'Anaphors, Gaps, and Questions in Situation Semantics', Center for the Study of Language and Information Working Papers, Stanford.
———: to appear a, 'Interpreting Questions', in D. Dowty, L. Karttunen, and A. Zwicky (eds.), *Natural Language Parsing Psycholinguistic, Computational, and Theoretical Perspectives*, Cambridge University Press.
———: to appear b, 'Parasitic Gaps, Resumptive Pronouns and Subject Extractions', *Linguistics* **23**, 3–44.
——— and Eva Ejerhed (eds.): 1982, *Readings on Unbounded Dependencies in Scan-*

dinavian Languages, Almqvist and Wiksell International, Stockholm.
Erteschik-Shir, Nomi: 1973, *On the Nature of Island Constraints*, unpublished Ph.D. dissertation, MIT.
———: 1982, 'Extractability in Danish and the Pragmatic Principle of Dominance', in E. Engdahl and E. Ejerhed (eds.), *Readings on Unbounded Dependencies in Scandinavian Languages*, Almqvist and Wiksell International, Stockholm, pp. 175–192.
Evans, Gareth: 1980, 'Pronouns', *Linguistic Inquiry* **11**, 337–362.
Fodor, Janet: 1970, *The Linguistic Description of Opaque Contexts*, unpublished Ph.D. dissertation, MIT. Distributed from 1976 by Indiana University Linguistics Club, Bloomington.
———: 1978, 'Parsing Strategies and Constraints on Transformations', *Linguistic Inquiry* **9**, 427–474.
———: 1980, 'Parsing, Constraints, and the Freedom of Expression', unpubished, University of Connecticut, Storrs.
———: 1982, 'The Mental Representation of Quantifiers', in S. Peters and E. Saarinen (eds.), *Processes, Beliefs, and Questions*, D. Reidel, Dordrecht, pp. 129–164.
——— and Ivan Sag: 1982, 'Referential and Quantificational Indefinites', *Linguistics and Philosophy* **5**, 355–397.
Frazier, Lyn: 1979, *On Comprehending Sentences: Syntactic Parsing Strategies*, unpublished Ph.D. dissertation, University of Connecticut. Distributed by Indiana University Linguistics Club, Bloomington.
———: to appear, 'Syntactic Complexity', in D. Dowty, L. Karttunen, and A. Zwicky (eds.), *Natural Language Parsing Psycholinguistic, Computational, and Theoretical Perspectives*, Cambridge University Press, Cambridge.
Gawron, J. M. *et al.*: 1982, 'Processing English with a Generalized Phrase Structure Grammar', *Proceedings of the 20th Annual Meeting of the Association for Computational Linguistics*, University of Toronto.
Gazdar, Gerald: 1979, 'English as a Context-Free Language', unpublished, University of Sussex.
———: 1981, 'Unbounded Dependencies and Coordinate Structure', *Linguistic Inquiry* **12**, 155–84.
———: 1982, 'Phrase Structure Grammar', in P. Jacobson and G. Pullum (eds.), *The Nature of Syntactic Representation*, D. Reidel, Dordrecht.
———, Ewan Klein, Geoffrey K. Pullum and Ivan A. Sag: 1982, 'Coordinate Structure and Unbounded Dependencies', in M. Barlow *et al.* (eds.), *Developments in Generalized Phrase Structure Grammar*, Indiana University Linguistics Club, Bloomington.
———, Ewan Klein, Geoffrey K. Pullum and Ivan A. Sag: to appear, *Generalized Phrase Structure Grammar*, Blackwell, Oxford.
——— and Geoffrey Pullum: 1982, 'Generalized Phrase Structure Grammar: A Theoretical Synopsis', Indiana University Linguistics Club, Bloomington.
———, Geoffrey K. Pullum, and Ivan A. Sag: 1982, 'Auxiliaries and Related Phenomena in a Restrictive Theory of Grammar', *Language* **58**, 591–638.
——— and Ivan A. Sag: 1981, 'Passive and Reflexives in Phrase Structure Grammar', in J. A. G. Groenendijk, T. M. V. Janssen and M. B. J. Stokhof (eds.), *Formal Methods in the Study of Language*, Mathematical Centre Tracts 135, University of Amsterdam.
Godard, Danièle: 1983, 'Anaphores et relatives en français', paper presented at the symposium on Levels of Grammatical Representation, Marseille, January 1983.
Grice, H. P.: 1975, 'Logic and Conversation', in D. Davidson and G. Harman (eds.), *The*

Logic of Grammar, Dickenson, CA.
Groenendijk, Jeroen and Martin Stokhof: 1981, 'Engdahl's Two Problems', unpublished, University of Amsterdam.
———: 1982, 'Semantic Analysis of *Wh*-Complements', *Linguistics and Philosophy* **5**, 175–233.
———: 1983a, 'Interrogative Quantifiers and Skolem Functions' in K. Ehlich and H. van Riemsdijk (eds.), *Connectedness in Sentence, Discourse and Text*, Tilburg Studies in Language and Literature 4, Tilburg University.
———: 1983b, 'On the Semantics of Questions and the Pragmatics of Answers', unpublished, University of Amsterdam.
Grosu, Alexander: 1980, 'On The Analogical Extension of Rule Domains', *Theoretical Linguistics* **7**, 1–55.
Hale, Ken: 1983, 'Warlpiri and the Grammar of Nonconfigurational Languages', *Natural Language and Linguistic Theory* **1**, 5–47.
Hamblin, C. L.: 1973, 'Questions in Montague English', *Foundations of Language* **10**, 41–53. Reprinted 1976 in B. Partee (ed.), *Montague Grammar*, Academic Press, New York.
Harlow, Stephen: 1981, 'Government and Relativization in Celtic', in F. Heny (ed.), *Binding and Filtering*, Croom Helm, London.
Hausser, Roland: 1978, 'Linguistic Cross-Connections', unpubished, Institut für Deutsche Philologie, Ludwig-Maximilians Universität, München.
——— and Dietmar Zaefferer: 1979, 'Questions and Answers in a Context-Dependent Montague Grammar', in F. Guenthner and S. Schmidt (eds.), *Formal Semantics and Pragmatics for Natural Languages*, D. Reidel, Dordrecht.
Hawkins, John: 1978, *Definiteness and Indefiniteness*, Croom Helm, London.
Heim, Irene: 1979 'Semantics and Pragmatics of Definite Noun Phrases', unpublished, University of Massachusetts.
———: 1982, *The Semantics of Definite and Indefinite Noun Phrases*, unpublished Ph.D. dissertation, University of Massachusetts, Amherst.
Hellan, Lars: 1977, '$\bar{X}$-Syntax, Categorial Syntax and Logical Form', in T. Fretheim and L. Hellan (eds.), *Papers from the Trondheim Syntax Symposium*, University of Trondheim, pp. 85–135.
———: 1980a, 'On the Logical Form of Infinitives and Gerunds', NELS X, *Cahiers Linguistiques d'Ottawa* **9**, 191–212.
———: 1980b, 'On Reflexives in Norwegian', *CLS Parasession on Anaphora*.
———: 1981a, 'An Argument for a Transformational Derivation of Passives', in A. Belletti *et al.* (eds.), Theory of Markedness in Generative Grammar, Scuola Normale Superiore, Pisa.
———: 1981b, 'On Semantic Scope', in F. Heny (ed.), *Ambiguities in Intensional Contexts*, D. Reidel, Dordrecht.
———: forthcoming a, 'Predication and Anaphoric Elements in Norwegian', in L. Hellan and K. K. Christensen (eds.), *Topics in Scandinavian Syntax*, D. Reidel, Dordrecht.
———: forthcoming b, *Reflexives in Norwegian and Theory of Grammar*.
Herslund, Michael: to appear, 'The Double Object Construction in Danish', in L. Hellan and K. K. Christensen (eds.), *Topics in Scandinavian Syntax*, D. Reidel, Dordrecht.
Higginbotham, James: 1980a, 'Anaphora and GB: Some Preliminary Remarks', NELS 10, *Cahiers Linguistiques d'Ottawa* **9**, 223–236.

———: 1980b, Pronouns and Bound Variables', *Linguistic Inquiry* **11**, 679–708.
——— and Robert May: 1980, 'Questions, Quantifiers, and Crossing', *The Lingustic Review* **1**, 41–80.
Hintikka, Jaakko: 1982, 'Questions with Outside Quantifiers', *CLS Parasession on Non-Declaratives*, Chicago.
Hirschbühler, Paul: 1978, *The Semantics and Syntax of Wh-Constructions*, unpublished Ph.D. dissertation, University of Massachusetts.
———: 1981, 'The Ambiguity of Iterated Multiple Questions', unpublished, University of Ottawa.
Hopcroft, J. and J. Ullman: 1979, *Introduction to Automata Theory, Languages, and Computation*, Addison-Wesley, Reading, MA.
Horn, George: 1974, *The Noun Phrase Constraint*, unpublished Ph.D. dissertation, University of Massachusetts.
Huang, James: 1982, *Logical Relations in Chinese and the Theory of Grammar*, unpublished Ph.D. dissertation, MIT.
Hudson, Richard: 1976, *Arguments for a Non-Transformational Grammar*, University of Chicago Press, Chicago.
Huntley, Martin: 1982, 'Imperatives and Infinitival Embedded Questions', *CLS Parasession on Non-Declaratives*, Chicago.
Ioup, Georgette: 1975, *The Treatment of Quantifier Scope in Transformational Grammar*, unpublished Ph.D. dissertation, City University of New York.
Jackendoff, Ray: 1977, *$\bar{X}$ Syntax: A Study of Phrase Structure*, MIT Press, Cambridge, MA.
Jacobsen, Bent and Per Anker Jensen: 1982, 'Some Remarks on Danish Weakly Stressed *der*', paper presented at the First Workshop on Scandinavian Syntax, Trondheim.
Jacobson, Pauline: 1977, *The Syntax of Crossing Coreference Sentences*, Ph.D. dissertation, University of California, Berkeley. Available from 1979 from Garland Publishing, Inc., New York.
———: 1982, 'Visser Revisited', *Proceedings from the Eighteenth Annual Meeting of the Chicago Linguistic Society*, pp. 218–243.
Janssen, Theo: 1981, 'Compositional Semantics and Relative Clause Formation', in J. A. G. Groenendijk, T. M. V. Janssen and M. B. J. Stokhof (eds.), *Formal Methods in the Study of Language*, Mathematical Centre Tracts 135, University of Amsterdam.
———: 1983, *Foundations and Applications of Montague Grammar*, proefschrift, Mathematisch Centrum, University of Amsterdam.
Johnson-Laird, Philip: 1982, 'Formal Semantics and the Psychology of Meaning', in S. Peters and E. Saarinen (eds.), *Processes, Beliefs, and Questions*, D. Reidel, Dordrecht.
——— and Alan Garnham: 1980, 'Descriptions and Discourse Models', *Linguistics and Philosophy* **3**, 371–394.
Joshi, Aravind: 1983, 'Factoring Recursion and Dependencies: An Aspect of Tree Adjoining Grammars (TAG) and a Comparison of Some Formal Properties of TAGs, GPSGs, PLGs, and LFGs', *Proceedings of the 21st Annual Meeting of the Association for Computational Linguistics*, MIT, Cambridge, MA.
Kamp, Hans: 1981, 'A Theory of Truth and Semantic Representation', in J. A. G. Groenendijk, T. M. V. Janssen and M. B. J. Stokhof (eds.), *Formal Methods in the Study of Language*, Mathematical Centre Tracts 135, University of Amsterdam. Reprinted in *Truth, Information, and Interpretation*, GRASS 2, Foris, Dordrecht.

Kaplan, Ronald and Joan Bresnan: 1982, 'Lexical-Functional Grammar: A Formal System for Grammatical Representation', in J. Bresnan (ed.), *The Mental Representation of Grammatical Relations*, MIT Press, Cambridge, MA.

Karttunen, Lauri: 1969, 'Pronouns and Variables', *Proceedings from the Fifth Annual Meeting of the Chicago Linguistic Society*, Chicago.

——: 1977, 'The Syntax and Semantics of Questions', *Linguistics and Philosophy* **1**, 3–44.

——: 1978, 'Questions Revisited', unpublished, University of Texas, Austin.

—— and Stanley Peters: 1976, 'What Indirect Questions Conventionally Implicate', *Proceedings from the Twelfth Annual Meeting of the Chicago Linguistic Society*, Chicago.

——: 1980, 'Interrogative Quantifiers', in C. Rohrer (ed.), *Time, Tense, and Quantifiers*, Niemeyer, Tübingen.

Kayne, Richard: 1981, 'Unambiguous Paths', in R. May and J. Koster (eds.), *Levels of Syntactic Representation*, Foris, Dordrecht.

Keenan, Edward and Leonard Faltz: 1978, 'Logical Types for Natural Language', *UCLA Occasional Papers in Linguistics* **3**.

——: 1985, *Boolean Semantics for Natural Language*, D. Reidel, Dordrecht.

Koster, Jan: 1978, *Locality Principles in Syntax*, Foris, Dordrecht.

—— and Robert May: 1982, 'On the Constituency of Infinitives', *Language* **58**, 116–143.

Kuno, Susumo: 1978, 'Subject, Theme, and the Speaker's Empathy', in C. Li (ed.), *Subject and Topic*, Academic Press, New York.

Ladusaw, William: 1979, *Polarity Sensitivity as Inherent Scope Relations*, Ph.D. dissertation, University of Texas, Austin. Available from Garland Publishing, Inc., New York.

——: 1982, 'Semantic Constraints on the English Partitive Construction', in D. Flickinger, M. Macken and N. Wiegand (eds.), *Proceedings of the West Coast Conference on Formal Linguistics*, Vol. **1**, Stanford, pp. 231–242.

Lakoff, George: 1970, 'Repartee', *Foundations of Language* **6**, 389–422.

——: 1971, 'On Generative Semantics', in D. Steinberg and L. Jakobovits (eds.), *Semantics*, Cambridge University Press, Cambridge, pp. 232–296.

Larson, Richard: 1983, *Restrictive Modification: Relative Clauses and Adverbs*, unpublished Ph.D. dissertation, University of Wisconsin, Madison.

Lasnik, Howard: 1976, 'Remarks on Coreference', *Linguistic Analysis* **2**, 1–22.

Lees, Robert: 1960, *The Grammar of English Nominalizations*, Mouton, The Hague.

Levelt, W. G. M. and S. Kelter: 1982, 'Surface Form and Memory in Question Answering', *Cognitive Psychology* **14**, 78–106.

Löbner, Sebastian: 1979, *Intensionale Verben und Funktionalbegriffe*, Gunter Narr, Tübingen.

McCawley, Jim: 1970, Paper presented to the Annual Meeting of the Linguistic Society of America.

——: 1978, 'Conversational Implicature and the Lexicon', in P. Cole (ed.), *Pragmatics, Syntax and Semantics* **9**, Academic Press, New York.

McCloskey, James: 1979, *Transformational Syntax and Model Theoretic Semantics*, D. Reidel, Dordrecht.

Maling, Joan: 1984, 'Non-Clause-Bounded Reflexives in Modern Icelandic', *Linguistics and Philosophy* **7**, 211–241.

―― and Annie Zaenen: 1978, 'The Nonuniversality of a Surface Filter', *Linguistic Inquiry* **9**, 475–497.

――: 1980, 'Notes on Base-Generation and Unbounded Dependencies', paper presented at the Sloan conference on Non-transformational Grammars, Stanford.

――: 1981, 'Germanic Word Order and the Format of Surface Filters', in F. Heny (ed.), *Binding and Filtering*, Croom Helm, London.

――: 1982, 'A Phrase Structure Account of Unbounded Dependencies in Scandinavian Languages', in P. Jacobson and G. Pullum (eds.), *The Nature of Syntactic Representation*, D. Reidel, Dordrecht.

Manor, Ruth: 1982, 'Answers and Other Reactions', *Theoretical Linguistics* **9**, 69–94.

May, Robert: 1977, *The Grammar of Quantification*, unpublished Ph.D. dissertation, MIT.

Miller, George and Noam Chomsky: 1963, 'Finitary Models of Language Users', in *Handbook of Mathematical Psychology*, II, chapter 13, John Wiley, New York.

Montague, Richard: 1974, in R. Thomason (ed.), *Formal Philosophy*, Yale University Press, New Haven.

Parsons, Terence: 1979, 'The Theory of Types and Ordinary Language', in S. Davis and M. Mithun (eds.), *Linguistics, Philosophy, and Montague Grammar*, University of Texas Press, Austin.

Partee, Barbara: 1975, 'Montague Grammar and Transformational Grammar', *Linguistic Inquiry* **6**. 203–300.

――: 1977, 'Comments on Bresnan's Paper' in P. Culicover, T. Wasow and A. Akmajian (eds.), *Formal Syntax*, Academic Press, New York.

――: 1978, 'Bound Variables and Other Anaphors', *Theoretical Issues in Natural Language Processing* **2**.

――: 1979a, 'Montague Grammar and the Well-Formedness Constraint', in F. Heny and H. Schnelle (eds.), *Syntax and Semantics* **10**, Academic Press, New York.

――: 1979b, 'Constraining Transformational Montague Grammar: A Framework and a Fragment' in S. Davis and M. Mithun (eds.), *Linguistics, Philosophy, and Montague Grammar*, University of Texas Press, Austin.

―― and Emmon Bach: 1981, 'Quantification, Pronouns, and VP Anaphora', in J. A. G. Groenendijk, T. M. V. Janssen and M. B. J. Stokhof (eds.), *Formal Methods in the Study of Language*, Mathematical Centre Tracts 136, University of Amsterdam.

Perrault, Ray: 1983, 'On the Mathematical Properties of Linguistic Theories', *Proceedings of the 21st Annual Meeting of the Association for Computational Linguistics*, MIT.

Peters, Stanley: 1979, 'Some Syntactic and Semantic Rules of English', unpublished, University of Texas, Austin.

――: 1982, 'The Situation in Question', *CLS Parasession on Non-Declaratives*.

―― and Robert W. Ritchie: 1973a, 'Context-Sensitive Immediate Constituent Analysis: Context-Free Languages Revisited', *Mathematical Systems Theory* **6**, 324–333. First published in 1969 in ACM Symposium on Theory of Computing, New York, pp. 1–8.

――: 1973b, 'On The Generative Power of Transformational Grammars', *Information Sciences* **6**, 49–83.

――: in preparation, 'Phrase-Linking Grammars', University of Texas at Austin Cognitive Science Working Paper and University of Washington Computer Science Technical Report.

Pinker, Steven: 1979, 'Formal Models of Language Learning', *Cognition* **7**, 217–283.

Pollard, Carl and Ivan Sag: 1983, 'Reflexives and Reciprocals in English: An Alternative to the Binding Theory', in M. Barlow, D. Flickinger and M. Wescoat (eds.), *Proceedings of the West Coast Conference on Formal Linguistics*, Vol. 2, Stanford University, pp. 189–203.

Postal, Paul: 1964, 'Limitations of Phrase Structure Grammars', in J. Fodor and J. Katz (eds.), *The Structure of Language: Readings in the Philosophy of Language*, Prentice-Hall, Englewood Cliffs.

——: 1971, *Cross-over Phenomena*, Academic Press, New York.

——: 1972, 'On Some Rules That Are Not Successive Cyclic', *Linguistic Inquiry* 3, 211–222.

——: 1974, 'On Certain Ambiguities', *Linguistic Inquiry* 5, 367–424.

Reinhart, Tanya: 1976, *The Syntactic Domain of Anaphora*, unpublished Ph.D. dissertation, MIT.

——: 1981a, 'A Second Comp Position', in A. Belletti *et al.* (eds.), *Theory of Markedness in Generative Grammar*, Scuola Normale Superiore, Pisa.

——: 1981b, 'Definite NP Anaphora and C-Command Domains', *Linguistic Inquiry* 12, 605–635.

——: 1983, 'Coreference and Bound Anaphora: A Restatement of the Anaphora Question', *Linguistics and Philosophy* 6, 47–88.

van Riemsdijk, Henk and Edwin Williams: 1982, 'NP Structure', *The Linguistic Review* 1.

Rizzi, Luigi: 1978, 'Violations of the *wh*-Island Constraint in Italian and the Subjacency Condition', Montreal Working Papers in Linguistics 11. Reprinted in L. Rizzi, *Issues in Italian syntax*, Foris, Dordrecht.

——: 1982, *Issues in Italian Syntax*, Foris, Dordrecht.

Rodman, Robert: 1976, 'Scope Phenomena, "Movement-transformations", and Relative Clauses', in B. Partee (ed.), *Montague Grammar*, Academic Press, New York.

Ross, John R.: 1967, *Constraints on Variables in Syntax*, unpublished Ph.D. dissertation, MIT.

——: 1970, 'On Declarative Sentences', In R. Jacobs and P. Rosenbaum (eds.), *Readings in English Transformational Grammar*, Ginn, Waltham, MA.

Sag, Ivan: 1976, *Deletion and Logical Form*, unpublished Ph.D. dissertation, MIT.

——: 1982, 'Coordination, Extraction, and Generalized Phrases Structure', *Linguistic Inquiry* 13, 329–836.

——: 1983, 'On Parasitic Gaps', *Linguistics and Philosophy* 6, 35–46.

Schiebe, Traugott: 1982, 'Critical Remarks on Engdahl's Semantic Analysis of Questions', Reports from Uppsala University Department of Linguistics, 9.

Selkirk, Elisabeth: 1977, 'Some Remarks on Noun Phrase Structure', in P. Culicover, T. Wasow and A. Akmajian (eds.), *Formal Syntax*, Academic Press, New York, pp. 285–316.

Seuren, Pieter: 1972, 'Autonomous Versus Semantic Syntax', *Foundations of Language* 8, 237–265.

von Stechow, Arnim and Thomas Ede Zimmerman: 1984, 'Term-Answers and Contextual Change', SFB 99 report 87, Universität Konstanz.

Taraldsen, Tarald: 1978a, 'On The NIC, Vacuous Application, and the *that-trace* Filter', Indiana University Linguistics Club, Bloomington.

——: 1978b, 'The Scope of *wh*-Movement in Norwegian', *Linguistic Inquiry* 9, 623–640.

——: 1981, 'The Theoretical Interpretation of a Class of "Marke" Extractions', in A.

Belletti et al. (eds.), *Theory of Markedness in Generative Grammar*, Scuola Normale Superiore, Pisa.
———: 1982, 'The Head of S in Germanic and Romance', in Th. Fretheim and L. Hellan (eds.), *Papers from the Sixth Scandinavian Conference of Linguistics*, Tapir, Trondheim.
———: to appear, '*som* and the Binding Theory', in L. Hellan and K. K. Christensen (eds.), *Topics in Scandinavian Syntax*, D. Reidel, Dordrecht.
Thomason, Richmond: 1974, 'On the Semantic Interpretation of the Thomason 1972 Fragment', unpublished, University of Pittsburgh. Distributed by Indiana University Linguistics Club, Bloomington.
———: 1976, 'Some Extensions of Montague Grammar', in B. Partee (ed.), *Montague Grammar*, Academic Press, New York, pp. 77–118.
———: 1977, 'Multiple Quantification, Questions, and Bach-Peters Sentences', unpublished, University of Pittsburgh.
Thráinsson, Höskuldur: 1976, 'Reflexives and Subjunctives in Icelandic', NELS 6, Montreal Working Papers in Linguistics **6**, pp. 225–237.
Vanlehn, Kurt: 1978, 'Determining the Scope of Engish Quantifiers', Artificial Intelligence Laboratory Report, AI-TR-483, MIT.
Wasow, Thomas: 1972, *Anaphoric Relations in English*, Ph.D. dissertation, MIT.
Webber, Bonnie Lynn: 1978, *A Formal Approach to Discourse Anaphora*, Bolt, Beranek and Newman. Published 1979 by Garland Publishing, Inc., New York.
Wessén, Elias: 1965, *Svensk språkhistoria* III, Almqvist and Wiksell, Stockholm.
Wilkins, Wendy: 1980, 'Adjacency and Variables in Syntactic Transformations', *Linguistic Inquiry* **9**, 709–758.
Williams, Edwin: 1977, 'Discourse and Logical Form', *Linguistic Inquiry* **8**, 101–140.
———: 1978, 'Across-the-Board Rule Application', *Linguistic Inquiry* **9**, 31–44.
———: 1980, 'Predication', *Linguistic Inquiry* **11**, 203–238.
Younger, D. H.: 1967, 'Recognition and Parsing of Context-free Languages in Time n^3', *Information and Control* **10**, 189–208.
Zaenen, Annie: 1980, *Extraction Rules in Icelandic*, unpublished Ph.D. dissertation, Harvard.
———: 1982, 'Contrastive Dislocation in Dutch and Icelandic: An Exercise in Comparative Syntax', paper presented at the First Workshop on Scandinavian Syntax, Trondheim.
———, Elisabet Engdahl and Joan Maling: 1981, 'Resumptive Pronouns Can Be Syntactically Bound', *Linguistic Inquiry* **12**, 679–682.
——— and Joan Maling: 1982, 'The Status of Resumptive Pronouns in Swedish', in E. Engdahl and E. Ejerhed (eds.), *Readings on Unbounded Dependencies in Scandinavian Languages*, Almqvist and Wiksell International, Stockholm, pp. 223–230.

INDEX OF NAMES

Allwood, Jens 150 n 35
Andersson, Lars-Gunnar 53, 54 n 2, 91, 141, 148 n 18, 149 n 24, 283 n 4
Anward, Jan 107, 145, 148 n 18, 149 n 24, 255 n 28
Aoun, Joseph 262, 283 n 8, 283 n 9
Åqvist, Lennart 252 n 1, 252 n 2

Bach, Emmon xi, 18, 46, 58, 60, 63–64, 95, 100, 146 n 2, 150 n 30, 197–198, 204–205, 207, 239, 247, 261, 273, 286, 291, 312, 320 n 2
Baker, Carl 81, 224
Barlow, Michael 19
Barwise, Jon xi, 19, 48, 66, 204, 242, 255 n 31, 319, 326
Bayer, Joseph 257 n 37
Belnap, Nuel 10, 154–155, 162, 167, 252 n 2, 253 n 5, 253 n 6, 254 n 13
Bennett, Michael 155, 162, 253 n 6
Berwick, Robert 19
Bílý, Milan 320 n 4
Borer, Hagit 262
Brame, Michael 18, 63
Bresnan, Joan 4, 13, 18–19, 34, 46, 63, 99, 234, 273

Carlson, Greg 240
Chao, Wynn 149 n 26
Chomsky, Noam 1–4, 6, 13, 17, 19, 45, 51, 56 n 23, 56 n 26, 58, 63, 117, 130, 132, 137, 150 n 38, 234 259–261, 263, 265, 267–268, 271, 279, 282 n 3, 283 n 9, 286, 317–319, 320 n 1, 320 n 5, 321 n 11
Christensen, Kirsti Koch 150 n 36
Church, Alonzo 29
Clifton, Charles xi
Cooper, Robin xi, xii, 2, 5–7, 19, 24, 34–39, 42, 47–48, 53, 55 n 11, 56 n 17, 56 n 20, 56 n 24, 57, 66–67, 72, 87, 117, 147 n 5, 147 n 10, 147 n 12, 149 n 23, 150 n 33, 170–172, 178–179, 182, 189, 198, 204–205, 242, 251, 253 n 8, 253 n 11, 255 n 23, 255 n 25, 255 n 31, 258 n 40, 312, 319, 324, 326
Cormack, Annabel 261
de Cornulier, Benoît 148 n 15
Cresswell, Max 253 n 11, 294

Dahl, Östen xi, 12, 107, 150 n 31, 253 n 10, 254 n 12, 255 n 28, 315
Doron, Edit 132, 149 n 26, 262
Dowty, David 13, 60, 65–66, 291–293, 312

van Eijck, Jan 150 n 31
Ejerhed, Eva xi, 53, 54 n 8, 56 n 24, 90, 132, 144, 146 n 3, 248, 262
Enç, Mürvet xi, 248–249, 251, 258 n 41
Engdahl, Elisabet 8, 11, 52–53, 54 n 7, 54 n 9, 55 n 15, 63, 87, 125, 129–130, 147 n 10, 148 n 13, 148 n 16, 149 n 26, 150 n 34, 150 n 37, 174, 184, 241–242, 253 n 10, 255 n 29, 257 n 33, 258 n 40, 258 n 44, 262, 282 n 2, 302, 319, 320 n 3, 320 n 5, 326
Erteschik-Shir, Nomi 125, 143
Evans, Gareth 253 n 8, 287

Faltz, Leonard 60
Flickinger, Daniel 19
Føllesdal, Dagfinn xi
Fodor, Janet D. 11, 22, 34, 44, 46, 71, 126, 145, 198, 247, 255 n 31
Frazier, Lyn xi, 11, 145, 150 n 37, 325

Garnham, Alan 312
Gawron, Mark 19

INDEX OF NAMES

Gazdar, Gerald xi, 3, 6–7, 18–20, 28–29, 33, 37, 53, 54 n 7, 55 n 14, 55 n 15, 56 n 19, 60, 63, 90, 122, 146 n 1, 234
Geggus, Jana xii
Godard, Danièle 321 n 11
Grice, Paul 84, 140, 148 n 17, 258 n 44, 279, 291–292
Grimshaw, Jane 234
Groenendijk, Jeroen xi, 10, 250, 252 n 1, 253 n 7, 253 n 10, 257 n 36, 258 n 44
Grosu, Alexander 150 n 38

Hale, Ken 56 n 22
Halvorsen, Per-Kristian xi
Hamblin, C. L. 151, 247, 279
Harlow, Stephen 262
Hausser, Roland 155, 253 n 3
Hawkins, John 254 n 16
Heim, Irene xi, 149 n 27, 189, 253 n 8, 254 n 16, 255 n 31, 258 n 42, 320 n 10
Hellan, Lars xi, 53, 54 n 6, 60, 65, 149 n 28, 150 n 31, 150 n 32, 251, 253 n 10, 255 n 27, 271, 273, 298, 308–309, 320 n 4, 320 n 10
Herslund, Michael 320 n 4
Higginbotham, James 114, 147 n 6, 154, 198, 257 n 34, 259, 270, 278–282, 284, 287–288, 303–306, 309, 312–313, 315
Hintikka, Jaakko 8
Hirschbühler, Paul 81, 156, 224
Hopcroft, J. 28
Horn, George 13
Huang, James 56 n 23, 262
Hudson, Richard 18
Huntley, Martin 53, 54 n 10, 94

Ioup, Georgette 71

Jackendoff, Ray 19, 210
Jacobsen, Bent 123
Jacobson, Pauline 65, 302
Janssen, Theo 100, 117
Jensen, Per Anker 123
Johnson, Eyvind 121
Johnson, Mark 53, 54 n 9
Johnson-Laird, Philip 12, 312, 315
Joshi, Aravind 19

Kameshima, Nanako 148 n 14
Kamp, Hans xi, 12, 19, 87, 149 n 22, 150 n 31, 253 n 8, 316
Kaplan, Ronald 34
Karttunen, Lauri xi, 19, 24, 47, 66, 148 n 15, 151–152, 154, 156–161, 167–168, 170, 180–181, 239, 246–247, 250–251, 252 n 2, 253 n 4, 255 n 25, 255 n 30, 255 n 31, 257 n 35, 279–280, 282
Kaufman, L. 125
Kayne, Richard 320 n 9
Keenan, Edward 60
Kelter, S. 255 n 25
Kirkpatrick, Charles 320 n 6
Klein, Ewan 30–32, 53, 54 n 7, 55, 55 n 14
Koster, Jan 45, 270
Kratzer, Angelika xi, 258 n 43
Kuno, Susumo 142
Kuroda, Yuki 56 n 18, 148 n 14

Ladusaw, William xi, 2, 53, 54 n 9, 60, 147 n 5, 206, 257 n 32, 312
Lakoff, George 5, 210, 283 n 6
Landman, Fred xi
Larson, Richard 236
Lasnik, Howard 63, 286–287
Lees, Robert 239
Levelt, W. G. M. 255 n 25
Linell, Per 124, 149 n 24
Löbner, Sebastian 253 n 11

Maling, Joan 22, 27, 89, 119, 122, 125, 148 n 18, 149 n 26, 150 n 29
Manor, Ruth 10, 148 n 17, 253 n, 253 n 3
May, Robert 5, 45, 147 n 7, 154, 197, 255 n 31, 259–260, 267, 276, 278–282, 303, 324
McCawley, James 5, 291
McCloskey, James xi, 2, 20, 58, 60, 262, 312
ter Meulen, Alice xi, 254 n 12
Miller, George 137
Montague, Richard 2, 24, 35, 58, 60, 65–67, 95, 151, 157, 174

Parsons, Terence 205
Partee, Barbara H. xi, 4, 53, 54 n 9, 58, 60,

66–67, 95, 100, 147 n 6, 197–198, 204–205, 207, 254 n 12, 257 n 38, 258 n 39, 261, 286, 288, 291, 312, 320 n 10
Perrault, Ray 18
Perry, John xi, 204, 255 n 31, 319, 326
Peters, Stanley xi, 3, 6–7, 12 n 1, 18–19, 41–42, 45, 53, 54 n 5, 55 n 12, 58, 66, 72, 145–146, 147 n 12, 149 n 26, 160–161, 167–168, 253 n 4, 280, 312, 322
Pinker, Steven 33
Platzack, Sven 320 n 4
Pollard, Carl 55 n 13, 55 n 14
Postal, Paul 17, 114, 271, 283 n 6, 287, 303, 307
Prince, Alan 295
Pullum, Geoffrey 19, 53, 54 n 7, 55

Reinhart, Tanya 3, 262, 269, 284, 286–294, 297–299, 299–300, 313, 320 n 1, 320 n 3, 320 n 10
van Riemsdijk, Henk 263, 271, 283 n 7, 308–309
Ritchie, Robert W. 6–7, 18, 34, 41, 45, 53, 54 n 5, 58, 145–146, 147 n 12, 322
Rizzi, Luigi 262–263, 265
Rodman, Robert 5
Rooth, Mats xi, 258 n 40
Ross, John R. 4, 137–138, 159
Russell, Bertrand 173

Sag, Ivan 2, 19, 29, 54, 54 n 7, 55 n 14, 132, 198, 255 n 31, 261
Schiebe, Traugott xi, 253 n 10

Selkirk, Elisabeth 206
Sells, Peter 149 n 26
Seuren, Pieter 5
Shieber, Stuart 54 n 9
Sportiche, Dominique 231 n 12, 318
von Stechow, Arnim xi, 10
Stokhof, Martin xi, 10, 250, 252 n 1, 253 n 7, 253 n 10, 257 n 36, 258 n 44

Taraldsen, Tarald 53, 54 n 2, 89, 120, 130, 148 n 18, 231 n 13, 263, 265
Thomason, Richmond 55 n 13, 58, 63, 65, 207, 282, 286
Thráinsson, Höskuldur 150 n 29

Ullman, J. 28

Vanlehn, Kurt 71, 198, 210

Wall, Robert 66, 312
Wall, S. 125
Wasow, Thomas 114, 313
Webber, Bonnie 315, 320 n 10
Weinberg, Amy 19
Wessén, Elias 149 n 24
Wilkins, Wendy 65
Williams, Edwin xi, 2, 65, 122, 239, 258 n 42, 261, 263, 265, 271, 283 n 7, 308–309

Zaefferer, Dietmar 155, 253 n 3
Zaenen, Annie xi, 22, 27, 34, 89, 119, 122, 125, 148 n 18, 149 n 26, 283 n 4
Zimmerman, Ede 10

INDEX OF SUBJECTS

absorption 280
accessibility 306–307
Across-the-board 122
admissibility conditions 19, 42, 56 n 19
agreement 17, 20, 46, 56 n 24, 157
  morphological 97, 99
ambiguity 35, 41
  scope 67, 324
  temporal 245–250
analysis trees 286
anaphors 113
  in non-argument positions 274
  in dislocated constituents 6–7, 11, 113
  interpretation of 30, 269
antecedent-anaphor relations
  stores for 192
autonomy of syntax 1, 147 n 12

Bach-Peters sentences 282
base generation 7–8, 13, 33, 57, 273, 322
Basque 45
binding
  accidental 28, 100, 116, 286
  in GB, definition of 274
  indirect 227
  semantic 100
binding operators 38–39, 41, 48, 85–86, 147, 147 n 12
  as placeholders 36
  interrogative 147 n 12
  Binding Theory (in GB) 273–275, 303, 321 n 11
bounding nodes 263

c-command
  definition of 269
casemarking 47
categorial grammars 60, 146 n 1, 146 n 2
Celtic languages 262

center embedding 23
Chinese 262
closure 176
  illustration of 184
  of interrogative quantifiers 176, 184–185
coindexing 52, 271, 273
Comp 16, 45, 71, 89,˙255 n 29
  WH phrases in 231, 257 n 32
Comp-to-Comp movement 51
comparison of grammars 19
complete answers 154–155, 180, 241, 279
completion functions 253 n 9
Complex NP Constraint 6, 13, 125, 137, 262
complex symbols 19
compositionality 24, 29, 36, 48, 250
computational efficiency 53, 54 n 8
configurational languages 45
conjoined questions 156
constituent questions 13, 45, 83, 156
  rules for 24, 65
constraints
  form of 11, 87
  non-structural 113, 141
  on binding of pronouns 114–119,
  on extractions 34
  processing motivated 143
  structural 137
constructivistic semantics 12
containment 270, 275, 306
context-free grammars 6, 18–19, 22, 28, 33, 43
context-free languages 54 n 5, 57
context-sensitive grammars 43, 54 n 5
context-sensitive languages 28
contrastive dislocation 283 n 4
contrastive stress 55 n 16
control 63–64

Coordinate Structure Constraint 122
coreference 88, 97
  accidental 97, 287
Crossing Constraint 305
cross-over 114, 272, 283 n 10, 302–312, 315
  and processing 312
  and the Binding Theory 317
  condition on reindexing 305, 308
  semantic account for 309–312

D-structure 52, 260
Danish 120, 123, 150 n 35
definite descriptions 173, 204, 253 n 9, 320 n 10
deictic pronouns 95–96, 98, 117, 169, 276
  see also pronouns, free
deletion rules 263–264
descriptive adequacy 18
derived categories, see slashed categories
designated variables 21, 24, 26
direct generation, see base generation
direct interpretation 312
direct questions 155
  meaning of 155
disambiguated representation 71, 312, 324
disambiguation strategies 127–129
discourse model 315
Discourse Representation Structures (DRS) 149 n 22, 150 n 31
Discourse Representation theory 316
disjoint reference 119, 272, 283 n 10, 285, 320 n 1
dislocated constituents 48
  in embedded structures 93
  interpretation of 77
  translation of 24
  with anaphors 16, 29–30, 49, 55 n 13, 55 n 14, 113, 269
  with quantifiers 55, 55 n 15
dislocated positions 45, 71, 147 n 11
  for subject 147, 147 n 11
donkey sentences 172, 253 n 8
double object constructions 320 n 4
Dutch 283 n 4

echo questions 71–72

embedded questions 6, 45
  derivation of 72
empty nodes, see gaps
epithets 102, 189, 254 n 19
  binding of 103–104
  deictic 103
exhaustive answers 54, 154, 181, 252 n 2
explanatory adequacy 18, 266, 282 n 2
extractions 13, 138
  acceptability of 140
  out of noun complements 138
  number of 6, 15, 23–24, 133–134
  out of embedded questions 6, 134
  out of relative clauses 138
  see also unbounded dependencies

feature instantiation 20
filler-gap dependencies 126–129, 135
  morphological mismatches 135
  resolution of 126–129
fillers 22, 150 n 37
finite state grammars 23
finlandssvenska 124
Finnish 239
Fixed Subject Constraint 99
Focus 45
FOOT features 20
fragments of natural language 19
functional structures 34
functions
  from individuals to individuals (W) 168, 173
  from sets of i.c. to sets of i.c. (F) 242
functions-in-intension 174, 237, 254 n 13

GB see Government-Binding theory
GPSG see Generalized Phrase Structure Grammar
Game-Theoretical semantics 8
gaps 13, 22, 24, 30, 37, 174
  alternation with pronouns 121
  interpretation of 37, 39, 174
  multiple 25, 41
  position of 47
  schema for 26
  subject 16
  translation of 30

INDEX OF SUBJECTS

gender agreement 47
Generalized Phrase Structure Grammar (GPSG) 5, 19, 53, 56 n 19, 132
  adequacy of 23, 28, 32
  comparison with GB 57
generalized quantifiers 48
generative capacity 18
Germanic languages 263
governing category 273
Government-Binding theory (GB) 51–52, 56 n 23, 87, 150 n 34, 150 n 38, 257 n 36, 261
  comparison with non-transformational approaches 57
grammaticality judgments 134

Head Feature Convention (HFC) 20, 146 n 1
Hungarian 45

Icelandic 107, 122, 150 n 29, 283 n 4
  Old 120
ID, reindexing rule 304
if questions 83, 148 n 16
indexed languages 28
indexing 2, 27, 41, 257 n 34, 309
  correspondence 28, 267
  token 86–87
indirect questions *see* embedded questions
individual concepts 253 n 11
individual instantiations 158
infinitival questions 22, 25, 45, 53, 54 n 10, 91
  embedded 92, 94
  matrix 92, 94
  rules for 94
  subject 93–94
infinitival relatives 45, 92–93
Intensional Logic (IL) 24, 66, 68, 326
intensional verbs 167, 236, 248
interpretation-by-substitution 38, 53
interpretive filtering *see* semantic filtering
interpretive rules 263, 266, 268
interrogative phrases 39
  interpretation of 39
  translation of 27
interrogative pronouns 180

interrogative quantifiers 77, 169, 175
  derivation of 184, 193, 228
  interaction with other quantifiers 195–206
  interpretation of 184
  n-ary 280
  restriction on 176
  scope of 165, 199, 225, 236
  similarities with pronouns 172
  with anaphors 190, 193
  with bound variables 157, 276
intersecting dependencies 22, 263
intervals 249, 258 n 41
Italian 119, 263, 265
iterated questions 220

Japanese 82, 85, 119, 148 n 14, 293

kinds 240

LF *see* logical form
LFG *see* Lexical Functional grammar
lambda abstraction 24, 26, 156
lambda conversion 24, 28–30, 55 n 15, 167
  illustration of 115
language processing 33
learnability 33
left dislocations 264, 282 n 3, 283 n 4
Leftmost Constraint 302
lexical categories 46
lexical entries
  format of 60
Lexical Functional Grammar (LFG) 5, 34
lexical insertion 37
  null 37
linear precedence 178
linguistic theory 1, 5
link child 42–43
link convention 49–50, 114, 203, 235
  illustration of 74, 115
link parent 42–43
link paths 42–43, 48
linked trees 42, 58, 86, 235, 322
  definition of 44
  for iterated questions 76
  for questions 75–76, 323
  illustration of 186, 193, 323

interpretation of 49, 175
  with anaphors 193
  with pied-piping 235
  with reflexives 111
  with resumptive pronouns 99–100
linking rules 21
  translation rules for 55, 55 n 13, 55 n 15
local dependencies 13, 130
logical form (LF) 52, 254 n 22, 260
  as disambiguated representation 324
  conditions on 304
  need for 260, 312, 325
long-distance dependencies *see* unbounded dependencies
long-distance reflexives 110

Marathi 119
meaning 8, 24, 29, 48, 152
  and truth conditions 152
metarules 19
model theoretic semantics 12, 34
Montague grammar 1–2, 4, 8, 48, 84, 174, 248, 326
move α 4, 50–51, 56 n 26, 261, 267–268
movement rules 36
multiple questions 28, 78, 80–81, 83, 154, 156, 161, 166, 220
Multiple WH Quantification 224, 255 n 30
  rule for 80, 223

negative quantifiers 161, 166, 258 n 44
nested dependencies 22, 263
Nested Dependency Constraint 22, 46
node admissibility conditions *see* admissibility conditions
non-argument positions 56 n 23
  with anaphors 274
non-coreference 119, 285–286, 320 n 1, 320 n 3
  pragmatic accounts 286–293, 320 n 3
  semantic accounts 286
  syntactic accounts 286
non-transformational grammar 3, 7, 322
Norwegian 120, 122, 148 n 18, 149 n 28, 255 n 27, 263, 265
NP quantification 147 n 7
  rule for 70

NP Storage Convention 68
NP structure 283 n 7
NP-movement 51, 272

opaque contexts 167, 248
operators 231 n 13, 321 n 11

PLG *see* Phrase Linking grammar
parallel processing 43
parameters 262
parasitic gaps 129–132, 130, 150 n 38, 293, 320 n 5, 320 n 9
  and bound anaphora 293–302
  and reflexives 297–299
  and resumptive pronouns 130
  and weak cross-over 314
parsing 11, 53, 87, 320 n 8
  efficiency of 34, 43, 56 n 20
parsing strategy 127
parsing time 33
partial answers 155
partitives 210–211, 258 n 42
  interpretation of 211
passive 130
paycheck sentence 170
performance limitations 23
performative hypothesis 159
persuade 64
phrasal categories 46
Phrase Linking grammars (PLG) 41–51, 53, 58, 132, 147, 147 n 12, 322–323
  and coordination 132
  comparison with Cooper 47
  comparison with GB 57
  comparison with GPSG 42
  semantics of 48
phrase structure grammars 5, 322
phrase structure rules 17, 53, 60
  context-free 53
  context-sensitive 53, 56
pied-piping 38, 147 n 12, 234, 257 n 35, 268, 323
Portuguese 119
possessives 206–210
  translation of 255 n 24
possible answers 151
PP complements 210

translation of 255 n 24
pragmatic strategies 291
predicate nominals 236, 238–239
predication 266, 282 n 3, 298, 320 n 4
presupposition 149 n 23
   in *which*-questions 154, 280
preposed constituents *see* dislocated
PRO 318–319
pro drop 119, 315
processing 312
   of complex utterances 135
   of questions 11
processing strategies 325
   semantic 325
Projection Principle 52
promise 64
pronominalization 307
pronoun-gap alternation 263
pronouns 114, 180
   alternation with gaps 121
   binding of 38
   bound 49, 55 n 15, 95, 98–100, 117, 169, 183, 310
   difference between personal and interrogative 173
   free 95
   interpretation of 284–319
   interrogative 172
   relational interpretations of 149 n 21
   subscripted 35, 156
   translation of 171, 253 n 9
proto-questions 253 n 4
psych-movement 317
PTQ 35–36, 60, 65, 67, 71, 151, 156, 178, 248, 253 n 11, 255 n 26, 255 n 31

quantification 35, 48
   common noun 147, 147 n 6
   controlled 35, 71, 77, 80–81, 86, 147, 147 n 8, 231
   free 35, 66–67
   higher order 181
   interaction of free and controlled 200
   over functions 282
   over individuals 277–278, 282
   over *n* place functions 168–169, 277
   vacuous 231

Quantifier Raising (QR) 147, 147 n 7, 254 n 22, 260, 324
quantifier scope 197
   restrictions on 197–198, 285–86
quantifiers 55
   and anaphoric relations 320 n 10
   as answers 240
   order of 55, 55 n 16
quantifying-in 35, 70, 115, 156, 160, 163
question-answering systems 252
quiz-questions 255 n 23

reconstruction 236, 257 n 36, 267–268, 323
recursion 23, 53, 54 n 8
recursive languages 18
reflexive pronouns 149 n 28
   complex 149 n 28
reflexives 7, 107, 109, 157, 164, 190
   binding of 29–30, 55 n 15
   control of 217
   derivation of 109
   distribution of 107
   in dislocated constructions 191, 270
   in interrogative quantifiers 157
   interpretation of 29–30, 106, 191–192, 254 n 21, 285
   interpretation of in GB 270
   long-distance reflexives 107
   processing of 112
   rule for 192
   rule for NP internal 218
   topicalized 29–30, 55 n 14, 111
reflexivization
   rule for 108
relational answers 163
relational interpretation 325–326
   in GB 277
relational questions 11, 163–164
relative clauses 13, 36–37, 45, 137
   center-embedded 23, 137
   extraposition of 55 n 15
   infinitival 92–93
resumptive pronouns 53, 90–91, 98, 125, 130, 149 n 24, 262, 264
   distance requirement 125
   in linked tree 101
   in processing 125

in subject position 121
zero 265
retrieval 245
  of binding operators 36
right-node raising 55, 89
  GPSG rules for 55 n 15
rightward dependencies 55
  schema for 55 n 15
Romance languages 262–263
rule-to-rule approach 59

SAC *see* Store Address Convention
S-structure 52, 260, 321 n 11
Scandinavian language 6, 13, 51, 107, 120, 122, 262, 265
scope 35, 178
  of tense operators 248
  of WH phrases 30, 75, 165
SELF 31
semantic competence 152
semantic filtering 37, 50, 53, 146–147, 147 n 12
semantic types 66, 156, 237
Semitic languages 262
shallow structure 271–272, 308
short-term memory 23, 112
sig, reflexive pronoun 108
  interpretation of 108
sin, possessive reflexive 7, 17, 31, 50, 165
Situation Semantics 8, 48, 174, 255 n 31, 326
SLASH 20, 53
  number of 54 n 9
Slash Termination Metarules 53, 54 n 7
slashed categories 20–21
  elimination of 21
  introduction of 21
slashed categories 20–21
  elimination of 21
  introduction of 21
sloppy identity 288–289, 300
som 148 n 18
  in subject questions 88–91
Spanish 119
speech acts 155
storage 35, 55, 55 n 11, 67, 147, 147 n 5, 324 v. ti 2 obligatory 49, 175

store 53
Store Address Convention (SAC) 116, 285–286, 311
  and cross-over 311
  rule for 116
structure preserving 273
subjacency 6, 13, 51, 262–263, 282 n 2
subject position 16, 99
subject questions 88
substitution 37
surface structure 18, 321 n 11, 326
syntactic categories 19–20
  and semantic types 84
  finite number of 53
  for questions 84, 156
syntactic derivations 35, 56 n 26
syntactic domain 289, 296, 320 n 8
syntactic features 19–20, 25, 31, 43, 53, 54 n 6, 105, 157
  in GB 319
syntactic islands 13
syntactic processing 44
syntactic representation 5, 8, 97
  indexed 87, 97
  levels of 58, 260–261, 324
syntactic rules
  format of 59

tell 153
tense operators 246, 249
  scope of 248
theta (θ) role 51
topicalization 13, 264
  rules for 24, 65
tough complements 27
Trace Introduction Metarule 53, 54 n 7
Transformational grammar 1–3, 7, 33, 58, 259
  adequacy of 18
  semantic interpretation 259
transformations 5
  arguments for 17
  need for 5
true answers 152
Turkish 119, 293

unambiguous paths 320 n 9

unbounded dependencies 4–6, 11, 13–54,
   54 n 6, 55–57, 65, 323
   binding 266
   constraints on 13
   morphological mismatches 135
   processing of 128
unmoved *wh*-phrases 28, 78–79, 82–83,
   90, 147 n 12, 148 n 16, 148 n 17,
   221, 224, 227, 255 n 31
   interpretation of 56 n 25

valence 48, 147, 147 n 12
value loading 255 n 31
variable binding operators *see* binding
   operators
variables 4, 37, 169
   accidental binding of 28, 116, 286
   binding of 4, 55 n 13
   distinguished 99–100
   essential 4
   free 29, 96, 171, 185, 286
   in GB 231 n 13, 321 n 11
   indexed 27
   individual 175, 196
   locally free 286
   over functions (*W*) 169
   over functions (*F*) 242
   over property-denoting expressions 171
   relational 171, 173–174, 196, 226, 326
   sorted 97
   types of 66, 207, 237, 253 n 11
VP deletion 260

W function 168–169, 173, 177–179, 182–
   183, 186, 195, 203–204, 236, 253 n
   11, 254 n 17

infinite number of 182
valence of 185
weak crossover 254 n 20, 282 n 3, 312–317
Well-formedness Constraint 67
WH phrases 41
   complex 228–234
   internal structure of 206
   scope of 75, 272
   scope of dislocation 41
   see also interrogative quantifiers
WH quantification 78, 85, 147 n 10, 157,
   176, 225, 253 n 4
   rule for 72, 176, 225
wh in situ *see* unmoved *wh*-phrases
wh-interpretation in GB 267
   adequacy of 275
wh-Island Constraint 6, 13, 125, 137, 262,
   282 n 2
wh-movement 4, 6, 51, 147, 147 n 10, 245,
   254 n 22, 262–263, 322
   as an interpretive rule 263–264
   characteristic properties of 261, 266
   in Chinese 56 n 23
   obligatory 85
whether questions 92, 148 n 16
which 242
   as a quantifier 241
   translation of 242
who 157
   interpretation of 157
whose 39, 208
wide scope 35, 53, 147, 147 n 7, 158–161,
   174, 183, 204
wonder 50, 153

yes/no questions 83, 148 n 15, 148 n 17

STUDIES IN LINGUISTICS AND PHILOSOPHY

formerly *Synthese Language Library*

1. Henry Hiż (ed.), *Questions*. 1978.
2. William S. Cooper, *Foundations of Logico-Linguistics. A Unified Theory of Information, Language, and Logic*. 1978.
3. Avishai Margalit (ed.), *Meaning and Use*. 1979.
4. F. Guenthner and S. J. Schmidt (eds.), *Formal Semantics and Pragmatics for Natural Languages*. 1978.
5. Esa Saarinen (ed.), *Game-Theoretical Semantics*. 1978.
6. F. J. Pelletier (ed.), *Mass Terms: Some Philosophical Problems*. 1979.
7. David R. Dowty, *Word Meaning and Montague Grammar. The Semantics of Verbs and Times in Generative Semantics and in Montague's PTQ*. 1979.
8. Alice F. Freed, *The Semantics of English Aspectual Complementation*. 1979.
9. James McCloskey, *Transformational Syntax and Model Theoretic Semantics: A Case Study in Modern Irish*. 1979.
10. John R. Searle, Ferenc Kiefer, and Manfred Bierwisch (eds.), *Speech Act Theory and Pragmatics*. 1980.
11. David R. Dowty, Robert E. Wall, and Stanley Peters, *Introduction to Montague Semantics*. 1981.
12. Frank Heny (ed.), *Ambiguities in Intensional Contexts*. 1981.
13. Wolfgang Klein and Willem Levelt (eds.), *Crossing the Boundaries in Linguistics: Studies Presented to Manfred Bierwisch*. 1981.
14. Zellig S. Harris, *Papers on Syntax*, edited by Henry Hiż. 1981.
15. Pauline Jacobson and Geoffrey K. Pullum (eds.), *The Nature of Syntactic Representation*. 1982.
16. Stanley Peters and Esa Saarinen (eds.), *Processes, Beliefs, and Questions*. 1982.
17. Lauri Carlson, *Dialogue Games. An Approach to Discourse Analysis*. 1983.
18. Lucia Vaina and Jaakko Hintikka (eds.), *Cognitive Constraints on Communication*. 1983.
19. Frank Heny and Barry Richards (eds.), *Linguistic Categories: Auxiliaries and Related Puzzles. Volume One: Categories*. 1983.
20. Frank Heny and Barry Richards (eds.), *Linguistic Categories: Auxiliaries and Related Puzzles. Volume Two: The Scope, Order, and Distribution of English Auxiliary Verbs*. 1983.
21. Robin Cooper, *Quantification and Syntactic Theory*. 1983.
22. Jaakko Hintikka and Jack Kulas, *The Game of Language*. 1983.
23. Edward L. Keenan and Leonard M. Faltz, *Boolean Semantics for Natural Language*. 1985.
24. Victor Raskin, *Semantic Mechanisms of Humor*. 1985.
25. Gregory T. Stump, *The Semantic Variability of Absolute Constructions*. 1985.
26. Jaakko Hintikka and Jack Kulas, *Anaphora and Definite Descriptions*. 1985.
27. Elisabet Engdahl, *Constituent Questions*. 1985.
28. M. J. Cresswell, *Adverbial Modification*. 1985.